MW00356475

STATUS SIGNALS

STATUS SIGNALS

A SOCIOLOGICAL STUDY OF MARKET COMPETITION

JOEL M. PODOLNY

PRINCETON UNIVERSITY PRESS

PRINCETON AND OXFORD

Copyright © 2005 by Princeton University Press

Published by Princeton University Press, 41 William Street, Princeton, New Jersey 08540

In the United Kingdom: Princeton University Press, 6 Oxford Street, Woodstock, Oxfordshire OX20 1TW

All Rights Reserved

Second printing, and first paperback printing, 2008
Paperback ISBN: 978-0-691-13643-1

The Library of Congress has cataloged the cloth edition of this book as follows

Podolny, Joel M. (Joel Marc)
Status signals : a sociological study of market competition / Joel M. Podolny.
p.   cm.
Includes bibliographical references and index.
ISBN-13: 978-0-691-11700-3 (alk. paper)
ISBN-10: 0-691-11700-4 (alk. paper)
1. Economics—Social aspects.   2. Markets—Social aspects.   3. Social status.   4. Social networks.   5. Social values.   I. Title.

HM548. P63 2005
658.8'02—dc22   2004027237

British Library Cataloging-in-Publication Data is available

This book has been composed in Times Roman
Printed on acid-free paper. ∞
press.princeton.edu

Printed in the United States of America

10   9   8   7   6   5   4   3   2

To Tamara

CONTENTS

ILLUSTRATIONS

TABLES

ACKNOWLEDGMENTS

STRUCTURAL SOCIOLOGISTS are supposed to maintain a strong sensitivity to how an actor's position impacts on what that actor achieves. When I turn this sensitivity to my own life and consider whatever achievement is encapsulated in this book, it is clear that I have had the good fortune to occupy positions that have afforded me access to tremendous support and wisdom.

Almost fifteen years have passed since I began, as a doctoral student in Harvard's Sociology Department, working through the ideas that have ultimately culminated in this book. As a doctoral student, I had the good fortune to have a remarkable dissertation committee. Peter Marsden chaired the committee and set me on the intellectual path that has carried me to this day. Now that I have returned to Harvard as a faculty member, I am grateful that I can turn to Peter for his insight, counsel, and friendship. Peter provided some extremely helpful comments on the early chapters of the book. The late Aage Sørensen was also on my dissertation committee; more than anyone else, Aage taught me what it meant to think like a sociologist. Bob Eccles also was extremely helpful in challenging me to understand my empirical context.

Between being a doctoral student at Harvard and returning as a faculty member, I spent more than a decade at the Graduate School of Business (GSB) at Stanford, and I owe a tremendous amount to the institution and to the people there. The list of colleagues who helped push my thinking is long, but four deserve special mention: Bill Barnett, Jim Baron, Mike Hannan, and Ezra Zuckerman. For the first five or so years, a week never went by without Bill and I chatting about research; if we spoke less about research in the subsequent years, it was partly due to the fact that we had each so internalized the other's thinking that we could anticipate the other's concerns, comments, and queries. I cannot overstate my debt to Mike; Mike always seemed to be able to find time to listen to my half-baked ideas, discuss my analytical concerns, and then offer advice that could push me in a fruitful direction. As a colleague, Mike was an extraordinary blend of eclecticism, penetrating insight, and positive support. Finally, whenever I felt that I had thoroughly worked through an analysis or line of reasoning, I would turn to Jim, who would patiently work through the argument, insightfully pointing out weaknesses or uncovering additional empirical implications that had to be there if my argument was valid. I am indebted to Ezra on many dimensions. I have often said that when Ezra arrived at Stanford, it was a true breath of fresh air; he brought tremendous imagination and energy not only to the institution but to the field of economic sociology more broadly. Perhaps more than anyone else, he gave me tremendous optimism that the field itself could flourish. I am also incredibly fortunate that

Princeton University Press asked Ezra to be one of the reviewers for this book; his extremely detailed and insightful reading of the first draft greatly enhanced the final document.

Though Glenn Carroll and I overlapped at Stanford only for a relatively brief time, I am thankful to Glenn for his comments and thoughts on several papers; those comments were extremely helpful in pushing my thinking forward. I am thankful to Roberto Fernandez for always being available to chat about research. Jeff Pfeffer offered me institutional advice was that was especially helpful along the way, and I felt extremely blessed to have been able to receive Jim March's periodic counsel.

In order to work through how I, as a sociologist, could help contribute to the understanding of markets, it was critical to have access to economists at Stanford who could enhance my understanding of their discipline and challenge my thinking from their perspective. I am particularly indebted to Jon Bendor and Garth Saloner for their patient insight, and I consider myself extremely fortunate to be the beneficiary of the wisdom and friendship of David Kreps and John Roberts. Bob Gibbons provided some extremely thoughtful comments during the year that he was at the Center for Advanced Study in the Behavioral Sciences, and he has continued to offer equally thoughtful remarks over the years.

Other especially supportive colleagues at Stanford include Pam Haunschild, Rod Kramer, Joanne Martin, Mike Morris, Maggie Neale, Charles O'Reilly, and Jim Phills. Finally, I wish to thank Mike Spence, who provided me tremendous support in his capacity as Dean of the Stanford GSB and whose research on market signals was extremely influential in shaping my thinking.

Some of my greatest intellectual debts from my years at Stanford are to my (then) students and (now) colleagues with whom I have collaborated on the research projects that are the foundation for this work: Toby Stuart, Beth Benjamin, Damon Phillips, Douglas Park, and Fabrizio Castellucci. Shortly after I arrived as a new assistant professor at the Stanford Business School, Toby walked into my office, asked me to run through the list of projects on which I was working, and then told me that he thought the "patent" project had "potential" and that he would be willing to work with me on it if I were interested in doing so. As amusing as Toby's brashness was, it was indicative of an honesty and forthrightness from which I have always benefited. Moreover, as he was a star doctoral student, Toby took a great risk in investing his time and energy in working with a new assistant professor, and I feel that my career has benefited as much if not more from Toby's efforts as his career has benefited from my efforts. The research in chapter 6, on status processes in the technological domain, was truly a collaborative endeavor. As a doctoral student, Beth spearheaded our joint work on the wine industry and, through her efforts, pushed me to think about a broader literature than I had previously considered. Beth's energy and positive attitude in the face of a dauntless data collection effort were inspiring to me then; her continued drive to focus on issues of real importance continues to inspire me today. My joint work with Beth constitutes the bulk of chapter 5. I am thankful to Damon for putting in the time to enable the status growth models in chapter 4 and for his thoughtful comments and insights over the years. Douglas Park showed incredible stamina in collecting decades worth of tombstone data without which the analyses in chapter 8 would not be possible. Joint work with Fabrizio helped lay the foundation for the analysis that is reported in chapter 9, and subsequent work with Fabrizio on the Formula 1 industry has been helpful in pushing my thinking. I also am thankful to Greta Hsu and Ozgecan Kocak for deepening my understanding of how markets operate.

In addition to the former students noted above, I would like to thank Fiona Scott Morton for the enjoyable and productive collaboration that gave rise to the analyses reported in chapter 7. Fiona revealed great open-mindedness in her willingness to intellectually engage across the disciplinary divide and, in the process, showed that it is indeed possible for an economist and a sociologist to have a productive research collaboration.

I began writing this book in earnest when I returned to Harvard two years ago, and I am incredibly thankful to my colleagues in the Sociology Department and the Organizational Behavior Group at the Business School for their support and encouragement. While I can honestly say that I have been overwhelmed by the positive sentiments of so many, I especially feel the need to thank Max Bazerman, Frank Dobbin, Jack Gabarro, Boris Groysberg, Linda Hill, Rakesh Khurana, Jay Lorsch, Nitin Nohria, David Thomas, Mike Tushman, Mary Waters, Chris Winship, and, as I mentioned above, Peter Marsden. My thanks go to Dorothy Friendly and Tom Barrow for their assistance in preparing the manuscript. Finally, I am grateful to Kim Clark, Bill Kirby, and Krishna Palepu for providing me with considerable resource support, and I am thankful to the institution more broadly. Adding my years as an undergraduate, graduate student, and now faculty member, I have been at Harvard for almost twelve years. I know of no other place that provides as fertile terrain for the development of ideas.

Although I have spent most of my career at Harvard and Stanford, I did spend one quarter at the University of Chicago. I am indebted to Ron Burt for providing me with the opportunity to be there and for the numerous stimulating conversations. There are others in the discipline who have also been extremely helpful along the way. Peter Bearman has been a wonderful teacher, supporter, and friend since the time that I took an undergraduate seminar that he taught in 1985; were it not for Peter, I would never have decided to become a sociologist. Peter provided some very helpful feedback on some of the earlier chapters. Harrison White has also been warmly supportive for the entire fifteen years that I have been on this intellectual odyssey. Perhaps more than any other scholar, Harrison inspired me to consider the field of economic sociology as my area of specialization. I am thankful to Mark Mizruchi for going way beyond the call of duty as a reviewer. As was the case for Ezra, Mark provided extremely detailed feedback on all the chapters in this book.

I wish to thank those at Princeton University Press. Ian Malcolm provided extremely supportive stewardship throughout the process. Linny Schenck and Carolyn Hollis were also extremely helpful and responsive in helping to turn the manuscript into a book. Will Hively provided an exceptionally detailed reading and copyediting of the manuscript, for which I am truly grateful.

Finally, I wish to thank those closest in my life. I thank my parents for fostering a love of learning and a confidence that has enabled me to pursue a career in which one has to continually affirm a belief in the long-term benefits of the investments one makes on a daily basis. I thank my children, Aaron and Asa, for enriching my life and making me so proud. And, finally, I reserve my greatest thanks for Tamara, my wife, my strongest supporter, and closest friend. She has given me so much, and she has taught me that knowledge and understanding rest as much on a willingness to engage the heart as a willingness to engage the mind. I dedicate this book to her, knowing that it is only a small signal of everything that she has done for me.

Joel M. Podolny
Cambridge, Mass., 2004

Introduction

AN EMERGENT PERSPECTIVE FROM
AN EMERGENT FIELD

W<small>E ARE ALL FAMILIAR</small> with the popular image of the academic researcher, high atop an ivory tower in serene and sublime contemplation. While this image provides fodder for those who are critical of the alleged detachment of higher education from practical concerns, it also is probably one of the initial attractions for those who choose academia as a profession. Certainly, I found the image strongly appealing when I decided to pursue a Ph.D. more than fifteen years ago. However, in the intervening years, I have come to the conclusion that academic research has all the serenity and sublimity of a wrestling match. Ideas and research findings do not float in through the tower window on a breeze; rather, like Gulliver's Lilliputians, they tug, pull, taunt, and elude easy capture. An idea that seems downright insightful on one day turns out to be completely wrongheaded the next. Sometimes one happens upon an unanticipated empirical finding that suggests a promising research path; however, after a week or longer, the promising path turns into a dead end. Often there is the challenge of pulling together what initially seemed to be a disconnected smattering of findings—some of which were anticipated and some of which were not. In order to be able to make significant progress, one is forced to transform sublime contemplation into active obsession, allowing half-formed ideas and initial findings to keep a grip on one's thoughts long enough that one can finally discern a pattern or clarify a concept. If one begins to believe in the mirage of well-specified ideas flowing in through the window on a breeze, there are well-meaning colleagues and blind reviewers to quickly and unsympathetically bring one back to one's senses.

Since roughly 1990, I have been wrestling with understanding how various facets of the concept of status relate to the market. Usually, we think of status in the context of relations among individuals or groups of individuals—for example, the pecking order among cliques in a U.S. high school, the deference displays in medieval courts, or the restrictions and constraints on interaction in a caste society. We think of status less often as a property that firms possess. Sometimes we might make passing reference to status distinctions among firms—noting for example that a bank is particularly prestigious, a law firm is a "white-glove firm," or that a brand has "class." Yet, even in those instances when we acknowledge status differences among firms, we generally do not give much attention to understanding how these status distinctions arise, are maintained, or are changed over time.

Like others, I had not given the concept of status in markets much thought, but when I was a graduate student at Harvard, I read a book on the investment banking industry by Robert Eccles and Dwight Crane called *Doing Deals*. In one of the chapters, the authors observed that investment bankers obsess about how their status compares with the status of other banks. As I discuss in chapter 3, the investment banking industry is unique in that it has "tombstone advertisements" that serve as tangible indicators of firm status in this industry. However, the more that I thought about Eccles and Crane's observation on the status obsession itself, the more that it seemed that this obsession was probably not unique to investment banks. As I looked at books and articles on different industries—from accounting to fashion to toys—it became clear that firms, like individuals, are deeply concerned with their status. However, none of these industry studies provided much in the way of systematic information about the underlying causes, consequences, and mechanisms related to those distinctions. Nonetheless, because sociologists had thought deeply about the concept of status among individuals, it seemed reasonable to try to extend and apply sociological thought on status to understanding the way in which status operates in the market.

I started along this path after being excited and inspired by the research that had emerged in economic sociology during the 1980s. Since Harrison White asked in a provocative 1981 *American Journal of Sociology* article "Where do markets come from?" a large number of sociologists have been seeking to demonstrate that the operation of the market can be better understood if it is conceptualized as a social mechanism. For example, White conceived of the market as a structure in which the production volumes and revenues of producers could be better understood if one modeled producers as occupying interdependent roles. According to White, producers do not perceive demand curves; rather, they perceive the choices of other producers and pick a pricing/volume combination that places them somewhere between those producers acknowledged to be slightly lower in quality and those slightly higher in quality. By way of analogy, White (1981) observes that shortly after Roger Bannister broke the four-minute mile—a record many considered unattainable—a number of others did the same. While there clearly are alternative explanations for the quick followers on Bannister's achievement, such as improvements in training and diet, the analogy is nonetheless relevant insofar as it helps connect White's market model to sociological accounts of the role structures within groups. For example, in *Street Corner Society* (1981), a famous ethnography of a city street gang, William Whyte (1981) observed how the bowling scores of group members were constrained by their position in the social pecking order of the gang. In markets, as in athletic competitions or social groups, "what is possible" is in large measure socially defined by qualitatively differentiated peers looking to each other for cues regarding appropriate aspirations and performance.

While there is general agreement that economic sociology is one of the burgeoning subfields within the discipline, there is a clear lack of consensus regarding the scope of the "new economic sociology" (Swedberg 2003). I would assert that a defining characteristic of economic sociology as it is currently unfolding is that it draws on sociology's broader corpus of analytical constructs to rethink the operation of the market.

One branch of the "new economic sociology" seeks to make clear that the existence of a market mechanism for the allocation of resources is not the inevitable consequence of individuals pursuing their own interests but is instead the consequence of collectivities pursuing a common interest (typically at another collectivity's expense), dominant cultural understandings, as well as state action. This line of research has deep historical roots in Polanyi's classic work *The Great Transformation* (1944) but has gathered new momentum through the work of Dobbin (1994), Carruthers (1996), Beckert (2002), and Fligstein (2001).

In addition to this line of research exploring the institutional underpinnings of the market, there is a second line of research—the line of research into which this book falls—that focuses on how a market actually operates. At its most fundamental level, the market is a mechanism for matching. However, what determines which buyers are matched with which sellers? What determines the terms of trade—price, quality and quantity of effort—that arise between a particular buyer and seller?

In the standard general equilibrium model of economics, the mechanism for matching and setting prices is what has come to be called the "Walrasian auctioneer," who sets prices so that the market clears (i.e., there is no excess demand at the set prices for goods). The Walrasian auctioneer—named after the French scholar who is considered the father of general equilibrium economics—is simply an analytical convenience, an assumption that is necessary for the general equilibrium model to make predictions about prices. However, since the Walrasian auctioneer does not exist in real markets, basic questions about the market's operation remain: What does determine who exchanges with whom? What are the determinants of the terms of trade?

I think it is fair to say that economic sociologists have not developed a parsimonious account of a matching mechanism to serve as an alternative to the Walrasian auctioneer. However, they have emphasized several aspects of the market's operation that do affect the patterns of exchange and the terms of trade. For example, Espeland and Stevens (1998) highlight processes of commensuration, whereby qualitatively dissimilar goods are made comparable through the establishment of a common metric. Zelizer (1994) shows how culture and institutions shape the "mental accounts" that we reference when we calculate what we are willing to pay for particular goods and services, and even what we think should carry a price at all. Above all, however, economic sociologists emphasize networks of relations between individuals and corporate actors. One of the cleanest demonstrations of the effect of social networks on market outcomes is Wayne Baker's (1984) analysis of the floor of the commodity exchange in Chicago. Economic models of markets generally posit that market efficiency increases with the number of participants and that one of the manifestations of increasing efficiency is a reduction in the volatility of prices. However, Baker argued that individuals do not have the cognitive capacity to process countless buy and sell offers. Accordingly, when the number of traders of a particular commodity increases beyond some threshold, the market tends to fragment into distinct groups of traders who focus primarily on the buy and sell orders within their clique. Such fragmentation increases price volatility; in effect, cognitive limitations cause actors to rely on personal networks for information, and this reliance on personal networks influences the operation of the market. Mizruchi and Stearns (2001) show how a similar reliance on personal networks in a context of uncertainty affects the terms that relationship managers in banks are willing to provide to corporate clients.

More generally, networks are central analytical constructs in the "embeddedness" tradition within the new economic sociology—first articulated by Granovetter (1985) and subsequently developed by others, such as Raub and Weesie (1990), Portes and Sensenbrenner (1993), and perhaps most notably by Uzzi (1997). In the embeddedness tradition, social ties among market actors are seen as conduits for information about exchange opportunities and conduits for trust; stronger social relations allow for the sharing of more complex information between buyer and seller than simply price and quantities, ultimately allowing for a better match of interests. Padgett and McLean (2002) have recently extended and enriched the embeddedness perspective by arguing that particular patterns of exchange relations can be understood as manifestations of logics that transpose from one context to another. So, for example, the pattern of relations defined by marriage may come to be seen as an appropriate pattern for exchange relations in a particular market, with strong implications for who can exchange with whom.

Networks are also central to Burt's (1992) theory of structural holes, in which an actor's autonomy from exchange partners depends on the degree to which the exchange partners are themselves disconnected from one another. To the extent that the actor's exchange partners are disconnected from one another, the actor is able to obtain highly favorable terms of trade for the information and resources that the actor provides.

As these and other scholars show, ideas about social networks are central to the new sociological rethinking of the market. In each of the cited references, networks are important to markets in a particular way. They shape outcomes insofar as they are conduits for the flow of information or resources; metaphorically, they are channels or "pipes" through which "stuff" flows. So, in Baker's study, networks are conduits for the flow of information about buy and sell offers.

While this research certainly makes a compelling case that networks influence patterns of exchange and terms of trade by serving as pipes for the flow of information and research, there is another way in which network ties can be relevant to market outcomes. Not only can a tie between two actors facilitate flows between those two actors; that tie can also be relevant to market outcomes when others in the market make inferences about the qualities of those two actors on the basis of the tie. For example, in a study of day care centers, Baum and Oliver (1992) argue that consumers' perceptions of a day care center are strongly influenced by whether the day care center has a tie to a legitimate institution like a church or school. The significance of the tie does not hinge on information or resources that pass between the day care center and the legitimate institution but on third parties' perceptions of the tie and the inferences that those third parties draw about the quality of the day care center based on its presence.

Insofar as the presence or absence of a tie between two actors becomes the basis on which third parties make inferences about underlying qualities of those actors, the overall pattern of relations in a market becomes an important guide to market actors as they seek out exchange partners and decide on appropriate terms of trade. If the metaphor of a pipe is appropriate for the first characterization of network ties, then the metaphor of a prism seems appropriate to this second characterization because ties serve as the basis for splitting out and inducing differentiation among one set of actors as perceived by another. In effect, the pattern of ties becomes the lens through which the differentiation in the market is revealed.

As I shall discuss in more detail shortly, an actor's status is fundamentally a consequence of the network ties that are perceived to flow to the actor. Accordingly, in highlighting the relevance of status for markets, I have sought to broaden the way in which the field has come to understand the relevance of networks to market outcomes—to encourage sociologists to look to a focal actor's ties as a fundamental basis on which others (not necessarily connected to the focal actor) make inferences about the quality of that focal actor. Put simply, I have sought to highlight the importance of networks, not simply as conduits for the flow of information and resources, but as constituent elements of identity.

Status is, of course, not the only aspect of identity that is influenced by an actor's network of relations; nor is status the only aspect of identity relevant to market outcomes. For example, Rao, Davis, and Ward (2000) look at how firms affiliate with either the NASDAQ or New York Stock Exchange to affect how others perceive them. A particularly provocative demonstration of how an actor's pattern of relations becomes the informational basis on which third parties make inferences about the qualities of the actor comes from Zuckerman

(1999, 2000), who examines how the conceptual categories of financial analysts affect the divestitures and stock prices of firms. A financial analyst at a securities firm does not follow and predict the performance of all firms. Instead, the analyst focuses on some particular subset of firms that conforms to an institutionalized cognitive category within the profession. A category such as food stocks may be institutionalized, but a category like entertainment might not. Zuckerman argues that analysts are less likely to track firms whose portfolio of assets cuts across the boundaries of these cognitive categories, because such boundary spanners lack a clear reference group for the purpose of evaluation. In effect, one can think about a firm's acquisitions and diversifications as constituting its pattern of exchange relations across and within categories, and the analysts make inferences about the firms based on that pattern. A lack of attention from analysts translates into a lack of attention from the investment community, which in turn gives rise to an increase in the cost of capital. Therefore, even if there is an economic justification for a portfolio of assets cutting across these boundaries, a firm is penalized by the capital markets for having a pattern of exchange relations that is inconsistent with the institutionalized categories of the market. Insofar as Zuckerman's work underscores how a firm's pattern of exchange relations shapes how that firm is perceived, Zuckerman's work also underscores the prismatic function of market networks—where the pattern of ties induces identities.

Nevertheless, while there are other aspects of market identity that can and should be explored in order to better understand the operation of the market mechanism, the central premise of this book is that there is considerable analytical leverage from an explicit focus on status.

In 1993 I published my first paper using the concept of status as a lens with which to examine market competition. The paper appeared in the *American Journal of Sociology* and was titled "A Status-Based Model of Market Competition." From the time of that article, I have—either alone or with collaborators whom I recognize more fully in the acknowledgements—considered the relevance of status in a diverse array of market contexts: investment banking, wine, semiconductors, shipping, venture capital, and currently Formula 1 racing. The results of the studies have now appeared in a number of journal articles or books chapters.

Although each of these markets afforded an opportunity to turn a clear analytical lens on one or two particular facets of status, none alone provided an opportunity to articulate the full set of relevant questions or to highlight the methodological concerns common to almost any investigation of status processes in markets. Moreover, given that different markets required different measures of status, it was not always obvious to others or even to me how the various studies related to one another.

In bringing together the results of these various empirical studies, I have tried to construct a whole that is greater than the sum of the parts. Though I provided a formulation of the status-based model of market competition in the

1993 paper, my thinking has evolved over the years as a result of the studies that followed. At the same time, other scholars have conducted research that furthers our understanding of status and related constructs.

Because my own thinking has evolved and because there has arisen considerable related work, this book has multiple objectives. The first is to more clearly articulate the concept of status as a signal. In particular, there are some important differences between my conception of a signal and the conception of a signal in the economic literature. I work through these distinctions most clearly in chapter 2.

The second objective of this book is to more clearly integrate findings from various papers that I have authored or coauthored. In integrating the various studies, I seek not only to elicit a richer appreciation of the status dynamics within markets but to highlight the interdependence of status distinctions that arise in the market and those that arise in other domains, most notably in the social sphere and in the domain of technological innovation among corporations. As I shall discuss in more detail, one of the distinctive features of status is that it "leaks"; an actor's status is affected by the status of those with whom the actor associates. Similarly, status leaks across different domains in which the same actors may interact. For example, the status that leaders of firms possess in the social sphere can spill over and have consequences for the status of the firms with which those leaders are associated. Therefore, while the first empirical analyses in chapters 3 through 5 focus exclusively on status dynamics within the market, chapters 6 and 7 broaden the scope of inquiry to demonstrate the market consequences of status distinctions that arise in related, interdependent domains.

A third objective of this book is to pose an orienting set of questions for the examination of status dynamics in markets and to highlight some recurring empirical concerns that arise in exploring those status dynamics. Some of the most central analytical questions include the following:

- What are the primary market mechanisms by which a status ordering in the market is sustained?
- How do status distinctions in other related domains spill over into the market and influence market competition?
- What inequalities in economic rewards are engendered by the status ordering?
- What environmental conditions determine whether the engendered economic inequalities are greater or less?

Some of the recurring empirical concerns are

- identifying central deference acts from which status distinctions arise;
- modeling the effect of signals besides status on which market actors could rely to make inferences about the quality of potential exchange partners.

A fourth and final objective of this book is to relate my work on status to the work of others. Over the years, I have been asked how my conception of status relates to the economic concept of reputation or the marketing concept of brand. In chapter 1, I discuss the difference between status, on the one hand, and reputation and brand, on the other. In chapter 2, I discuss hypotheses and predictions that follow from a conception of status but do not follow from the prototypical conceptions of reputation and brand. In addition to clarifying distinctions between my understanding of status and related constructs from other academic fields, I also aim to clarify connections and draw distinctions between my work and other work within my own field of sociology. Since the publication of "A Status-Based Model of Market Competition," a number of other sociologists have found status to be a useful construct in their own research on market dynamics. Throughout this book, I try to integrate the research of these scholars with my own. There is also, of course, a rich tradition of work on status outside of markets. In addition to appearing as an important theme in classic works by Weber (1948), Veblen (1953), and Blau (1964), among others, the concept of status figures prominently in an experimental tradition known as expectation states theory (Berger et al. 1977), and in a recent paper Gould (2001) develops a provocative formal model of status hierarchies in groups. While these writings have had a strong effect on my thinking at a general level and therefore exert an influence on ideas throughout this book, I provide a particularly focused discussion of the similarities and differences between their conception of status and my own near the end of chapter 2. I also try to establish more explicitly connections to other perspectives in economic and organizational sociology, such as the "embeddedness" tradition (Granovetter 1985), Ronald Burt's (1992) theory of structural holes, and organizational ecology (Carroll and Hannan 2000), as well as a rather diffuse literature on the evolution of technology (Hughes 1987; Pinch and Bijker 1987). Even though these other research traditions are not centrally concerned with status dynamics, they do draw attention to features of firms and markets that are relevant to a full understanding of status dynamics within markets. Accordingly, it seems appropriate to integrate their insights with mine. Therefore, after laying out the core theoretical arguments in chapters 1 and 2 and offering empirical analyses in chapters 3 through 5 that focus solely on status dynamics within the market, I present analyses in chapters 6 through 9 that draw on these other literatures for a more multifaceted understanding of status dynamics in markets. Chapter 6 focuses on how status distinctions associated with the evolution of an industry's technology affect the status dynamics of the market. Chapter 7 links a concern with status dynamics in markets to the embeddedness perspective on markets. Chapter 8 relates a concern with status dynamics to organizational ecology, and chapter 9 considers the relevance of status to market competition in conjunction with Burt's theory of structural holes.

I am confident that a thoughtful reader will be able to quibble with a particular operationalization or offer an alternative explanation for a given finding. I certainly know I had my own concerns with some of the empirical analyses;

indeed, the concerns that arose in one study typically paved the way for the study that followed. In writing this book, I have tried to highlight the complementary nature of the various empirical examinations; my aspiration is that the reader's concerns about a particular analysis will be assuaged by encountering the other analyses. Even if the reader finishes the book with residual concerns, these need to be set against the payoff of the diverse array of market phenomena that are glimpsed more clearly through the lens of status. To the extent that the lens helps us to focus on aspects of market phenomena that are otherwise obscured by the dominant images of markets, I feel comfortable that this book consti-tutes a contribution to the emerging field of economic sociology.

Chapter One

STATUS, REPUTATION, AND QUALITY

Wᴇ ʜᴀᴠᴇ ᴀʟʟ had the experience of entering a room filled with unfamiliar people. Such experiences are especially likely to arise at key transition points in our lives—starting in a new school, beginning a new job, or entering a new community. Most of us find such moments to be fraught with anxiety. Questions—floating between the conscious and subconscious levels—form in our minds: With whom should I talk? Whom should I avoid? How will I be perceived if I spend too long without talking to anyone? How will I be perceived if I end up talking with the wrong person? What is the upside of being here? Is this "just for fun" or is this an opportunity to meet people who will be important to me in this new environment? What is the downside of being here? If I say the wrong thing or am seen associating with the wrong person, will others' judgments of me start to crystallize in a way that will taint my future interactions?

To answer such questions, we search the room, looking for cues and signals. A typical first response to such uncertainty is to see if there is anyone that we know. If the transition is taking on a new job, we look to see if there are any individuals whom we met during the interview process. If such an individual is indeed in the room, we draw on our experience with that individual to make some initial inferences. If we liked that person, we assume that the individuals with whom that person is talking are probably likable themselves. If we did not have a positive interaction with that person, we shift our attention and perhaps even move to another part of the room to ensure that our first encounter is not an awkward one.

If we truly know no one, there are other cues and signals on which we can rely. Who seems to be central in conversations? Who seems to be isolated? Who is surrounded by a circle of friends? Whose comments are being ignored? Who controls the conversation? Even distinctions like the laughter induced by a joke can serve as cues regarding the social landscape. When the golfer Lee Trevino was once asked about the difference between being a rookie and being an established professional, he supposedly said, "When I was a rookie, I told jokes, and no one laughed. After I began winning tournaments, I told the same jokes, and all of sudden, people thought they were funny." Such cues are the earmarks of status distinctions and deference relations, and they help us navigate through the social terrain. They help us make inferences about whose opinion we should value or at least be perceived as valuing. At a more fundamental level, they help us make inferences about the character of those in the room—who is smart, who is stupid, who will make a good friend, who is to be avoided.

And just as we are trying to read the signals being sent by others, we know that others—also at a level that floats between the conscious and subconscious—are trying to read the signals that we cannot avoid sending. In talking with some, ignoring others, and simply waiting on the words of still others, we create a tangible basis for those in our presence to make inferences about the quality of our character.

Even if such inferences are invalid, we know that they can engender a self-fulfilling prophecy. When an individual tells a joke and no one laughs, the individual grows uncomfortable and awkward in the telling of future jokes. Others are more likely to ignore the individual when they sense a joke coming on. As a consequence, the individual is more likely to be a peripheral player in the group even if the initial interaction was just bad luck.

The same applies simply to the comments or observations that an individual makes in a social setting. If the individual's comments are challenged, ignored, or ridiculed, the individual grows insecure or disheartened. Others feel more emboldened to challenge the individual if there is any ambiguity about the veracity of her comments. Again, such initial interactions simply can be the result of bad luck, but because of the expectational dynamics that they set in motion, such interactions will have consequences that carry on long after the initial interaction. Of course, all luck is not necessarily bad. Some individuals may have the good fortune to be perceived as smarter or funnier than they actually are, and the positive reinforcement from the initial interactions will encourage such individuals to make investments—like staying abreast of the latest gossip or checking the Web for the latest jokes—that will allow them to occupy a central location in the group for some time.

For more than fifty years, sociologists have found the concept of status to be extremely helpful in understanding the social dynamics of scenarios like the one above. Indeed, many of the greatest sociologists of the twentieth century, such as Weber (1948), Blau (1964), Homans (1951), Merton (1968), and Parsons (1963) found the concept of status to be extremely useful in understanding action in a broad array of social settings. The concept of status invokes the imagery of a hierarchy of positions—a pecking order—in which an individual's location within that hierarchy shapes others' expectations and actions toward the individual and thereby determines the opportunities and constraints that the individual confronts.

This book applies this most sociological of concepts to the study of markets, using the image of a status hierarchy as a way to conceptualize the producer side of markets. The focus on the producer side of individual markets is important in delimiting the scope and contribution of this book. From Veblen (1953) through Bourdieu (1984), sociologists have been interested in how the status concerns of individuals shape their consumption patterns. In such accounts, the market is an essential input to the status-based competition that plays out in other domains—such as among neighbors on the street, parishioners in a church, or employees in a firm. In contrast, this book focuses on the competition within the market itself, positing that one need not go beyond the interaction of producers and consumers within that market to observe the relevance of status.

A Story of Status

As an initial illustration of the importance of status considerations on the producer side of the market, consider a story that appeared on the cover of the *Wall Street Journal* on July 19, 2002. The article recounts the dilemma of high-end jewelers faced with spiraling demand for turquoise. Turquoise is formally regarded as a "semiprecious" stone. Of course, even a semiprecious stone can be integrated into jewelry that costs many thousands of dollars, and turquoise is no exception. Not only can one purchase pieces of turquoise at prices in excess of ten thousand dollars; the turquoise pieces of the best Native American artists are on display in prestigious museums throughout the country. At the same time, however, this particular semiprecious stone is stigmatized by "its close proximity to 25-cent postcards and $2.99 shot glasses at souvenir shops such as Desert Images, located inside Phoenix's Sky Harbor International Airport" (p. A6).

Faced with a spike in demand, high-end jewelers have adopted one of three strategies. Some, such as the "venerable New York retailer" Fortunoff, expand their collections of turquoise considerably. Others continue to maintain the same small collections of turquoise that they have always maintained. For example, according to the article, Tiffany & Co., which has always offered turquoise pieces for sale, "scoffed at the idea" of expanding its collection in response to an increase in demand. Finally, other high-end jewelers, who presumably have never sold the stone before, refuse to offer any turquoise to meet such demand. Indeed, the article opens with an account of Lane Jewelers. This Chicago store "prides itself on superior service, but it has its limits. Any client looking for turquoise—the must have gem of the moment—will have to look elsewhere." Steve DeMarco, the owner of Lane Jewelers, is even willing to tell potential customers where they can go to find turquoise jewelry: "by the side of the road in Arizona." In contrast to Fortunoff, Tiffany and Lane were concerned about how the expansion or, in Lane's case, even the introduction of turquoise into its product line would affect their image.

While it may seem obvious why a high-end jeweler might become concerned about its image being tarnished if it offers a semiprecious stone, the issue is worth pondering. How is the jeweler's image being threatened? Will Lane Jewelers be unable to provide superior service if it offers a semiprecious stone? Of course not. In fact, Lane's ongoing customers arguably may find Lane's refusal to sell the jewelry a sign of poor service. If they truly desire turquoise, they now need to find some other jeweler whom they can trust to provide them with a turquoise piece.

Is the jeweler's image being threatened because "expensive" is a critical element of its image and turquoise is a comparatively inexpensive stone? Perhaps Tiffany and Lane are concerned that their stores would become crowded with "run-of-the-mill" shoppers looking for a bargain, and that this would sour the shopping experience of those who spend thousands, tens of thousands, or even hundreds of thousands of dollars on jewelry. There are two problems with this explanation. First, as noted above, a high-end jewelry store can expand its turquoise collection while offering only pieces priced above, say, five or ten thousand dollars. Indeed, the *Wall Street Journal* article makes reference to Eiseman Jewels of Dallas, a jeweler whose customers spend an average of nine thousand dollars per purchase, which adopted precisely this approach. According to the article, Richard Eiseman looked through more than fifty collections of turquoise stones before finding turquoise that was consistent with the image of his store, but he believed that he had found such stones. Second, at least in the case of Tiffany, the store is already offering some turquoise pieces. It is hard to believe that Tiffany faces a threat of more "run-of-the-mill" shoppers if it doubles or triples the size of its turquoise collection, especially if the pieces remain above a reasonably high price threshold.

We could think through other facets of these stores' reputations, but it seems that Lane and Tiffany should be able to undertake actions that contribute to the qualities that their customers have grown to expect—service, cleanliness, high-price items, serene shopping environment—and, simultaneously, expand their turquoise collections. So, to repeat the question: Why is it that these stores feel their image is threatened?

The answer turns in part on the conceptual difference between reputation—a term that is often employed by economists in their analyses of markets—and status, the concept that is central to this book. When economists use the term reputation or when the term is used colloquially, it denotes an expectation of some behavior or behaviors based on past demonstrations of those same behaviors. So, in saying that Lane has a reputation for superior service and a serene atmosphere, we are saying that the knowledgeable public believes that Lane will offer superior service and a serene atmosphere because this level of service and atmosphere has been manifest in the behavior of the salespeople and the customers in the past. Stated abstractly, if an actor—be that actor an individual or some collection of individuals such as a firm—has a reputation for "X," it is because that actor has engaged in behavior that constituted evidence of "X" in the past. However, when we use the term status, we use the term to refer to an actor's position in a hierarchical order. That position reflects some diffuse sense of better or worse that is indirectly tied to past behaviors, but it is more directly tied to the pattern of relations and affiliations in which the actor does and does not choose to engage.

The problem for the higher-end jewelers is clearly articulated in the quotes noting that the image of turquoise is tarnished since it is sold alongside Arizona highways and in the same retail establishments that sell inexpensive shot glasses and postcards. To the extent that a high-end jeweler trades in turquoise, the jeweler becomes perceptually associated with the low-status purveyors of shot glasses. Consumers—either consciously or unconsciously—start to wonder whether the high-end jeweler is actually a lower-quality merchant than they previously thought, and the high-status jeweler accordingly runs the risk of a loss of status.

As sociologists and anthropologists (Blau 1955, 1964; Dumont 1981) have well documented, status flows through associations and through relations that involve either exchange or deference. Exchange relations are characterized by an implicit, loose equality in the value of that which is transferred between parties; exchanges can involve material goods and payments, but they need not. For example, a friendship can be characterized as an exchange relation in which each partner alternates between roles of giver and receiver as the friendship is played out. Deference relations are characterized by inequality: one person engages in behavior directed toward another that can be interpreted as an acknowledgment that the other should be regarded as superior in some sense. Some scholars interpret journal citations as deference relations since a citation is generally an implicit acknowledgment that the author of the cited work has made an important contribution.

When an actor engages in behavior that can be interpreted by others as an exchange or association with another actor, the status of each affects the status of the other. If the high-status actor associates with low-status others, then the high-status actor experiences a status loss. A particularly vivid example of such a status loss comes from Elias and Scotson's (1994) work *The Established and the Outsiders*, an examination of social dynamics in an English village. In the text, Elias and Scotson write about a newcomer's arrival to and subsequent ostracism within one of the better-off sections of town:

> Newcomers who settled in the "good streets" of the village were always suspect unless they were obviously "nice people." A probationary period was needed to reassure good families that their own status would not suffer by association with a neighbour whose standards were uncertain. The ostracized "black sheep" was in this case a woman who had recently moved into the neigbourhood and who made the following comments when she herself was asked about her relations with her neighbours: "They're very reserved. They speak on the streets but nothing else." She then told how she had asked the "dustmen in for a cup of tea one cold day," soon after she arrived. . . . "They saw it. That shocked them around here."

In this example, one party (the workmen) have established identities, and the other party (the home owner) has no identity. Therefore, the workmen have a stronger impact on the home owner's identity than the home owner has on the workmen's identity. If both parties to an exchange have reasonably fixed identities, then one would expect that the lower-status party would generally experience an increase in status, whereas the higher-status party would generally experience a decline in status. So, in studies of caste systems, scholars will note that an intermingling of castes is viewed by those in the higher-status caste as polluting their status. In a later analysis of status change among investment banks, I will provide some evidence of precisely this type of status contamination or leakage between partnering banks.

Status also flows through deference relations. When a high-status individual exhibits deference to another—for example, telling a large group that they should all listen to the words of the other—that other experiences a gain in status. Indeed, receiving deference from a high-status actor generally has a greater impact on one's own status than receiving deference from a low-status individual. If the CEO tells the employees in a company that they should really listen to the advice of a new recruit, such a gesture of deference will have a greater impact than if a line employee does the same.

Not only does status leak between actors within a given domain—for example, between two individuals in an organization or community—status distinctions can also leak across domains. Status distinctions in the social domain can spill over and have implications in the political or economic domain. One can observe movie celebrities endorsing politicians, politicians (or at least ex-politicians) publicly endorsing companies, and employees of prominent law firms and banks "borrowing" the prestige of their employer to impress someone in a bar.

In short, when two actors are involved in an association, exchange, or deference relation with one another and when others perceive that linkage, status leaks through the linkage. If the linkage is among peers of equal status, neither actor gains or loses in status, and accordingly the status of both remains the same. However, if the linkage is between actors of unequal status, the higher-status actor will tend to experience a drop in status while the lower-status actor will tend to experience a gain. To be sure, there are exceptions or modifications to this rule, and modifications to the rule arise when the identity of one of the parties is more established than the other; however, as a broad generalization, status leaks through linkages, and this leakage is precisely what concerns the higher-end jewelers. Even though high-status jewelers may be able to maintain their reputation for exceptional service, fine products, as well as numerous other characteristics that their customers find desirable, the higher-end jewelers are concerned that their status will decline through the associations implicit in the predominantly low-status turquoise trade.

This emphasis on the way in which status flows through exchange relations draws a sharp distinction between the sociological conception of status and economic conceptions of reputation. This emphasis should also sharpen the distinction between the sociological conception of status and the marketing conception of brand. Marketing scholars and advertisers use the term brand to reflect the overall market perception of a firm or product. Brand is an all-encompassing concept; there are a variety of factors that can shape the perception of brand—a firm's product, the music that is used in the firm's advertising, the propensity of the firm's employees to engage in illegal behavior, the firm's country of origin, and so on. Brand is affected by a firm's reputation on a number of dimensions (e.g., reliability, friendliness, innovativeness); similarly, brand is affected by status. However, precisely because brand is so all-encompassing, it is not a particularly helpful construct in sharpening our understanding of the particular mechanisms by which perceptions are formed. In contrast, analytical constructs like status and reputation (at least when the term "reputation" is followed by "for____") do draw attention to particular mechanisms.[1] Of course, having opened up the analytical distinction between reputation and brand, on the one hand, and status, on the other, a new question arises: if status is distinct from a higher-end reputation for service, serenity, and so on, why should the jeweler care about the loss of status? Should not rational consumers simply focus on those traits for which the jeweler has a reputation and ignore this more ephemeral attribute of status? Put more directly, if a consumer is confident that Lane Jewelers can provide him with excellent service and a serene shopping experience, why should the consumer even focus on status?

One possible answer is that the consumer values the status of the jeweler because the status of the jeweler facilitates his or her own conspicuous consumption. That is, if others know that an individual has purchased a particular piece from Lane Jewelers, they will be more impressed than if the individual purchased the same piece from a lower-status jeweler. While this answer could be part of an explanation, there is considerably less visible branding in jewelry than in other objects that are conspicuously consumed, such as automobiles or clothing. A store like Tiffany might have some pieces that are distinctly identified with its name, but this is the exception rather than the rule. Accordingly, while particular jewels—such as diamonds or rubies—may contribute to conspicuous consumption, the identity of the jeweler will typically have minimal impact.

The answer, I will argue, begins with a simple observation: even if an actor—be it an individual or a firm—has a reputation for a particular quality, potential exchange partners of that actor will frequently encounter some uncertainty about that quality and the associated reputation. There can be many causes for this uncertainty. At a fundamental level, regardless of the average level of quality

---

[1] One exception to my claim that the term brand is too general to highlight any particular mechanism underlying perceptions of quality is Douglas Holt's (2004) work *How Brands Become Icons: Principles of Cultural Branding*. Holt argues that the most powerful brands arise from the creation of "identity myths" that ease collective anxieties about social change. While Holt does posit a particular mechanism—indeed a mechanism with strong roots in sociological work on the impact of modernization on identity—this mechanism is very different from the mechanisms that are central in a study of status dynamics.

displayed by an actor on a particular dimension, there will inevitably be some variance around that level. For example, if the quality of concern is service, a firm will have different salespeople who will differ in their service ability, and even the same person can have a good day and a bad day.

Another reason that potential exchange partners may be uncertain about a particular quality or reputation is that it may be too costly to collect reliable information. If an individual is purchasing a car, the individual may find it worth the time and expense to gather information from a variety of sources to obtain a reliable estimate of the car's quality. However, if the individual is interested in buying a ten-dollar bottle of wine, that individual may have a much smaller interest in nailing down the bottle's quality or the winemaker's reputation.

A third source of uncertainty is that the value of a producer's product may hinge in large part on others' perceptions of its value. So, in the case of jewelry, the value of a piece of jewelry is exclusively a function of resale value, and this resale value is, of course, contingent on others' perceptions. If an individual purchases a $100,000 diamond necklace from Tiffany, but others—especially those who can and do spend $100,000 on pieces of jewelry—would be willing to spend only $20,000 or so, then the individual feels that he has been deceived by the jeweler. So, while a jeweler obviously would like to obtain as high a price as possible for the jewelry that she sells, the reputation of the jeweler as trustworthy is primarily a function of whether that price can be sustained over time. In this sense, a jeweler is like an art dealer: a critical quality of an art dealer is the ability to find work whose value will appreciate (or at least not decline) over time. Of course, as the example of turquoise illustrates, people's tastes change over time, and thus there is always some uncertainty about whether the jeweler is offering a "fair" price.[2]

We have run through a few reasons why market participants may be uncertain about the qualities or reputation of a firm; in the chapters that follow, we will consider a number of others. For the purpose of this book, an exhaustive tabulation of the sources of uncertainty is unimportant. All that is important is

---

[2] One can think about this particular source of uncertainty as being linked to the "winner's curse." When there are multiple potential buyers of an item in a competitive bidding situation (e.g., auction), some of the buyers are likely to underestimate the good's value while others are likely to overestimate its value. The winner of the auction is the one that is willing to pay the highest price and the one that is most likely to overestimate its value—hence, the curse. See Thaler (1994) for a more explicit discussion of the winner's curse. While the winner's curse is most commonly considered in competitive bidding situations, any buyer of an item may have reason to worry that she is overestimating the value of a good if the value that she places on the good depends in part on the value that others place on the good. So, if an individual values a particular piece of jewelry because of its perceived resale value at auction or simply because the individual values the envy of others who do not have an expensive piece of jewelry that the individual owns, then the individual needs to worry about the winner's curse. That is, the individual needs to worry that piece of jewelry will not have the anticipated resale value or will not evoke the desired level of envy. The trustworthiness of the jeweler hinges in part on the individual not being subject to this type of curse.

that one recognize the following fact: the existence of a reputation for a valued quality does not necessarily eliminate the uncertainty that market participants have about the presence or extent of that valued quality.

Given uncertainty about the presence of that valued quality, potential exchange partners of that producer will have a reason to look for other tangible indicators of that quality. As long as there is some positive correlation between an actor's status and the valued quality, then the actor's status can serve as such an indicator, and there are two reasons to believe that there will generally be a positive correlation between status and valued qualities. First, just as in any social setting, a valued quality can give rise to associations and relations that buoy an actor's status. For example, if an individual's wisdom and humor are traits that encourage others to defer to that individual, then on average there will be a positive correlation between status and wisdom and between status and humor. Similarly, if the quality of a producer's product draws deferential behavior from other producers—such as imitating those qualities in their own products—then there will be a positive correlation between status and quality. Of course, the causality can flow in the opposite direction, and the pattern of relations and associations underlying an actor's status can enhance the qualities that the status is supposed to represent. In elaborating on the scenario of a newcomer entering a group, I made reference to self-fulfilling prophecies in social settings. Such self-fulfilling prophecies can also occur in market settings. If individuals expect that a jeweler is likely to be correct about the fair price of a piece of jewelry, then they will be more willing to pay that price, which in turn will reinforce the belief that the jeweler sells pieces only at a fair price.

So, we are now in a position to answer why—or more accurately when—rational consumers will look to status to make inferences about underlying quality. If quality is imperfectly observable, if reputation is no better than an imperfect indicator of the unobserved quality, and if there is reason to anticipate a positive correlation between status and quality (regardless of the direction of causality), then rational consumers will look to status to further reduce their uncertainty. Such conditions regarding the relevance of status to market decisions can be framed in the form of a hypothesis that can be regarded as the central claim of this book: *the greater market participants' uncertainty about the underlying quality of a producer and the producer's product, the more that market participants will rely on the producer's status to make inferences about that quality.*

Several corollaries follow from the basic claim that market participants rely on a producer's status to make inferences about quality to the extent that quality is difficult to observe. For instance, if the central claim is true, it should also be true that the returns from status increase with greater uncertainty about the underlying quality of a producer and the producer's product. One could apply this corollary to the jewelry market. It seems reasonable to assume that there is greater uncertainty about the quality and value of a piece of a jewelry that is composed of many gems linked by gold and silver than about the quality and value of any particular gem. So, in the case of diamonds, DeBeers has devoted considerable resources to promulgating a well-defined set of criteria by which the relative value of a diamond might be assessed.[3]

There do not exist similarly well-defined standards for comparing the quality of art in different gem-laden bracelets. The best one might hope to do is to use the aggregate value of the gems and minerals embodied in the bracelet to establish a benchmark for its value, but such a procedure still does not reflect the artistic merit of creating the composite piece. Accordingly, one would expect that a jeweler's status would have more impact on the price that she could obtain for a composite piece than on the price that she could obtain for an individual stone.

Consider another corollary: if the returns from status increase as this uncertainty increases and if status "leaks" in the manner noted above, an increase in the uncertainty about the quality of what producers bring to market should drive an increase in status-based stratification. That is, the greater the uncertainty about the quality of producers in a market, the greater will be the reluctance of high-status actors to enter into relations or associations with lower-status counterparts.

These are only a few of the specific implications of the basic claim that we will explore in later chapters. But, at a broader level, the aspiration of this book is to convince you, the reader, of the benefit of analyzing a market with the same conceptual lens that is used to interpret and predict unfolding action in a social setting like that of a newcomer entering a room. The jeweler and the newcomer are in an analogous situation. Each knows that there exists uncertainty about her underlying qualities, and each knows that past enactments of those qualities will not entirely remove the uncertainty about whether those qualities exist today. Given this uncertainty, each knows that others will look to her status, as revealed through associations and relations, as a signal of that underlying quality.

Of course, even if one is convinced that there is value in extending the conceptual lens of status to the jewelry market, one still might question the broader applicability of the lens to other market contexts. Although I have already asserted that the low level of branding in jewelry ensures that the jeweler's name will generally not affect the conspicuous consumption of a particular jewel, one cannot deny that jewels are themselves objects of conspicuous consumption. It is thus entirely reasonable to ask whether the concept of status is usefully

---

[3] These criteria are known as the "four Cs"—cut, clarity, color, and carat weight. Beneath each "C" are further institutionalized distinctions. For example, a "classic round brilliant cut" is one in which there are 58 facets to the diamond—33 on the upper half, 24 on the lower half, and 1 point at the bottom know as the culet. Or, consider the way in which the clarity of a diamond can be defined as "flawless" only when no inclusions can be seen under a jeweler's $10 \times$ loup.

applied only to markets for goods that are typically understood to be "status goods."

In the chapters that follow, we will look at status dynamics in a number of industries—investment banking, wine, shipping, venture capital, and semiconductors. Although wine may be considered a status good that individuals purchase at least in part to enhance others' perceptions of themselves, investment banking, venture capital, shipping, and semiconductors are not. Therefore, by the end of this book, it will become clear that the lens of status has analytical utility even in markets for goods that are not generally considered status goods. However, at this point, one brief vignette drawn from one of these industries is probably useful to at least suggest the broader applicability of this lens.

In the 1980s, Drexel Burnham Lambert pioneered the high-yield debt market, which is more colloquially known as the "junk bond" market. What distinguishes the junk debt market from the more traditional investment-grade market is that the issuers of junk debt are smaller, less financially secure corporations than the issuers of investment-grade debt. Whereas "blue chip" corporations like GE or IBM are issuers of investment-grade debt, companies like Levitz (a furniture manufacturer) or Bally Entertainment have been issuers of junk debt. Of course, because junk bonds are a riskier investment, they also generate a higher return, and the commission—technically known as a "spread"—that Drexel earned on junk debt made Drexel the most profitable firm on Wall Street for a time even though Drexel was not one of Wall Street's elite firms.

Historical accounts of the leading Wall Street firms in the 1980s reveal that the emergence of the junk bond market posed a tremendous dilemma for the higher-status banks in the industry. Firms like Goldman Sachs and Morgan Stanley had traditionally refused to serve as underwriters for firms like Levitz because of the fear that such an association would tarnish their image.

When Morgan Stanley could resist entry no longer, the firm issued a press statement claiming that Morgan Stanley would "gentrify" the junk bond market (Chernow 1990). The status concerns underlying such a statement are apparent. As Phillips and Zuckerman (2001) and Hewitt and Stokes (1975) observe, high-status actors are more likely than low-status actors to offer disclaimers for behavior that would be considered deviant. In this case, Morgan Stanley was essentially trying to adopt the same stance vis-à-vis the high-yield debt market as Eiseman Jewels of Dallas was trying to adopt vis-à-vis the turquoise market. While each was willing to enter the market, each was seeking a way to draw a distinction between its particular connections within this market and the connections that others were willing to make. So, Eiseman would participate in the turquoise market, but it would devote considerable resources to searching for the finest stones. Similarly, Morgan Stanley would participate in the junk bond market, but it would exercise considerable discretion in choosing to underwrite for some and not for others. In fact, the statement implies that Morgan intended to be sufficiently discreet in this market that one could look to Morgan as a guide to the segmentation of the market. Morgan's junk clients would be the "gentry," whereas others' clients will be the riffraff.

Of course, such a gentrification of the market can only be an aspiration for Morgan Stanley, since Morgan Stanley's status is ultimately a function of how the financial community receives Morgan Stanley's entry. If the other high-status actors continue to associate with Morgan Stanley and if lower-status actors continue to defer to Morgan Stanley, then Morgan Stanley will be able to preserve its status. If, on the other hand, the reception of Morgan Stanley is more akin to the reception given to the newcomer in Elias and Scotson's English village after she invited the workmen to tea, then Morgan Stanley's status will by definition suffer.

In the third chapter, we will take a more systematic look at how the status of an investment bank's exchange partners affects the bank's own status as well as some of the economic consequences of a bank's status position. Nonetheless, this example does provide some initial indication that the conceptual lens of status is as relevant to investment banks as it is to jewelers or to a newcomer entering a room.

Chapter Two

THE MATTHEW EFFECT (UN)BOUNDED

THE PREVIOUS CHAPTER underscored two features of status that are critical to understanding its relevance in markets. First, potential exchange partners regard an actor's status as a signal of that actor's underlying quality when there is uncertainty about the underlying quality and when reputation is only an imperfect indicator. Second, status "leaks" through relations. In this chapter, I discuss consequences of these two features for generating inequality in key valued outcomes—such as profits—and how such consequences, in turn, affect status hierarchies over time. For the purpose of elucidating some of the central dynamics underlying the generation of inequality, I will reference what has come to be known as the "Matthew Effect," as manifest in markets.

The Matthew Effect is one of the many terms introduced into the sociological vernacular by Robert Merton. Merton (1968) coined the phrase with reference to a line from the first book of the New Testament: "For unto everyone that hath shall be given, and he shall have abundance; but from him that hath not shall be taken away even what he hath." Merton applied the phrase to the considerable discrepancy in esteem accorded high- and low-status scientists for similar accomplishments. For example, the likelihood that an article will be widely read and cited is positively correlated with the author's status. Similarly, when two scientists of unequal status are coauthors of a work that is deemed to be of high quality, others will ascribe more credit to the higher-status author even if there is no evidence that the higher-status author is more responsible for the content of the work. Put simply, the higher one's status, the more rewards—whether in the form of praise from colleagues, research grants, or simply the attention and acknowledgment of the field at large—that the scientist is likely to receive for effort of a given quality.

It is possible to provide other specific illustrations of the Matthew Effect in science, but the term has acquired a meaning that extends beyond the domain to which Merton first applied the term. More generally, the term refers to the fact that higher-status actors obtain greater recognition and rewards for performing a given task at a given level of quality and lower-status actors receive correspondingly less. The term has been applied to a diverse set of social phenomena, such as education (Wahlberg and Tsai 1983; Kerckhoff and Glennie 1999), the life course (Dannefer 1987), intraorganizational power (Kanter 1977), prostitution (Mansson and Hedin 1999), development planning in third world economies

(Okowa 1989), and the dispensation of mental health resources (Link and Mil-carek 1980).

On the producer side of the market, the Matthew Effect is a direct consequence of status being a signal of quality, and the Matthew Effect manifests itself in terms of higher-status producers experiencing higher prices and, even more important, lower costs for providing a good or service of a given level of quality. The fact that higher status would be associated with higher prices is not surprising; the fact that higher status can be associated with lower costs is probably less intuitive. As will become clear shortly, the validity of this second assertion depends very much on the qualifier "providing a good or service of a given level of quality." However, to fully understand how the Matthew Effect follows from the notion of status as a signal of quality and why the Matthew Effect manifests itself in terms of higher prices and/or lower costs, it is helpful to begin with a rigorous understanding of what a signal actually is.

According to Spence (1974), a signal is any observable indicator of an (unobservable) quality that meets the following criteria: (1) the indicator must be at least partly manipulable by the actor, and (2) the marginal cost or difficulty of obtaining the indicator must be inversely correlated with the actor's quality level. A college diploma is a signal of productivity because its attainment is at least partly within an individual's control and because it is more difficult for those who lack organizational skills (or other such attributes that constitute productivity) to obtain a college degree. Similarly, a warranty is a signal of quality because it is more costly for those who manufacture a low-quality good to issue a warranty than for those who manufacture a high-quality good.

While Spence's criteria can be regarded as strictly definitional, the definition embodies a powerful insight for contexts in which underlying quality differences are not observed. In order for a higher-quality actor to distinguish herself from a lower-quality counterpart, the higher-quality actor must find something that is easier or less costly for her to obtain. Otherwise, the lower-quality counterpart will simply mimic the higher-quality actor, and a potential exchange partner—considering offers of the lower- and the higher-quality actors—will be unable to make inferences about the underlying differences in quality. To distinguish situations in which the high-quality actor can and cannot distinguish herself from a low-quality imitator, economists use the terms "separating" and "pooling" equilibria, respectively.

Though the definition of a signal embodies this insight, the insight is more general than the definition. While Spence writes that a signal may be any observable indicator whose cost is inversely associated with quality level, it is also true that an indicator can serve as a signal yielding a separating equilibrium if (1) the indicator is not available to all actors desiring to signal high quality and (2) the cost of producing a good or service of a given level of quality is inversely associated with the possession of the indicator. That is, rather than the *cost of the indicator* differing between high- and low-quality actors, it is possible for the *cost of quality* to differ between those who possess the indicator and those who do not.

As an initial illustration, let us assume that an employer is hiring for a position in which an individual's personal networks will affect the ease with which the individual can perform in that position at a particular level of quality, and the employer is trying to decide between an applicant who has an MBA and an applicant who does not. Say, for example, that the position is an investment counselor, and the individual's network can affect job performance in three ways: (1) providing potential clients, (2) providing information and advice that can be passed on to clients, and/or (3) providing experiences that will be helpful to the individual in relating to potential clients and/or potential sources of valuable information.

Presumably, an individual can acquire such a network regardless of whether the individual goes to business school. However, to the extent that being in a business school makes the costs of acquiring such a performance-enhancing network cheaper or easier, the MBA will signal quality to the extent that the salary associated with such a position adequately compensates the MBA applicant for the difficulty of acquiring her network but does not adequately compensate the non-MBA for the difficulty of acquiring his network. If the salary for the position becomes sufficiently high that both the MBA and the non-MBA would be adequately compensated for the difficulty of acquiring this high-performance network, then the MBA degree would no longer serve as a signal yielding a separating equilibrium.

Economic reasoning should lead one to question whether a state of the world can exist in equilibrium. Specifically, one should ask the following question: if the salary associated with being an investment counselor is sufficient to justify acquiring an MBA (but not sufficient to justify acquiring such a network without an MBA), then should not all individuals who would regard this career choice as favorable invest in an MBA? As a result, in equilibrium, there should be no individuals without MBAs applying for such a job.

Hence, the relevance of the boundary condition, which is that the "indicator not be available to all actors desiring to signal high quality." As long as not all actors seeking to be investment counselors can obtain an MBA, the MBA can continue to serve as a signal distinguishing those who will be able to bring a high-performance network to bear on the job from those who will not.

Most economists would look at such a brute-force boundary condition and question the extent to which it is sensible. If the MBA market operates with a modicum of efficiency, the market should be able to expand to accommodate those who wish to signal that they are high-quality investment counselors. The economist might say, "Sure, one can just assert that the market won't expand sufficiently, but one needs to be very careful about making assertions that violate our basic expectations about the way the (capitalist) world should work. Before you know it, we are moving down a slippery slope to where someone could assert, 'As long as the moon is made of cheese, we can design spaceships that will help cure world hunger.'" Stated less colorfully, one needs to be careful about the assumptions that are implicit in the boundary conditions underlying one's theories or concepts. If a concept is relevant only when a questionable condition holds, then the concept is of little practical use in making inferences about the world.

Therefore, we need a reason why the indicator will not be available to all who desire to signal high quality. In the case of MBAs and investment counselors, we may or may not have a good reason. However, there are some desired goods, services, objects, or entities that by definition cannot be available to all regardless of the efficiency with which the capitalist system operates. In his work *The Social Limits to Growth* (1976), Fred Hirsch distinguishes between two types of goods—material goods and positional goods. Material goods are those whose "output is amenable to continued increase in productivity per unit of labor input . . . [they are] physical goods as well as such services as are receptive to mechanization or technological innovation without deterioration in quality as it appears to the consumer. It is assumed that . . . [the] final output obtained per unit of raw material will be sufficient to contain emerging shortages of raw materials as a result of technological progress, which is broadly what has happened until now." In contrast, positional goods are those that "are (1) scarce in some absolute or socially imposed sense or (2) subject to congestion or crowding through absolute use." Veblen's (1953) conspicuous consumption goods, such as originals from clothing designers—are necessarily positional. To the extent that the original is worn by hundreds or thousands, the value to any particular individual declines.

Leadership positions within an organization are another example of positional goods. No matter how many financial resources flow into an organization and no matter how those financial resources are allocated, not everyone can have an equal claim to increasing leadership within that organization. To be sure, one can try to decentralize authority and distribute it more evenly within the organization, but one cannot expand the total amount of leadership to be distributed within an organization or within an economy without bound.[1]

Within any social system, status is—like Hirsch's positional goods—zero-sum in character. One actor cannot increase his status without another losing status. As a consequence, to the extent that status is the indicator of interest, it is necessarily the case that high status will not be available to all actors within a social system. Therefore, the first condition for the alternative, non-Spencian type of signal is met. Indeed, with Hirsch's distinction between material and

---

[1] Some may argue that leadership within an organization is not zero-sum. That is, there may be some organizations in which many individuals feel empowered as leaders and some organizations in which few or any feel empowered as leaders. However, the fact that leadership within in an organization is not zero-sum does not imply that it can expand without bound.

positional, we could rewrite the conditions for this alternative type of signal as follows: an indicator can serve as a signal yielding a separating equilibrium if (1) the indicator is positional in character and (2) the cost of producing a good or service of a given level of quality is inversely associated with the possession of the indicator.

So, status meets the first condition. What about the second condition? The actor possessing this indicator must find it less difficult or less costly to produce a good of a given quality. In considering this second condition, let's return to the domain in which Merton first elaborated the concept of the Matthew Effect—the domain of science. Above, I referenced Merton's observation that a high-status scientist generally receives greater recognition for a work of a given quality than a lower-status counterpart would receive for that same work. At the same time, the high-status scientist should find it easier—*that is, less costly*—to generate a work of a given quality. Higher-status scientists are more likely to receive (paid) invitations to present their work at high-caliber institutions and thereby receive focused feedback from a broad range of colleagues, enabling the high-status scientist to more easily improve the work. At one of those talks, the high-status scientist may receive a critical comment that will result in a tremendous improvement in the work; the low-status scientist, without this attention, will find it much more difficult to make those improvements. Higher-status scientists will generally be able to garner positions at more heavily endowed universities that can afford to offer the scientist an employment contract with a lighter teaching load and thus more time to generate the work of a given quality. These same heavily endowed universities are also more likely to provide the scientist with a flow of PhD students who, in an effort to further their own career, will put time and energy toward collaborative activity from which the high-status scientist will receive most of the credit. As an extreme example of the benefit afforded by those collaborators, consider Stanford professor Carl Djerrasi, the famed "father of the birth control pill," who is an author on over 1,200 papers, most of them coauthored with various combinations of more than three hundred graduate students and postdoctoral colleagues.

Of course, scientists do not begin their career as high-status actors. At an early stage in her career, the eventual high-status scientist has to generate work of sufficient quality to start her on a high-status path. In elaborating on the Matthew Effect, Merton did not argue that there is no causal impact of quality on a scientist's status. Rather, he simply wished to underscore the cumulative advantage that accrues over time to the higher-status actor. Small, initial differences between two scientists—perhaps due to differences in ability or perhaps just due to the luck of one scientist's first experiment turning out very well and another's turning out poorly—become magnified over time. So while initial differences in status may be attributable to quality differences, those differences in status will augment those quality differences by making the costs of quality higher for the lower-status actor.

Notably, the inverse relation between status and costs holds for any quality level of output. The high-status scientist clearly has the resources to more easily embark on the pathbreaking work that will appear in the leading journals like *Nature* and *Science*. At the same time, the high-status scientist can more easily publish a relatively insignificant book chapter because the high-status scientist is likely to receive many more invitations for such chapters than her lower-status counterpart. Thus, in the domain of science, the second condition seems to hold: the costs of a given quality of output are lower for the higher-status scientist than for the lower-status scientist.

What about the costs of quality in the market? The direct impact of status on costs is obscured by the fact that higher-status producers are generally of higher quality and higher-quality goods are often more costly to produce. Therefore, the zero-order relationship between status and costs is often positive. However, *if one controls for the quality of a good or service*, it almost necessarily follows from the conception of status as a signal that the effect of status on costs is negative. If consumers and relevant third parties to a transaction perceive status to be a signal of unobservable quality, then they will be more reluctant to enter into a transaction with a low-status producer than they would be with a high-status producer even if both claim to offer the same quality of good or service for the same price. So, somewhat ironically, the second condition—that the costs of quality be inversely correlated with status—follows inevitably from the expectational differences that are induced by the signal.

Empirically, this greater reluctance to accept the quality claims of lower-status producers is manifest in several cost advantages for the higher-status producer. First, and perhaps most important, if consumers or relevant third parties—such as retailers—require "proof" that the product confronting them is of a given level of quality, status lowers the transaction costs associated with the exchange between buyer and seller. Implicit and explicit promises of a higher-status producer are more likely to be accepted; therefore, the higher-status producer need not devote as much time or expense to convincing the buyer or relevant third parties of the validity of its claims. A particularly vivid example of the inverse relationship between status and transaction costs is afforded by Stevens's (1991) account of competition among what in 1991 were the "Big Six" and now are the "Big Four" accounting firms for the audits of major for-profit and nonprofit corporations. While price competition among the six highest-status accounting firms often drove competing bids for the business of the most significant clients to the range of their costs and thus effectively eliminated most if not all positive rents from status, the lower-status firms were still unable to compete for the audit opportunities in the high-status niche.

In one instance, Stevens details how SBO Seidman, a second-tier accounting firm beneath the so-called Big Six, attempted to compete for the audit of a major charitable organization. Even though SBO Seidman was fully capable of performing the audit, its request to present a bid to the corporation was denied.

Only the Big Six were invited. As Stevens comments, "The charity's selection committee limited its competition to the Big Six not because the Big Six stand for superior professional standards . . . but because the world has stamped a 'Good Housekeeping Seal of Approval' on their audits" (1991: 237). In effect, SBO Seidman could not pay transaction costs high enough to compensate for the status differential between it and the highest-status firms. In the next chapter, I will highlight an example of the goodwill that investment banks give to one another in working on deals together; higher-status banks are more likely to have their claims accepted, and this greatly facilitates their ability to coordinate multibank deals.

In a study of the market for legal services, Uzzi and Lancaster (2004) offer a similar example of the transaction-cost-reducing effects of status. The following is an illustration from an attorney as to how the inside counsel for a firm might go about choosing a law firm:

> The tax director says to herself, You know, I could get this [legal expertise] somewhere else. I can use a medium-sized firm in Kentucky, and they're fine. But, I think I'd like to be able to tell my directors I got Baker & McKenzie—a high-status firm. There's less to justify before the deal and after the fact if something goes wrong.

Especially in light of the attention that Williamson (1985) and others have given to transaction costs in exchange relations, the inverse relationship between status and transaction costs for a good or service of a given quality is noteworthy. Another, related type of costs are what might be called "advertising" or "marketing" costs. If transaction costs are the costs that are involved in consummating the exchange, then advertising costs are those costs that a producer pays to make potential consumers aware of its presence and products in the market. For the higher-status producer, advertising costs for attracting a given volume of business are lower. More customers simply flow to the producer without the producer actively seeking them out, and often the higher-status producer receives "free" advertising that the lower-status producer is unable to obtain. Examples of this free advertising abound. Publications from highly regarded academic presses are more likely to receive reviews in academic journals than publications from less highly regarded presses (Powell 1985). Business journalists are more prone to ask the employees of prominent firms within a market to offer insights into market trends than they are to ask employees of less prominent firms.

A third type of costs lowered by status are financial costs. While not particularly explicit about the mechanism, Fombrun and Shanley (1990) note how status enhances a firm's ability to obtain capital from either commercial banks or from issuing securities in the financial markets and thereby lower its costs in those markets. One possible mechanism is that transaction costs in financial markets are lowered in the same way that they are lowered in the product or service market in which a firm makes its offering. Zuckerman's (1999, 2000) research also speaks to the issue of financial costs.[2] While Zuckerman focuses more on how a firm's configuration of economic assets affects its legitimacy rather than its status, status and legitimacy are obviously closely related concepts; firms lacking legitimacy are in general going to be perceived as lower status than firms possessing legitimacy. Therefore, when Zuckerman finds that firms with an illegitimate configuration of economic assets are less likely to be tracked by financial analysts and therefore have lower market value, his work at least indirectly points to a similar relation between status and financial costs.

Notably, these advantages in transaction, advertising, and financial costs, which accrue from status, all derive solely from the view of status as a signal that reduces the reluctance of market participants to enter into an exchange relationship with a particular producer. However, if one is willing to draw on Frank (1985) and make the additional and arguably very realistic assumption that employees are willing to accept lower monetary compensation in exchange for higher status, then one can specify a fourth source of lower costs. If an employee does indeed value the status of her workplace, she should be willing to accept a lower wage or salary to work for a higher-status firm. Of course, a higher-status firm may actually offer higher salaries than lower-status competitors because it wishes to have employees (perceived to be) of higher quality. However, controlling for the (perceived) quality of the potential employee, the higher-status firm should be able to acquire an individual at a lower cost.[3] Phillips (2001) offers another reason why higher-status firms may face lower labor costs, controlling for the quality of labor. In a phenomenon that he labels "the promotion paradox," Phillips finds that higher-status firms promote their employees at a slower rate than lower-status firms. Phillips argues that higher-status firms are able to do so because their chances of financial success are higher than those of their lower-status counterparts; specifically, rational employees are willing to stay longer at a lower rank in a higher-status firm because the expected returns to promotion are greater in the higher-status firm owing to the higher-status firm's greater likelihood of financial success. Therefore, even if employees do not value status as an end in itself, they may still be willing to accept a lower grade (and accordingly) lower-paying position because the discounted value of remaining with the higher-status firm is higher.

In short, the consideration of these different costs confronted by producers in a market suggests the following: given two producers at a particular point in

---

[2] See more detailed reference to Zuckerman's work in chapter 1.

[3] While highlighting Frank's (1985) observation that individuals are willing to exchange money for status, I wish to distinguish my view from Frank's analysis of intrafirm differences in compensation. Frank argues that, because individuals value status, those in a higher position in the firm are willing to accept less than their marginal productivity. Conversely, those in a lower-status position demand a salary or wage in excess of their marginal productivity. In contrast to Frank, I frame the individual's "pond" not as a single firm but as either all firms or a subset of firms within the market.

time, the costs for a given quality of output will be lower for the higher-status producer than the lower-status producer as long as consumers and other potential exchange partners—such as financial intermediaries or retailers—regard status as a signal of quality.

Though status can influence both price and costs, the discussion so far has obviously focused primarily on its cost-related benefits. The reason for this focus is not only that the cost-related benefits are less intuitive than those pertaining to price, but that the cost-related benefits can actually be of greater significance to the high-status producer. These cost-related benefits afford the producer insulation from the competitive pressure of lower-status producers even in the context of intense price competition. The previous example of competition among auditing firms makes the case in point. Even though the high-status audit firms were not earning positive rents from their status, their lower transaction costs enabled them to prevent lower-status firms from establishing ties to prestigious clients and thereby entering the higher-status segment.

It is important to reiterate one aspect of my argument. The fact that higher-status actors can provide a good or service of a given quality at a lower cost does not mean that the costs of the higher-status actors will be lower. In general, higher-status actors will produce higher-quality goods, and higher-quality goods will be more costly than lower-quality goods. My argument is only that higher-status actors will be able to offer goods *of a given quality* at a lower cost.

Above and beyond the implications of status for costs and price, there are some additional benefits of status that are worth noting. For example, higher-status actors often have a greater ability to set the rules of the game and define the parameters of product quality. For example, when governments seek to protect the environment through legislation, they will typically turn to leading firms in the affected industries for advice about both the environment and the economic consequences of the legislation. Thus, the higher a firm's status, the more that firm can influence what product qualities are allowed and what product qualities are disallowed. While such advantages are no doubt important and provide even further amplification of the Matthew Effect, I here emphasize these advantages less than the cost-related advantages because the cost-related advantages are the ones that follow logically from the conception of status as a signal. Later, especially in chapter 6, I emphasize one way in which a firm's status enhances its ability to define quality, but at this point I simply wish to unpack the cost-related advantages that are implicit in the understanding of status as a signal.

An astute reader might be concerned about the tautological nature of the narrative so far. Status meets the definition of a signal of quality because the costs of producing a good of a given quality are inversely correlated with status; however, the reason that that the costs of producing a good of a given quality are inversely correlated with status is that the producer's potential exchange partners look to status as a signal of quality.

There is considerable validity in the assertion that the argument so far is simply tautological. At this point in the chapter, all I have done is elaborate how this particular tautology manifests itself in markets and highlight the parallels with how the same tautology manifests itself in other contexts. Merton's observations on the Matthew Effect in science can be largely reduced to the same tautology. Status meets the definition of a signal of quality in science because the costs of producing scientific work of a given quality are inversely correlated with status, but the reason that the costs of producing scientific work of a given quality are inversely correlated with status is that those in the field of science who hand out rewards—from grants to lighter teaching loads to publishing opportunities—look to status as a signal of quality.

At least in the market, an interesting paradox arises out of this tautology. If higher-status producers can produce any quality of good at a lower cost and receive a potentially higher revenue, then the Matthew Effect clearly applies in markets. Over time, the higher-status actors should accumulate a disproportionate share of the rewards. However, if status is a signal of quality and the Matthew Effect therefore applies, why is it that higher-status producers do not invariably eliminate their lower-status counterparts from the market? Why can't the second half of the quote from Matthew—"from him that hath not shall be taken away even what he hath"—be taken more literally?

In the world of science, there are fundamental human limitations on the cumulative advantages of status. Unless the norms of science would permit high-status scientists to hire ghostwriters, ghost researchers, and ghost teachers, there is simply a limit to the volume of activity that can be undertaken by the higher-status scientists. There are simply physical limits on the number of students that a Nobel laureate can teach, the number of research projects in which the Nobel laureate can be involved, and the number of papers that a Nobel laureate can write. Moreover, even if a high-status scientist can keep building cumulative advantage through leveraging coauthorship relations and building a huge supporting infrastructure in a lab, retirement or ultimately death provides an end to the cumulative advantage.[4]

Are there similar human limitations on the operation of the Matthew Effect in markets? Price theory suggests that there might be with the notion of "diseconomies of scale." If higher-status firms exhibit long-run diseconomies of scale as they expand into the market such that price per unit rises above the market value of the good, then there may be constraints on the expansion of the high-status producers. Possible sources of long-run diseconomies of scale

[4] Despite these human limitations on the ability of high-status individuals to dominate an entire market, it is at least worth observing that elite educational institutions began to worry during the emergence of the Internet boom that Internet-based learning would provide individuals with a way to overcome limitations on the number of students that they could teach. There was considerable fear that firms would hire away the highest-status instructors from the leading universities and then broadcast their teachings globally. Unext, for example, hired Nobel Prize winner Gary Becker.

are inherent limitations on a factor of production or a loss of managerial control. However, one of the earliest results of the industrial organizations literature was the lack of evidence of long-run diseconomies of scale with respect to production costs (Bain 1956; Johnston 1960). Therefore, at least within the production ranges of these studies, there is no empirical grounding for the assertion that limitations on the high-status producers emerge from diseconomies of scale.[5]

Moreover, one can simply perform a mental experiment in which a high-status firm acquires a low-status competitor and changes nothing other than the low-status competitor's name to reflect its high-status affiliation. The low-status firm will continue to produce the same quality of output for the same consumers that it has always supplied, except under the higher-status name. With no communication of substance between the acquirer and the acquired, it is hard to see where diseconomies are likely to arise.

So, from where do the bounds on the operation of the Matthew Effect come? What prevents one or a few high-status firms from gradually expanding their presence in the market and driving out all the lower-status competitors?

One might posit that if a high-status firm moves into the niche occupied by low-status competitors by offering quality comparable to that of the low-status competitors, then the lower quality being offered will undercut the firm's status. That is, even though the high-status firm can offer lower quality more cheaply than the lower-status competitors, it undercuts its status with the low-quality offer.

However, there is at least one problem with this explanation: it denies the ability of high-status firms to differentiate the quality of their products through explicit or implicit announcements. In 1994, Mercedes introduced the C-class sedan into the United States at an entry-level luxury car price below $30,000. While this sedan was and remains more expensive than a large number of family sedans manufactured by Toyota, Ford, and a number of other competitors, this new C-class model was clearly of lower quality than other Mercedes sedans: the E-class, which sold for $50,000 and up, and the S-class, which sold for $70,000 and up. The C-class lacked many features of Mercedes' higher-end models; however, the introduction of the C-class did not lead to confusion about the quality of the E-class or S-class. Mercedes used the letter designation to draw clear distinctions between the quality of a product offered in the

---

[5] It is important to distinguish diseconomies of scale that arise from growth within a particular market from diseconomies of scope, which might accrue from growth through expansion across markets. The dismantling of diversified corporations in the 1980s was taken by many as evidence of managerial inefficiencies that result from combining firms producing in separate markets. Even if one ignores recent studies that challenge the assertion that unrelated diversification is invariably inefficient (e.g., Chevalier 2000), there is not to the best of my knowledge anyone who has challenged the basic conclusion from Bain (1956) and Johnston (1960) that within a particular market there is no evidence for diseconomies of scale.

$30,000 price range and the quality of products being offered in the higher price ranges.

To return to the example of jewelry in the previous chapter, there is no reason that Tiffany or Lane Jewelers could not put a special case of turquoise jewelry in a corner, leaving the displays of the higher-quality diamonds completely unaffected by the turquoise.

Of course, I do not want to assert that declines in the average quality of offerings will have no impact on the status of the firms making such offers. Before concluding this chapter, I will return to the question of the linkage between status and quality. Here I wish only to point out that high-status producers should be able to sufficiently differentiate among their higher and lower-quality offerings that status can remain a signal of quality within—and not just across—quality segments of a market. While upper-end luxury cars will invariably be of higher quality than entry-level luxury cars and while diamonds will invariably be regarded as higher-quality stones than turquoise, it should be possible for the higher-status firm to enter any lower-status/lower-quality segment of a market and—to the extent that it can leverage its lower costs and potentially higher revenue within that segment—compete effectively within that segment.

However, the problem for the higher-status firm is that it cannot enter that lower-status/lower-quality segment and leverage its lower costs and potentially higher price. If it enters that lower segment, it runs a significant risk of forfeiting some status. The reason comes from a consideration of the nature of status itself—more specifically, from the second key aspect of status noted in this and the previous chapter. In addition to being a signal of quality, status leaks. To the extent that the high-status producer expands its presence in the market to those niches occupied by the low-status actors, the high-status actor ceases to be perceived as high-status. Just like the woman who has tea with her workmen and suffers a loss of status as a result, the high-status firm suffers a loss of status when it "plays" in the lower-status sandbox. Although Mercedes can preserve the reputation of the E-Class and S-Class for quality when it begins to sell the C-Class, the status of the Mercedes name and the "three-pointed star" that appears on Mercedes cars is almost certain to experience some decline. Mercedes may decide that the decline is economically justifiable, and later I will offer some general reasons when and why a producer may decide that a decline in its status is justifiable, but regardless of whether it is economically justifiable, it is practically inevitable that when a high-status producer enters niches that are occupied by lower-status actors—whether those actors be low-status consumers or low-status producers—that producer runs a risk of losing status.

There are other explanations one might offer for why a high-status firm cannot simultaneously be an effective competitor in a high-status/high-quality segment and low-status/low-quality segment. In my view, some of the more convincing alternative explanations focus on the administrative and organizational complexity associated with operating in very distinct segments as well as the equity considerations that may arise among employees within the firm. For example, if a high-status investment bank acquires a lower-status competitor and then seeks to offer the same quality of service with the same quality of employees, the high-status bank is likely to find that the employees in the acquired entity will want salaries comparable to those that the acquirer offers to its own employees. The high-status firm then faces the dilemma of paying its acquired employees more than they received from the low-status firm (and hence lowering the benefit that its status brings to the new operation) or trying to manage disgruntled employees.

Another alternative, suggested by Zuckerman and Kim (2003), is that high-status firms face a "slumming" discount because the clients in those niches suspect that the higher-status producer will not be sufficiently motivated or knowledgeable to serve them well. Such a constraint is analogous to that of job overqualification, whereby an individual is bypassed for a job not because of capability but because the individual is perceived to be a flight risk.

While such alternatives may be part of the explanation, these alternatives will not give rise to the same predictions that arise from a consideration of status as a relationally based signal of unobservable quality. Therefore, rather than trying to rule out such alternatives, I will in later chapters simply set these alternatives aside and focus on the predictions that arise from the understanding of status that I have elaborated in this chapter.

But before we get to these analyses, a few concluding observations are in order. The purpose of this chapter has been to "unpack" the concept of status. In unpacking the concept, we have seen how status creates both advantage and constraint. There is a tendency to see the advantage as integral to occupancy of a higher-status position and constraint as integral to a lower-status position. However, such an understanding of the relevance of status would be mistaken. The relational underpinnings of status protect the low-status actors from the high-status ones just as much as they protect the high-status actors from their low-status counterparts.[6]

---

[6] If such a protection effect is not clear, momentarily assume that status did not have any relational underpinnings; that is, assume that a producer could be high-status and participate in any segment of the market. Then, in fact, the high-status firm should be able to expand into all niches. Not only could Mercedes introduce a $30,000 car; it could introduce a car at every price level until it was competing with Hyundai. Indeed, if status could be reduced to the economist's conception of reputation, this should be precisely what Mercedes could and should do. On account of having a superior reputation for quality that it built up through its luxury cars, it should be able to establish a reputation for quality at every price level. Sure, quality at the $10,000 level would be different from quality at the $70,000 level, but as long as Mercedes developed a reputation for delivering high quality for a given price, it should be able to compete effectively at any price level since it would have lower costs than its lower-status counterparts. However, because of its relational underpinnings, status cannot be reduced to reputation, and Mercedes cannot enter the lower-status niche without negatively affecting how it is perceived and therefore how it can compete in the high-status niche.

In unpacking the concept of status, we have rearranged the relationship between costs, signals, and quality initially posited by Spence (1974). As noted at the outset of this chapter, according to Spence, the marginal cost of a signal is by definition inversely associated with quality. However, for status, it is the marginal cost of quality that is inversely associated with the existence of the signal. The greater one's status, the more profitable it is to produce a good of a given quality. More simply put, whereas the economic view of signals begins with differences in quality between producers and then derives as signals those attributes for which the marginal cost of the signal is greater for the low-quality producer than the high-quality producer, the sociological view takes as its point of departure the reality of the signal and then derives differences in quality on the basis of who possesses the signal and who does not.

Embracing the sociological view does not require that one deny the economic one. In arguing that status differences induce distinctions in quality, we can also allow distinctions in quality to induce status differences. The view of status as a relationally based signal of quality that in turn induces differences in quality falls apart only if any change in quality is immediately followed by a corresponding change in status. If any quality change were immediately reflected in a status change, then there would be no barrier to low-status firms making an investment in quality and then immediately reaping the benefits of that status. In effect, there would be no impediment to upward status mobility; status distinction would not imply status barrier.

However, whereas the view of status elaborated here requires that past manifestations of quality not perfectly determine status, this view of status is entirely compatible with the existence of a *loose* (albeit positive) *linkage* between quality and status, with changes in the former having some though not completely determinate impact on the latter. In fact, if changes in quality had no impact on changes in status, then high-status producers would have a strong incentive to free ride on their status—that is, to stop investing in the resources needed to make high-quality goods—since they would possess the signal of quality regardless of their actual investments in quality.

So, to summarize, the conception of status as a signal of quality rests on the following understanding:

1. Quality is not perfectly observable.
2. There is a loose, positive linkage between past manifestations of quality and present status.
3. Status leaks through exchange and deference relations.
4. Potential exchange partners look to status to make inferences about quality.

While I have elaborated this conception of status in a way that hopefully clarifies its relation to the economic conception of a signal and the economic conception of reputation, it is also important to underscore that this conception of status is quite similar to other conceptions of status or prestige found in the sociological literature. Since Weber (1948), an essential feature of status systems has been the property of closure, in which there are restrictions on mobility and affiliations between status groups, and the standing of a particular status group in the broader society is a function of the deference or "honor" given to those within that particular group.

In classic studies of groups and social exchange (e.g., Blau 1955; Goode 1978; Whyte 1981), status differences are strongly correlated with differences in the quality of an individual's contributions to the group of which the individual is a part. In some instances, the status differences induce self-fulfilling prophecies in terms of performance. For example, Whyte observed how status differences among a group of young adult males engendered differences in athletic performance that, in turn, reinforced the initial status differences. Similarly, the expectation-states tradition (Berger et al. 1977) highlights the extent to which personal characteristics can become the basis for status distinctions, which induce corresponding differences in demonstrated ability.

There are also some strong points of overlap between the concept of status elaborated herein and the concept of status in an especially provocative model of group dynamics recently developed by Gould (2001). What makes Gould's model so provocative—and my reason for commenting on the model in some detail—is that Gould develops a general model of status hierarchies within groups from some axiomatic assumptions about people's desires. He then derives from this model and tests several propositions about affiliation patterns within groups.

Gould's formal model proceeds from two basic assumptions about what people desire: they wish to affiliate with others who are of high quality, and they wish to affiliate with others who are likely to reciprocate an affiliation attempt. An actor's status can be understood as the deference one implicitly receives owing to the ratio of affiliation attempts received versus affiliations given. While individuals wish to affiliate with those who are of high quality, Gould assumes that there is uncertainty in quality judgments, and people look to others' evaluations to address this uncertainty. By implication, individuals wish to affiliate with high-status others since status is indicative of quality.

Because high-status individuals are likely to be the targets for disproportionate numbers of affiliation attempts, they are unable to reciprocate all these attempts. Since the high-status actors also wish to affiliate with high-quality others, they will show a preference for affiliating with other high-status actors. Accordingly, the more that low-status actors value reciprocation, the less that they will seek out the attention of the high-status members of their group, and the more that the group will be characterized by status-based homophily.

Like the conception of status that I have proposed, Gould's conception of status implies a loose, positive correlation between status and quality. In both models, the highest-status actors are on average the highest-quality, and discrepancies in quality do not perfectly correspond to discrepancies in status.

Moreover, in Gould's model, the Matthew Effect can largely be understood as the fundamental reason why discrepancies in quality do not correspond to discrepancies in status. Since all actors are looking to one another's affiliation attempts to resolve their uncertainties about quality, any differences in the affiliation attempts received by actors (i.e., any differences in the status across actors) accentuate the perception of quality differences.

The major difference between Gould's conception of status and the one that I propose concerns the check on the self-reinforcing nature of the Matthew Effect. In my conception, the fundamental check on the Matthew Effect is that high-status actors fear a loss of status due to any association with the low-status actors. Were it not for the risk of their status leaking through exchange relations, the high-status actors would permeate all market niches. In Gould's model of status hierarchies, status does not leak. The fundamental check on the Matthew Effect is that high-status actors are constrained in the total number of ties that they can form, and low-status actors are averse to forming ties with high-status actors who do not reciprocate their affiliations. However, if the actors in Gould's model have little desire for reciprocation, then the highest-status actors would dominate the market insofar as they would be the sole targets for all attempted affiliations.

So, to summarize, both conceptions of status imply a loose correlation between status and quality; the major difference between the two models is that Gould posits a capacity constraint on the part of high-status actors and a desire for reciprocation on the part of low-status actors, whereas I posit a leakage of status through exchange relations. When actors are individuals, it may be reasonable to assume that high-status actors would have a well-defined capacity constraint in the volume of ties that they can form; however, when actors are corporate entities, it is harder to justify such a capacity constraint. Tiffany's avoidance of ties to purveyors and buyers of turquoise cannot really be understood in terms of Tiffany's lack of resources for forming such ties or the distaste that purveyors of turquoise might feel for lack of proper reciprocation from Tiffany's if those purveyors attempted an affiliation.

Having made this observation, I think it would be a mistake to conclude that the model of status I propose is relevant to corporate actors whereas Gould's model is relevant to natural persons. In the previous chapter, I referenced Elias and Scotson's example of the newcomer whose status was tainted after she was seen to have invited workmen for tea. Such an example clearly points to the fact that status can leak between natural persons as easily as it can between organizations.

Before concluding this discussion of the way in which the conception of status as a signal relates to other conceptions, I would like to comment briefly on one way in which my conception of status differs from at least some of the classic accounts of status. Scholars such as Weber (1948), Blau (1955), and Goode (1978) contend that status can be valued as an end in itself (rather than as a signal of underlying qualities). Though some sociologists might argue that the conception of status as a signal is more economic and implicitly less sociological than a conception of status that does posit that status is valued as an end in itself, a number of economists have developed accounts of status in which a desire for status is incorporated into actors' utility functions (e.g., Hirsch 1976; Frank 1985). Therefore, it would be a mistake to conclude that the distinguishing element of a sociological perspective on status is that status is valued as an end. What distinguishes the sociological perspective on status is the focus on the mechanisms by which status distinctions arise; Hirsch (1976) and Frank (1985), by contrast, both simply posit status distinctions as arising from formal distinctions in hierarchies without paying any attention to the relational foundations of these distinctions.

More important, while the conception of status as a signal does not require that actors value status as an end in itself, the conception of status as a signal does not preclude actors from desiring status for its own sake. One can think about the value that actors place on status as an end as providing some baseline value for status; however, to the extent that status serves as a signal, it will provide value above this baseline level to the degree that there is uncertaintly about quality.

In the next chapter, I use the conception of status as a signal as a guide to analyzing market dynamics in the investment banking industry. In particular, I focus on the implications of status for costs, revenues, and the pattern of exchange relations within the investment banking industry.

In shifting from a theoretical discussion of the reasons that status *can* be regarded as a signal to an empirical analysis of whether status *is* regarded as a signal, it will become important to try to control for other signals on which market actors can rely to make inferences about underlying quality. If the linkage between status and quality is necessarily loose, it is possible that there are other signals of quality for which there is a tighter linkage. For example, in certain product markets, it may be possible for high-quality firms to signal their higher quality with warranties. If the linkage between quality and a signal like a warranty is sufficiently tight, then uncertainty is effectively removed, and status becomes irrelevant to the decisions of market actors.

To the extent that status is an important signal of quality in the investment banking industry, we should find evidence of the following (even controlling for reliance on other signals):

- An inverse relationship should exist between status and the costs of making an offering of a given quality.
- The returns to status should increase with the uncertainty that consumers have about the ability of banks to make a quality offering.
- Previous exchange partners of an investment bank should rely less on status as a signal of quality to make inferences about the desirability of a subsequent exchange relation since they have private knowledge of the bank's quality.

To the extent that status leaks through the exchange relations among banks, we should find evidence of

- status-based homophily in partnership arrangements among investment banks (i.e., high-status banks partnering disproportionately with other high-status banks and low-status banks partnering disproportionately with other low-status banks);
- an increase (decrease) in the level of homophily when an investment bank's exchange partners have reason to be more (less) uncertain about quality and thus look more (less) to status as a signal of quality;
- an increase (decrease) in a bank's status when it enters into exchange relations with partners that are higher (lower) in status.

Though these expectations will serve to guide the analysis of the investment banking industry in the next chapter, the examination of the investment banking industry will not be limited to these particular considerations. In addition, we will focus on the subjective importance that the banks attach to status as well as to any direct or indirect information about how status relates to costs for a given level of quality.

Chapter Three

GETTING MORE FOR LESS IN THE INVESTMENT BANKING INDUSTRY

THE PREVIOUS two chapters provided the initial theoretical foundation for this book. They elaborated the concept of status as a signal that is grounded in deference relations and leaks through exchange relations, and they developed some of the implications of this leaky signal for market outcomes. Though the first chapters contained passing references to different empirical contexts, this chapter—which examines the relevance of status in investment banking markets—will be the first detailed empirical examination of status in a particular market context.

I focus first on the investment banking industry primarily because it offers an exceptional indicator of status in the form of what are called "tombstone advertisements," which I shall discuss in more detail shortly. In addition, data services tracking the investment banking industry provide considerable data on the exchange relations on the producer side of the market as well as the prices that investment banks charge to their clients.

Investment banking is one of many industries in the financial sector of the economy—a sector that has received much attention from scholars associated with the new economic sociology (Abolafia 1996; Adler and Adler 1984; Baker 1984; Davis and Mizruchi 1999; Jensen 2003a, 2003b; Mizruchi and Stearns 1994; Rao, Davis, and Ward 2000; Zuckerman 1999). One can safely conclude that the financial sector has received such attention from sociologists for two related reasons. First, financial markets would seem to provide a compelling test case for establishing the relevance of sociological ideas to market phenomena. Few if any sectors contain markets that better conform to assumptions associated with the economic model of perfect competition—specifically, the profit maximization of firms, the utility maximization of individuals, and perfect information about the opportunities for exchange. While profit-maximizing firms and utility-maximizing individuals might be reasonable baseline assumptions in a number of other sectors, the markets in the financial sector seem unique in the extent to which they are alleged to closely mirror the information assumptions. The belief in the appropriateness of the information assumptions is strongly reflected in Eugene Fama's influential efficient market hypothesis (1970), which states that individual investors cannot "beat the market" over the long run, because at any particular time the price of a stock reflects all the available information on the stock. Fama argues that since all investors have the same information, no single investor can have an advantage in predicting a return on a stock.[1] As a measure of the influence of this hypothesis on the literature, the initial review paper in which Fama elaborates the hypothesis has received over one thousand citations in the *Social Science Citation Index*. Although many economists and noneconomists have challenged the efficient market hypothesis, just the formulation of the hypothesis and the importance of the hypothesis to financial theory are sufficient to underscore the effect of strong disclosure requirements, which push market conditions in the direction of those assumptions underlying the model of perfect competition.[2] Legal requirements and the interests of individuals converge in trying to ensure that the information available to some is available to all. So, for example, every time that bonds or stocks are issued in the United States, there is a public record of the issuance. There is not a similar public record, for example, of every car or dishwasher that is sold. Thus the financial sector would seem to represent a theoretically compelling arena for sociological inquiry into market dynamics. Analyses documenting the relevance of sociological ideas to the financial sector would seem to imply the broad applicability of such ideas to other sectors as well. Accordingly, for both theoretical and empirical reasons, the financial sector has been one that has attracted considerable sociological interest.

This chapter is organized as follows. First, it provides some institutional details on the investment banking industry itself. Second, it discusses how status was manifest at least through the late 1980s in artifacts known as tombstone advertisements. Third, it provides some illustrative information on how status lowers investment banks' costs and potentially increases their revenues. The chapter concludes with a systematic examination of the relationship between status and "spread"—essentially the price that investment banks charge for underwriting securities.

---

[1] Contrary to what sociologists sometimes believe, perfect information does not imply omniscience, an ability to tell which future states of the world will be realized. Rather, the assumption of perfect information implies a commonly held awareness of the probabilities of the possible future states of the world. Moreover, the assumption of perfect information implies that market actors are aware of all exchange opportunities and that there is implicitly no uncertainty about the quality of each opportunity. Put in the form of a cliché, you see all opportunities, and what you see is what you get.

[2] Some might take recent insider trading and stock manipulation scandals as evidence that the informational assumptions of the efficient market hypothesis are not valid approximations of reality. Such scandals underscore the strong interests of well-placed individuals in keeping information private. However, even if the occurrence of these scandals shows that there are attempts to subvert public disclosure requirements, the fact that such attempts have come to light as scandals also is a testament to the strong concern in these markets with making information public. If a car designer has private information that a car that he has designed is inferior, he can purchase another car without this information being public. If the CEO of a firm is worried about the prospects of his company and sells stock, his selling of stock must be public.

WHAT DO INVESTMENT BANKS DO IN THE PRIMARY SECURITIES MARKETS?

Investment banks participate in a broad array of activities; this chapter focuses on only one of them, the competition among investment banks in what are called the primary securities markets. Stated broadly, the business or function of investment banks in the primary securities markets is to reduce the transaction costs associated with market exchanges. In these markets, transaction costs can be roughly defined as the costs of "getting together" securities issuers and investors. This function is analytically distinct from the brokerage activity that investment banks undertake in the secondary markets, where previously issued securities are traded among investors. This function is also analytically distinct from the facilitation of mergers and acquisitions activity among corporations.

There are two general classes of corporate securities that investment banks underwrite in the primary securities markets: equity and debt. A purchaser of equity gains stock, or an ownership stake, in the corporation and a share of the profits of the firm. A purchaser of debt acquires a bond that specifies terms of repayment for an initial loan to the corporation. There are two types of offering within each of these two broad classes. Equity is divided into initial public offerings (IPOs) and common stock offerings. An IPO is a company's first sale of stock to the public; a common stock offering is a sale of equity by a publicly traded firm that by definition has previously had its initial public offering. Debt is divided into investment-grade and non-investment-grade securities, the latter of which may be labeled high-yield or "junk" debt. What distinguishes investment-grade debt from high-yield debt is the risk that the issuing corporation will default on the loan repayment to the bondholder. The risk is determined by the major bond-rating agencies: Moody's and Standard & Poor's, who apply systematic formulas to the assets and liabilities of the firm in order to determine the ultimate rating.

In the primary securities markets, investment banks perform this function of getting issues and investors together by paying the issuers for the securities and then selling those securities to investors. The activity of purchasing and reselling securities is called underwriting, and the fee that a bank earns for this activity is called the *spread*. A variety of factors—most important, the size of the offering or the risk associated with placement—affect whether the spread is especially large or small, but underwriting spreads (at least over the period covered by my data) typically range from 0.1 percent of the dollar value of the offering to about 4 percent of the value.

While formally the process of underwriting seems to simply involve the transfer of a security between different parties, the success of a bank in underwriting depends to a large extent on whether the bank can bring the decisions of market actors closer to the assumption of perfect information at the core of the efficient market hypothesis. Since no issuers and few investors are always in the primary markets looking for exchange partners, both sets of actors face the difficult problem of locating actors from the other side of the market with whom to trade. Even if issuers and investors can identity potential exchange partners, issuers face risk and uncertainty about the nature of demand on the investors' side, and investors confront considerable risk and uncertainty regarding the financial soundness of the issuers. Rather than searching for actors from the other side of the capital market and establishing a price themselves, issuers and investors seek and are sought by investment banks that, in turn, compete with one another by trying to reduce issuers' and investors' uncertainty about each other.

In saying that investors confront both "risk" and "uncertainty," it is important to emphasize that these are distinct analytical constructs, and for the purposes of understanding the role of status not only in investment banking but in all markets, uncertainty is the concept of more analytical relevance. Following a definitional convention that goes back to Knight (1921), I use the term "risk" to denote contexts in which there is a known probability distribution of outcomes though the actual outcome is not yet known, and I use the term "uncertainty" to denote contexts in which the underlying probability distribution is unknown. One can draw on gambling as an example to illustrate the distinction. When an individual plays roulette in a casino, it seems appropriate to use the term risk to characterize the decision about where the individual places his chips, because there is a clear probability distribution of outcomes; however, it is more appropriate to use the term uncertainty to reflect the possibility that the wheel has somehow been rigged or that there are rules at this particular roulette table of which the individual is unaware.[3] In financial markets, as in casinos, risk is inherent in practically all decisions, and agencies such as Moody's and Standard & Poor's provide information on debt offerings that allows investors to calculate the likelihood that a firm will default on its debt payments. However, above and beyond the risk associated with the purchase of individual securities, issuers and investors confront uncertainty in their selection of an investment bank as an intermediary of exchange. For example, the issuer depends

---

[3] It is important to acknowledge that the distinction that I am elaborating is still a controversial one in economics. While there are economic and noneconomic scholars who are persuaded that empirical (Camerer 1995) or theoretical research (Kreps and Porteus 1978) has provided compelling support of this distinction, there are still economists who believe that all uncertainty can be properly conceptualized as risk. In part, this desire to conceptualize uncertainty as risk derives from the fact that the mathematics of risk are more tractable than the mathematics of uncertainty, and one can assume that complete ignorance about the probability distribution can be replaced with an assumption that all possible future states of the world are equally likely. It seems both impossible and inappropriate to try to resolve this debate in the context of the book. I think it is safe to say that sociologists are generally comfortable with the distinction and see uncertainty as fundamental to market processes (e.g., White 2002; Kocak 2003; Podolny and Hsu 2003).

on the bank for advice regarding the optimum price for that particular security. If the price is too low, the issuer will not receive as much capital for the offering as it otherwise could have. If the price is too high, the issuer will still receive all of the capital from the investment bank or syndicate for the security, but a quick fall in the value of the security will anger investors and make them fearful of investing in, and thus providing money to, that issuer in the future. If the security is not adequately distributed to a sufficiently large number of investors and if the bank does not facilitate the trading of the securities in the secondary markets, the price of the security will decline, and again investors will be much more hesitant to direct financial resources to the issuing company in the future. Since there are not well-established probability distributions for the adequacy of a bank's pricing decisions or for the quality of its efforts in the secondary markets, the term uncertainty is appropriate in characterizing the decision-making of an issuer when selecting an investment bank.

Investors are obviously at risk, because there is risk inherent in any security; they look to the underwriting bank to at least give them an accurate perception of the risk inherent in a particular security, but there is uncertainty about the extent to which the bank will provide them with accurate information about the risk. However, like the issuers, investors also confront uncertainty about the support that the bank will provide for trading the security in the secondary markets.

Banks reduce the uncertainty confronted by market actors through two interrelated activities. First, they develop an extensive network of relations with issuers, investors, and even other investment banks. Second, and more important for the first purpose of this book, they cultivate a distinct status vis-à-vis their competitors, which provides a tangible basis for the rational calculations of exchange partners. We shall consider each of these interrelated activities in turn.

Strong and varied connections to a relatively large number of issuers and investors, a state sometimes referred to as "being in the deal stream," provides a bank with an intimate knowledge of supply and demand in the market (Eccles and Crane 1988). The greater this knowledge, the better the bank can take on the role approximating that of the mythical Walrasian auctioneer in general equilibrium economics, finding possible exchange partners and setting a market-clearing price for an issue.

In addition to cultivating an extensive network of relations with investors and issuers, investment banks—from the emergence of the U.S. banking industry in the late 1800s through at least the 1990s—would invariably form extensive ties to one another through participation in syndicates, a collection of banks that jointly underwrite a security offering. Despite intense competition among investment banks for the opportunity to lead a security offering, the selected bank would typically not underwrite the entire offering itself. Rather, it would form and lead a syndicate. The leader of a syndicate is referred to as the lead manager. Either by itself or with the assistance of one or several banks that receive the title of comanagers, the lead manager determines the composition of the syndicate and the proportion of securities to be allocated to each syndicate member. Occasionally an issuer will request that a manager include a particular bank or set of banks as comanager(s) on an issue because of some connection between the issuer and the chosen comanager, such as common regional affiliation or prior business dealings; however, the choice of comanagers is usually at the discretion of the lead manager.

When one takes a broad cross-sectional and longitudinal view of the investment banking industry, one sees considerable variation in the use of syndicates across banks and across time. Indeed, a particular salient dimension along which banks differ in organizational form is the degree to which they depend on ties internal or external to the firm for the distribution and trading of securities. For example, if one looks across banks during the 1980s—the period on which I have gathered considerable systematic data—Morgan Stanley was at one extreme in that its connections to investors were mediated by large syndicates. As it had done since the turn of the century, Morgan Stanley relied almost exclusively on these syndicates for distribution and trading in the secondary markets. At the other extreme during the 1980s were Merrill Lynch, which internalized the ties to the investor side of the market through the development of an extensive in-house sales network, and Salomon Brothers, which internalized connections through the development of a vast trading force. Those firms with internalized networks of exchange relations still used syndicates, but their extensive internal resources allowed them to rely on smaller syndicates or to underwrite a moderately sized offering alone if the need arises.

Over the history of the investment banking industry in the United States, prior to the 1980s, syndicates had been the predominant form of underwriting. However, in March 1982, a Trojan horse appeared when the SEC enacted Rule 415, which allowed a practice called "shelf registration." This practice would usher in a declining use of syndicates. Prior to Rule 415, issuers had to register every new security issue separately, and during the time of registration of a large issue from a blue-chip company, a lead bank would put together a large syndicate to help underwrite the issue. However, Rule 415 allowed blue-chip companies to register a large block of securities, any fraction of which could be sold off during the two-year period following the registration. Shelf registration allowed blue-chip companies to take advantage of sudden fluctuations in interest rates. For banks, the consequence was that they no longer had time to put together a large syndicate; rather, they needed to rely to a much greater degree on their own internal distribution channels.

Though shelf registration existed side by side with a strong reliance on syndicates for most of the decade, large syndicates began to become increasingly atypical in the 1990s. As I will soon discuss, institutional details associated with the syndicate form of organization provide valuable clues regarding the status distinctions among securities markets. Therefore, if one is interested in the systematic examination of status dynamics in investment banking, it is appropriate to focus on a period in which there was still a strong reliance on syndicates. The analyses in this chapter accordingly draws on data from the 1980s, arguably the last decade in which the syndicate system remained a critical organizational form in the primary markets.

When a bank is trying to put together a syndicate, potential syndicate members confront uncertainty that is similar to that faced by investors. The potential member banks depend on a lead manager's ability to select offerings for which there is enough demand that the offerings can be placed at a price that will allow the banks to earn a sufficient spread. Thus a lead manager confronts three potential constituencies, each of which faces some uncertainty in its decision to enter into an exchange relation with the lead manager.

A bank's external ties to investors, issuers, and to other banks enables the bank to reduce its *own* uncertainty about market conditions by providing itself with knowledge of supply and demand for particular securities as well as the qualities of the firms providing those securities. However, to restate and hence emphasize an important point: a bank's competitive success is contingent not only on the reduction of its own uncertainty about market conditions; it depends even more directly on its ability to serve as a guide through the uncertainties that permeate the decisions of other actors in the market. Therefore, in addition to developing ties that enhance its own knowledge of a given primary securities market, a bank tries to reduce the uncertainties confronted by its three constituencies through the formation of a distinct identity or status vis-à-vis the other banks.

STATUS DETERMINATION IN THE INVESTMENT BANKING INDUSTRY

Part of a bank's status is determined by the bank's performance in underwriting securities. Banks that demonstrate superior competence in the underwriting function will be regarded as higher-status than banks that do not demonstrate this superior competence. However, past performance is often difficult to evaluate. Market participants can engage in considerable speculation over such questions as whether a bank might have underwritten an offering at terms more favorable to the issuer or whether problems encountered in an offering were due more to factors within a bank's control than to factors beyond the bank's control. Such speculation is enhanced by the fact that the investment banking arena is an extremely dynamic—even volatile—environment. As a result, the connection between past performance and present ability is often considered quite tenuous. In a way that is quite consistent with the theoretical relationship between status and quality posited in the previous chapter, there is a "loose linkage" between a bank's status and the qualities or attributes for which that status might be regarded as a signal.

On account of that loose linkage, a bank's status is not only a function of the bank's performance but also a function of the relational position that the bank cultivates in the market. Investment bankers are extremely concerned about the identity of actors with whom their bank is associated because such associations affect how the bank is perceived. The clearest evidence of such a concern comes from a consideration of *tombstone advertisements*, announcements of security offerings that appear in the major financial publications such as the *Wall Street Journal, Institutional Investor*, and *Investment Dealer's Digest*. Figure 3.1 presents an example of such an advertisement. The figure depicts the tombstone advertisement for a debt offering of the Chrysler Corporation, when then CEO Lee Iacocca was in the process of leading the corporation back from the verge of bankruptcy. The advertisement lists the issuers, the type and size of the offering, and the banks involved in underwriting the offerings.[4]

Although the decline in the use of syndicates in the 1990s has made such advertisements with a large number of listed banks an increasing rarity, such advertisements appeared for practically every major security offering from the turn of the twentieth century until the 1990s.[5] At the beginning of the twentieth century, such advertisements served to inform investors of the existence of a new security offering. However, even after the emergence of an electronically integrated market in which major investors were aware of an offering minutes after its release, these advertisements—which appeared in the financial publications the day after the announced security offering took place—persisted. Accordingly, the term "advertisement" became an increasing misnomer, leading a number of scholars to conclude that the primary purpose of these visual announcements was to clarify and reinforce the status distinctions among the banks (Hayes 1971, 1979; Eccles and Crane 1988; Chernow 1990).

There are well-defined norms for the allocation of banks to positions on the tombstone. The highest-status position on the tombstone is the one that is

[4] These announcements acquired the moniker *tombstone* advertisement because they were listed opposite the obituaries when they first appeared in publications at the turn of the last century.

[5] It is important to emphasize that the decline in syndicates and accordingly the decline in the appearance of tombstone advertisements does not imply any less concern with status. To this day, market participants still use such terminology as "bulge bracket" to distinguish the elite firms from the rest, and bankers still obsess about their standing vis-à-vis other firms. Thus, the concern with status has not declined; all that has declined has been the appearance of this particular visible manifestation of status. Bankers still look, for example, to partnering relations among banks as indicators of status even if such partnering relations are not visibly represented in a one-page advertisement in the *Wall Street Journal*.

This announcement is neither an offer to sell nor a solicitation of an offer to buy these securities.
The offer is made only by the Prospectus Supplement and the related Prospectus.

New Issue / February 13, 1985

$100,000,000

12⅛% Subordinated Notes due February 15, 1990

Price 100% and accrued interest from February 15, 1985

Copies of the Prospectus Supplement and the related Prospectus may be obtained
in any State in which this announcement is circulated only from such of the
undersigned as may legally offer these securities in such State.

Salomon Brothers Inc   **Merrill Lynch Capital Markets**

The First Boston Corporation   **Goldman, Sachs & Co.**

Lehman Brothers   **Morgan Stanley & Co.**
Shearson Lehman / American Express Inc.   Incorporated

ABD Securities Corporation   **Bear, Stearns & Co.**   **Alex. Brown & Sons**
                                                                     Incorporated

Deutsche Bank Capital   **Dillon, Read & Co. Inc.**   **Donaldson, Lufkin & Jenrette**
Corporation   Securities Corporation

Drexel Burnham Lambert   **EuroPartners Securities Corporation**
Incorporated

E. F. Hutton & Company Inc.   **Kidder, Peabody & Co.**   **Lazard Frères & Co.**
                                     Incorporated

PaineWebber   **Prudential-Bache**   **L. F. Rothschild, Unterberg, Towbin**
Incorporated   Securities

Smith Barney, Harris Upham & Co.   **Swiss Bank Corporation International**
Incorporated   Securities Inc.

UBS Securities Inc.   **Wertheim & Co., Inc.**   **Dean Witter Reynolds Inc.**

American Securities Corporation   **Daiwa Securities America Inc.**

A. G. Edwards & Sons, Inc.   **Interstate Securities Corporation**   **McDonald & Company**
                                                                        Securities, Inc.

Moseley, Hallgarten, Estabrook & Weeden Inc.   **The Nikko Securities Co.**
                                                          International, Inc.

Nomura Securities International, Inc.   **Thomson McKinnon Securities Inc.**

Tucker, Anthony & R. L. Day, Inc.   **Yamaichi International (America), Inc.**

FIGURE 3.1. Example of a tombstone advertisement

the uppermost and farthest to the left. The lead manager of the syndicate always occupies this position. Salomon Brothers is the lead manager in figure 3.1. If there is one comanager for an offering, that comanager is invariably listed to the right of the lead manager. Merrill Lynch is the comanager for the Chrysler offering. If there is more than one comanager, they will be arranged beneath the name of the lead manager. The manager's and comanagers' relations are among the most visible and significant in the syndicate. Managers and comanagers will underwrite a much larger share of the offering than other participants. Comanagers may assist the manager in performing due diligence; they may help recruit additional syndicate managers, and they may help to make a market for a security once it is issued.

Following the comanagers are the rest of the banks in the syndicate arranged hierarchically into brackets; the higher the bracket, the more prestigious the position. The number of brackets varies, depending primarily on the number of banks. There may be as few as one or as many as ten.

One can observe banks in the management or comanagement positions that are lower-status than the nonmanagement banks in a syndicate. However, status distinctions among the nonmanagement positions are strictly enforced. The highest bracket on many ads is labeled the bulge bracket or special bracket because its members' names historically have appeared in larger type than the names of banks in the lower brackets. Over the history of the industry, the bulge bracket has been reserved for the names of the roughly five or six highest-status firms in the industry. Over the period of the 1980s, the bulge bracket firms were Morgan Stanley, First Boston Corporation, Goldman Sachs, Salomon Brothers, and Merrill Lynch.

Banks are listed alphabetically within each bracket. For example, in figure 3.1, the first bracket begins with the First Boston Corporation and ends with Morgan Stanley. ABD Securities Corporation is the first bank listed in the second bracket, and Dean Witter Reynolds is the last bank in this bracket (since Dean is a first name, and not a last name, this firm is listed alphabetically by Witter). Finally, the third bracket begins with American Securities Corporation and ends with Yamaichi International (America), Inc. There are, therefore, no formally designated status distinctions within brackets. However, the fact that banks are listed alphabetically to downplay any possible status distinctions within brackets does not mean that there is a complete absence of such subtle distinctions. For example, at least during the early and mid-1980s, Merrill Lynch was considered a special-bracket firm, but it was typically regarded as being slightly lower in status than other banks in the special bracket, as suggested by an article revealingly titled "Will the Sun Ever Shine on Merrill's Investment Bankers?" (Kadlec 1986).

If such informal distinctions become sufficiently acknowledged, then a bank's typical bracket position comes to reflect its change in status. Even out-of-order brackets exist for the one or two banks in a syndicate that occupy an intermediate status between two relatively large brackets of banks. There may be minor fluctuations in a bank's bracket position that are due not to changes in its status but to the fact that a bank has obtained an unusually large or small share of an offering for some idiosyncratic reason, such as a regional connection between the bank and the issuer. For example, in figure 3.1 Lehman Brothers appears with the bulge bracket firms in a position that is slightly higher than is typical. As recently as the mid-1970s, such shifts due to share size were extremely infrequent. Though they became much more common throughout the late 1970s and early 1980s, these fluctuations were invariably limited to one bracket higher or lower than the bank's typical position in such an advertisement.

Position in the tombstone is not a trivial matter. There are economic advantages associated with bracket position; the higher a bank's bracket, the greater the share of the offering that is allocated to the bank to underwrite. Nevertheless, concern with position extends beyond the desire to obtain a large share of the offering. A bank's concern with the status associated with the tombstone is sufficiently great that it will withdraw from an offering if it is given a position in the syndicate and thus a placement on the tombstone that the bank's managers believe to be incommensurate with the bank's status. For example, in a 1985 offering for which it was lead manager, Goldman Sachs sought to divide the bracket directly beneath the bulge bracket into two distinct brackets. However, nine of the firms that would have ended up in the lower division refused to participate in the offering (Monroe 1986). Similarly, in 1987, five high-status firms refused to participate in a $2.4 billion financing for the Farmers Home Administration when thirteen regional, small minority-owned firms were to receive a larger share of the offering and thus a higher place on the tombstone (*New York Times*, September 21, 1987). In both of these examples, banks preferred to withdraw from deals rather than accept a tombstone position they felt to be diminutive.

Since a bank's underwriting ability is a function of its position in the "deal stream" and since participation in syndicates is historically one of the ways that a bank can accurately assess the supply and demand for particular securities, such a refusal to appear in a syndicate underscores the tension between activity that is conducive to the better performance of the bank and behavior that enhances or at least preserves the status of the bank. Although underwriting ability and status ought to be positively correlated, the relational component of status and market knowledge occasionally forces a bank to sacrifice an improvement in one for enhancement of the other.

Just like the bracket positions beneath them, the manager and comanager positions carry status implications. For example, from at least the turn of the century until the late 1970s, Morgan Stanley was generally regarded as the flagship firm of the investment banking industry. Even the other special-bracket firms were not considered to be on a par with Morgan Stanley's status.

Consistent with such an image, Morgan Stanley not only refused to accept any position on a tombstone less than that of the lead management position but also refused to accede to a given issuer's request to allow any comanager on the offering.

To preserve its policy, Morgan Stanley would forgo what could be quite lucrative business opportunities from such potential corporate clients as Houston Industries and Singer and even from such political entities as the government of Japan (Chernow 1990). The test of the policy came in 1979, when IBM, one of the world's largest corporations and a Morgan Stanley client for twenty years, insisted that Morgan Stanley accept Salomon Brothers as comanager. Morgan Stanley was to receive approximately $1 million in underwriting fees for leading this issue; however, Morgan Stanley refused to accept Salomon Brothers as comanager. IBM responded not only by using Salomon Brothers as the sole manager for this issue but also by relying on Salomon as its primary underwriter throughout the 1980s. Following the confrontation with IBM, Morgan Stanley gradually revised its policies. By 1981 Morgan Stanley had agreed to appear in a syndicate role beneath a lead manager and comanager, but it had to be in its own bracket—listed before the other bulge bracket firms. By the late 1980s Morgan Stanley was routinely appearing in alphabetical order with the other bulge bracket firms.

Importantly, such preoccupation with tombstone position has broader significance. It is simply a particular manifestation of a bank's more general concern with which actors are seen as its peers. Journalistic accounts will highlight the prestige that accrues to a rising bank when it occupies a management or comanagement position on an offering that would typically be managed only by one of the special-bracket firms. For example, a 1976 *Forbes* article on the investment banking firm Bache Halsey Stuart noted that on May 18, "American Telephone and Telegraph announced that Bache Halsey Stuart would co-manage its huge 12-million-share offering scheduled for June 16th. In cracking AT&T's traditionally exclusive fraternity of investment bankers—Morgan Stanley, Goldman Sachs, Merrill Lynch, and Salomon Brothers—Bache gained new status."[6]

Such articles are notable not only because they emphasize the importance that bankers ascribe to status but also because they highlight the relational underpinnings of status. Status comes not just from performance or underwriting volume but from association with others of a given status, as suggested in the reference in the *Forbes* article to AT&T's exclusive fraternity of bankers. For

---

[6] While one might look at such examples as being inconsistent with the equilibrating dynamics implicit in the status-based model of market competition, there is nothing about the status-based model of market competition that prevents change because of luck or exogenous shocks. In later chapters, I will discuss the topic of change more directly; at this point, I simply wish to note in passing that status distinctions can be self-reinforcing but there can still be exogenous or random sources of change in the status ordering.

Bache Halsey Stuart, having a client as prominent as AT&T reflected positively on the firm. Conversely, for a bank to be in a bracket position lower than its status reflects negatively on the bank.

So far in this chapter, we have observed that both risk and uncertainty accompany the decisions of actors in the primary securities markets. We have seen that investment banks develop networks that function to reduce risk and uncertainty. By serving as conduits for the flow of information, these networks improve a bank's own knowledge about facets of the market. At the same time, the patterns of exchange and deference among the actors in the market—most notably among the banks themselves—yield a tangible status ordering. Finally, we have considered qualitative evidence that banks seem to care deeply about their status.

Yet, the conception of status as a signal, as elaborated in the previous two chapters, implies not that banks care about status primarily as an end itself. The conception of status as a signal has clear implications for a bank's costs and price (spread). The higher a firm's status, the lower will be its costs for products or services of a given quality. The more that a bank's exchange partner is uncertain about whether any bank can provide products or services at a given level of quality, the greater will be the returns that the bank can derive from status. We now consider these economic implications of status—first by drawing on some vignettes from the industry and then in a more rigorous analysis.

The Economic Implications of Status: Some Illustrations

Illustrations of the potential revenue implications of status are relatively straightforward. Indeed, we have already observed a way in which status enhances revenues when we discussed the distribution rules for shares among syndicate members. The higher a bank's status, the larger the share of an offering to which the bank is entitled. Moreover, to the extent that the largest, most prestigious issuers (like AT&T in the aforementioned example) are looking to partner with high-status banks, status carries with it increased access to the blue-chip firms that issue the lion's share of securities.

What about the cost implications? Chapter 2 highlighted several cost advantages that can accrue from status: for a given quality of output, higher status can result in lower transaction costs, advertising costs, financial costs, and labor costs. In the primary securities markets, a clear example of the inverse relationship between status and transaction costs was provided in an interview that I conducted with the head of a middle-size investment banking firm about procedures involved in putting together an underwriting syndicate. In forming a syndicate, the lead manager, along with the issuer, may participate in quite a number of "due diligence" meetings, where syndicate members "kick the tires" of the corporation to assess the financial viability of the offering. They hold these meetings as a way of maintaining financial responsibility to investors.

When asked about the advantages of status, the executive replied:

> Typically if you hear that Goldman Sachs or Salomon or whatever is doing an underwriting, they usually have pretty stringent requirements, and it is usually a plus for the company that they are doing work for that Goldman Sachs wants to be their investment banker or underwriter or whatever, [that is] a plus with reference to the market place. Half the time, if Goldman Sachs calls or Salomon call us and says [they] are going to be an underwriter for Ford Motor or whatever and asks, "Do you want to be part of the underwriting group?" we almost don't have to do any diligence; you just say yes. On the other hand, if a smaller firm which just doesn't have the credentials calls us, we will probably do more diligence and be less likely to follow suit.

This investment banker points to an inverse relationship between the status of a bank and the transaction costs associated with facilitating the exchange between issuer and investors. The higher the status of the bank, the easier and hence the less costly for a bank to put together a syndicate for a given issue.[7]

A higher-status bank not only realizes such advantages in its relations with syndicate members; it accrues them in its relations with investors as well. Just as the potential syndicate member is more likely to believe that an issue is of high quality because its offering is being led by a high-status underwriter, so an investor is more likely to believe that an issue is of superior quality if it is underwritten by a higher-status firm rather than a lower-status firm. Given that the primary function of an investment bank is to reduce the transaction costs associated with placement of securities, such transaction costs are quite significant.

Banks can also realize transaction cost advantages in the form of free advertising when the business press turns disproportionately to high-status banks for insights and opinions on the market. In the previously mentioned article "Will the Sun Ever Shine on Merrill's Investment Bankers?" investment bankers from Merrill Lynch lamented the fact that though they had a larger market presence than several of the special-bracket firms, their comparatively lower status meant that they were frequently ignored by the business press, which sought advice from industry leaders on trends in the primary securities markets (Kadlec 1986). In order for Merrill Lynch to acquire a comparable

---

[7] One could be concerned, as one reviewer was, that this example suggests that the real cost savings are for the low-status bank, since the low-status bank does not need to perform due diligence but the high-status bank does. However, one needs to recall that the lead bank receives a disproportionate share of an offering, and the disproportionate share of the offering should more than compensate the bank for the added transaction costs of leading the offering. The important fact is that the high-status bank realizes transaction cost savings insofar as it does not need to devote as much time and effort to convincing others to join the syndicate.

presence in the leading trade publications, it would have had to take out paid advertisements.

There is also illustrative evidence that for a given quality of employee, labor costs are lower for the higher-status banks. Again, Merrill Lynch is a case in point. In seeking to recruit MBAs from top business schools during the 1980s, Merrill Lynch had to offer more appealing compensation arrangements to potential recruits than other special-bracket firms were offering to retain the same talent.

It is thus clearly possible to come up with illustrations, first, of how status increases aggregate revenue and, second, of how status lowers costs (controlling for quality). Notably, however, these illustrations do not speak to the systematic relationship between status and profitability (i.e., spread) on any particular exchange. It is possible, for example, that high-status firms can have larger market share than lower-status firms, have lower costs for a given level of quality, and yet still find themselves in intense price competition. Indeed, the previous chapter made reference to the competition among the top accounting firms in the audit market, where this seemed to be the case. As Stevens (1991) observed, the high-status audit firms had access to clients to which the lower-status firms did not, and yet the high-status firms were bidding close to their costs. Over time, auditing services had become increasingly commoditized, and there was accordingly little uncertainty about whether a firm could perform an adequate audit.[8] Therefore, while the high-status accounting firms retained some of the cost advantages associated with status (e.g., lower labor costs for a given quality of employee and lower transaction costs of "getting in the door" to bid on the business of a prominent client with the hope of converting a commodity relation into a more lucrative consulting relation), higher status did not result in higher prices or even margins on individual transactions.

These last observations on the relationship between status, costs, and price can perhaps be further clarified with a minimal amount of formalism. If p_h and p_l are the prices charged by a high-status producer and a low-status producer, s_h and s_l are the statuses of the two producers, and Θ is the premium that a buyer is willing to pay for each unit increment of status, then the pricing mechanism reproduces the hierarchical ordering in the market to the extent that

$$p_h < p_l + \Theta(s_h - s_l). \qquad [3.1]$$

If the advantages of status are strictly on the cost side, then Θ equals zero and the inequality reduces to p_h and p_l, indicating that the high-status producer will actually have lower prices than the lower-status producer. The high-status

---

[8] Stevens's observations predate the Anderson/Enron scandals. It will be interesting to observe whether the scandals will decommoditize the auditing market by reintroducing uncertainty about whether an audit is above a given quality threshold.

producer could still have higher revenue than the low-status producer because of a higher overall volume; or, as in the auditor example, the high-status firm could try to leverage its lower costs and prices to gain entrée to exchange opportunities associated with a different service market. Thus, the conception of status as a signal does not imply an unconditional relationship between status and price. Rather, it is more accurate to say that the conception of status as a signal implies that status yields lower costs for a given level of quality, and the importance of status to market outcomes increases with uncertainty about underlying quality differences between producers. While these differences in costs can have implications for price, price is ultimately only a variable of "intermediate" significance on route to what firms really care about—profitability, and any specification of the implications of status for price requires that one first consider the institutional features of the market on which one is focused. Accordingly, as we now move from vignettes about the economic implications of status to a quantitative analysis of the relationship between status and price (i.e., spread) in the debt markets, it is important to consider the features of these markets in more detail.

THE EFFECT OF STATUS ON PRICE IN THE INVESTMENT-GRADE MARKET

We will initially focus on what is clearly the most commoditized of the primary securities markets—the market for investment-grade debt. The issuers of debt in the investment-grade market are necessarily those firms that are regarded as being extremely sound financially and, accordingly, have an extremely high likelihood of paying back their debt. Investment-grade debt has for some time been given the nickname "vanilla debt," a label that reflects the lack of complications involved in underwriting this issue. One banker from a prestigious firm commented to me that he personally could successfully execute a typical investment-grade issue even after he had left the firm. All such an issue would require would be a few phone calls to major institutional investors.

One should not take this somewhat facetious comment to mean that there is no difficulty involved in the placement of investment-grade debt. Particularly as issues get larger, the challenge of placement becomes greater and requires more extensive knowledge of and connections to the demand side of the market. Two bankers associated with a comparatively small firm noted the size of an issue as a reason why their firm would neither be willing nor able to underwrite a given issue. Nevertheless, apart from the factor of size, which is relevant in any of the primary securities markets, the prestigious banker's comment is illustrative of the low level of difficulty that bankers attribute to underwriting in this particular market.

A low level of difficulty implies little quality difference across underwriters, and little quality difference across underwriters tends to imply that price is extremely important in an issuer's selection of an investment bank in the primary securities markets. This clearly was the case in the investment-grade market during the 1980s. Eccles and Crane (1988) note that the phrase "loyalty is a basis point" was a particularly common phrase among investment bankers over that time period. A basis point is 0.01 percent of the value of an offering. Though the phrase was probably an exaggeration, it reflected the bankers' strong belief that price (i.e., spread) was an extremely important factor in the exchange relationship between issuer and underwriter. An issuer would switch investment banks if it could find a slightly lower price in the market. Just as in the auditing market, intense price competition did not necessarily imply equal access for all. Status would still be relevant as a determinant of which half dozen or so banks could get a foot in the door to make a bid. But for any given offering, there could be multiple potential exchange partners, and there would be intense price competition among them.

Each observation in this analysis involves an issuer–lead manager pair. That is, the regression incorporates variables denoting characteristics of the issuer and the lead manager. Implicitly, such a specification assumes that the comanager and other syndicate managers are chosen after the spread on the offering is determined. Discussions with investment bankers indicated the reasonableness of this assumption.

Most of the data for this analysis come from the Securities Data Corporation (SDC) database on the primary securities markets between the years 1982 and 1987. These data were graciously made available to me by Professors Robert Eccles and Dwight Crane, who used the data as a basis for their book on the investment banking industry, *Doing Deals*. The SDC data contain extensive information on all the corporate security offerings underwritten by investment banks over that period. In particular, for each issue, data are available for the type of offering, type of registration, spread, volume, bond rating, and the lead manager and comanagers. The primary purchasers of the SDC data are the investment banks themselves, who use the data mostly to assess their share of the market and their penetration into particular industrial sectors. For the investment-grade market, the SDC database contains information on 3,541 investment-grade offerings between 1982 and 1987.

While the SDC data contain considerable information on the transactions in the primary securities markets, they do not contain information on the status distinctions between investment banks. As noted above, status distinctions are reflected in the tombstone advertisements; however, an obvious question is how one abstracts quantitative measures of these status distinctions from the advertisements. For the purpose of the analysis in this chapter, I collected the tombstone ads that appeared in the *Wall Street Journal* in 1981, the year before the six-year span covered by the SDC data base. During this period, there were 180 tombstones for investment-grade issues.[9]

In making use of the tombstone data, I apply one of the standard measures for relational data on status, Bonacich's (1987) $c(\alpha,\beta)$ measure. Because I rely on this measure for quantifying status distinction not only in this analysis but in a number of subsequent analyses, it seems appropriate to devote a few paragraphs to explicating the measure.

Formally, the measure is defined as follows:

$$c(\alpha,\beta) \equiv \alpha \sum_{k=0}^{\infty} \beta^k \mathbf{R}^{k+1} \mathbf{1}, \qquad [3.2]$$

where α is a scaling factor, β is a weighting factor, $\mathbf{R}$ is a relational matrix, which is 0 along the main diagonal and in which cell r_{ij} summarizes the relative superiority (or inferiority) of i with respect to j, and $\mathbf{1}$ is a column vector of ones. For the purposes of this analysis, a given cell r_{ij} is equal to the following proportion: the number of offerings in which bank i and bank j jointly appear in nonmanagement positions and i appears in a bracket above that in which j is located, divided by the number of offerings in which bank i and bank j jointly appear. In other words, r_{ij} is the proportion of offerings in which i appears above j when i and j are in the offering but neither is in a manager or comanager position. The sum of cells r_{ij} and r_{ji} will equal 1 only if i and j never appear in the same bracket; otherwise, the sum will be less than 1.[10] Given this definition of the relational matrix and the additive infinite sequence specified in equation [3.2], this measure implies that a focal bank's status is a positive function of the number and status of the bank's "subordinates," where subordinates are defined as banks that appear in lower, nonmanagement bracket positions than the focal bank. The status of these subordinates, in turn, is a positive function of the number and status of their subordinates, and so on.

The absolute value of the weighting factor β must be between 0 and the absolute value of the reciprocal of the maximum eigenvalue. The closer that β is to the reciprocal of the maximum eigenvalue, the more that a bank derives

[9] One might argue that to assess the effects of status in the later years of the sample, it would be better to collect not just the tombstone 1981 data but also the data from the following years. However, one would expect that any bias resulting from the failure to collect additional years of tombstone data would be in the direction of minimizing status effects. Hence, to the extent that the 1981 data show a significant impact of status on economic outcomes in the later years, it would seem reasonable to infer that the effects of status would be no less significant if the later years were taken into account.

[10] Banks that made fewer than three appearances in the tombstone data over 1981 were excluded from the analysis; 170 banks appeared in more than three syndicates. Invariably the excluded banks were relatively minor foreign banks that appeared in syndicate offerings because the issuer was based in their country.

indirect status from the status of those banks that are beneath it, which in turn derive more status from the status of those banks beneath them, and so on. Ultimately, the choice of β depends on whether one believes that being superordinate to a high-status actor confers more status than being superordinate to a low-status actor. If the only determinant of status is the number of others that a focal actor is directly superordinate to, then β should be closer to 0. However, if the status of those subordinates affects the focal actor's status, then β should be closer to the maximum eigenvalue. In this particular context, it seemed reasonable to set a high value for β. We know that banks were much more concerned with their position vis-à-vis other banks than with the aggregate number of other banks they were above. In the analyses of the investment banking industry, I set β at ¾ of the reciprocal of the maximum eigenvalue. However, given that there is no theoretical or empirical basis for arriving at an exact value, I experimented with several values for β, and the results that I discuss below remain substantively the same across these values.

Table 3.1 represents selected status scores from the investment-grade market in 1981. Bonacich's $c(\alpha,\beta)$ measure is standardized such that a score of 1 means that a bank has approximately average status. An examination of the scores in table 3.1 suggests the face validity of the measure. Those familiar with the industry will recognize the "bulge bracket" firms—Morgan Stanley, First Boston, Goldman Sachs, Merrill Lynch, and Salomon Brothers—as being at the top of the status ordering, and there is a fairly clear break between the bulge bracket and the next tier of firms. Major Wall Street banks dominate the twenty or so highest status positions. As one moves into the lower-status positions, one observes an increasing number of small, typically regionalized firms.

Given this measure of status, we now proceed to measure the impact of status on percentage spread. Percentage spread is the gross spread divided by the dollar amount of the offering. For example, suppose that a syndicate of banks purchase $200 million in bonds from an issuer for $199.5 million; the spread would be $500,000, and the percentage spread would be 0.25. Use of percentage spread rather than gross spread allows for greater comparability across offerings; moreover, among industry participants, percentage spread is the more commonly referenced measure of "price."

Control variables in the analysis of the effect of status on price.   Though the SDC database lists 3,541 investment-grade offerings between 1982 and 1987, the information on percentage spread is available for only 2,782 of the issues. Careful inspection of the data suggests that the pattern of missing information is not random; the likelihood that data are missing is frequently correlated with the size of the issue and the revenue of the issuer. Because of this significant amount of missing data on the dependent variable, selectivity bias is a potential danger in the analysis. Following Berk (1983), I correct for the selectivity bias via a two-stage procedure. Using a dichotomous logistic model, I construct

TABLE 3.1
Selected Status Scores in the Investment-Grade Debt Market

Bank	Status Score	Rank
Morgan Stanley	3.30879	1
First Boston Corporation	3.03206	2
Goldman Sachs	2.87465	3
Merrill Lynch	2.84215	4
Salomon Brothers	2.82667	5
Lehman Brothers Kuhn Loeb	2.19846	6
Paine Webber	2.10382	7
Prudential Bache Securities	2.09874	8
Dean Witter Reynolds	2.04583	9
Warburg Paribus Becker	2.02556	10
Smith Barney Harris	2.01689	11
Dillon Read	2.01074	12
Bear Stearns	2.00232	13
Kidder Peabody	1.99902	14
Shearson	1.99621	15
E. F. Hutton	1.99388	16
Donaldson Lufkin & Jenrette	1.99863	17
Lazard Freres	1.98856	18
Wertheim Securities	1.98685	19
L. F. Rothschild, Unterberg	1.98629	20
Drexel Burnham Lambert	1.98431	21
UBS Securities	1.86799	22
M. A. Schapiro and Co.	1.68572	23
Bell Gouinlock	1.57457	24
Atlantic Capital	1.23710	25
Burns-Fry and Timmins	.85649	50
Robert W. Baird and Co.	.66863	75
Sanford C. Bernstein and Co.	.44116	100
Folger Nolan Fleming Douglas	.21968	125
Anderson & Strudwick	.07925	150

a "selection equation" that estimates the probability that an observation has information on spread. I incorporate the *predicted probability of observed data on spread* as a regressor in the main equation.

To assess the effects of status on percentage spread, it is necessary to include several control variables in addition to this predicted probability of inclusion in the sample. One of these is the *size of the offering*, which is measured in terms of logged dollars. Though it is more difficult to underwrite a large offering than a small offering, the marginal difficulty of underwriting each additional dollar increment decreases with the size of the offering. As a result, it seems reasonable to expect that the size of the offering should have a negative effect on the percentage spread.

In the investment-grade market, the *rating of the bond* is also an important determinant of spreads. A higher rating implies lower risk, which results in lower spreads. Standard & Poor's ratings for investment-grade debt range from AAA to BBB+. Rating information is available for all the offerings between 1982 and 1986. For those years, indicator variables are constructed for all ratings above BBB+, with BBB+ forming a residual category. Ratings information was not available for offerings in 1987; accordingly, a separate indicator variable is constructed denoting missing information on rating.

I also control for the recent joint transaction history of the underwriting bank and issuing company in all product markets. It seems reasonable to expect that prior or concurrent transactions with a bank will lower the spread owing to "client-specific economies." Superior information about an issuer accumulated from prior transactions should allow the bank to underwrite an offering at a lower cost. Two indicator variables are used to account for this transaction history. One of these denotes whether *the bank and issuer were involved in another transaction at the time of the offering*. I select a 120-day window around the date of the offering; if the bank led an offering for the corporation in any of the primary securities markets or gave merger/acquisition (M&A) advice to the issuer during this period, this indicator variable is coded 1 and 0 otherwise. Discussions with bankers revealed that the process of deciding on a particular issue and bringing the issue to market can often take about 120 days. Accordingly, if a bank managed two offerings for the same firm over this time, I regarded the issues as "simultaneous." However, if the *bank managed an offering or assisted in M&A more than 120 days but less than one year prior to the offering*, I regarded this as a "recent (though not simultaneous) transaction" that could yield client-specific economies. Accordingly, an additional indicator variable is set to 1 if the bank consummated a transaction with the issuer more than 120 days but less than a year prior to the current transaction.

An additional variable relevant to the spread is whether the *offering was negotiated or competitive*. In the latter, competing banks submit sealed bids to the issuer, and the lowest bid wins the offering. Though this type of offering is not particularly common for corporate securities, many public utilities are required by law to solicit bids in this form. In negotiated offerings, the issuing firm selects a bank on the basis of discussions with one or several investment banks. Price is still an important factor underlying the exchange between bank and client, though it need not be the only factor that affects the corporation's decision to choose a particular bank. Because competitive offerings are awarded strictly on the basis of price, it follows that sealed bids typically have lower spreads. Therefore, an indicator variable is constructed to denote whether the issuer selected a bank through a competitive bid process. Note that even in a sealed-bid competitive offering, status can be relevant to market processes to the extent that it leads to a reduction in costs.

It is important to control for *whether the security was "convertible."* Some corporations issue bonds that they are willing to convert into stock at a pre-determined conversion rate. This feature reduces the risk of holding the bond and presumably, therefore, also decreases the spread. Thus an indicator variable is also constructed to denote whether the bond was convertible.

A final and especially important variable that we need to consider is the competing signal of *recent underwriting volume*. In the previous chapter, we observed that there is necessarily a loose linkage between status and underlying quality. This loose linkage engenders the "stickiness" in status ordering, and without this stickiness, status would simply be epiphenomenal. However, we also observed that the decoupling of status from underlying quality creates the possibility that there might be other signals more tightly coupled to underlying quality. For example, in certain product markets, it may be possible for high-quality firms to signal their higher quality with warranties. If the linkage between quality and a signal like a warranty is sufficiently tight, then uncertainty is effectively removed, and status becomes irrelevant to the decisions of market actors. In the investment banking industry, there is one clear alternative signal: the recent volume history of the bank. The link between short-term volume history and underwriting quality is quite tight since a bank's quality with respect to both issuers and investors is contingent on the bank's insight into the market, which in turn depends on the extent to which it has been participating in the deal stream. Insofar as underwriting volume is a quantitative indication of the degree to which a bank is in the deal stream, such volume is a clear determinant of quality. Underwriting volume is also a signal of quality properly defined; the marginal difficulty and cost of underwriting a given issue at a given point in time is inversely associated with recent underwriting volume, since lower volume implies less knowledge. A bank with less knowledge of the market exposes itself to greater risk in seeking to make competitive bids for a given issue.

There are several institutional manifestations of recent underwriting volume as a signal. Perhaps the most important are the league tables, which provide annual or quarterly rankings of banks according to their volume of underwriting activity in the various primary markets. They are published at quarterly intervals in the major trade journals. One interviewed banker commented that the banks are so obsessed with their position in the tables that they call the SDC and *Investment Dealers Digest* (IDD) information service to ensure that the services have not forgotten to include a deal that they have managed. While this banker believed that the importance ascribed to the rankings was unjustified, he also pointed out that many bankers perceived that any decline in the league tables resulting from such an omission could undercut a bank's standing in the eyes of market participants.

Banks change position in league tables much more frequently than they change position in the tombstone advertisements. This comparatively greater movement would seem to be another reason that the linkage between volume and quality could be tighter than the linkage between status and quality.

Given that the status order and volume rankings are two informational orders in which decisions are potentially embedded, the constraining effects of status ultimately depend on the degree to which the status order exerts an independent effect on outcomes beyond that exerted by underwriting volume. If decisions are based more on the yearly fluctuations in volume and less on the stickier positional status distinctions encoded in the tombstone advertisements, then the time lag between shifts in quality and shifts in perception will necessarily be shorter, and the significance of the Matthew Effect for the investment-grade debt market will be minimal. Recall that it is the lag between shifts in quality and shifts in perception that insulates a given producer from the competition of those who are lower in status. If a low-quality bank can come to be regarded as identical to a high-quality bank simply by increasing underwriting volume over a short time frame, then it faces essentially the same cost and revenue profile as that of the high-quality bank. It may have to absorb some short-term costs to expand at a rapid rate, but ultimately there is no persistent constraint on its ability to invade the high-quality niche. In this case, status would simply be a by-product of underlying economic processes. It is only when the lower-quality bank must confront a relatively disadvantageous cost-and-revenue profile over an extended time frame that the status ordering and the Matthew Effect can be considered relevant.

I measure recent underwriting volume as the dollar amount of offerings in the investment-grade market for which a bank was lead manager in the twelve months prior to the month in which the deal was issued.[11] Volume history is therefore a moving one-year window that is updated monthly. Obviously, any particular choice of window length is arbitrary; I selected one year because the league tables rarely summarize more than one year of information. Because of a positive skew in the distribution of the variable, underwriting volume is converted to logged dollars.

Though underwriting volume over the past year is included as the primary signal of the short-term informational order, it is important to note that the interpretation of the coefficient for volume history cannot be unambiguous. To the extent that economies of scale are relevant, the volume history measure summarizes such effects; moreover, insofar as the volume measure necessarily implies greater knowledge of the supply and demand conditions at the moment of the offering, these knowledge effects are also bound up in this variable.

---

[11] Because the SDC data do not report every bank that appears in a syndicate and accordingly do not report how shares are divided among the syndicate, it is not possible to construct an annual volume measure that includes volume underwritten in a nonmanagement position.

However, since we are not so much interested in clearly interpreting the effect of volume as in determining whether the inclusion of this variable eliminates the effect of status, such ambiguity about the meaning of this variable does not detract from the central inferences that we can draw from the analysis.

Basic Results

Columns 1 and 2 of table 3.2 present the basic results. Column 1 excludes the variable of recent underwriting volume; column 2 includes this variable. In discussing these results, I will ignore most of the control variables since they are of little sociological interest. The exceptions to this general statement are the variables denoting client-specific economies and, of course, underwriting volume over the previous year. Both of the variables denoting client-specific economies have a negative effect on spread, though the effect of "simultaneous" transactions with the same issuer is not statistically significant. The negative effect is consistent with the view that a firm can derive economic benefits from seeking to embed exchange relations in ongoing relations.

Focusing on the variable of main interest, we observe that status has statistically significant and negative impact on price at the .01 level. A unit change in status leads to a reduction in spread of 0.080. While the substantive impact of the coefficient may not seem considerable, it is important to evaluate the apparently small magnitude of the coefficient in light of the phrase "loyalty is a basis point" and in light of the difference in status scores across banks. If we refer back to table 3.1, we see that the difference in status between, for example, second-ranked First Boston and fourteenth-ranked Kidder Peabody is 1.03. The difference between these two banks translates into an ability and willingness of the former to underbid the latter by eight basis points. Even controlling for volume underwritten in the last year, the effect of status remains negative and significant, though the magnitude of the status effect declines from –0.080 to –0.062.

This negative effect of status on price is no doubt counterintuitive; yet, it is important to recall the earlier observation that the impact of status is necessarily indeterminate since price is not tantamount to profitability, and it is easy to make sense of this finding by considering features of the market context as well as the effect of status on costs. As has been repeatedly emphasized, price is very important to an issuer's selection of an investment bank in the investment-grade market. Intense price competition necessarily implies no revenue advantages from high status on a given transaction. If issuers are choosing primarily on the basis of price, then the banks should not be able to command a premium for status. Even if issuers would prefer an extremely high-status firm to a comparatively low-status firm, they may be indifferent to minor status variations between those five or six banks at the top of the hierarchy, leading those top banks to compete among themselves on the basis of price in much the same way that the

TABLE 3.2
Relationship between Status and Spread in the Investment-Grade Debt Market

Variables	1		2		3		4	
Intercept	1.244	(.153)	1.221	(.152)	8.608	(.750)	14.298	(2.239)
Status	−.080	(.013)	−.062	(.013)	−2.813	(.274)	−2.271	(.287)
Status × log(size of offering)		—		—	.151	(.015)	.121	(.016)
Log(recent underwriting volume)		—	−.006	(.0008)	−.006	(.0008)	−.126	(.162)
Log(recent underwriting volume) × log(size of offering)		—		—		—	.007	(.001)
Log(size of offering)	−.0116	(.008)*	−.007	(.008)*	−.413	(.412)	−.451	(.041)
Convertible security	.679	(.0275)	.679	(.027)	.665	(.026)	.658	(.027)
Bond ratings								
AAA	.004	(.025)*	−.012	(.025)*	−.018	(.025)*	−.021	(.025)*
AA+	−.101	(.027)	−.105	(.027)	−.124	(.027)	−.134	(.027)
AA	−.086	(.024)	−.093	(.023)	−.090	(.023)	−.096	(.023)
AA−	−.084	(.025)	−.079	(.024)	−.080	(.023)	−.087	(.024)
A+	−.053	(.025)	−.055	(.025)	−.054	(.024)	−.062	(.024)
A	−.086	(.023)	−.090	(.023)	−.089	(.022)	−.093	(.022)
A−	−.045	(.026)	−.044	(.025)*	−.040	(.024)*	−.052	(.025)
Missing data on bond rating	−.111	(.021)	−.091	(.021)	−.088	(.020)	−.096	(.020)
Bank/issuer transaction within last 120 days	−.008	(.003)	−.007	(.003)	−.008	(.002)	−.008	(.002)
Bank/issuer transaction between 120 days and 1 year	−.001	(.003)*	-9×10^{-4}	(.003)*	−.002	(.003)*	−.002	(.003)*
Competitive offering	−.186	(.018)	−.178	(.0173)	−.172	(.0170)	−.173	(.017)
Predicted probability of observed data on spread	−.492	(.105)	−.444	(.105)	−.459	(.103)	−.459	(.102)
R^2	.27		.29		.31		.32	

$N = 2{,}787$. Numbers in parentheses are standard errors.
*Not significant at the .05 level

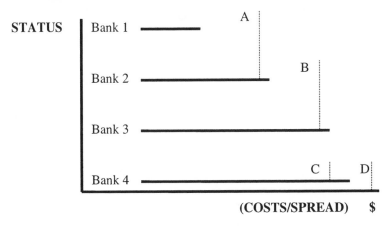

FIGURE 3.2. Hypothetical scenario of four banks

highest-status accounting firms competed with one another in the earlier example of the audit markets.

However, the lack of benefits in terms of price does not preclude benefits on the cost side. As previously noted, higher status leads to lower transaction costs in forming syndicate and investor relations. Since members of the syndicate and investors are more likely to accept the word of a high-status firm that an offering is above some quality threshold and engage in less due diligence, the high-status firm has lower transaction costs. In addition, as we have observed, the higher-status firm is likely to have lower labor costs for a given quality of employee. With status yielding benefits on the cost side but not on the revenue side, the relationship between status and price is negative.

If such a result still seems counterintuitive, a hypothetical scenario may help to illustrate how such a negative relationship between status and spread can occur. Assume that there are only four investment banks in the industry. They are of different status; they each have the opportunity to compete with one another for every issue, and as suggested by the discussion of the industry, they compete only on price. Figure 3.2 provides a graphical representation of the cost profiles for the four banks in such a situation. The vertical axis denotes increasing status; the horizontal axis indicates dollar values expressed in some arbitrary unit. The horizontal line for each bank represents its costs for performing an underwriting at a given quality level. If a bank successfully bids a dollar amount that falls to the right of the point where the horizontal line ends, then it earns a profit.

Assume that all four banks want to lead a particular offering. If bank 4 makes a bid at D, it earns a profit; an expected bid at C, however, would result in losses. In a situation where all four banks desire the deal, bank 1 can practically guarantee that it will win the deal by issuing a bid at point A, just below bank 2's costs. Another bank will be able to win the deal only if it takes a loss.

Assume now that the four banks are considering a second deal. Bank 1 decides that it is not worth the investment, but the other three banks desire the deal. In this case, bank 2 bids at point B and wins the deal to the extent that other firms are not willing to take a loss. If we make the reasonable assumption that firms cannot consistently take losses on their offerings, then this competitive situation in the context of cost differences based on status results in the observed negative relationship between status and spread.

A comparison over the past year of the magnitude of the effects of status and underwriting volume on price is worthwhile. The relative magnitudes of these two effects provide insight into how much a lower-status bank would have to exceed a higher-status bank in underwriting volume in order to bid the same as the high-status bank. The coefficient for status is 10 times that of the coefficient for volume history, implying that a given bank would have to underwrite $\exp(10) = 22,026.5$ times the volume of a bank one unit higher in the status order in order to compensate for the preexisting status differential. When considered in these terms, the 0.6-unit difference in status between fifth-ranked Salomon Brothers and sixth-ranked Lehman Brothers Kuhn Loeb clearly seems impenetrable to a strategy of "eating" deals to signal quality. Even a 0.005-unit difference in status, such as that between seventh-ranked Paine Webber and eighth-ranked Prudential Bache Securities, seems difficult to overcome simply by increasing volume. Importantly, this conclusion holds even if one interprets volume as something other than a signal of quality. Even if one interprets underwriting volume as denoting scale economies, the fact remains that the cost reduction and therefore the enhanced bidding ability from increased volume are insufficient to overwhelm even minor differences in the status order. The effect of status, even after the inclusion of the volume variable, means that a lower-status bank cannot simply buy its way into a high-status niche by increasing its volume over the short term.

Even though the strong negative main effect for status is initially counterintuitive, it is an important result insofar as it provides strong evidence of the cost advantages of status. It also shows how the pricing mechanism can become a central element in the reproduction of a status ordering. To the extent that higher-status firms can make an offering of a given quality at a lower cost than their lower-status competitors, the lower-status competitors are effectively blocked out of the high-status niches.

At the same time, as I have stressed, the status-based model of competition does not imply that the relationship between status and price is necessarily negative. The status-based model, as elaborated in previous work and in this book, does not make a prediction about a *main* effect of status on price. Rather, the fundamental prediction involves how the effect of status on price changes with uncertainty. The greater a potential exchange partner's uncertainty, the more that the potential exchange partner should be willing to pay for status. In this context, the greater the uncertainty associated with a particular issue, the greater the spread that the bank should receive.

To focus on this contingent effect, we will consider two factors: the size of the offering and the financial soundness of the issuer. We will focus first on how the effect of underwriter status on spread changes with the size of the offering. We will then look at the effect of status on spread in the non-investment-grade market, where the issuers are by definition less financially sound than the issuers in the investment-grade market.

The Joint Impact of Status and Offering Size on Underwriting Spread

So far, the results show that, on average, higher-status banks underbid lower-status banks for a given deal in the investment-grade market. Such a result is consistent with the issuer's concern with price in their selection of underwriter, whereas potential syndicate members and investors are more concerned with status. These last two groups have more reason than the issuer to be more concerned with status. They are creditors, whereas the issuer is the debtor. As creditors, they have comparatively more to lose if the issue falls in value because of the poor performance of the bank. The issuer, on the other hand, will make the same interest payments regardless of how the security is placed.

Nevertheless, the issuer still has some reason to worry about the quality of the placement. If investors or syndicate members lose money on a particular offering, they will almost undoubtedly be less likely to purchase a security from the same issuer in the future. As a result, a poor performance by the underwriter will make it more costly for the issuer to raise money in the financial markets; the issuer will have to compensate the purchasers of the security for what they perceive to be additional risk associated with holding that security.

Consequently, there might be some reason to expect a positive return on status, especially for the larger offerings. As previously noted, not all issues are considered to be of the same difficulty; in particular, the larger an issue, the more challenge is involved in its placement and the more questions that there would be about a given bank's ability to successfully accomplish the task. For the RJ Reynolds/Nabisco junk-bond offering, Kohlberg Kravis Roberts and Co. (KKR) doubted very much if even Salomon Brothers, a special-bracket firm and the bank with the second-largest underwriting volume in the junk market, could effectively lead the offering (Burrough and Helyar 1990). The RJ Reynolds offering was indeed an exceptionally large offering, and although it involved non-investment-grade securities, it does raise the issue of whether there are positive returns to status for increasingly large issues. The fact that higher-status banks underbid the lower-status banks on average does not preclude the possibility that higher-status banks may be able to derive a premium from underwriting the larger, more difficult issues.

Column 3 of table 3.2 reproduces the regression in column 2 with the inclusion of an interaction term between status and the size of the offering. Column 4 is the same as column 3 except that it adds an additional interaction term between the size of the offering and the bank's underwriting volume over the past twelve months. In both regressions, the interaction term between status and the size of the offering is positive and statistically significant.

In column 4, the effect of status in the investment-grade market is

$$-2.27 + 0.121 \times \log(size\ of\ offering).$$

Through algebraic manipulation of terms, it can be easily shown that the effect of status becomes positive when the offering is greater than \$140 million. This amount is clearly within the range of observed values; the median offering size across all banks is \$100 million. At \$200 million, or the seventy-fifth percentile in terms of offering size, a one-unit difference in status, such as that which existed between First Boston and Kidder Peabody, translates into a four-basis-point benefit for the former over the latter.

Considering these results in conjunction with the results from columns 1 and 2 of table 3.2, we observe that higher-status banks on average underbid the lower-status banks; however, for the larger issues, the latter must do so from a relatively disadvantageous cost structure. The result is significant because it illustrates the fact that for larger, more difficult issues, status in the investment-grade market is relevant not only to the investor and the potential syndicate members but to the issuer's decision as well.

For an additional test of whether the returns to status increase with uncertainty, we now shift to an examination of the relationship between status and spread in the non-investment-grade debt market. However, before undertaking such an analysis, it is necessary to provide some institutional details on how the non-investment-grade market differs from the investment-grade market.

The Relationship between Status and Spread in the Non-Investment-Grade Market

Non-investment-grade debt differs from investment-grade debt in terms of both risk and uncertainty. By definition, there is greater risk associated with the underwriting and ownership of non-investment-grade debt. As noted above, non-investment-grade debt, which can alternatively be called "junk" or "high-yield" debt, is so categorized because the probability that the issuer will default on debt payments is greater than for issuers of investment-grade debt.

While a number of financial models allow actors in the primary securities markets to quantify risk in terms of security price differentials, there can be more or less uncertainty about the underlying parameters of the models used to calculate this risk. Throughout the 1980s, there were often quite disparate estimates for the values of important parameters in the models used to price non-investment-grade securities (Blume and Keim 1987; Altman 1989; Asquith, Mullins, and Wolff 1989). Securities analysts simply did not agree on the amount of risk associated with particular non-investment-grade securities, and such lack of agreement about how to even calculate risk necessarily implies uncertainty.

One reason for the uncertainty is that issuers of junk debt are often not well-established companies; they often have only short histories on which analysts can base their estimates of a company's likelihood of debt repayment. A second reason for the high level of uncertainty during the 1980s was that the market it-self was quite new. Whereas the investment-grade market had been in existence since before the turn of the century, the first non-investment-grade issue was underwritten in 1977, and the market did not emerge as a separate entity until the early 1980s. One firm in particular, Drexel Burnham Lambert, developed this market. Indeed, the idea of a market for high-yield debt was the brainchild of one of Drexel Burnham Lambert's bankers, Michael Milken. Prior to 1977, the only non-investment-grade issues were so-called fallen angels, issues that were initially investment grade but were subsequently downgraded by the major bond-rating services in response to a decline in the financial status of the issuer. Lack of experience with the issuers and with the market itself impaired ana-lysts' ability to assign probabilities of performance outcomes confidently to non-investment-grade securities.

Such uncertainty about the level of risk associated with a non-investment-grade security is likely to translate into greater uncertainty about banks' abilities to place securities. Greater uncertainty about the risk of a security will generally imply less consensus on an appropriate price for the security, and this lack of consensus will in turn create greater uncertainty about a bank's ability to place the security at a price that investors will accept. Thus, whether one considers the securities themselves or the abilities of the underwriters, there was much greater uncertainty in the non-investment-grade market than in the investment-grade market during the period of this study.

To see whether the increase in uncertainty led to greater returns from status, I estimate essentially the same model that I used to predict percentage spread in the investment-grade market. The SDC data list 8,081 non-investment-grade offerings between 1982 and 1987, though information on percentage spread is available for only 2,004 of those offerings. Once again, a selection equation is used to construct a variable that controls for the probability that an observation has information on spread and therefore is in the sample.

As was the case for status in the investment-grade market, status is measured using the tombstone advertisements that appeared in the *Wall Street Journal* in 1981; in that year, there were 101 advertisements for high-yield issues. Table 3.3 presents selected status scores for banks in the non-investment-grade market

TABLE 3.3

Comparison of Representative Status Scores from the Investment-Grade and Non-Investment-Grade Debt Markets

Bank	Investment-Grade Debt		Non-Investment-Grade Debt	
	Status Score	Rank	Status Score	Rank
Morgan Stanley	3.30879	1	3.99696	1
First Boston Corporation	3.03206	2	3.69273	2
Goldman Sachs	2.87465	3	2.58810	4
Merrill Lynch	2.84215	4	2.51190	5
Salomon Brothers	2.82667	5	2.42783	6
Lehman Brothers Kuhn Loeb	2.19846	6	2.31416	9
Prudential Bache Securities	2.09874	8	3.03846	3
Dean Witter Reynolds	2.04583	9	2.17970	14
Warburg Paribus Becker	2.02556	10	2.16743	20
Smith Barney Harris	2.01689	11	2.17789	17
Dillon Read	2.01074	12	2.17666	18
Bear Stearns	2.00232	13	2.26895	8
Kidder Peabody	1.99902	14	2.22815	10
Shearson	1.99621	15	2.17894	16
E. F. Hutton	1.99388	16	2.19418	11
Donaldson Lufkin & Jenrette	1.98863	17	2.17939	16
Lazard Freres	1.98856	18	2.16955	19
Wertheim Securities	1.98685	19	2.18137	12
L. F. Rothschild, Unterberg	1.98629	20	2.18054	13
Drexel Burnham Lambert	1.98431	21	2.15789	21
Alex, Brown and Sons	1.07966	28	1.21547	25
Burns-Fry and Timmins	.85649	50	.80712	46
Nikko Securities	.62842	80	.72837	50
Sanford C. Bernstein and Co.	.44116	100	.49928	65
Cyrus J. Lawrence	.34032	110	.22257	100
Anderson & Strudwick	.07925	150	.00177	154
Thomas & Company	.01166	162	.01606	150

alongside their status scores in the investment-grade market. One hundred fifty-three banks appeared in both markets, and for these banks, the Spearman correlation between the status scores in the two markets is quite high, .96. This high correlation does not result from a required consistency in bracket positions across markets.

One can point to examples of banks that appear in higher brackets in one market than in another market. For example, Hambrecht & Quist, a San Franscisco–based investment banking firm, achieved considerable stature in the market for initial public offerings (IPOs) in the 1980s because of its association with many Silicon Valley companies. As a result, Hambrecht & Quist would appear in higher brackets in IPOs than in debt offerings. Table 3.3 contains several examples of banks whose status ranking in one debt market differs from its status ranking in the other debt market by more than ten or twenty positions. Thus, there is no requirement that a bank's bracket in one market be identical to its bracket in another.

The high correlation most likely suggests that a bank's initial status position in the junk market originated largely from its status position in the investment-grade market. It is possible at least informally to point to other examples in which a producer's initial status in one market derived in large measure from its status in a related market, such as IBM's entry into the personal computer market (Anderson 1995). Particularly notable in the case of the non-investment-grade market is the fact that Drexel Burnham Lambert, the bank that founded this market and continually led the market in underwriting volume from its inception up through the period covered by the data, was ranked twenty-first in status in the non-investment-grade market even four years after its first non-investment-grade issue. As table 3.3 shows, this rank is the same as Drexel's rank in the investment-grade market.

While the measure of status in the high-yield market is the same as the measure of status in the investment-grade market, 272, or 14 percent, of the 2,004 high-yield offerings were led by banks that never appeared in the tombstone advertisements. In comparison, in the investment-grade market, only 42, or 1.48 percent, of the 2,830 offerings were underwritten by "nontomb-stone" banks. Because of the comparatively large number of high-yield offerings underwritten by banks that never appeared in the tombstones, it is appropriate to include an indicator variable denoting that the lead manager is a nontombstone bank.[12]

I include the same control variables that I employed in the estimation of percentage spread in the investment-grade market. I include variables denoting the size of the offering and the one-year underwriting volume for the lead bank in the non-investment-grade market. I include the same two indicators of client-specific economies, an indicator variable denoting whether the offering can be converted to equity, and information on the bond rating of the offering. Of course, bond ratings in the non-investment-grade market are necessarily lower than those in the investment-grade market. Bond ratings are coded into the following five dummy categories: "BBB," "BB," "B," "C," and "no rating." Those issues that were missing specific rating information constitute the residual category. (Importantly, missing information is different from "no rating"; the latter simply means that we know the offering was not rated by the bond agencies.)

---

[12] When the lead manager is a "nontombstone," the status variable is set to a value of 0.

I add an indicator variable denoting whether Drexel Burnham Lambert was the lead underwriter for the offering. Though Drexel's status in the market as represented in the tombstones was comparatively low, Drexel—as the founder and pioneer of high-yield debt—occupied a relational position on the investor side of the market so superior to that of even the highest-status firms that it had a near monopoly on the high-volume issues that were eagerly sought by the higher-status banks. Drexel could place non-investment-grade issues that other firms simply could not place. The dummy variable is included to control for this monopoly effect.

Results for the analysis of the non-investment-grade market are presented in the first column of table 3.4. Selected variables from the full model for the investment-grade market, first depicted in column 4 of table 3.2, is reproduced alongside the non-investment-grade results (it is column 2 in table 3.4)

TABLE 3.4
Relationship between Status and Spread in the Non-Investment-Grade Debt Market

Variables	1	2
Intercept	31.13 (1.536)	14.298 (2.239)
Status	−2.722 (.750)	−2.271 (.287)
Status × log(size of offering)	.151 (.042)	.121 (.016)
Nontombstone bank	1.755 (.213)	N/A
Log (recent underwriting volume)	−.962 (.084)	−.126 (.162)
Log(recent underwriting volume) × log(size of offering)	.056 (.005)	.007 (.001)
Log(size of offering)	−1.653 (.090)	−.451 (.041)
Bond ratings		
BBB	−.982 (.146)	N/A
BB	−.332 (.165)	N/A
B	.282 (.121)	N/A
C	.753 (.198)	N/A
No rating	−.168 (.123)*	N/A
Drexel is underwriter	.676 (.102)	N/A
Competitive offering	−.469 (.270)*	−.173 (.017)
Bank/issuer transaction within last 120 days	−.054 (.045)*	−.002 (.003)*
Bank/issuer transaction between 120 days and 1 year	−.104 (.037)	−.008 (.002)
Convertible security	.527 (.091)	.658 (.027)
Predicted probability of observed data on spread	−.360 (.152)	−.459 (.102)
R^2	.48	.32

$N = 2,003$. Numbers in parentheses are standard errors. N/A denotes not applicable in investment-grade analysis.

*Not significant at the .05 level

to facilitate comparison. As was the case in the investment-grade market, the interaction effect between status and size of offering is positive and statistically significant in the non-investment-grade market. Higher-status banks earn a greater spread relative to lower-status banks as the offering size increases. Specifically, the effect of status is

$$-2.72 + 0.151 \times \log(\textit{size of offering}).$$

The results bear a striking resemblence to those in the investment-grade market. First, there is evidence that at least over a good range of offering sizes, the relationship between status and spread is negative. At an offering size of $25 million (the twenty-seventh percentile in terms of offering sizes), one increment in status is associated with a decrease in spread of 15 basis points. Moreover, we observe that the tombstone banks consistently underbid the nontombstone banks. Since those banks never appearing in a tombstone are almost necessarily lower in status than those that do appear in the tombstone advertisements, such a result further shows how the cost-reducing consequences of status are serving to block out an especially low-status group. Therefore, just as in the investment-grade market, there is evidence that higher-status banks use the cost-related benefits of status to underbid the lower-status banks over a considerable range of offerings.

At the same time, as was the case in the investment-grade market, the relationship between status and spread increases with the size of the offering. If we compare the interaction between status and size across the two markets at a given offering size, we see that the relationship between status and spread is more (less) positive (negative) in the junk market than in the investment-grade market. For example, for a $100 million offering, the effect of status on spread in the non-investment-grade market is 0.06; for an investment-grade offering of that size, the effect is −0.04, a difference of 10 basis points. The major difference between pricing dynamics in the non-investment-grade and investment-grade markets is that the "baseline" premium for status shifts in a positive direction with increasing uncertainty.

To summarize, analyses of both markets reveal that higher-status banks underbid lower-status banks over a significant volume range, an outcome that results from the negative relationship between status and costs. However, as the difficulty of placement increases from either the size of the offering or the lower rating of the bond, the bank is able to command a premium from issuers for status.

In their study of the market for legal services, Uzzi and Lancaster (2004) find similarly that the effect of status on price increases with the complexity of legal work. Specifically, they compare the effect of law firm status on the prices charged by partners and associates, arguing that partners are generally performing more complex and challenging work than associates, and they find

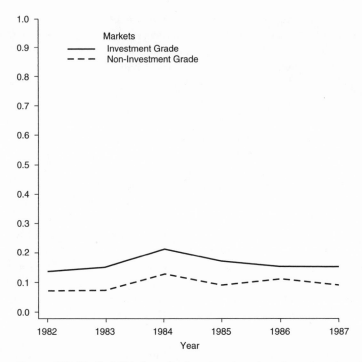

FIGURE 3.3. Herfindahl indexes for investment-grade and non-investment-grade debt, 1982–1987

that the effect of status on a law firm's partner price is significantly greater than the effect of status on a law firm's associate price.

We thus have evidence that status does seem to act as a signal in the market. The value of status increases with risk and uncertainty, and the existence of an alternative signal—in this case, underwriting volume—that is arguably more tightly coupled to quality does not eliminate the reliance on status as a signal. To be sure, one might be concerned that even though the analysis controls for this alternative signal, the analysis does not control for actual quality differences. Such a concern is reasonable; however, as investment banking is a service business, it is notoriously difficult to develop an adequate measure of quality for one bank or a small number of banks—let alone systematic measures of quality over an entire industry for a number of years. In chapter 5, I will conduct an examination of the wine industry, where it is indeed possible to obtain reasonable measures of actual quality. We can presumably take some comfort in the fact that the absence of systematic quality information for the researcher also means that the decision-makers themselves similarly lack systematic quality information and are therefore forced to rely on the same signals on which researchers rely. That is, the informational cues on which we rely are the same informational cues to which market actors have ready access, and even in the presence of the informational cues that are captured in the league tables, status lowers costs and provides increasing returns as risk and uncertainty increase.

However, if status lowers costs and potentially increases revenues, we are immediately presented with the paradox in this context that we raised at a more general level in the previous chapter. Since potential exchange partners should prefer a high-status bank to a low-status bank, the high-status banks should dominate the market. Yet, the year-to-year correlation of market share between 1982 and 1987 in the two debt markets is quite high. In the investment-grade market, the correlation is .91; in the non-investment-grade market, the correlation is .88. Figure 3.3 shows the macro-level consequences of these high year-to-year correlations by depicting the Herfindahl indexes for these two markets over this period. The Herfindahl index approaches 0 as the market nears a perfectly competitive situation with an infinite number of producers possessing an infinitely small market share; the measure approaches 1 as the market becomes an absolute monopoly. Except for the rise in concentration in 1984, the index reveals no consistent trend toward increasing concentration in either market. Why is it that the higher-status banks do not use their lower costs and potentially higher revenues to eliminate the others from the market?

In the previous chapter, I proposed a general answer deriving directly from the relational conception of status elaborated therein. High-status firms cannot enter into relations with low-status exchanges without encountering a reduction in their own status. In the next chapter, we test this broad proposition.

Chapter Four

TO MINGLE OR *NOT* TO MINGLE WITH
THE HOI POLLOI: *THAT* IS THE QUESTION

THE FIRST TWO CHAPTERS elaborated a two-sided conception of status. Status is (1) a signal of quality that (2) leaks through exchange relations. Drawing on data from the investment banking industry, the previous chapter documented cost and revenue consequences that follow from the fact that status is a signal. Drawing on data from the same industry, this chapter documents implications of the leakiness of status.

In saying that status leaks through exchange relations, I obviously have been somewhat loose in my use of language. A more precise way of articulating the same observation would be to say that there is a *forced alienation* of status that occurs when two parties enter into an exchange that can be verified by third parties. To the degree that the goods, services, and/or payments flow between actors, there is necessarily a latent transfer of status in which each party gives some of her status to the other.

In settings more acknowledged as fully social, this latent transfer of status is well acknowledged (Whyte 1981; Blau 1989; Homans 1951). A higher-status actor cannot enter an exchange relation with a lower-status actor without running the risk of diluting status. The central proposition of this chapter is that the same latent transfer of status is endemic to market exchange as well. In the first chapter, we considered the dilemma of high-status jewelers confronted with the rising popularity of turquoise, a stone that is affiliated with shops by the side of the highway in Arizona. The high-status jeweler has a choice about whether to enter into an exchange relation with a purveyor of turquoise, but if the high-status jeweler does choose to purchase turquoise stones, the high-status jeweler cannot control the flow of status between them unless the jeweler somehow hides the result of the exchange from third parties (i.e., does not display the stone for sale, does not tell others that he has entered into this exchange, and somehow ensures that the purveyor of turquoise will not tell others), and the jeweler obviously cannot make a profit on the exchange if he hides all evidence of it. When a high-status jeweler engages in an exchange with the purveyor of this stone, some of the status of the jeweler flows to the purveyor, and some of the status of the purveyor flows to the jeweler. To the extent that the purveyor has less status than the jeweler, the jeweler will experience a net loss of status, and the purveyor of the turquoise will experience a net gain.

The reason that the parties to the exchange have little ability to limit or enhance the flow of status is that the ascribed flow is actually at the discretion of the third parties who are aware of the exchange. One does not need to assume that there is active deliberation among these third parties in which they form a formal judgment in order for such ascription to take place, though such active deliberation is not ruled out either. One needs only to assume that the third parties behave like an audience that uses what is observable to make inferences about what is unobservable.

The assertion that the transfer of status depends on the attributions of third parties may sound rather banal. However, it has an important analytical implication. Contrary to some perspectives on market phenomena, such as transaction cost economics (Williamson 1975), this observation implies that the dyad cannot be the fundamental unit of analysis for economic transactions. Because the value that each party derives from the exchange is not independent of the attributions made by third parties, the value of the exchange cannot be understood by treating the exchanging parties as an isolated dyad.

The rest of this chapter explores the implications of the proposition that status flows through exchange relations in the context of manager-comanager relations in the investment banking industry. Recall from the previous chapter that the manager-comanager relations are the most visible and significant exchange relations in the syndicate. The lead managers and comanagers typically underwrite a much larger proportion of the security offering than the other members of the syndicate. In addition, comanagers may assist the lead manager by performing "due diligence" to validate the financial soundness of the corporation, recruiting banks into the syndicate, determining the allocation of securities among syndicate members, or "making a market" for a security once the security has been distributed to investors and is being bought and sold in the secondary markets.

First, we look at the non-investment-grade market for evidence that the status of a bank is affected by the status of the other banks with which it enters into exchange relations. To the extent that a bank's status is affected by the status of its exchange partners, it seems reasonable to expect that a bank's willingness to enter into exchange relations with lower-status partners will be a direct function of the value that status provides to the bank. Since the value of status increases with uncertainty, it follows that banks will be more willing to enter into exchange relations with lower-status partners when there is less uncertainty in the market.

GROWTH (AND DECLINE) OF STATUS

A Model of Status Growth (and Decline)

To explore how the status of a bank is influenced by the status of its partners, it is necessary to begin with a model of how the status of a bank can change over time. Let S_{it} denote the status of bank i during period t. We are interested in the relative change in status that occurs between two time periods: $(S_{i,t+1}/S_{it})$. The following specification provides a baseline model:

$$\frac{S_{i,t+1}}{S_{it}} = S_{it}^{\rho} w_{i,t+1};$$ [4.1]

or, alternatively,

$$S_{i,t+1} = S_{it}^{\rho+1} w_{i,t+1},$$ [4.2]

where $w_{i,t+1}$ is a log-normally distributed error term. The parameter ρ is essentially an endogenous feedback effect. If $\rho < 0$, then there are diminishing returns to increases in status. If $\rho = 0$, the growth in status is consistent with what is known as Gibrat's law, which posits that growth is random and independent of size (or, in this case, the amount of status), though the magnitude of fluctuations is proportionate to size. If $\rho > 0$, growth in status has a positive effect on itself and is therefore explosive. If $\rho = 0$ or $\rho > 0$, there is no endogenous bound on the amount of status that an actor can have. This general baseline model is the same as those employed in models of organizational growth (e.g., Barnett 1994; Barron, West, and Hannan 1994).[1]

Clearly Merton's Matthew Effect is consistent with $\rho > 0$. If $\rho > 0$, then high-status organizations increase their status at a faster rate than low-status organizations. Merton's Matthew Effect is also consistent with $\rho = 0$ since the absolute status difference between a low-status organization and a high-status organization will increase if both organizations have the same growth rate.

Exogenous covariates can be incorporated into the model using a log-linear specification as follows:

$$S_{i,t+1} = S_{it}^{(\rho+1)} e^{(b_0 + b_1 A_i + b_2 P_i + b_3 A_i P_i)} w_{i,t+1},$$ [4.3]

where A_i denotes the average status of bank i's management partners prior to $t + 1$ and P_i refers to bank i's contribution/performance prior to $t + 1$. The log-linear specification of exogenous effects ensures that the predicted growth

---

[1] As one reviewer pointed out, there is a lack of independence across observations since the status of every firm in a market is formally interrelated to the status of other firms as specified in equation [3.2] in the previous chapter. As the number of firms in the market increases, any specific interdependencies between any two observations will decline. Moreover, this issue of observation independence is not unique to status. Whenever one is studying multiple competitors, there is an implicit interdependence insofar as the share of the market acquired by one firm is unavailable to the other firms. Accordingly, while I do not deny the lack of independence, the lack of independence is not unique to the study of status dynamics; it is simply a factor that must be acknowledged when analyzing a population of competitors.

rate for status is nonnegative. By taking the logarithm of both sides of the equation, this model can be estimated using OLS (ordinary least squares) techniques.[2]

The above equation specifies that an actor's status is a function of its past status, its past performance, the status of its exchange partners, as well as an interaction of the performance and status of exchange partners. One obviously expects that a higher level of performance should result in higher status (i.e., $b_1 > 0$). Moreover, the conception of status as a property that leaks through exchange relations implies a main positive effect for A_i (i.e., $b_2 > 0$). However, one might reasonably wonder why it makes sense to include an interaction effect between the status of past management partners and performance. Assume that you are "a third party"—an investor, an issuer, or even another bank—trying to decide how much status you should accord to two banks. The banks are alike in terms of their market performance; they have underwritten an equivalent volume of securities at a level of competence that seems close to identical. However, the first bank generally has partners that you consider to be generally higher in status than the partners of the second bank. What inference would you draw about the relative abilities of the two banks?

A reasonable inference is that the bank with the higher-status partners has had an easier time riding on those partners' coattails, whereas the lower-status bank has had to do more work on its own. The bank with the higher-status partners thus deserves less credit for the performance and, accordingly, the status that one would accord for a given level of performance. Along similar lines, it is noteworthy that it in his initial elaboration of the Matthew Effect, Merton (1968) focused on coauthor relations. Like the management-comanagement relations in a syndicate, coauthor relations are inherently collaborative activities in which a relevant audience either implicitly or explicitly makes judgments about the relative contributions of the different parties. Merton (1968) observed that the higher-status coauthor receives more credit for the value of a joint product even when the lower-status actor may in fact have been responsible for more of the product. To the extent that the same holds in the context of the investment banking industry, we expect a bank's status to reflect a negative interaction between the status of the bank's affiliates and the bank's past performance. To summarize, given the specification in equation [4.3], the following pattern of coefficients should be observed:

$$b_1 > 0; \quad b_2 > 0; \quad b_3 < 0.$$

[2] An alternative specification for this model would replace A_i with $(A_i - S_{it})$. This specification posits that a firm's growth rate should increase if the average status of a focal firm's partners is greater than the focal firm's status and that the growth rate should decrease if the average status of those partners is less than the status of the focal firm. The disadvantage of this specification is that it makes the effect of S_{it} on the growth rate quite complicated. That being said, analyses were conducted with this alternative specification, and the effects of the exogenous covariates were qualitatively similar to those that are reported in the analysis in this chapter.

Constructing the Variables for the Model of
Status Growth (and Decline)

The previous chapter provided some qualitative evidence that status leaks through a bank's relations with issuers, but there is no measure of issuer status that is as good as the measure of bank status obtainable from the tombstone advertisements. Accordingly, to test the model, we will focus on manager-comanager relations in the non-investment-grade market.

The status of the banks is measured at two time points, 1981 and 1987. As was the case for the 1981 status scores, which were discussed in the previous chapter, the status scores for 1987 are derived from the tombstones for all non-investment-grade offerings displayed in the *Wall Street Journal* in that year. There were 132 non-investment-grade tombstones in 1987, somewhat fewer than the 180 that appeared in 1981.

The reason for focusing on the non-investment-grade market is that status distinctions in this market are likely to be less institutionalized, owing to the newness of the market. Previous work on the investment banking industry suggests that seven years is not a particularly long time to study changes in status as reflected in tombstone position (Hayes 1971, 1979). However, the newness of the high-yield market hopefully engenders more variance than is typical for this comparatively short time frame. Table 4.1 provides some representative status scores for those firms in the non-investment-grade market. As is clear from an examination of the illustrative scores in the table, there is obviously some similarity in bank status between the two years, but there is also some movement as well.

A variable of central analytical interest is the *average status of a bank's management partners* between 1981 and 1986, inclusive. The SDC data contain complete information on the manager-comanager relations over this period. The average status of a bank's management partners from 1981 to 1986 is calculated by using the status scores of those partners in 1981 as a proxy for their status in subsequent years. Using the 1981 scores introduces some unwanted noise in the data, but it would have been quite time-consuming to collect status information for the intervening years between 1981 and 1987, and there seems no clear way in which this additional noise biases the results in favor of our hypotheses.

The analysis includes two measures of a bank's performance: *the total dollar volume of offerings for which a bank has been lead manager or comanager between 1981 and 1986* and *the number of offerings on which a bank has been lead manager or comanager between 1981 and 1986.* Both measures are computed using SDC data. As discussed in the previous chapter, the dollar volume of deals managed is the standard performance measure reported at quarterly and annual intervals in trade publications such as *Institutional Investor* and *Investment Dealer's Digest.*[3]

---

[3] The astute reader will recognize a slight difference between the way that underwriting volume is measured in this analysis and the way that it was measured in the previous chapter. In the previous

TABLE 4.1

Representative Status Scores for Banks in the Non-Investment-Grade Debt Market in 1981 and 1987

Bank	'81 Status Score	'81 Rank	'87 Status Score	'87 Rank
Morgan Stanley	3.99696	1	2.26507	7
First Boston Corporation	3.69273	2	5.87647	1
Prudential Bache Securities	3.03846	3	.13885	14
Goldman Sachs	2.58810	4	2.69464	4
Merrill Lynch	2.51190	5	2.61348	5
Salomon Brothers	2.42793	6	2.59099	6
Lehman Brothers	2.31415	7	3.04878*	3
Bear Stearns	2.26895	8	3.18736	2
Paine Webber	2.26499	9	.32452	10
Kidder Peabody	2.22815	10	.28730	12
E. F. Hutton	2.19418	11	.13375	16
Wertheim Securities	2.18137	12	.12783	17
L. F. Rothschild Securities	2.18054	13	.12281	19
Dean Witter Reynolds	2.17666	14	.11139	15
Shearson American Express	2.17897	15	3.04878*	3
Smith Barney	2.17789	16	.13945	13
Dillon Reed	2.17666	17	.11139	20
Lazard Freres	2.16955	18	.11126	21
Warburg Paribus Becker	2.16955	19	N/A	
Drexel Burnham Lambert	2.15789	20	.34947	9
New Court Securities	1.19376	25	N/A	
Robinson Securities	.72837	50	.00904	32
Robertson Securities	.21183	101	.10015	22
Anderson Securities	.00177	150	N/A	

*Shearson and Lehman merged between 1981 and 1987. Accordingly, the two banks have the same status score in 1987.

N/A denotes that this bank is no longer present in the 1987 tombstones.

As discussed in the previous chapter, the introduction of shelf registration led to a large reduction in the average number of participants in a typical underwriting syndicate. The reason for this decline in the number of participants is beyond the scope of this analysis, but the consequence is that the

---

chapter, underwriting volume was measured with volume as lead manager. In this chapter, underwriting volume is measured with volume as lead or comanager. The reason for the difference is that the previous chapter focused on price, which is negotiated between a particular lead manager and an issuer. Accordingly, the volume as lead manager seemed most relevant in that context. In contrast, in this analysis, we are focused more on general perceptions of a bank among its peers, and accordingly it seems reasonable to include comanagement volume since comanagement positions are regarded as significant opportunities to demonstrate performance.

TABLE 4.2
Likelihood of Inclusion in 1987 Population of Banks

Variables	Estimate
Intercept	.47 (.60)
Log(number of offices)	.35 (.21)*
Among the top 100 banks	1.99 (.65)*

$N = 171$; $\chi^2 = 67.99$ with 2 d.f. Numbers in parentheses are standard errors.
*$p < .05$, one-tailed test

number of firms participating in non-investment-grade syndicates decreased dramatically over the period of our study. Of the 171 banks that had participated at least minimally as members of non-investment-grade syndicates in 1981, only 68 were members of such syndicates in 1987.[4] Because of the large decline in the number of participants, it is important to control for possible selection bias in estimating status growth and decline. It is possible to construct a selection equation by using the log of the number of offices that the bank operated in 1981 as a predictor of the likelihood that the bank will be included in the 1987 sample. The number of offices is a good proxy for the size of a bank's sales force, and the size of a bank's sales force is an important determinant of a bank's ability to underwrite security offerings in an era of shelf registration. Data on number of offices for the largest one hundred banks in any given year are published in *Institutional Investor*. If a bank is not one of the largest one hundred, then it is assigned a value of 0 for number of offices, and a dummy variable is constructed identifying those banks that are not among the largest one hundred. Through this coding, it is possible to estimate how being (or not being) among the one hundred largest banks affects the likelihood of remaining in the high-yield market in 1987, and then—contingent on being one of those one hundred banks—how the number of offices affects the likelihood of inclusion. Table 4.2 presents the results of this regression, and the predicted probability of inclusion is then entered as a control variable in the growth model.

Results for the Model of Status Growth (and Decline)

Table 4.3 presents descriptive statistics for the variables used in the analysis. Table 4.4 presents the regression results. Let's begin by considering the baseline equation in column 1 of table 4.4, where the exogenous covariates are excluded from the analysis. The point estimate for ρ, the endogenous feedback

---

[4] Banks were categorized as being participants in the market if they participated in at least 3 non-investment-grade offerings.

TABLE 4.3
Descriptive Statistics for Variables in Growth Model in Debt Markets

Variables	Mean
Focal bank's status, 1981	1.10 (1.03)
Average status of management partners, 1981–86	1.91 (1.74)
Number of offerings managed, 1981–86	37.57 (66.81)
Underwriting volume managed, 1981–86 (millions of $)	4054.0 (3265.0)

$N = 68$. Numbers in parentheses are standard deviations.

coefficient, is positive, though the effect is not significantly different from 0. The fact that we cannot rule out Gibrat's baseline hypothesis of proportionate growth is noteworthy. To the extent that high-status and low-status firms experience identical growth rates in status, the absolute status difference between high- and low-status firms increases over time, and this increase is unchecked by any endogenous bound. As noted above, such a result is consistent with Merton's Matthew Effect.

When the exogenous covariates are included in the model, the point estimate for ρ declines dramatically from 0.03 to −0.82 (in column 5), which is significantly *less* than 0. By substituting a value of −0.82 into equation [4.3], it can be shown that this value for ρ leads to relatively rapid convergence toward some fixed level of status.[5] We can interpret this result as signifying that the bounds on a focal bank's growth in status are strictly determined by the status of a bank's affiliates and by the bank's past performance. Banks can sustain status growth only to the extent that they are able to form affiliations and generate performance outcomes that are consistent with a higher level of status. If the average status of a bank's management partners and the bank's performance do not increase, then growth in status is quickly checked.

Since we know from column 1 that the unconditional growth rates are essentially independent of current status level, we can conclude that higher-status banks find it no more difficult than lower-status banks to achieve a given increment in either the average status of their exchange partners or their performance outcomes. The consequence is that the absolute difference in status between higher- and lower-status banks increases over time. However, given the results in columns 2 through 5, it should be clear that the upper bound on this process is set by the size of the market and by the inherent tension between expanding one's market share and entering into exchange relations only with those who are highest-status. This point becomes even clearer after explicit consideration of the exogenous coefficients, on which we now focus.

[5] In substituting, it is important to remember that there is a 5-year interval between S_t and S_{t+1}.

TABLE 4.4
Growth Rate Models for Status in Debt Markets

Variables	Model				
	1	2	3	4	5
Intercept	−7.30*	−12.23*	−16.82*	−16.87*	−17.96*
	(.90)	(1.18)	(2.90)	(2.88)	(3.06)
ρ	.03	−.57†	−.91*	−.93*	−.82*
	(.41)	(.36)	(.38)	(.38)	(.39)
Average status of management partners, 1981–86		2.38*	1.56*	1.69*	1.98*
		(.44)	(.58)	(.60)	(.63)
Number of offerings managed, 1981–86			.025*	.11†	.12*
			(.015)	(.07)	(.07)
Log(underwriting volume managed 1981–86)			.24*	.22†	.25*
			(.14)	(.14)	(.14)
Management partner status × number of offerings managed				−.019	−.021†
				(.015)	(.015)
Exclusion probability					−.95
					(.91)
R^2	.00	.31	.36	.38	.39

$N = 68$. Numbers in parentheses are standard errors.
†$p < .10$, one-tailed test; *$p < .05$, one-tailed test

As predicted, the effects of the two performance measures and the average status of the focal bank's management partners are positive and statistically significant. Each additional deal for which the focal bank is a lead manager or comanager increases the status growth rate by $\exp(0.12) = 1.12$ times. Each additional one-unit increment in the average status of the bank's management partners increases the status growth rate by $\exp(1.98) = 7.24$ times.

Also, as anticipated, the interaction between number of underwritings and average status of management partners is negative and significant at the .1 level.[6] Given that a one-tailed t-test at the .1 level signifies a t-ratio of only 1.3, one probably wants to be cautious in drawing an especially strong conclusion that a higher-status partner will receive more credit for past collaborative performance than a lower-status partner.

Yet, more generally, the growth model provides evidence of the Matthew Effect in markets at the same time that it reveals that the bounds on a focal bank's

[6] The interaction between average status of management partners and total underwriting volume was also analyzed, but the interaction term was highly collinear with total underwriting volume and therefore did not yield reliable estimates.

growth in status are determined by the status of a bank's affiliates. Given the evidence that a bank's status is determined by the status of a bank's affiliates, and given the benefits of status, the obvious question that arises is why a bank would ever form ties with banks lower in status than itself.

There are a number of reasons why a high-status bank might wish to form ties to banks lower in status than itself. For example, in competing for the right to lead-manage an offering of a particular issuer with headquarters outside New York, a high-status lead manager (fearing the potential loss of the deal) might offer to bring in a regional comanager that would be of lower status than other potential comanagers but that could credibly commit to trying to build or maintain a regional market for the issuer's security. A high-status lead manager might wish to give business to a lower-status comanager because it felt less competition in the league tables with the lower-status comanager and did not want to give a significant volume of business to one of its higher-status counterparts. If a high-status bank is a potential recipient of a comanagement position from a low-status bank rather than a giver of such a position, the high-status bank will have an interest in comanaging the offering if only because the comanagement opportunity will provide the bank with increased revenue. Thus, there are a number of reasons why a bank might be willing to enter into management-comanagement relations with banks lower in status than itself, but in doing so the bank faces a trade-off of increased economic opportunity in the short term against a potential loss of status in the long term. Such a trade-off is no different from the trade-off faced by the high-status jeweler trying to decide whether it should purchase turquoise for sale.

What determines how a bank responds to this trade-off? When will a bank be willing to act on its interest in engaging in relations with banks lower in status than itself? Arguably, a bank's willingness to risk a loss of status should be inversely proportional to the value of status. The lower the future value of status, the more likely that a bank will opt for the short-term benefit that it can gain from crossing status lines.

So, this question begets another: what determines the long-term value of status? To the extent that status is a signal of quality, the long-term value of status declines as uncertainty about quality declines. Banks should be more willing to enter into economic exchange with those of lower status than themselves when there is less uncertainty about quality. We now undertake a comparative examination of market share and management-comanagement relations to test this basic contingency.

STATUS AND MARKET SHARE IN THE TWO DEBT MARKETS

We begin by focusing on the relationship between bank status and market share in the two debt markets. Because the issuers of investment-grade debt are the "blue-chip" firms with established histories, CEOs and boards that are part of the "establishment," and a history of strong financial performance, the issuers of investment-grade debt are almost necessarily higher-status than the issuers of "junk" debt. Indeed, the nomenclature of "junk" is illustrative of the way in which the issuers in this market were viewed. If one wants even further qualitative evidence that the issuers of "junk" debt were regarded as low-status, one would need only to look at Morgan Stanley's press announcement when it decided to enter the market for non-investment-grade debt. Like other high-status banks, Morgan Stanley was reluctant to enter this market despite the huge profits that the market's pioneer, Drexel Burnham Lambert, was earning. In chapter 1, I noted that when Morgan Stanley finally decided to enter the market, it announced that it would "gentrify" the market through its entry (Chernow 1990). It is hard to imagine a term that could better convey Morgan Stanley's view that this market was populated by low-status actors as well as its belief in the relational foundations of status.

Figures 4.1 and 4.2 show how the cumulative percentage of offerings was distributed across the banks in both debt markets between 1981 and 1987. Recall that there were 3,278 investment-grade issues during this period and 8,081 non-investment-grade issues. Status scores from 1981 are represented on the horizontal axes of both figures; the vertical or response axes denote the cumulative percentage of offerings led by those banks in a given percentile rank and lower. Precise comparisons are difficult because, as table 4.1 shows, the distributions of status scores in the two markets are not identical. Nevertheless, even given the different ranges on the horizontal axes, it should be reasonably clear that the lower-status banks underwrote a greater percentage of offerings in the non-investment-grade market than in the investment-grade market. This result is entirely consistent with the claim that there ought to be greater status-based homophily in a more uncertain context. In the more uncertain context, the higher-status banks are more reluctant to dominate the market because of the threat to their status of being at "the lower end" of the market.

Of course, such a result involves a high-level comparison of distributions across two market contexts. For a more fine-grained result that focuses on the exchange relations of individual firms, I turn once again to the exchange relations between lead managers and potential comanagers. The central analytic question is: What affects the likelihood that a given bank appears as comanager on an offering led by a particular lead manager? In answering this question, I model the management-comanagement pairing on an offering as the result of two joint decisions: the lead manager's decision to choose a particular comanager and the comanager's decision to accept the offer. The central concern in this model is whether status exerts a greater impact on pairings in the non-investment-grade market than in the investment-grade market. That is, do we observe greater status-based homophily in manager-comanager relations in the high-yield context than in the investment grade context?

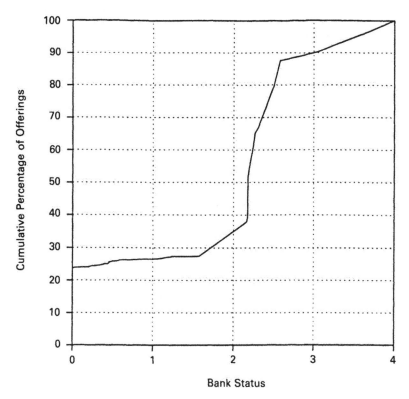

FIGURE 4.1. Distribution of offerings by status in the non-investment-grade debt market

Analysis of Manager-Comanager Pairings

Using the SDC data available on individual transactions in the debt markets between 1981 and 1987, I model the probability of a match between a lead manager and a particular comanager in each of the debt markets by using a logistic regression model in which each observation is a lead manager/potential comanager pair that is coded 1 if the lead manager chooses the particular bank as comanager for the offering and 0 otherwise. Accordingly, each offering in the investment-grade market contributes approximately 169 observations (170 banks in the investment grade market − 1 lead manager = 169 choices) to the analysis, since each manager has 169 "tombstone" banks from which it can select a comanager. The exact number of potential choices varies slightly because of failures or mergers among the banks during the study period. Similarly, since there are 171 tombstone banks in the high-yield market, there are 170 observations associated with each offering. If a lead manager were required

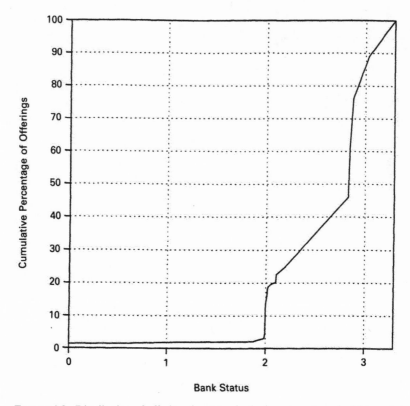

FIGURE 4.2. Distribution of offerings by status in the investment-grade debt market

to select a certain number of comanagers for a given offering, then the multiple observations per offering would violate the standard nonindependence assumption in a regression analysis, but because a lead manager can choose no comanager, one comanager, or multiple comanagers, there is not a strict dependence across observations related to a particular offering.

While I draw on the SDC data from 1981 through 1987 for the purpose of the analysis, a number of the variables—especially those pertaining to the relationship between a lead manager and potential comanager—require lagged terms that provide historical information over some time period. For the purpose of this analysis, I use a twenty-four-month lag. Accordingly, data from years 1981 and 1982 enter in largely for the purpose of history.[7]

To a large degree, the variables in this analysis are similar to the variables employed in the analysis of spread in the previous chapter and the growth

---

[7] I also conducted analyses using a 12-month window. Results were substantively uninfluenced by the length of time chosen.

model in this chapter. Accordingly, I will only quickly discuss the variables that are common across analyses and will devote more attention to the variables that are unique to this particular regression.

Status.   The central effect in which we are interested is the effect of status differences on the probability of an exchange relationship. As the status difference between two banks becomes larger, the likelihood of an exchange relationship should decline, and this decline should be more pronounced in the more uncertain context (i.e., the market for non-investment-grade debt.)

The status of a bank is measured the same way that it has been measured in the previous analyses. I draw on Bonacich's $c(\alpha, \beta)$ measure to distill a quantitative indicator of a bank's tombstone position. I once again use the tombstone data from 1981 as a measure of status in both markets. One might reasonably ask why I do not use the 1987 tombstone data as the measure of status for the later observations. The primary reason is—as we have just observed in the previous analysis—that the 1987 tombstone locations are a consequence of the partnering relationships over the previous time period; accordingly, one might be confounding cause and effect by using the 1987 tombstone data for the later observations. A second, albeit less important, reason is that I have tombstone data for 1987 only in the non-investment-grade market. Since the analysis of lead management pairings is a comparative analysis across markets, use of the 1987 scores for one market and not the other would impede a clear comparison.

Because we are focusing on how the difference in status between a particular lead manager and a potential comanager affects the likelihood of an exchange relationship, the effect of a change in status of either member of the dyad is contingent on whose status is greater. On the one hand, if the lead manager's status is greater, then an increase in that bank's status enlarges the status gap and therefore lowers the likelihood of an exchange relation. On the other hand, if the lead manager's status is less than the potential comanager's, an increase in the lead manager's status reduces the status gap between the lead manager and potential comanager and therefore raises the probability of an exchange relationship. To test for this functional relationship, I adopt a spline specification (Johnston 1984). I use one coefficient to measure the effect of the lead manager's status when the lead manager's status is greater than the potential comanager's, and I use another coefficient to measure the effect of the lead manager's status when the lead manager's status is less than the potential comanager's. To the extent that there is status-based homophily, the first of the coefficients should be negative and the second should be positive. To the extent that there is greater uncertainty in the non-investment-grade market than in the investment-grade market, the absolute value of each coefficient should be greater in the analysis of the non-investment-grade market than in the investment-grade market.

Similarly, the effect of an increase in the potential comanager's status on the probability of exchange will depend on whether the potential comanager's status is greater than or less than the lead manager's. Again, I use a spline specification: one coefficient to model the effect of a change in the potential comanager's status when it is greater than the lead manager's and one to model the effect of a change when the comanager's status is less than the lead manager's. As with the lead manager's status, the first of these coefficients should be negative and the second should be positive, and the absolute value of these effects should be stronger in the high-yield market than in the investment-grade market. These predicted effects are summarized in table 4.5.[8]

Previous exchange partners. In investigating the likelihood that a particular lead bank is matched with a potential comanager, it is obviously very important to control for the extent of a relationship between the banks in the past as well as relationships between the issuing corporation and the banks. I use several variables to test for such relationship-specific effects.

The first is *the number of times that the lead manager has chosen a potential comanager over a twenty-four-month period* prior to the offering date for the

TABLE 4.5

Hypothesized Determinants of the Probability That a Lead Manager (LM) Chooses a Potential Comanager (PCM)

Variables	Expected Direction of Effect under Uncertainty	Effect in Non-Investment-Grade (NIG) vs. Investment-Grade (IG) Markets
Number of times PCM has chosen LM on offerings over past 2 years	+	NIG > IG
Number of times over past 2 years PCM has managed or comanaged offering for issuer	+	NIG > IG
LM's status when LM's status is less than PCM's	+	NIG > IG
LM's status when LM's status is greater than PCM's	−	NIG < IG
PCM's status when PCM's status is less than LM's	+	NIG > IG
PCM's status when PCM's status is greater than LM's	−	NIG < IG

[8] Given the complexity of the specification laid out in this table, one might reasonably ask whether it is possible to examine these status effects using one parameter and a difference variable, such as the absolute difference between the lead manager's and potential comanager's statuses. The problem with this alternative approach is that such a specification would result in an identification problem. One could not be sure whether the positive effect for the coefficient was due to the difference between the two variables or simply to changes in the levels of one or both of the variables. By using the dual spline formulation and thereby using up four degrees of freedom rather than one, it is possible to overcome this identification problem.

issue managed by the particular lead bank. I (Podolny 1994) as well as others (Haunschild 1994; Kollock 1994) have argued that the greater the uncertainty, the more that we should observe market actors turning to those with whom they have transacted in the past as a means for addressing this uncertainty. In effect, a reliance on prior exchange partners is an alternative mechanism to a reliance on status as a signal. One would, therefore, expect that as uncertainty increases, past occurrences of the dependent variable for a particular lead manager/potential comanager pair would have an increasingly strong effect on the likelihood of an occurrence of the dependent variable. Unfortunately, however, there is an identification problem that confounds any substantive interpretation of this variable. Heckman and Borjas (1980) and Cox (1966) both demonstrated that to the extent that there is unobserved heterogeneity across observations, this unobserved heterogeneity will result in a positive effect of prior outcomes on the probability that the outcome will occur again. Because a positive coefficient may be due to unobserved heterogeneity, one cannot provide a unique substantive interpretation for a variable that measures past occurrences of a dependent variable. However, Heckman and Borjas (1980) argue that past occurrences of the dependent variable should still be included as an independent variable in a model because this variable serves as at least a partial control for unobserved heterogeneity.

While the effect of past occurrences of the dependent variable does not lend itself to substantive interpretation, the data allow for the construction of two other measures that are not confounded by unobserved heterogeneity. The first measures *the number of times that the lead manager has occupied a subordinate position in an offering led by the potential comanager over the past two years*. The effect of this variable denotes the tendency for the lead manager to reciprocate for management opportunities that have been provided to it by the potential comanager over the previous two years. To the extent that the development of enduring exchange relations is a function of uncertainty, this tendency to reciprocate will be greater in the in the non-investment-grade market than in the investment-grade market.

Interviews with investment bankers, as well as prior scholarly work (e.g., Eccles and Crane 1988; Chernow 1990), reveal that if an issuer has a strong relationship with an investment bank but does not use it as a lead manager for a particular offering, the issuer may still insist on that bank being a comanager. In fact, the previous chapter reported a particularly notorious example of such insistence when IBM insisted that Morgan Stanley use Salomon Brothers as comanager despite the fact that Morgan Stanley had previously never relied on comanagers. Accordingly, I use a variable that measures *the number of times that the potential comanager has occupied a management position in any offering that the issuing corporation has made over the previous two years*. To the extent that a repeated reliance on previous exchange partners is a function of uncertainty, this prior tie between the issuer and potential comanager will have a greater effect on the probability of a match between a lead manager and a potential comanager in the non-investment-grade market than in the investment-grade market.

Control variables.   The control variables all have their parallels in the previous analyses. Using the data from *Institutional Investor* discussed in the growth model, I include the *number of offices* maintained by a potential comanager as a proxy for retail capacity. Since *Institutional Investor* reports data only for the one hundred largest banks and since there are more than one hundred potential comanagers in each market, there are obviously a number of banks for which this information is missing. I therefore include an indicator variable that is coded 1 if the data are missing and 0 otherwise so that the estimate for the number of offices is not biased because of missing information.

I include two variables to measure a potential comanager's underwriting history: one that measures the logged dollar value of offerings for which the potential comanager was lead manager over the past two years and one that measures the logged dollar value of offerings for which the potential comanager was comanager for the past two years. As before, these variables are included because underwriting volume is an alternative signal of quality and volume is a determinant of quality insofar as it gives a bank a better knowledge of supply and demand conditions. Moreover, since volume in the capacity of comanager is necessarily a function of the degree to which an investment bank has been chosen as a comanager in the past, the bank's underwriting volume as a comanager is a partial control for unmeasured factors, such as research ability or network connections to prominent investors, that affect the marginal probability that the comanager will be selected by any lead manager. Thus, I include measures of volume history for largely the same reason that I did so in the previous chapter: to demonstrate that status concerns are a significant determinant of market relations even in the presence of alternative market indicators of past performance and ability.

Results

Table 4.6 lists the descriptive statistics for the analysis, and table 4.7 presents the regression results for both the investment-grade and the non-investment-grade markets.

The first column of results in table 4.7 reveals a considerable tendency toward status-based homophily in the non-investment-grade market. As expected, an increase in the lead manager's status has a positive effect on the probability of an exchange relationship when the lead manager's status is less than the potential comanager's status and a negative effect when it is greater than the potential comanager's status. Similarly, the effect of the comanager's status is contingent on whether it is greater or less than the lead manager's status.

TABLE 4.6

Descriptive Statistics for Analysis of Relations between Lead Managers (LMs) and
Potential Comanagers (PCMs)

Variables	Non-Investment-Grade Mean	Investment-Grade Mean
Previous exchange partners		
No. of times potential comanager (PCM) has given lead manager (LM) a subordinate management position over past 2 years	.071 (.470)	.496 (3.227)
No. of times issuer has used PCM over past 2 years	.001 (.058)	.017 (.223)
Status		
Lead manager's status	2.413 (.668)	2.720 (.437)
Potential comanager's status	.632 (.794)	.702 (.669)
Control variables		
Log(PCM's sales in lead manager position over past 2 years)	4.958 (8.338)	2.437 (6.646)
Log(PCM's sales in comanager position over past 2 years)	6.931 (9.176)	4.871 (8.725)
PCM's no. of offices	23.678 (83.508)	18.740 (64.981)
No. of times LM has selected PCM over past 2 years (occurrence-dependent term)	.105 (576)	.629 (3.328)
Sample information		
No. of offerings, 1983–87	5,228	2,821
No. of comanagers selected	1,125	3,523
No. of dyads	809,741	467,149

Numbers in parentheses are standard deviations.

When the comanager's status is less than the lead manager's, the effect is positive. When the comanager's status is greater than the lead manager's, the effect is negative.

It is important to underscore that the increase in the log-odds applies to each and every offering of the lead bank. Therefore, if one wants to know how the log-odds of a lead manager/potential comanager relationship increase over some time period, one needs to multiply the log-odds by the number of offerings made by the lead manager over that time period. If Goldman Sachs's status were to increase from 2.58 to 2.69 (as it did between 1981 and 1987), then its log-odds of entering into an exchange relation with a lower-status comanager decrease by $(2.69 - 2.58) \times 1.56 = 0.09 \times 1.56 = .14$ on each of the deals that it leads.

TABLE 4.7
Logistic Regression Results for Debt Markets

Variables	Non-Investment-Grade Coefficient	Investment-Grade Coefficient	Comparative Hypotheses
Intercept	-6.76 (.190)**	-9.62 (.24)**	
Previous exchange partners			
No. of times potential comanger (PCM) has given lead manager (LM) a subordinate management position over past 2 years	.133 (.020)**	1.5×10^{-4} (3.2×10^{-3})	NIG > IG**
No. of times issuer has used PCM over past 2 years	1.461 (.069)**	.773 (.021)**	NIG > IG**
Lead manager's status			
LM's status when LM's status is less than PCM's	.842 (.119)**	$-.032$ (.084)	NIG > IG**
LM's status when LM's status is greater than PCM's	-1.556 (.073)**	$-.114$ (.063)*	NIG < IG**
Potential comanager's status			
PCM's status when PCM's status is less than LM's	1.632 (.086)**	.804 (.062)**	NIG > IG*
PCM's status when PCM's status is greater than LM's	$-.843$ (.096)**	.665 (.085)	NIG < IG**
Control variables			
Log(PCM's sales in lead manager position over past 2 years)	$-.015$ (.008)	.041 (.005)**	
Log(PCM's sales in comanager position over past 2 years)	.112 (.009)**	.180 (.010)**	
PCM's no. of offices	3.2×10^{-4} (1.5×10^{-4})	1.8×10^{-4} (9.6×10^{-5})	
PCM's no. of offices is missing	.223 (.141)	.068 (.079)	
No. of times LM has selected PCM over past 2 years	.123 (.017)**	.022 (.003)**	
χ^2 for covariates	4347, 11 d.f.**	18,617, 11 d.f.**	

Numbers in parentheses are standard errors.
*$p < .05$; **$p < .01$; one-tailed test

While status homophily is obviously the phenomenon of the greatest substantive interest in the analysis, a few of the other coefficients in the first column are also worthy of note. The tendency of a lead manager to reciprocate for subordinate management opportunities provided to it over the past two years is positive and statistically significant. For each offering over the two-year historical window that the potential comanager led and chose the lead manager as a comanager, the log-odds that the lead manager would select the potential comanager for the current offering increase by 0.13.[9]

Prior contact between the issuing corporation and the potential comanager also has a positive effect on the probability that the lead manager chooses the potential comanager. For each time that the issuing company has used the potential comanager as either a lead manager or comanager on a junk offering in the past year, the odds that the potential comanager will be chosen increase by a multiplicative factor of $\exp(1.46) = 0.37$.

The second column of results in table 4.7 pertains to the investment-grade market. Though the direction of several of the coefficients is consistent with a principle of status-based exclusivity, the significance of these effects is generally quite low. The effects of the lead manager's status and the potential comanager's status on the probability of an exchange relation are only partly consistent with the proposition that firms are avoiding exchange relations with lower-status others. When the status of the lead manager is greater than the status of the comanager, a positive increment in the lead manager's status has the anticipated negative effect on the probability of an exchange relation. When the lead manager's status is less than the potential comanager's status, however, we cannot reject the null hypothesis that the status of the lead manager has no effect on the probability of an exchange relation.

Results for the potential comanager's status show that the potential comanager's status does have the anticipated statistically significant, positive effect on the probability of an exchange relation when the comanager's status is less than the lead manager's status. When the potential comanager's status is greater than the lead manager's, however, the effect is not negative. It therefore seems that potential comanagers do not avoid associations with

---

[9] To highlight the significance of this result, it is important to recognize that, because of the specification in the model, an increase in the probability of an exchange relationship applies to each offering by a lead manager for a two-year window after that lead manager was selected by the potential comanager. For example, Morgan Stanley led 54 syndicates in the non-investment-grade market between January 1, 1983, and December 31, 1984. If a focal bank selects Morgan Stanley as a comanager on December 31, 1982, the log-odds that Morgan Stanley will choose this focal bank as a comanager on at least one of these offerings from January 1, 1983, to December 31, 1984, increase by $54 \times 0.13 = 7.02$. The mean number of offerings underwritten by a lead bank during this two-year period was 24.16. Accordingly, if a focal bank selects the "mean underwriter" as comanager on December 31, 1983, the log-odds that the focal bank will be chosen by this mean underwriter over the two-year period increase by $24.16 \times 0.13 = 3.14$.

lower-status lead managers in the investment-grade market. There are perhaps two reasons for this. First, as reported, in figures 4.1 and 4.2, there are comparatively few offerings led by low-status banks in the investment-grade market, where 96 percent of the offerings were led by one of the twenty-one highest-status banks. In contrast, only 71 percent of the offerings in the non-investment-grade market were underwritten by the highest-status banks.[10] In effect, the differential selection of the higher-status banks into the lead management positions means that potential comanagers in the investment-grade market are rarely confronted with a situation in which they have the possibility of comanaging an offering that is led by a bank that is significantly lower in status. Second, just as the higher-status banks could occupy a greater proportion of lead management opportunities without fearing a loss of status in the investment-grade market, so the higher-status banks could also occupy a greater proportion of comanagement positions without fearing a loss of status.[11] A decline in status-based homophily implies greater market concentration, since higher-status comanagers are much less reluctant to expand market share.

In passing, it is worth observing that just as there is less concern with status in the investment-grade market, so there is less reliance on a prior tie as a basis for a subsequent exchange relation. While the two variables denoting the effect of a previous exchange relation have a positive effect, the one denoting the tendency of the lead manager to reciprocate is not statistically significant, and the point estimate is quite close to 0. Even though such effects are not of primary interest in the context of this book, the results are still noteworthy insofar as they provide further confirmation that in a context of greater risk and uncertainty, the relational underpinnings of the market are more important as determinants of exchange opportunities. With scholars such as Granovetter (1985), Mizruchi and Stearns (1994), and Uzzi (1997) emphasizing the embeddedness of economic transactions, a result like this one suggests that embeddedness is contingent on the level of uncertainty—just as the reliance on market status is contingent on uncertainty.

---

[10] I use the 21 highest-status banks, rather than a "rounder" number like 20, because Drexel Burnham Lambert, the bank with the largest market share in the non-investment-grade market, is ranked twenty-first in status in that market. Using a cutoff of 20 would have resulted in an even greater absolute difference between the two markets.

[11] This observed difference in the proportion of lead management positions occupied by the highest-status banks in the two markets raises the question of whether the less significant effects in the investment-grade market are strictly due to lower variance in the variables in the investment-grade market. By using the data presented in table 4.5 to construct coefficients of relative variation for the variables in the investment-grade and non-investment-grade market, one can easily observe that the lead manager's status is the only variable of substantive interest for which the coefficient of relative variation is noticeably less in the investment-grade than in the non-investment-grade market.

Yet while the results in the first two columns clearly suggest important differences between the two markets in the attention paid to status and to previous exchange partners, the results from the first two columns do not provide a formal statistical test of these differences. As I noted earlier, the hypothesized effects of uncertainty on the reliance on status can be operationalized in terms of the four status inequalities reported in table 4.5. While of less central interest, I similarly argued (and there now seems some suggestive evidence) that there is a similar inequality in the reliance on previous exchange partners between the two markets. To test for these inequalities more formally, I pooled the data from both markets and constructed six interaction variables between market type and the variables relevant to the effect of status and prior exchange relationships. I then repeated the analysis using the pooled data and simultaneously included all interactions between market type and the six variables. A statistically significant interaction between market type and a variable implies a statistically significant difference across the two markets with respect to the interacted characteristic. Though I do not report the coefficients, I do report the results of these tests in the last column of table 4.7. All the comparisons yield statistically significant differences in the expected direction.

Changing Uncertainty in the Non-Investment-Grade Market

I have treated differences in risk and uncertainty between the two debt markets thus far as being time-invariant; I would now like to focus on changes over time in the non-investment-grade market. The primary reason ties back to the distinction between risk and uncertainty elaborated in the previous chapter. Recall the Knightian distinction between risk (which denotes a context in which there is a known probability distribution of outcomes though the actual outcome is not yet known) and "uncertainty" (when the underlying probability distribution is unknown). We have observed that the effect of status on price and patterns of exchange relations is greater in the non-investment-grade market than in the investment-grade market, where the former is characterized by both greater risk and greater uncertainty than the latter. However, because the former is higher in both risk and uncertainty, it is difficult to disentangle whether these status effects are driven more by risk or more by uncertainty. To some degree, the interaction effect of offering size and status on spread at least begins to tease these apart. Investment banks and issuers do not maintain systematic information about how the size of an offering relates to the likelihood of a successful placement; accordingly, the positive interaction between bank status and size on spread reported in tables 3.2 and 3.4 provides at least some indication that uncertainty (and not just risk) drives the relevance of status. However, further evidence on this point comes from analyzing the pattern of exchange relations over time in the non-investment-grade market. Throughout the 1980s, the risk associated with high-yield offerings did not change. A bond with a CCC rating from Moody's in the earlier 1980s carried the same level of risk as a bond with that rating at the end of the 1980s. However, the uncertainty permeating this market did experience a considerable decline throughout the 1980s. Since Drexel pioneered this market in the late 1970s, the early 1980s were characterized by considerable uncertainty about the overall supply and demand for these securities. As noted, many of the highest-status firms were reluctant to even enter the market. However, by the late 1980s, the market was clearly institutionalized; all the major investment banks had high-yield departments that focused exclusively on this market. Accordingly, while the risk associated with securities did not change, since the risk was linked to the assets of the firms issuing the security, uncertainty did change. Therefore, the changing uncertainty in the non-investment-grade market gives us the ability to tease apart whether the reliance on status is driven primarily by risk or uncertainty.

Figures 4.3–4.5 depict the pattern of manager-comanager relations for three two-year time intervals: 1981–1982, 1983–1984, and 1985–1986. The lead manager's and comanager's statuses are depicted on the horizontal plane. The spikes along the vertical axis depict the number of deals jointly managed by a specific manager-comanager pair. The graphs demonstrate that, over time, the status-based homophily declined rather remarkably. This decline is most clearly demonstrated by looking at the section of the plane where the comanager's status score is greater than 2 and the manager's status score is less than 2. In the earliest two-year period, there is no offering for which the comanager is above 2 and the lead manager is below 2. In the middle period, there are three "spikes" in this region and in the latest period eleven spikes, with several of those spikes denoting more than one offering. As the market ages and uncertainty declines, high-status comanagers are apparently more willing to engage in exchange relations with low-status lead managers. Low-status manager/high-status comanager pairs violate two status-based expectations. First, they violate the expectation of status-based homophily. Second, they violate the expectation that higher-status banks will appear in positions superior to lower-status banks.

As these status-based violations increase over time, so, too, does the market presence of high-status firms relative to low-status firms. To illustrate this increasing domination of the market by high-status banks, I again use the status score of 2 to divide the banks into a high-status group and a low-status group. In 1981 and 1982, twenty-one banks with a status greater than 2 and thirty-four banks with a status less than 2 comanaged at least one offering. Comparing the number of offerings that these banks comanaged in the 1981–1982 period with the number that they comanaged in the 1985–1986 period reveals whether there was movement toward an increasing domination of the comanagement positions by the higher-status banks. The average bank in the high-status group

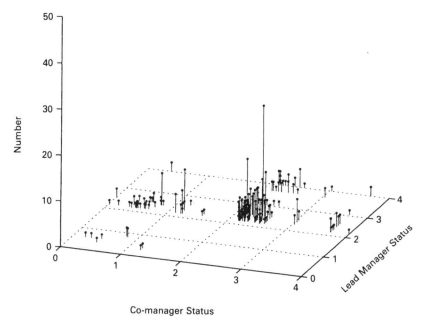

FIGURE 4.3. Non-investment-grade manager-comanager pairs, 1981–1982

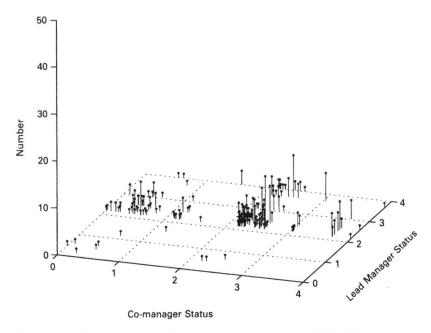

FIGURE 4.4. Non-investment-grade manager-comanager pairs, 1983–1984

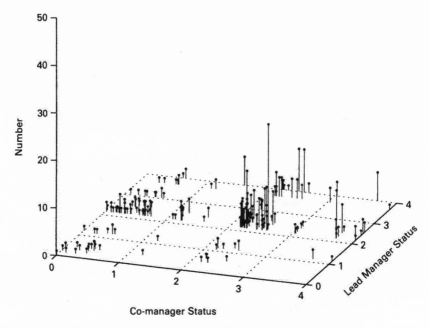

FIGURE 4.5. Non-investment-grade manager-comanager pairs, 1985–1986

increased the number of offerings for which it was a comanager by 199 percent from the 1981–1982 period to the 1985–1986 period, whereas the average bank in the low-status group increased its number by 162 percent. More generally, across these fifty-five banks, the correlation between status and percent increase in number offerings comanaged is .23, which is statistically significant at the .1 level. The decline in status-based homophily thus seems to be accompanied by a trend toward an increasing concentration of the market in the hands of the higher-status banks. The clear implication is that the relevance of status to the formation of exchange relations is directly affected by the level of uncertainty.

CONCLUSION

I noted at the outset that the focus of this chapter would be on the leakiness of status. We have observed that status does indeed leak through exchange relations, and we have observed that a firm's willingness to enter into exchange relations with those lower in status than itself is a direct function of whether such leakiness could have implications for future economic revenue. The less uncertainty in a particular context, the less value inhering in status as a signal and the more cross-status relations that are manifest.

Throughout the analyses, uncertainty has been treated as a characteristic of the market in a particular period, not a firm-level characteristic. There is no variance in the uncertainty that issuers, investors, or potential management partners have about the quality of the banks in a market at a given moment in time. I have essentially ignored interfirm differences in uncertainty because I have no systematic indicators of such differences. In chapter 6, we will consider differences in the technological niches occupied by firms, and one of the distinguishing characteristics of those differences is the level of uncertainty associated with the niche. Similarly, in chapter 7, I will focus on status dynamics surrounding British shipping cartels, a context in which differences in the age of firms provide at least some basis for making such inferences.

At the same time that uncertainty has been treated as a characteristic of the market, I have treated the extent of status segregation in the market as a general propensity for firms to engage in exchange relations with partners whose status is different from their own. Such a way of treating status is a decidedly micro-level approach in the sense that it tends to ignore salient divides or breaks in the status ordering. That is, in addition to focusing on the general tendency to homophily, one could also be concerned with the presence (or absence) of salient thresholds in the status ordering that tend to not be crossed. In order to observe such breaks, one needs to adopt a more macro-level perspective on the status ordering and consider the overall distribution of firms in the status ordering. In chapter 8, we will take up this analytical task.

However, before we proceed to considering interfirm variance in uncertainty or adopting a more macro-level perspective on status segregation, I believe it is important to focus in more detail on how consumers rely on status as a signal. It is now hopefully fair to say that the analysis of the investment banking industry has yielded considerable evidence supporting the conception of status as signal that I elaborated in the first two chapters. At the same time, an appropriately skeptical reader may have some concerns about the evidence thus presented. In the previous chapter, I mentioned one concern that I regard as especially important—the absence of rigorous controls for either quality or reputation. Maybe higher-status firms are just higher in quality, and maybe higher-quality firms try to preserve the quality of their services in the primary securities market by associating only with other banks that are also high in quality. Put simply, status might just be epiphenomenal, nothing but a reflection of true albeit difficult-to-measure quality differences of which industry participants are aware. One could then explain the cost advantages of high-status firms as spurious; the real cost advantage would be a reduction in transaction costs attributable to a reputation for quality, not to occupying a high-status network position.

One response to this critique of the results is that such a quality-based interpretation denies the phenomenological reality of the investment banking market. As Jim March, one of the leading figures of the "Carnegie School" tradition in organizational behavior and one of the greatest social scientists whom I have had the pleasure to know, has quipped: rationalization is not explanation. That is, even if one might try to rationalize the findings in terms of quality rather than status, this does not mean that quality is the explanation. To rely solely on quality differences as the explanation is to deny much of the qualitative data to which I alluded in the previous chapter. As we have seen in the previous chapter, there is much evidence that bankers care deeply about the status of their bank vis-à-vis the other banks in the market.

Another response draws on the fact that the higher-status banks have lower costs and do not dominate the market. As we discussed in chapter 1, reputation is not a constraint on a firm's ability to dominate the market. Just as a high-status jeweler should be able preserve its reputation for quality by sub-branding its turquoise offerings (e.g., putting them in a different case, making it clear that turquoise is a softer stone than a diamond, and so on), so a Morgan Stanley or Goldman Sachs should be able to underwrite offerings of the "lower-end" issuers and preserve its reputation for quality. To be sure, these lower-end issuers would be higher-risk investments, but this higher risk could be priced with a higher yield on the bonds and higher spread for the syndicate members. The only reason that a bank could not preserve its reputation by entering the lower end of the market would be that reputation has a relational component. However, if reputation has a relational component, then reputation essentially is status, and it is simply a question of semantics whether one wants to employ the terminology of status or of reputation-cum-relational component.

A third and final response to this critique that the observed status effects are simply spurious quality effects would be to leave the context of investment banking and to consider a context in which it is easier to obtain controls for quality and reputation. This is the response that I pursue in the next chapter—in an examination of the California wine industry.

Chapter Five

THE MEDIUM, THE MESSAGE,

AND THE SIGNAL

A COMMON SAYING in politics and marketing is that "the medium is the message." The saying denotes the belief that people are simply unable to filter out the broader context within which a message is situated. As a consequence, it is not possible to decouple the content of a message from the form in which the message is conveyed. The status-based model of market competition implies a similar idea. Insofar as the message that producers are trying to convey is a message about quality, the status ordering is the medium in which these messages are situated, and any claims regarding quality are ultimately filtered through this medium.

In economic models of reputation in markets, there is no medium that exists independently of the message. That is, reputation follows entirely from the actions of producers and not from a network position in a market that can be defined independently of those actions. So, for example, Shapiro (1983) constructs a model in which producers are differentiated by the quality of the goods they produce; these differences in quality are associated with differences in expectations on the part of consumers, and these differences in expectations imply sustainable differences in the level of operating profits across producers. In Shapiro's model, reputation flows entirely from the actions of the producer—a producer has a reputation for high quality to the extent that the producer chooses to make and sell high-quality goods.

Werner Raub and Jeroen Weesie (1990) have shown how such models of reputation can be given a sociological flavor by embedding the transmission of reputational information in the pattern of ties among a group of actors; however, even in Raub and Weesie's model, the ultimate source of information is the content of a particular act. Networks are not filters but—to draw on the metaphor in chapter 1—pipes that perfectly transmit information between the nodes in the network. To continue the metaphor, the pattern of pipe connections does not yield any independent information.

Given the existence of economic and sociological models that assume individuals attend to the message independently of the medium, an obvious and yet important question is: Why *would* individuals pay attention to the medium and not just the message? In politics and marketing, the answer typically has to do with either constraints on individuals' time and/or the willingness of individuals to at least implicitly allow others to act as agents on their behalf. So, while an individual may lack the time to thoroughly read the political platforms of the major political parties (especially when the cost of this time is weighed against the perceived difference that the individual's vote will have on the election outcome), it is easier for the individual, first, to simply attend to whether the symbolism in which the message is situated is a symbolism with which the individual can agree and, second, to trust that the party members are in fact writing a platform that is consistent with the individual's interpretation of the symbols. Put in economic terms, the search costs for accurate information on potential actions leave individuals in a situation in which they are looking to proxies that will be correlated—albeit imperfectly—with that information.

Chapter 1 offered a similar rationale for why individuals would look to status rather than simply to past actions to make inferences about quality. It may be too difficult for individuals to acquire information about past acts. Elias and Scotson's example of the woman who invited the dustmen for tea helped to serve as a case in point. Why did the established insiders of the town look at the woman's association with the dustmen to make an inference about the quality of this newcomer's character? Acquiring information on the quality of her character based on past actions would have been costly; they would have needed to find out the town in which she had previously resided. They would have needed to conduct inquiries of her previous neighbors about a variety of acts in which she did and did not engage, and if they lacked reliable ties to any of those previous neighbors, they would then have needed to figure out how they could validate the veracity of those sources. As a consequence, it was simply easier to attend to the symbolic significance of the woman inviting the dustmen to tea and make inferences about the woman as a result of the quality of company that she kept.

Even if individuals are willing and able to go to the trouble of acquiring information on past acts in order to make inferences about quality, it is sometimes difficult to provide an unambiguous interpretation for those past acts. If one buys a watch from a particular retailer and the battery runs out almost immediately, is this the fault of the watchmaker or the retailer? Was the watch defective? Or, did the retailer not manage his inventory appropriately—keeping this particular watch on the shelf for too long? To the extent that there is some ambiguity about the significance of past acts and events, status can still be relied on as a signal of quality.

In the examination of the investment banking industry, we observed investment banks behaving as if the medium mattered to the message. Specifically, we observed investment banks avoiding lower-status associations out of concern that the leakage of status through exchange relations would contaminate any claims or demonstrations of quality.

However, in assessing the effects of the medium of status on market outcomes, we had only loose proxies for past demonstrations of quality, such as the underwriting volume of the investment bank. Because these indicators of the "message" of quality were imperfect, it was not possible to look at the impact of the medium and the message simultaneously. In addition, it was also not possible to look at how a firm's status at one moment in time affected its investment in quality at a subsequent moment in time. Recall that chapter 2 drew a distinction between a Spencian and non-Spencian conception of a signal. According to Spence, the marginal cost of a signal is by definition inversely associated with quality. However, for status, it is the marginal cost of quality that is inversely associated with the existence of the signal. The implication is that the lower one's status at one time point, the less profitable and accordingly the less likely that one produces a good above a given quality threshold at a subsequent time point.

In this chapter, we focus on the impact of medium and message jointly, and the central claim of this chapter is the following: not only does the medium of status have an independent effect on market outcomes, as we observed in the examination of the investment banking industry; the medium of status moderates the economic returns obtained through past demonstrations of quality. The status ordering provides the lens through which past demonstrations of quality are perceived and accordingly affects both the returns obtained through those past demonstrations of quality as well as the likelihood of subsequent investments in quality.

The wine industry provides a uniquely appropriate context for such an examination because the existence of "blind taste tests" provides information on quality. Since the evaluator of a wine can examine the wine without knowing the identity of the producer, it is possible to obtain a measure of quality that is unbiased by expectations based on the winery's status. In this way, the message can be analytically decoupled from the medium. The empirical examination in this chapter will thus simultaneously fulfill two objectives. First, it will help address the nagging concern that status is simply a reflection of unmeasured past demonstrations of quality. Second, it will provide some empirical insight into the joint impact of medium and message.

THE JOINT IMPACT OF MEDIUM AND MESSAGE

If one looks for theoretical leads regarding the joint impact of status and past demonstrations of quality on individual outcomes, one can find such leads in sociological research outside of the market context. A number of scholars have argued that higher status associations or affiliations help to increase returns obtained from a given quality of output. This proposition is perhaps most clearly articulated in the sociology of science. Latour (1987) and Camic (1992) both asserted that a scientist is more likely to receive favorable evaluations of a given quality of work to the extent that he or she is able to associate the work with the efforts of high-status others. Similarly, in sociological studies of education, Bowles and Gintis (1976) maintained that a child's affiliation with a particular social class, rather than the child's past educational achievement, shapes expectations about his or her intellectual ability. Finally, in community studies like that undertaken by Elias and Scotson (1994), sociologists have frequently observed that evaluations of an individual's moral character have less to do with the individual's prior acts of morality than with the status of the company he or she keeps.

In these and other contexts, holding all else constant, the status accrued through one's associations should increase the returns obtained through an actor's past demonstrations of quality. Similarly, returns obtained in the market by producing output of a given quality should decrease to the extent that the market actor does not affiliate with high-status others.

There are two possible processes by which this might occur. First, status distinctions across actors may act as a screen or filter, drawing attention *away* from the demonstrations of quality by market actors with lower-status associations and toward demonstrations of quality by actors with higher-status associations. If the likelihood of observing a market actor's investment in quality increases with the status of the actor's affiliates, then those with lower-status affiliations will generally find it more difficult to recoup a given investment in quality. The claim that affiliations represent a screen or filter rests on the assumption that it is often easier to observe affiliations than it is to observe differences in quality. Though such an assumption may not be valid in all cases, it seems plausible in many. For example, in selecting a day-care facility to care for one's children, it may be easier to observe a facility's affiliations with other parents or community groups than to observe the quality of daily care (Baum and Oliver 1992). Or, in evaluating job applicants, it is often easier to observe educational affiliations and the status of an applicant's references than it is to immediately observe differences in individual performance.

A second way that the status of an actor's associations can affect returns to investments in quality is by biasing evaluations of quality. Theorists from a variety of disciplines agree that perceptions are largely influenced by the context in which they are embedded (Lewin 1935; Cohen, March, and Olsen 1972; Pfeffer and Salancik 1978; Ross and Nisbett 1991). Social structures and patterns of relation direct attention, dictate the information on which we focus, and shape the meanings, attributions, and emotional responses that such information elicits (Asch 1940). Empirical work supports these claims. Work in the area of construal and communicator credibility shows that arguments attributed to high-status actors produce greater attitude change than arguments attributed to low-status actors. Messages associated with high-status sources are attended to more closely, recalled more successfully, regarded as more accurate and reliable, and deemed more worthy of adoption than are the same messages when associated with low-status sources (Hovland, Janis, and Kelley 1953).

Extended to the market context, this logic suggests that claims of quality (either implicit or explicit) made by firms with high-status affiliations are more likely to be considered credible and trustworthy than similar claims made by firms with low-status affiliations. In essence, status distinctions may engender past and present beliefs about quality, which potential market participants not only use and are slow to revise but for which they are also willing to pay a premium.

The above discussion leads to the following proposition regarding how the status of a market actor's affiliates affect the returns to quality:

- The status of an actor's affiliates will increase returns to past demonstrations of quality.

Of course, if status enhances returns to quality, an obvious question arises: What prevents all actors from developing high-status affiliations and, in the process, diluting the status signal? In other words, what ensures that the pattern of status affiliations will remain in a stable equilibrium? For the status ordering to remain in equilibrium, those who have developed high-status affiliations in the past must somehow find it less costly or more rewarding to develop such relations in the future. Otherwise, status distinctions would cease to exist and would ultimately be irrelevant to market decisions and behavior.

Two mechanisms may explain how status distinctions remain relatively stable over time even if all actors prefer to affiliate with high-status others. The first mechanism follows directly from the analysis of comanagement relations among investment banks in the previous chapter. High-status firms have a vested interest in avoiding relations with low-status, low-quality producers because such relations threaten their own status. Firms with well-established high-status relations are likely to have more affiliative options from which to choose and thus are more likely to associate with others of similar status to preserve their relative advantage. Thus, one reason that low-status firms may find it more difficult or costly to affiliate with high-status firms is that high-status firms will actively avoid low-status affiliations. A second reason hinges on the previous assertion that demonstrations of quality by low-status firms are less likely to be noted or observed than the similar behavior of high-status firms. If there is a cost associated with affiliation, and if such low-status firms are less likely to be noted, then low-status firms will obtain lower returns and be less likely to invest. Thus, if a status ordering is to exist as a tangible structure, a second proposition must also apply:

- The higher (or lower) an actor's status, the greater (or less) the net benefit the actor will derive from subsequent high-status affiliation.

Stated another way, returns obtained through high-status affiliation will be lower for actors that have not established high-status affiliations in the past.

These two propositions will now be tested in an examination of wine prices in the California wine industry. Specifically, the outcome on which we will focus is the price that a producer commands for a bottle of its wine. With a clearly defined outcome like price, these propositions can be even more clearly specified when formalized as part of an equation. Letting P_{ijt} denote the price at which winery j sells bottle i at time t, the determinants of the price of a bottle of wine can be modeled using the following equation:

$$P_{ijt} = b_0 + b_1 q_{ijt} + b_2 s_{ijt} + b_3 Q_{jt,t-k} + b_4 S_{jt,t-k} + b_5 Q_{jt,t-k}$$
$$\times S_{jt,t-k} + b_6 s_{ijt} \times S_{jt,t-k} + \sum_{v=7}^{V} b_v \mathbf{X}_{vt} + u_{ijt}. \qquad [5.1]$$

Here q_{ijt} refers to the quality of bottle i sold by winery j at time t, s_{ijt} refers to the status of the appellation listed on bottle i, $Q_{ijt,t-k}$ refers to the average quality of winery j as revealed by its wine between t and $t - k$ (excluding the quality of bottle i), $S_{jt,t-k}$ refers to the average status of winery j's appellation affiliations between t and $t - k$ (excluding the appellation affiliation on bottle i), and $\mathbf{X}$ refers to a vector of control variables reflecting economic forces in the environment (e.g., annual demand for wine) and indicators of fixed and variable production costs (e.g., grape prices, vineyard acreage), and u_{ijt} denotes an error term.[1]

This specification implies that the price that a winery commands for a particular bottle of wine is a function of factors at three levels: the level of the bottle, of the winery, and of the market environment. For our purpose, the variables of greatest substantive interest are those at the level of the winery; the quality and status of the bottle as well as the features of the environment serve essentially as controls for assessing the joint impact of the winery's reputation for quality and the winery's status. The first proposition, that the status of an actor's affiliates will increase returns to past demonstrations of quality,

---

[1] Since the observations on the price of individual bottles are pooled across a number of vineyards, errors are likely to be correlated across observations. A random effects generalized least squares model is therefore employed for the analysis. The model interprets each regression intercept realization (for each winery at a given point in time) as a random draw from a population with a fixed mean and randomly distributed error term that varies by organization. This estimation technique allows an unbiased assessment of parameter estimates by factoring out nonrandom error variance across vineyards.

In other analyses throughout this book, "fixed effects models" are generally employed as a way to control for unit-specific error. Fixed effects models are generally more effective in controlling for unit-specific error because they employ one degree of freedom for each unit in the data, rather than one total degree of freedom. Therefore, I try to employ fixed effects models whenever possible. However, the problem with the fixed effects model is that it removes all between-unit variance for the purpose of estimation, and the removal of this between-unit variation can make reliable estimation problematic if there is comparatively little within-unit variation. This was the case in this particular analysis; accordingly, the random effects model was employed.

implies that $b_5 > 0$. The second proposition, that returns to high-status affiliation will be higher for actors that have established high-status affiliations in the past, implies that $b_6 > 0$. To test this model, it is necessary to have measures of quality and status. We now consider the operationalization of these variables.

THE CALIFORNIA WINE INDUSTRY

The data for the analysis consists of all California producers of red and white table wine listed in the *Connoisseur's Guide to California Wine* between 1981 and 1991, inclusive. The *Connoisseur's Guide*, published by C. Olkin & Company (Alameda, CA), is considered by many industry experts to provide the most comprehensive coverage of California wines available. During the period from which the data for this analysis are drawn, California winemakers owned approximately 88 percent of all U.S. wine acreage (Moulton 1984) and accounted for 90 percent of all U.S. wine production (Manfreda and Mendelson 1988). In 1990 alone, California wineries produced more than 320 million gallons of taxable wine (Gavin-Jobson, *Jobson's Wine Marketing Handbook* [New York, 1991]).

The *Connoisseur's Guide* seeks to review a broad array of products generally available to consumers from each market segment and to provide information on retail price, quality, and availability. Moreover, unlike other publications, the guide does not solicit wine from individual wineries but, rather, buys only finished products on the market in order to avoid upwardly biasing its selection. Moreover, the *Connoisseur's Guide* is virtually the only publication that consistently reports retail price and quality data in conjunction with a wine's appellation affiliation. Between 1981 and 1991, the *Connoisseur's Guide* provides information on 10,079 products made by 595 wineries affiliated with 73 different appellations over the eleven-year period.

Measuring quality.   The *Connoisseur's Guide* rates wine on a four-point rating scale under peer group, single-blind conditions.[2] This means that all wines of a similar type (e.g., Chardonnay) are rated together and that raters are blind with respect to the wine's producer and its price. Bottle quality (q_{ijt}) is the rating that is reported in the guide for a given bottle of wine. A vineyard's past quality ($Q_{jt,t-k}$) is operationalized as the average quality of all bottles of wine reported for the winery over the three prior years.

As noted at the outset, few industries have as many publicly available evaluations of product quality as the wine industry. In fact, an entire profession

---

[2] Though some sources measure quality using finer gradations than a 4-point scale, they lack the comprehensiveness and/or representativeness of the *Connoisseur's Guide*.

has arisen to provide consumers with expert ratings of wine quality across a wide variety of products. Of course, the abundance of such ratings does not ensure their validity. If such ratings are truly to denote quality, two conditions must hold. First, there must be some convergent validity across independent evaluations. That is, wines considered high quality according to one set of evaluators should generally be considered high quality by other evaluators. The lack of such convergent validity implies the absence of a clear, linear metric for the assessment of quality. Second, convergent validity must derive strictly from the aesthetic properties of the wine itself and not from external cues denoting the regional origin, producer, or price of the wine. If convergent ratings were contingent on such external cues, then it would not be possible to assert that the perceived quality differences are in fact real differences inherent in the properties of the wine.

The evaluations of wine do in fact meet these two criteria. As with the rating of most products—especially aesthetic ones—there are sometimes discrepancies across evaluations. In general, though, discrepancies in wine ratings appear to be no more frequent or severe than discrepancies in evaluating product quality in any industry. Wine experts agree in their evaluations of wine much more often than they differ. As one well-known wine writer noted, "To the general public, 'wine tasting' has always been tinged with romance and obscurity. But serious professional wine judging is, in fact, a highly systematized procedure" (Roy Brady as quoted in Thompson 1984: 469).

The systemization of wine rating is due, in large part, to a variety of scientific methodologies, strict classifications, and traditional terminologies that wine experts have developed for the purpose of evaluation. "People who make wines, or blend wines, or sell wines need to make command decisions to determine differences among wines. They use . . . an array of sensory tests to reach conclusions: score cards, ranking, paired tests, and so on. And, if they are wise, they analyze the results by appropriate statistical procedures for their significance" (Amerine 1984: 452). The existence of such rigorous standards of evaluation helps to ensure convergent validity. Moreover, because professional evaluations are typically performed under controlled conditions by panels of experts who are blind with respect to a wine's identity and price, we can be relatively certain that the convergent validity we observe is not due to external earmarks such as a wine's origin or price. Though there may be slight differences in opinion among individual rankings because of stylistic preferences, experts tend to demonstrate remarkable reliability overall, invariably agreeing on wines that are average, poor, or exceptional (Thompson 1984).

Of course, while there is a general view that expert assessments do have convergent validity and while interviews with winery owners and vintners suggested that the *Connoisseur's Guide* provides quality ratings that are reasonable and well respected within the industry, it seems appropriate to assess whether *Connoisseur's* ratings display convergent validity with at least one other source.

One way to do so is to compare the *Connoisseur's* ratings with the ratings of another wine publication, the *Wine Spectator*. The *Wine Spectator's Ultimate Guide to Buying Wine* (New York, 1992) provides a compilation of the tasting results published in the *Wine Spectator* since 1980. The *Spectator* relies on two types of tasting for its quality ratings: (1) weekly blind tastings performed by the *Spectator*'s tasting panel and (2) special tastings of a particular type or vintage of wine conducted by the *Spectator*'s senior editors, frequently on location at the winery. A random selection of 198 wines rated by both provides the basis for an assessment of the reliability of the quality measure. There was disagreement in only 21 percent of the cases.[3]

Measuring status.   While blind taste tests exist for wines from all regions of the world, unique features of the appellation system in the California region have allowed for the emergence of an elaborate status ordering across subregions within the state. Areas such as Napa Valley or Sonoma Valley have emerged as high-status regions, and the wineries affiliated with the regions acquire status via the association. There are a few other regions of the world that also have status orderings, such as the Bordeaux region in France; however, unique features of the Californian appellation system give rise to deference relations across subregions within the state, and these deference relations can be used to derive quantifiable distinctions in the status ordering.

California wineries associate with formally recognized regions, or appellations, in their efforts to increase status and enhance their identities in the marketplace. Established in 1978 by the Bureau of Alcohol, Tobacco and Firearms (ATF), the American appellation system is a formally recognized governance system that dictates the viticultural designations that can be placed on a wine's label. The intention behind the ATF system is to enhance the perceived value of American wine in the international marketplace by establishing the credibility of the appellation designations placed on its labels. According to ATF

---

[3] Because tasters for the *Wine Spectator* rate wines on a 100-point scale and the *Connoisseur's Guide* uses a 4-point scale, the standard assumption of equal variation among the two samples did not hold. In lieu of a traditional rank correlation analysis, a series of pairwise comparisons was performed to determine the extent to which the two sets of ratings agreed in their relative rankings of the wines within the sample by considering all possible dyadic combinations of the 198 bottles. Since each bottle can be paired with 197 others, there are $(198 \times 197)/2 = 19,503$ such pairings. For each pair i and j, the guides are coded as disagreeing if one guide gave i a rating that was superior to j and the other guide gave j a rating that was superior to i.

This 21 percent figure is a conservative estimate and would likely be much lower in a fully random sample. Unlike the *Connoisseur's Guide*, which rates a wide spectrum of California products, the *Wine Spectator* rates products that are submitted to it for review by wineries, or products that are sufficiently well known to be of interest to the well-informed oenophile. As a result, the sample of wine reviewed by the *Spectator* is likely to be skewed toward higher-end, higher-priced wines that are less representative of the overall market. This skew, in turn, likely leads to an underestimate of the agreement across the two rating guides.

rules, a winery may place a "politically designated" region (i.e., a nation, state, or county) on its label if not less than 75 percent of the grapes that go into the wine originate from the designated area. The appellation system also governs the establishment and use of "viticultural areas." A viticultural area (another appellation category) is defined as a delimited grape-growing region, distinguished by geographic features that set it apart from surrounding areas. Once an area is legally established, a producer may place an appellation designation on its label if not less than 85 percent of the grapes that go into the wine comes from the specified region. By 1990, 128 viticultural regions had been established throughout the United States, 62 of which were located in California (Figiel 1991; U.S. Department of the Treasury, *Code of Federal Regulations,* "Laws and Regulations under the Federal Alchohol Administration Act," Title 27 [Washington, DC, various years]). Well-known examples of viticultural regions include Napa Valley, Sonoma Valley, and Alexander Valley. Together with the 58 politically designated state and county regions, California wine producers could choose among 120 different appellations during the period of our study.

As wineries publicly affiliate with various regions, a clear status or deference ordering emerges. Regions become subordinated to other regions as wineries within them engage in cross-regional affiliation. When a winery in one region— for example, Sonoma Valley—decides to designate another region on its label— for example, Napa Valley—the decision constitutes a clear act of deference, much like the decision of one firm to hire another's employee or the decision of one graduate department to hire another's student.

Contributing to the deferential significance of the act is the fact that wineries can exercise considerable discretion in choosing appellations. Wineries are not required to designate where their grapes originate, nor are they required to place an appellation designation on their label, though when they do designate a region on their label they must actually use grapes from that region in their product. Only if wineries choose to produce a varietal wine are regional designations mandated, but even then wineries have considerable latitude in the designations they select, since appellations often overlap, making it common for a given product to be eligible for multiple designations at once. Nor do wineries have to be physically located within an appellation to place the appellation affiliation on the bottle. In fact, the practice of crossaffiliation is quite common, as wineries are required only to use the mandated percentage of grapes in their product to claim affiliation. Based on data discussed below, almost 50 percent of the bottles that use the Napa Valley designation originate from wineries located outside the Napa Valley region.

It is widely recognized that the motive force behind most viticultural affiliations lies in the perceptual impact that such affiliations have on consumers' assessments of quality and the economic impact that such perceptions have on the winery's ability to price its wine. According to the Wine Institute, the wine industry's primary industry association, "viticultural area designation confers upon growers and wineries within such area a cachet of quality that may well raise the price of their grapes and wine" (Figiel 1991: 32). By affiliating with a particular appellation, or deferring to it, wineries signal that their wine is of a quality consistent with the wine of other producers who also affiliate with that same appellation.

A particularly visible attempt at such an association is Gallo Vineyard's efforts to associate with the Sonoma County appellation. Gallo is the largest producer of wines in the United States; in 1997, approximately one-fourth of the wine consumed in the United States was produced by the Gallo winery. At the same time, Gallo has traditionally been regarded as a maker of low-quality "jug" wines and, perhaps more notoriously, the Thunderbird brand. Yet throughout the 1990s, Gallo sought to improve perceptions of its wine, and in late 1997 Gallo began a large-scale advertising campaign in which it identified its new generation of products as "Gallo of Sonoma."

When a winery places an appellation on its bottle to signify the geographical origins of its wine, the exchange relation through which the winery acquired its grapes becomes visible to consumers and takes on a dual significance. First, the exchange relation affects consumers' perceptions of the winery. Over time, through multiple acts of affiliation, a winery acquires a distinct status or identity. Second, the exchange relation influences consumers' perceptions of the overall status ordering of appellations. The more that wineries seek to visibly affiliate with a particular region, thereby showing a certain deference to the superiority of the region, the higher the region's status becomes in the eyes of consumers.

The appellation system creates a framework by which wineries in one region defer to wineries in another. Together, these deference relations form a network of strategic association that creates meaning by directing constituents' attention and shaping subsequent attributions (Granovetter and Swedberg 1992). The deference ordering thus yields a context within which wineries may establish higher or lower status affiliations. A winery that continually affiliates with high-status regions, such as Napa Valley or Sonoma Valley, will have higher status than a winery that persistently affiliates with low-status regions, such as Ybarra County. Of course, appellations will vary by quality as well as status. The thoroughness of the data on quality will allow us to partial out any quality differences deriving from appellation affiliation.

A noteworthy difference between the wine industry and the investment banking industry is that the "ability to pay" is the only determinant of the ability to acquire a high-status affiliation. Any winery can affiliate with a high-status region if it has the money to do so. Grape growers are not refusing to sell their grapes to particular wineries because the wineries are not of sufficiently high status. One might conclude that this fact should lead to more volatility in status ordering among wineries than among investment banks. However, this observation misses the point that the factor cost of the raw materials is not the fundamental determinant of the stability in the status ordering; rather, it is the transaction costs associated with convincing consumers that the final product—the wine—is above a given threshold of quality. If the origin of the grape were the only determinant of the quality of the wine and if a winery could then offer a perfect signal of quality by placing the appellation on the bottle, then it is true that there would be no transaction cost difference for wineries of different status, and status distinctions would either be extremely volatile or collapse entirely. Precisely because the grape is not the only input that determines the quality of the wine, higher-status wineries will still face lower (transaction) costs for developing a wine of a given quality because their history of past affiliations will make it easier for them to signal that quality.

Given this appellation system, individual wineries are able to acquire their status by affiliating with appellations of a given position in the overarching status hierarchy. The status hierarchy itself arises from the pattern of cross-regional affiliations that wineries engage in through the appellation designations they place on their labels. These cross-regional ties provide the basis for constructing a relational matrix, $\mathbf{R}_t$, which can then be used to generate status scores. Each cell r_{ijt} in the matrix represents the number of wineries in geographical region i that use the appellation of geographical region j in year t. $\mathbf{R}_t$ is a square, asymmetric $n \times n$ matrix, where n denotes the number of appellations. The main diagonal is set to 0. Given the data in this matrix, one can then construct status scores for each region using Bonacich's $c(\alpha,\beta)$ measure, discussed in detail in chapter 3.[4]

Calculation of status scores for appellations in year t requires complete information on all winery affiliations made during that year, in addition to the wineries' geographic locations. While it is not possible to obtain full information on all wines produced within a year, it is possible to obtain complete information on all affiliations. The ATF requires all producers to obtain a Certificate of Label Approval if they intend to ship their products interstate or a Certificate of Exemption from Label Approval if they do not (U.S. Department

[4] One of the only differences between the application of the measure in this analysis and the application of the measure in the investment banking analysis is that we standardized scores in this analysis so that the highest-status region in year t has a status score of 1 (rather than the "average status" region having a score of 1). The reason that we standardized at the maximum is that the number of appellations at the low-status end of the distribution increased considerably over the time period studied. One consequence of an increase in the number of appellations is that it leads to greater variation in status if Bonacich's measure is standardized at the average; those regions at the upper end of the distribution (e.g., Napa) receive a boost to their status simply because of the proliferation of a large number of low-status regions over time. Such a boost would interfere with our ability to accurately measure changes in the status of wineries affiliated with those regions.

of the Treasury, *Code of Federal Regulations*, "Laws and Regulations under the Federal Alcohol Administration Act," Title 27 [Washington, DC, various years]). Each year, wine producers register thousands of labels with ATF. ATF inspects all labels, determines whether they meet required guidelines, and then retains a final copy of each for its archives.

As was the case with the tombstone data for banks, the enormous amount of work involved in collecting even one year of wine label data is a deterrent to collecting such data for each year of the analysis. Accordingly, the data on the appellation affiliations of all California red and white table wines are collected from four years staggered evenly throughout the sample period: 1981, 1984, 1987, and 1990. California wineries registered 22,027 labels across the four different years. Because many of these labels reflected different labeling designs for the same bottle of wine, labels reporting the same producer, varietal, vintage year, and appellation in a given year were consolidated, reducing the total to 7,641 unique alignments across seventy-three designated appellations.[5]

Table 5.1 presents representative status scores for a number of appellations in 1990. To validate the status scores derived from the cross-regional affiliation patterns, seven industry experts were surveyed in 1993 for their perceptions of appellation status at that time. The correlations between the average evaluations of the experts and the status scores for the regions was .81.[6]

These results suggest that perceptions of well-informed participants correlate strongly with the patterns of cross-regional affiliation we observe in our

[5] While the geographic origins of the grapes can be determined from the appellation affiliations on the bottle label, the geographic location of the winery cannot. Geographic locations for the various wineries were therefore determined using two viticultural maps: Raven Maps and Images' 1989 *Vineyards and Wineries of California* and Compass Maps' *1992 Winery Guide to Northern and Central California* (Modesto, CA). Phone calls were made to wineries to validate the information in the maps. Together, the geographic location information and the ATF affiliation data enabled the construction of the R_t matrices used in determining the status scores.

[6] These experts were located through officials at the Wine Institute, the wine industry's major trade organization and its internal publication *Consumer Media Guide*. Usually available only to the institute's members, the *Consumer Media Guide* lists over 375 writers, editors, and reporters who regularly cover wine and the wine industry for newspapers, magazines, food and wine programs, and other consumer audience media throughout the United States. Fifteen experts were selected from the *Media Guide*; these experts were well known for their writing on the industry, or associated with a well-known publication, and were familiar with both northern and southern California wine regions. Ten of the experts we contacted agreed to participate, and seven of these completed surveys. These experts consisted of wine writers, critics, and legal representatives active in establishing the appellation system and many of the viticultural areas within it.

A principal component factor analysis of the ratings given by the experts was first performed to determine the aggregate level of agreement. The factor analysis yielded a single factor solution, with all experts loading between .72 and .90, which indicates a strong consensus among the raters. Having established interrater reliability, we calculated the mean expert rating for each appellation and then ranked the mean ratings. The Spearman correlation between these ranks and the status order obtained from the relational matrix calculations on the 1990 ATF data was .81.

data. Yet, despite the high correlation between the expert evaluations and the status scores, individuals familiar with the California wine industry may be surprised by some features of table 5.1. There is a considerable break in status between the three highest-status regions and the rest. Also, there are some orderings that may seem nonintuitive. Napa Valley's fourth-place ranking, for example, surprises some wine followers, who expect it to be higher.

There are a number of ways to respond to such concerns. First, we can investigate whether the "surprising" results are incorrect by speaking with industry experts. So, with respect to Napa Valley's fourth-place ranking, some industry experts noted that the lower-than-expected ranking can be attributed to the potentially diluting effect of numerous other appellations that have been established within its boundaries. As winery owners and grape growers have established smaller, more specialized subregions within the larger Napa Valley, many of these regions have seen their status grow, while Napa Valley's status has diminished.

Still, it is impossible to refute all objections to any status ordering, and the measure of status in this industry is just not as compelling as the measure of status in the investment banking industry. However, one should be able to take

TABLE 5.1

Representative Status Scores in the California Wine Industry, 1990

Appellation	Status	Appellation	Status
Alexander Valley	1.0000	Cienega Valley	.0217
Sonoma County	.7656	Knights Valley	.0212
Russian River Valley	.7052	Monterey County	.0210
Napa Valley	.4491	San Luis Obispo County	.0182
Los Carneros	.2637	Northern Sonoma	.0178
Sonoma Valley	.2489	Santa Maria Valley	.0170
Mendocino County	.2163	Santa Barbara County	.0167
Dry Creek	.1927	Amador County	.0157
North Coast	.1461	Santa Clara County	.0146
Chalk Hill	.0559	Edna Valley	.0138
Mendocino	.0546	South Coast	.0124
Sonoma Mountain	.0519	Santa Clara Valley	.0116
Monterey	.0501	Solano County Green Valley	.0080
Napa County	.0413	Clarksburg	.0076
Central Coast	.0397	Lake County	.0068
Howell Mountain	.0391	McDowell County	.0067
Anderson Valley	.0376	Santa Ynez Valley	.0059
Sonoma Coast	.0280	Ventura County	.0000
Stags Leap	.0264	Mount Veeder	.0000
Sonoma County Green Valley	.0254	Trinity County	.0000
Paso Robles	.0224		

some comfort from the .81 correlation between the status ranking and the ranking of expert ratings. Moreover, to the extent that status is improperly measured by our network measure, the error in measurement should only reduce, not enhance, our ability to test and support our hypotheses.

But to provide even greater confidence in the analysis, it seems appropriate to repeat the analysis of the effects of status on price using the mean ratings of the experts rather than the network scores. Since the experts provided ratings in 1993 only—whereas the network scores were compiled for 1981, 1984, 1987, and 1990—this analysis relying on expert scores cannot be considered a rigorous test of the central propositions in this chapter, nor a definitive validation of our status measure; however, to the extent that the results of this additional analysis remain largely consistent with the original one, the analysis provides another confirmatory check of the robustness of the network measure and main results.

Using the status scores derived from the cross-regional affiliations, it is fairly straightforward to specify the status of a given bottle's affiliation, as well as the average status of affiliations that a winery has maintained over time. A bottle's status in year t (s_{ijt}) simply derives from the most recently measured status score of the appellation with which the bottle is affiliated. For example, a bottle produced in 1982 is given the status of the bottle's appellation in 1981, since 1981 is the most recent year for which we have information on the appellation's status. Wineries produce multiple products each year. They may choose to use a mix of appellation affiliations across products or, alternatively, to affiliate with a single appellation for all products. As with the measure for past demonstrations of quality, the average status of a winery's appellation alignments ($S_{jt,t-k}$) is operationalized with a three-year moving window. For example, if a winery produced a bottle in 1982 from an appellation with a status score of .023, another bottle in 1982 with a status score of .05, a bottle in 1983 with a status score of .10, and a bottle in 1984 with a status score of .08, its status in 1985 is $(.023 + .05 + .10 + .08)/4 = .0633$. The status reflected by this three-year window should have an independent effect on price, should positively interact with the three-year quality window in affecting price, will positively interact with subsequent affiliations in affecting price, and should have a positive effect on the subsequent quality of wine produced by the vineyard.

Control variables.   Other factors besides quality may affect the price that a winery charges for its products. First, demand should vary by *varietal*, the type of grape from which the wine is made. Chardonnay, Cabernet, and Merlot are all examples of varietals. There are seventeen varietals or blends of varietals in the data. Some grapes, like Chardonnay and Cabernet, are in extremely high demand; others, like Syrah, are in much lower demand. To allow for these differences in demand across varietals, differences that may affect price, dummy variables are included for each varietal. The varietal information was obtained from the *Connoisseur's Guide*. Second, since demand could vary temporally, increasing or decreasing over time, the analysis also includes dummy variables denoting the year in which the bottle of wine was sold.[7]

Some industry experts assert that wine producers use a standard markup or cost-plus pricing strategy to set wine prices (e.g., Kramer 1992). Such explanations oversimplify the pricing decision, since most wineries consider many factors in setting their pricing policies and use a variety of strategies depending on their pricing objectives, but it would be difficult to deny that a producer's costs are extremely relevant to price. As Stuller and Martin (1989: 39) noted, "Winery economics, as much as market considerations, are often the major factor in the price of a given wine. The quality of the raw materials and enological skill that go into a wine are critical if it is to successfully remain in a price segment. But where it's placed in a segment can often depend on when a winery was built, how it's financed, equipped, and operated." Thus, it is important to include indicators of a firm's production costs in our examination of price formation.

Any focus on costs must begin with a consideration of *the cost of the grapes*. Grapes typically represent a winery's single largest production cost. For some superpremium vintages, grapes may account for up to 60 percent of a winery's operating costs, though for most small wineries grapes average about 40 percent of operating expenditures (Stuller and Martin 1989). It seems reasonable to expect wineries to charge higher prices for wines produced from more expensive grape varietals and for wines produced in years when the cost of grapes was relatively higher. Grape prices were obtained from the *Final Grape Crush Report*, 1981–1991, a publication produced by the California Department of Food and Agriculture (Sacramento, CA, various years) in compliance with Section 55601.5 of the Food and Agriculture Code. From the report, it was possible to obtain information on the average price per ton of the primary grape used in a given wine (as indicated by the varietal, appellation, and year listed on its label) for approximately one-third of the bottles in the sample. Accordingly, for this third of the sample, the cost of the grape was used as a proxy for the cost of the wine. For the rest of the observations, cost is set equal to 0, and an indicator variable is coded 1 if information was missing on cost and 0 otherwise. As in the analysis of the investment banking industry, use of such an indicator variable for missing data allows for unbiased estimates of the effect of cost and does not require excluding numerous cases with missing cost data.

Economic models assert that a firm's costs are not only a function of its primary inputs but also a function of economies that the firm is able to realize.

---

[7] Although it might be reasonable to include interactions for fluctuations in demand by varietal and by year, in case demand for some varietals increases while demand for others declines, examinations of year-varietal interactions for the more common varietals revealed no evidence of such interaction effects.

The economies most relevant to the wine industry are learning economies and economies of scale. Learning economies refer to the reduced production costs that accrue from learning about the production process over time. The *log of the winery's age* is incorporated into the model as a proxy for these learning economies. Newer wineries have higher costs than older wineries if only because they do not have as good an understanding of the production and distribution of wine. Because the log of age should have a negative effect on costs, the log of age should also have a negative effect on price.

Economies of scale refer to the reduction in per-unit cost that accompanies increased production volume. Moulton (1984) found that production costs per case of wine generally decline as winery size expands. His estimates suggest that costs fall by approximately 27 percent as production increases from 5,000 to 100,000 cases and by an additional 35 percent as production increases to 3 million cases. A number of proxies for scale economies figure in the analysis: *the number of acres owned by the winery, the storage capacity of the winery,* and *the number of brands produced by the winery*. The number of acres owned by the winery and its storage capacity are both direct indicators of the winery's size and volume. To the extent that an increase in scale leads to a decrease in cost, these measures should have a negative effect on price. The number of brands used by the winery is a further proxy of size and potential scale economies. Since a winery's size will be an important determinant of its capacity for producing multiple brands, the number of brands should be at least a partial reflection of scale economies.

Results

Table 5.2 presents the means and standard deviations. Table 5.2 also reports the correlation matrix for all variables of interest. The correlations in this analysis seem especially important to report because an examination of the matrix allows insight into the relationship between the status and quality variables. While the correlations between the variables denoting quality and status are all positive and statistically significant, the strongest correlation between the two most robust variables—three-year status and three-year quality—is only about .6. The absence of a stronger correlation among the status and quality variables reinforces the basic claim that status and quality are not interchangeable.

Table 5.3 depicts the effects of status and quality on price. Model 1 is a baseline model including only the effects of quality and the appellation listed on the bottle. Results show that the quality of the bottle has a significant positive effect on price. Since price is expressed in terms of dollars, interpretation of the effects is rather straightforward: a one-unit increase in bottle quality produces a $1.27 increase in the price of a bottle of wine. As a point of comparison, the average bottle of wine in our sample costs $10.65.

TABLE 5.2
Means, Standard Deviations, and Correlations* among Wine Industry Variables

Variables	Mean	S.D.	1	2	3	4	5	6	7	8	9
1. Status of appellation on bottle	.50	.42									
2. Avg. appellation status over prior 3 years	.39	.40	.484								
3. Avg. quality of wine	.58	.76	.151	.155							
4. Avg. quality of wine over prior 3 years	.41	.45	.156	.568	.262						
5. Wine price ($)	10.65	5.25	.175	.259	.341	.352					
6. Grape cost ($ per ton)	712.65	265.41	.466	.660	.213	.479	.415				
7. Age of winery (years)	20.08	31.82	.003	-.006	-.073	-.079	-.096	-.069			
8. Size of winery (storage capacity in thousands of gallons)	1,566	1,632	-.053	-.052	-.051	-.065	-.078	-.033	.137		
9. Vineyard acreage	252.83	570.56	-.017	-.006	-.068	-.082	-.113	-.062	.495	.174	
10. Number of brands	1.40	1.19	-.034	.004	-.033	-.037	-.063	-.069	.154	.435	.243

*All correlations whose absolute value is above .02 are statistically significant at $p < .05$.

TABLE 5.3
Regression Models of Effects of Status on Wine Price

Variables		Status as Network Measure			Status as Expert Assessment
	1	2	3	4	5
Status of appellation on bottle	.135	−.146	−.298	−.770**	.201*
	(.060)	(.059)	(.167)	(.287)	(.093)
Quality of bottle	1.269*	1.221**	1.225**	1.227**	1.212**
	(.060)	(.059)	(.059)	(.059)	(.059)
Avg. appellation status over prior 3 years			.731*	−.195	−.238
			(.258)	(.403)	(.130)
Avg. quality of wine over prior 3 years			1.323**	.797**	−.115
			(.159)	(.294)	(.657)
Three-year status × 3-year quality				.898*	.262**
				(.415)	(.117)
Three-year status × bottle status				.862*	.024
				(.413)	(.015)
Grape cost		.0044**	.0042**	.0042**	.0038**
		(.0004)	(.0004)	(.0004)	(.0003)
Log(age of winery)		−.001	−.0003	−.0002	.013
		(.001)	(.003)	(.003)	(.085)
Size of winery		−.135*	−.132*	−.134*	−.00005
		(.063)	(.061)	(.061)	(.00001)
Vineyard acreage		−.0002	−.0001	−.0001	−.0004*
		(.0002)	(.0002)	(.0002)	(.0002)
Number of brands		−.187**	−.150*	−.147*	−.117*
		(.061)	(.060)	(.060)	(.058)
R^2	.39	.41	.42	.42	.42

$N = 7,358$. Numbers in parentheses are standard errors. Indicator variables for years, missing values, and varietal effects are not shown.
    *$p < .05$; **$p < .01$

Model 2 adds control variables for the cost of the grapes, learning economies, and economies of scale. The cost of the grapes has a significant, positive effect on the price of the wine. There are three separate variables to control for economies of scale: storage capacity of the winery, vineyard acreage owned, and the number of brands owned by the winery. Although the coefficients associated with all three variables are negative and thus consistent with the existence of scale economies, vineyard acreage is not statistically significant. Because wineries can purchase grapes in addition to or in lieu of growing their own, acreage may not always be directly indicative of a winery's actual economies. Finally, while a negative coefficient for log-age is consistent with the notion of learning economies, the effect is also not significant.

Model 3 reports the main effects for winery status and winery quality. The quality of the winery, as measured by the average quality of all wine it has produced over the three prior years, has a positive and significant effect on price that is distinct from the effect of bottle quality. It seems reasonable to think of this variable as a reputation effect, since it represents the quality of the winery's past performance and is thus consistent with the economic definition of reputation.

While our central interest is in the interactive effect of winery status with, first, winery quality and, second, bottle status, we should first focus on the main effect for winery status, which is positive. Although this effect is not significantly different from 0 in model 4, the inclusion of the interaction variables in model 4 means that one cannot consider the main effect independently from the level of the variables with which vineyard status is interacted. Hence, the results of model 3 provide a more straightforward test of the main effect for winery status, since this model essentially reports the average effect of winery status across all the observations. Moreover, even if one uses the results in model 4, one can evaluate the effect of vineyard status at the mean value of vineyard quality and the mean value of bottle status. The effect is as follows: $-0.195 + (0.898 \times 0.41) + (0.862 \times 0.50) = 0.604$, which is close to the average value reported for model 3.

Recall that the two propositions that motivated this particular analysis were the following:

- The status of an actor's affiliates will increase returns to past demonstrations of quality.
- The higher (or lower) an actor's status, the greater (or less) the net benefit the actor will derive from subsequent high-status affiliation.

The first of these propositions is tested by the interaction of winery status and winery quality. The second of these propositions is tested by the interaction of winery status with bottle status. Model 4 reveals positive and significant effects for the interaction of winery status with winery quality and for the interaction of winery status with bottle status.[8] The positive interaction is consistent with the

---

[8] Given the inclusion of two interaction terms in model 4, an appropriate concern is multicollinearity. Belsley, Kuh, and Welsch (1980) propose a set of multicollinearity diagnostics that are available in SAS version 6.1. The approach computes a condition index and coefficient estimates for each effect. The diagnostics produced results that fell well below Belsley, Kuh, and Welsch's recommended cutoffs, thereby suggesting that multicollinearity concerns were minimal.

Though not reported in the table, each interaction was positive and significant when entered into the analysis individually as well.

proposition that high-status affiliations increase returns to past demonstrations of quality. The positive and significant interaction between winery status and bottle status indicates that high-status wineries derive greater returns from a given high-status affiliation than do lower-status wineries. Wineries with a history of the highest status affiliations (i.e., *winery status* = 1) can charge 86.2 cents more per bottle for a given affiliation than wineries with a history of the lowest status affiliations (i.e., *winery status* = 0), holding all else constant.[9]

Notably, there is no significant main effect for the status of the bottle's appellation when the interaction term between winery status and bottle status is excluded from the analysis and bottle status is entered alone. Affiliating with a high-status appellation for the production of a single wine produces no positive benefit if a winery has not invested in high-status relations in the past. This result supports the basic contention that the value of an affiliation cannot be assessed in isolation but can be understood only in the context of other affiliations formed by that winery.

If one takes the point estimates literally, then only the highest-status wineries can command higher prices for higher-status appellation affiliations. Specifically, the effect of the status of the appellation listed on the bottle is as follows: $-0.770 + 0.862 \times winery\ status$. This point estimate suggests that only those wineries with a status greater than $0.770/0.862 = 0.89$ should benefit from higher-status affiliations. Given that there is a broad confidence interval around this interaction, however, it would be a mistake to interpret the point estimate too literally. For example, if one uses estimates for the main and interaction effects that are only one standard deviation above the point estimate, then the joint effect is $(-0.770 + 0.287) + (0.862 + 0.413) \times winery\ status = 0.483 + 1.275 \times winery\ status$. In this case, all wineries with an average status above $0.483/1.275 = 0.378$ would derive a positive benefit from higher-status affiliations. In either case, the results remain sufficient to reject the null hypothesis that high-status and low-status wineries receive the same net benefit from affiliating with appellations of a given status. In rejecting this null hypothesis, the results indicate that high-status vineyards are able to command higher prices for an affiliation of a given status, thereby enabling high-status wineries to outbid their low-status competitors for grapes from high-status regions.

---

[9] Since R^2 does not show a marked increase with each model, we questioned whether the inclusion of the additional variables was justified. We concluded that it was, for two reasons. First, a t-test is equivalent to an F-test with one additional variable; hence, a significant t-statistic denotes a significant improvement in R^2 even though the improvement may not be registered at the second decimal place. Second, we decided to enter the variables in the model in this particular order to establish a baseline model that would allow us to determine whether there was any net effect for the status variables after the controls were entered. Obviously, the amount of variance attributed to a particular variable is contingent on order of entry. If vineyard status and the interaction terms were entered into the regression first, then more of the increase in R^2 could be attributed to these variables, but such an approach would not allow us to assess a net effect for the variables of interest.

Similar results obtain when the expert assessments of status are substituted for the measures derived from the deference relations across regions. Model 5 portrays the full model using the expert assessments as the basis for the status measure. The measure of bottle status based on expert assessments has a correlation of .73 with the measure of bottle status derived from the network measure and a correlation of .82 with the measure of three-year winery status based on the network measure. In interpreting the results of model 5, it is important to bear in mind two features of the analysis. First, the scale for expert assessment, which can range between 1 and 7, is different from the scale for the network measure of status, which can range between 0 and 1. Bottle status based on expert assessment has a mean of 4.88 and a standard deviation of 2.01. Winery status based on expert assessment has a mean of 4.78 and a standard deviation of 1.96. Second, though there are some differences in the main effects, the main effects cannot be interpreted independently from the interaction terms. When considered with the interaction terms, the results using the expert assessments are largely consistent with the results based on the network measure. The interaction between three-year status and three-year quality is positive and statistically significant. In the results reported for model 5, the interaction between three-year status and bottle status is positive and just beyond conventional significance levels ($p = .11$). If nonsignificant control variables are removed from the model, however, the interaction between three-year status and bottle status becomes significant at the .10 level, indicating that the higher-status wineries derive a greater return from a high-status affiliation. Given that the status ordering experienced some changes over the eleven-year period and that the expert ratings were administered at the conclusion of that period, it seems reasonable to assume that results can be interpreted as consistent with the network-based status results: namely, a history of high-status affiliations provides a positional advantage for high-status wineries, which, at an aggregate level, facilitates the reproduction of the overall status orderings.[10]

How Differential Returns to Quality Affect Subsequent Quality Choice

So far we have observed that higher-status wineries obtain greater returns for a given quality of product. This first result implies that higher-status wineries will be able to outbid lower-status wineries for the higher-quality grapes. If

---

[10] When the interaction terms are excluded from the analysis, the only difference from the results based on the network measure is that the main effect for bottle status is positive and significant, whereas the main effect for 3-year status is positive and not significant. Since there are good theoretical reasons for believing that the effect of 3-year status interacts with other variables and since model 4 provides some empirical support for this prediction, there seems little reason to focus on differences in what is clearly an incomplete model.

market actors with low-status affiliations bid for inputs that are necessary to produce high-quality goods, it is likely these actors will be outbid by their competitors with higher-status affiliations, since this latter group will be able to command higher prices for the goods that follow. As a result, low-status actors may face greater barriers and have less incentive to pay the costs associated with producing higher-quality products, whereas high-status actors will have fewer barriers and thus greater incentive to produce higher-quality products. Thus, as was the case in the investment banking industry, pricing dynamics become a mechanism by which the status-based inequality is reproduced.

However, because the wine industry provides such compelling data on quality, it is possible to test this implication. That is, we know that high-status wineries obtain greater returns for a given quality of wine, but does this affect the extent to which they make investments in quality? Put another way, does the status of an actor's affiliations also influence the quality level at which that actor subsequently chooses to produce?

Modeling the effects of past affiliations on a producer's subsequent choice of quality is somewhat more complicated, because the quality of wine produced is ultimately a function of multiple choices that can be grouped into two categories: (1) choices about the cost or quality of raw materials used and (2) choices about the production process or the conversion of raw materials into the final product. Since the status of a winery's affiliations can influence both access to and the ability to afford higher-cost raw materials, as well as decisions to engage in higher-quality production techniques and/or use higher-quality talent, it is necessary to assess the effects of past affiliations on quality choice in two stages.

Although data are not available on the costs of all raw materials, we have already noted that data are available on the cost of the primary grape used in production, and the grape used is an important determinant of the final costs. Accordingly, to assess how status affects the cost of the input, the following model is estimated:

$$c(g_{ijt}) = b_0 + b_1 Q_{jt,t-k} + b_2 S_{jt,t-k} + \sum_{v=3}^{V} b_v X_{vt} + u_{ijt},$$ [5.2]

where $c(g_{ijt})$ is the cost of the grape used for bottle i produced by winery j in year t. The coefficient of central interest is b_2, which specifies the effect of status (as revealed through the pattern of appellation affiliations between time t and $t - k$) on the cost of the grape used in the wine. The same control variables will be included in this analysis as in the analysis of the wine price, except of course for the cost of the grapes in the bottle since that variable is now the dependent variable.

To assess whether past affiliations have an effect on wine quality, controlling for the raw materials used in the wine, the following model is then estimated:

$$q_{ijt} = b_0 + b_1 Q_{jt,t-k} + b_2 S_{jt,t-k} + \sum_{v=3}^{V} b_v X_{vt} + u_{ijt}. \qquad [5.3]$$

As in the other analyses, quality (q_{ijt}) is defined as the *California Connoisseur's Guide* rating for a particular bottle of wine. Because the *Guide* rates the quality of each bottle on a four-point rating scale, our dependent measure, quality, is categorical and ordinal. Thus, an ordered logistic regression model is an appropriate model for assessing the effect of past status on subsequent quality. The ordered logistic regression is simply a generalization of the dichotomous logit, in which there are $N - 1$ intercepts for N categories. The advantage of the ordered logit over an ordinary least squares model is that it does not require the assumption of constant intervals between categories and cannot give rise to predicted values that are outside the range of possible values for the dependent variable.

As in the equation estimating the cost of the grapes used in the bottle, the central coefficient on which to focus in this equation is b_2, which specifies the effect of status on subsequent quality choice (controlling for winery quality averaged over the three previous years as well as a number of other baseline control variables). If the effect is positive, this indicates a positive effect of status on subsequent quality choice. After this baseline model is estimated, two additional explanatory variables will be included in the model: the cost of the grapes used in the wine and the status of the appellation from which the grapes derived and with which the winery chose to affiliate. If the effect of past affiliations remains significant, then we can conclude that past affiliations affect not only the quality of inputs but also the quality of the process of converting those inputs to outputs. If the effect of affiliations becomes insignificant when these two variables are included, however, we should infer that the primary mechanism by which past affiliations affect quality is through the choice of higher- or lower-cost (and presumably quality) raw materials.

Table 5.4 reports the regression results for the effect of past status on the cost of the grape used in the wine. The number of observations is smaller because data on grape costs are available for only approximately one-third of the cases. The results of model 1 show that three-year status has a positive effect on the cost of grapes used in the product. Superior returns afforded by status appear to lead higher-status producers to purchase higher-quality grapes as inputs.[11] Conversely, because lower-status producers cannot obtain as great a return, they do not purchase more expensive, higher-quality grapes.

---

[11] Ideally one might wish to construct a selection equation to control for the effects of missing data on this analysis. However, I could not think of any variables to be employed in a selection equation that would not also predict cost.

TABLE 5.4

Regression Models of Effect of Status on Price Paid for Grapes

Variables	Model 1	Model 2
Average appellation status over prior 3 years	419.89**	396.97**
	(13.17)	(22.35)
Average quality of wine over prior 3 years	64.62*	31.49
	(10.03)	(27.96)
Three-year status × 3-year quality		41.83
		(32.96)
Log(age of winery)	−4.96	−5.07
	(5.57)	(5.58)
Size of winery	5.7×10^{-8}	9.7×10^{-8}
	(4.2×10^{-7})	(4.2×10^{-7})
Vineyard acreage	−.013	−.013
	(.010)	(.010)
Number of brands	.878	.943
	(3.77)	(3.77)
R^2	.39	.39

$N = 2,079$. Numbers in parentheses are standard errors. Indicator variables for year and varietals are not shown.

$*p < .05; **p < .01$

Because there was a positive interaction effect of three-year status and three-year quality on bottle price, it seems appropriate to examine whether such an interaction also influences subsequent quality through the purchase of higher-quality grapes. Since higher-status affiliations increase the returns to past demonstrations of quality, these affiliations should also increase the extent to which that quality is maintained and enhanced through the purchase of superior inputs. The results of model 2 show that the effect is positive but not significant ($p = .20$). Hence, while the direction of effects is as anticipated, it is not possible to rule out the null hypothesis that there is no joint effect of quality and status on grape price.

Let's now turn to the examination of the quality of the wine bottle. Table 5.5 reports the results. The analysis includes controls for past quality, grape price, relevant vineyard characteristics, and year and varietal effects. Model 1 shows the effect of past affiliations without the inclusion of the price of the grapes and bottle status as controls. Model 2 includes the cost of the grapes and the status of the bottle as explanatory variables. The effect of three-year status is positive and significant in model 1 but loses significance in model 2. The implication of this result is that the effect of past affiliations on subsequent quality typically plays out through the selection of the quality of the raw material input. Because lower-status vineyards cannot obtain the same returns from a high-quality grape, they do not purchase expensive, high-status grapes. More generally, these results suggest that, *on average*, status of affiliation affects subsequent selection of inputs but not necessarily the quality of the process of converting inputs to outputs.

The only exception to this average effect occurs when the raw material is of high quality. Model 3 includes an interaction term between three-year status and grape cost. The interaction is positive, indicating that three-year status has a positive and significant effect on final quality when the raw material is a high-price and implicitly high-quality grape. In effect, when the raw input is of sufficiently high quality, superior returns from past affiliations enable high-status wineries to hire superior winemakers or to buy superior equipment to realize the potential of their high-quality inputs, while low-status wineries cannot do so.

Taken together, the results in tables 5.4 and 5.5 provide evidence that an actor's position may significantly influence and constrain important attributes of

TABLE 5.5
Regression Models on Bottle Quality

Variables	1	2	3
Bottle status		.454**	.476**
		(.082)	(.083)
Average appellation status	.449**	.0216	−.060
over prior 3 years	(.071)	(.098)	(.104)
Average quality	1.333**	1.309**	1.310**
over prior 3 years	(.060)	(.060)	(.060)
Grape price		.0004*	−.0001
		(.0002)	(.0002)
Average appellation status over			.0004**
prior 3 years × grape cost			(.0002)
Log(age of winery)	−.002*	−.002*	−.002*
	(.001)	(.001)	(.001)
Storage capacity	−.013	−.017	−.019
	(.017)	(.017)	(.018)
Vineyard acreage	−.00001	$−7.4 \times 10^{-6}$	9.9×10^{-6}
	(.0006)	(.0007)	(.0007)
Number of brands	.006	.006	.006
	(.023)	(.020)	(.020)

$N = 7,592$. Numbers in parentheses are standard errors. Varietal and year effects are not shown.
*$p < .05$; **$p < .01$

that actor, namely, the quality of its inputs, production, and final products. These particular results take us back to the distinction between the Spencian and non-Spencian type of signal elaborated in chapter 2 and referenced in the first paragraphs of this chapter. Whereas Spence's conception of a signal rests on ex ante quality distinctions, the status-based model of market competition allows for quality differences to arise endogenously in a context of status differentiation. In both Spence's conception of a signal and the status-based model of market competition, there is alignment between possession of the indicator—in this case, status—and underlying quality differences, but the status-based model allows for differences in the possession of the indicator to induce differences in quality, and this is precisely what this analysis of the California wine industry has just shown.

More generally, the results from this analysis complement those from the previous chapter. Insofar as wine and investment banking are very different types of industries, the relevance of status in these two contexts points to the general applicability of status as a signal across a broad variety of markets. Wine is a consumer product for a mass market; investment banking is a service by and for corporate actors. Wine purchases are typically on the order of ten to twenty dollars; investment banking services typically involve multimillion-dollar transactions. Wine is generally regarded as a conspicuous consumption good; investment banking is generally not regarded in this fashion.

Because wine is a conspicuous consumption good (Veblen 1953), it is at least worth using this fact as an opportunity to comment on the difference between the understanding of status as market signal and the more traditional understanding of status as a basis for conspicuous consumption. Wine may be purchased from a high-status producer not only because the producer's status signals high quality but also (or more importantly) because the act of consuming such a wine strengthens the individual's ability to claim higher social status. So, for example, an individual may choose to buy a bottle of Opus One rather than a different, lower-price wine he or she believes to be of equal quality because he or she would like to be perceived as the type of individual who drinks Opus One.

There is no underlying incompatibility between these two understandings of status. Status may serve both as a signal of quality and as a tool of conspicuous consumption. If an individual's social standing is enhanced by drinking wine from a high-status winery, then the individual should be willing to pay a higher price for that wine. Moreover, if the individual perceives that one's social standing is enhanced by drinking wine affiliated with a particular region, or by drinking wine from a winery that has affiliated with that region for a substantial period of time, it is quite likely that the individual will be willing to pay substantially more for a product that offers both the current and past associations.

Despite their consistencies, the conspicuous consumption rationale and the status-based model remain distinct in some important and defining ways. The most notable distinction is the role that quality plays in determining price and the decision to purchase. Whereas the signaling model predicts that status increases returns to past investments in quality and incentives to invest in future quality, the conspicuous consumption view downplays quality concerns. An act of conspicuous consumption consists precisely in the demonstration of wealth through the throwing away of money on more expensive goods that provide no greater utility but cost significantly more. Thus, the conspicuous consumption rationale would not explain why a vineyard's status would vary with the underlying level of the vineyard's quality. In short, while it would obviously be difficult to deny that conspicuous consumption may be an important motive underlying the purchase of wine, such a view alone does not lend itself to the propositions tested in this chapter.

The analyses of the two markets discussed in this and the previous chapter not only complement one another because of the substantive differences in their contexts; the analyses also complement one another because of the comparative strengths and weaknesses in data. The investment banking industry afforded a uniquely superior measure of status and enabled us to observe how the relevance of status varied systematically with the level of uncertainty. Whereas the wine industry did not possess as strong of a measure of status or as systematic information on the level of uncertainty, it afforded a much better measure of quality. As a consequence, the analysis of the wine industry has allowed us to disentangle the effects of the medium of status from the message of quality. Framed less metaphorically, the central claim of this chapter has been that the consequences of quality choices are not independent of the tangible status ordering in which market participants are situated. A firm's position in the status ordering influences the attention that others pay to quality, their assessment of quality, and their regard for the product more generally. Relative to lower-status firms, higher-status firms therefore derive greater benefit from producing a given quality of product. As a consequence, the status ordering helps to determine which firms will develop reputations for quality and which will not. In many cases, reputation differences may not be ascribable solely to differences in the underlying capabilities of producers but, rather, may be ascribable to differences in the pattern of affiliations. That is, where a firm is located in the social structure of a market and who the firm affiliates with may strongly influence the perceived quality of the firm within the market.

Such a conclusion does not imply that differences in structural position are completely exogenous, nor that differences in quality have no effect on structural position. There is undoubtedly a reciprocal relationship between the level of quality that a firm achieves and the structural position that a firm obtains. I simply assert that the existence of the status ordering constrains how firms can develop reputations for quality. Specifically, a firm receives lower returns from its investment in quality to the extent that it fails to establish affiliations that reflect that investment. More important, highly discrepant shifts in quality, affiliation, and status do not appear to achieve returns capable of sustaining a firm's investment. A firm's history or pattern of affiliations over time constrains the returns available to subsequent affiliations and quality decisions. More generally, the existence of a status ordering creates disincentives for individual firms to improve quality in ways that do not contribute to the reproduction of the status ordering.

One interesting consequence of the alignment of quality with status pertains to innovative behavior on the part of firms. In the context of this study of the wine industry, the existence of the status ordering means that wineries have little incentive to develop high-quality wines that are not simultaneously high-status. Suppose, for example, that a winery could develop a more well-balanced and thus higher-quality wine by blending equal proportions of grapes from two distinct regions, say Mendocino County and Sonoma County. In this case, the winery by law would not be allowed to use either region's appellation, since neither region would contribute 85 percent of the grapes that went into the wine. Recognizing that consumers look to the appellation listed on the bottle and its status relative to other appellations in making inferences about a wine's quality, wineries have a disincentive to develop high-quality blends that draw from diverse regions. In essence, the status ordering inhibits high-quality, low-status innovations, thereby restricting the range of potential innovations that may be considered in a given market.[12]

Such an effect of status on innovation is highly idiosyncratic to this industry, but the observation does provide a point of departure for a more general consideration of the relevance of status to innovative activity within an industry. We shall turn to this consideration in the next chapter.

---

[12] This example is drawn from an interview with a Mendocino winemaker who stated that such trade-offs between blending for higher quality or choosing not to blend so as to maintain the appellation affiliation are quite common. He reported that on many occasions both he and other winemakers choose to maintain the appellation affiliation rather than blend away imperfections in their products.

Chapter Six

STATUS AND INVENTION

IN HIS WORK on markets, Harrison White (2002b) draws on the metaphor of a "pump" to characterize the way in which producer identities can serve as an interface between the dispersed inputs that go into market products and the consumers desiring those products. Such a metaphor is compatible with the status-based model of market competition as elaborated in the previous five chapters. Whether the focus is on a service like investment banking or a product like wine, the differentiated status ordering of producers acts as a sorting mechanism, enabling previously dispersed activities and materials to congeal into differentiable products whose underlying quality is sufficiently easy to infer that each consumer can rapidly pair up with the output that best fits her identity, preferences, and budget.

Indeed, the value of a status ordering to the consummation of market exchanges can be made even clearer by briefly considering the dynamics in a market without such an ordering. Given the absence of a tangible status ordering but the presence of uncertainty about quality, there would be insufficient focal points for the scattered array of inputs to rapidly self-organize into differentiated outputs or for those outputs to find their matches among consumers. Because market actors would lack clear guidance on finding appropriate exchange partners, the velocity of consummated exchanges would slow to the point that the market could no longer be considered a pump. Actors would be less likely to enter the market, and upon entering, they would find it difficult to find a "satisficing" exit. Consummated exchanges would drip rather than flow through the market.

In highlighting the importance of the market mechanism to facilitating matching in a context of uncertainty, White's metaphor captures an essential facet of what the economist Friedrich Hayek (1949) first argued that markets are fundamentally about—providing information to guide searching and matching. Of course, White goes beyond Hayek in emphasizing the fact that the essential information for matching is not fully reflected in prices and quantities of isolated commodities.

This chapter shows that, at least in some markets, the image of a status ordering as the fundamental channeler of buyers and sellers captures only one part of a two-part story about status dynamics in markets. In numerous markets—especially those that go under the label of "high-technology markets"—technological invention is one of the fundamental determinants of quality. At the same time that stable status positions are providing guidance for matching in these contexts, inventive activity on the part of producers is constantly changing the meaning of quality. That is, while the identities of producers are serving as focal points for the pumping out of products, the producers themselves—along with other actors, such as universities, individual inventors, and even producers from other industries—are engaging in innovative activity that over time transforms the qualities being signaled. For example, at the same time that a status ordering of television manufacturers reproduces itself, the characteristics implicit in a high-quality television evolve. The image that is regarded as sharp, clear, and large continues to evolve as producers build on each others' inventions as well as the inventions of relevant third parties and the inventions of other industries.

However, while the inventions of different producers will over time transform the meaning of quality, not all producers will contribute equally in this collective albeit competitive endeavor. Some producers will be more likely to develop inventions that are ignored; others will develop inventions that become the foundation on which others build. Consider the technological domain behind a market such as microelectronics or biotechnology. To the extent that the actors that develop those technological areas devote their energies to one particular pursuit, they will in general be unable to devote those same energies to other undertakings. In effect, ideas and inventions compete with one another for the allocation of resources and attention. Some technological solutions will become "winners" in this competition, drawing the interest and effort of those actors involved in the development of the technological domain. These winners are likely to become a foundation for the future advancement of technological knowledge. Others will be "losers" in this competition in the sense that they will become technological dead ends. While the distinction between winner and loser should be regarded as endpoints on a continuum rather than as a dichotomy, this distinction helps to underscore the fact that the constituent elements of quality evolve over time and producers will differ in the extent to which they can exert a positive impact on this evolution.

As this simple example makes clear, competitive dynamics in the technological domain differ in important respects from competitive dynamics in the market domain. In technical domains, competition plays out between evolving trajectories, as firms choose to place bets on some trajectories but not on others. There may be inherent quality differences among inventions associated with the different trajectories, but by themselves, these quality differences will not determine which trajectories flourish and which become dead ends. Rather, characteristics of the actors and features of the evolving technological paths will exert a significant impact on competition in the technological domain.

So alongside the image of a status ordering as a pump through which resources flow, this chapter introduces the image of an evolving "technological network" or "web" in which the nodes in that network are inventions and the ties are ideational connections linking inventions that build on one another. As the web unfolds through evolutionary inventive activity, the constituent elements of quality that are signaled by the status ordering change over time.

Given this image of a web of inventive activity alongside the status ordering of producers, the first proposition of this chapter is that just as status acts as a signal of the quality of products, so status acts as a signal of the importance of these inventions that ultimately shape the constituent elements of quality. The higher an actor's status, the more likely that an invention associated with that actor will be seen as promising and, as a consequence, the more likely that the invention will become an inspiration and foundation for subsequent inventive activity.

The second proposition of this chapter is the following: just as status distinctions guide and direct the evolution of inventive activity among producers in the industry, so status distinctions should also guide and direct the enthusiasm with which consumers embrace some inventions and reject others. In effect, the status-based interactions within the unfolding web should have consequences for the consumer payments that flow to the market pump.

In order to more clearly elaborate and test these propositions, it is necessary to develop this image of the unfolding technological web in more detail. Once the imagery is developed, it will then be possible to more fully elaborate on the way in which status affects the nature of the web's unfolding as well as the way in which the web's unfolding affects the payments that flow from consumers.[1] The semiconductor industry will provide the context for testing the ideas elaborated in this chapter.

NICHES IN A TECHNOLOGICAL WEB

The evolutionary imagery of an unfolding technological web has its origins in the literature on the sociology of technology. Through "thick description" of

---

[1] In focusing on the importance of status in guiding evolutionary invention, I do not want to suggest that revolutionary invention is unimportant. Indeed, if one is interested in significant changes in the status ordering, revolutionary invention may be the more important. However, I am not aware of any work that has been fully capable of endogenizing revolutionary invention. To be sure, there is considerable work that highlights differences in the responsiveness of firms to revolutionary inventions. For example, work by scholars such as Anderson and Tushman (1990), Tripas and Gavetti (2000), or Christensen (1997) certainly leaves the impression that high-status firms will be less likely than their lower-status counterparts to adapt to the new conditions generated by the revolutionary invention even if those inventions emerge from the high-status firms. However, at least to the best of my knowledge, such work does not answer such questions as whether high-status or low-status firms are more likely to generate such inventions. It seems reasonable to speculate that future work on status would make some headway on this question. One could imagine, for example, that instability or fragmentation in a status ordering might be associated with a higher likelihood of revolutionary change, especially if those who are lower in the status ordering are frustrated by their position and perceive invention as a way out. To the degree that hostile takeovers represented a revolutionary invention in the market for corporate control, Hirsch (1986) tells a story along these lines.

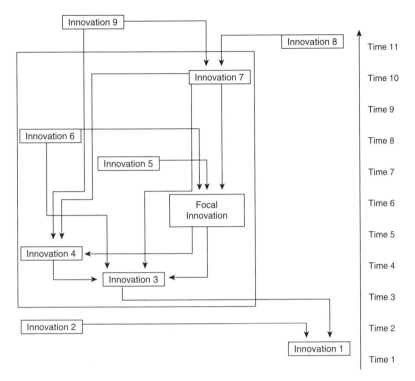

FIGURE 6.1. Example of a hypothetical niche

technological controversies and their resolution, those working in this tradition emphasize the rich connections among actors and their inventions in technological arenas. These scholars use the network image of a "seamless web" to describe the dense pattern of relations concatenating the inventions and associated actors in unfolding technological systems (Hughes 1987; Pinch and Bijker 1987). Drawing on this basic imagery of an unfolding technological web in which inventions are linked by common ideational content, it is reasonable to think of each invention's location within that network as defining that invention's niche. More specifically, one can think of each invention as occupying an "egocentric niche" that includes (1) the focal invention, (2) the inventions on which the focal invention builds, (3) the inventions that build on the focal invention, (4) the inventions that are sufficiently close to the focal invention in content that they help to circumscribe the focal invention's technological contribution, and (5) the technological ties linking these inventions.[2]

Figure 6.1 provides an example of such a niche. The egocentric niche includes all the inventions in the box and the technological ties between those inventions.

[2] I borrow the terminology of "egocentric niche" from Burt (1992).

I will use the term "tie" to denote technological commonalities among inventions. Invention A has a tie to invention B if the contribution of A incorporates, builds on, or is bounded by a technological contribution of B.[3]

Given this conception of an invention's niche, the full technological network can be conceptualized as a structure of interlocking niches. Each new invention represents both the emergence of a new niche in that structure and an entrant into one or more established niches. Because of this dual significance of each new invention, one could analyze technical change and the evolution of the constituent elements of product quality as a process of either niche emergence or niche entry. The analysis that follows will frame the phenomenon of technological change in terms of niche entry. In framing technical change in terms of niche entry, however, the search for the determinants of technical progress turns naturally to an examination of the niche itself, and the central question becomes: How do the characteristics of the niche affect the likelihood of a new entrant?

For the purpose of this investigation, there are three primary ways to characterize the structure and the composition of the technological niche. One is in terms of the inventions themselves, with purely technical features representing the important distinguishing criteria. The second way to categorize different niches is in terms of niche structure, where the term structure refers to the number and the pattern of relations that connect the inventions in a niche. The third way is in terms of the identity of the actors that own the inventions in a niche. The literature on the sociology of technology highlights the fact that a diverse community of actors is involved in the elaboration of every technological network. For applied technologies, this community is likely to include business firms with products that incorporate the technologies as well as universities, government-sponsored research labs, and research consortiums that together supply essential technological knowledge to manufacturing firms. As I shall discuss in further detail below, the concept of status affords a meaningful and generalizable basis for distinguishing among the actors involved in the elaboration of the technological network.

Like capital-rich entrepreneurs who might enter one of many organizational niches, inventors may perceive numerous niches into which they might enter. But given fixed resources and perhaps well-established competencies, these actors cannot pursue every possible avenue for future invention; instead they must adjudicate between niches, deciding to enter only those with the greatest perceived promise. Certain inventions will prove to be central to the advance

---

[3] Such technological ties between inventions can be regarded as a subset of knowledge-based ties between actors. The broader category of knowledge-based ties would include not only the linkages among inventions but also social ties among actors. Because the actors in our analysis are organizations, examples of knowledge-based ties would include such formal interorganizational alliances as patent cross-license agreements and technology exchanges. Informal knowledge-based ties would include such connections as personal relationships among technical personnel employed by different organizations.

of technological knowledge and thus of great economic or at least prestige benefit to the organizations that own them. However, others in the same technical arena will remain peripheral to this technological advance. Clearly, the decision to invest resources in a particular niche is one of large consequence to the actor. Let us now shift our attention to consider how the three attributes of the niche that we have identified are likely to affect the process of technical change.

Niche Attribute 1: The Quality of the Focal Invention

If the promise of an invention were an easily observable feature, then the decision of which niche to enter would be a relatively simple one. However, it is striking the degree to which inherent technical properties fail to serve as reliable guides for discerning the inventions that become most successful. For example, when Intel Corporation developed the microprocessor, one of the landmark inventions in the semiconductor industry, the company was unaware of its significance. According to Gilder's (1989) account of the microprocessor's development, at the time of the invention Intel's sales staff believed that the company would never sell more than ten thousand microprocessors, and the firm's board of directors expressed concern that the chip would distract Intel from focusing on its principal markets.

The observation that technical characteristics alone cannot sufficiently inform decisions about which technologies to develop is a claim that is not unique to academics; it is also made by participants and close observers in different technological domains. For example, consider the following article from *Electronic Business,* an electronics trade publication, that focused on a flurry of interest in flash memory, a technology that was important for the then inchoate market for personal digital assistants (handheld computers). Flash memory allowed a computer to write and quickly erase information from semiconductors that retained data even after their power supply had been cut. The author of the article writes, "Remember bubble memory? How about Josephson Junction? The chip industry is littered with products and technologies that were the subject of huge amounts of hype but never panned out. Despite these cautionary tales, the drum beats are growing even louder for . . . flash memory. Although flash seems likely to escape the disastrous fates of these earlier technologies, some healthy skepticism seems warranted" (Ristelhueber 1993: 99).

Pervasive uncertainty is not limited to the development of specific new product areas. It is often the case that technological debates surround even well-established, basic technologies. For example, a longstanding controversy in the semiconductor industry through the 1970s and 1980s pitched silicon against gallium arsenide (GaAs) as the choice material on which to engrave microscopic circuits (i.e., as the basic material for building integrated circuits). This debate persisted because silicon has certain properties that make it easier to pack a large number of circuits on a single chip, but GaAs circuits are faster at equal or lower power than silicon circuits. Furthermore, GaAs has properties that make it appealing for building optoelectronic semiconductors (devices that detect, amplify, or transmit light). Though silicon chips had dominated the industry for decades, many industry participants continued to foresee a larger role for GaAs chips. As the former head of IBM's Advanced Gallium Arsenide Technology Laboratory noted in 1990, many advocates of silicon referred to GaAs as "the technology of the future, always has been, always will be" (Brodsky 1990: 68).

Each of these examples points to a situation in which technical uncertainty surrounded a new invention, a technical controversy, or, more generally, a high-technology pursuit. It is precisely because of the uncertainty surrounding the potential success of inventions that the status of the actors associated with the inventions in the niche becomes an important determinant of which technological leads will be followed and which will be dead ends. However, even though status is the analytical construct of central concern, the impact of actors' status on investment decisions cannot be considered independently of structural properties of the unfolding web, because the structural properties of each niche determine the possibilities for new entrants. The status of an actor associated with an invention may signal that the invention is in a high-quality locale within the unfolding technological web; however, if there are no opportunities to develop new ideas in that space, then others cannot act on the information yielded by the status signal. Accordingly, before considering status directly, let us briefly consider how to conceptualize niche structure.

Niche Attribute 2: Structure

In focusing on the structure of the niche, the fundamental concern is relating the structure (i.e., the pattern of ties among the inventions within a niche) to the more latent property of competitive intensity, or crowding. Although competitive intensity is not a directly observable feature of a niche, ecologists (Hawley 1950) have long drawn on Durkheim's (1933) important insight that there is an inverse relationship between differentiation and competitive intensity. More recently, Hannan and Freeman (1989) have emphasized the importance of segregating processes in reducing the competitive intensity in the niche. Thus, the analytical property of crowdedness becomes transformed into the property of differentiation among the inventions within the niche.

How can differentiation be measured in a technological niche? Were there some analogue to physical or resource space, then it might be possible to simply count the number of inventions that surround a focal invention in that space. However, it seems implausible to assume that there is a fixed carrying capacity for a type of knowledge that is independent of the realized level of that knowledge. In the domain of technological knowledge, there is no clear

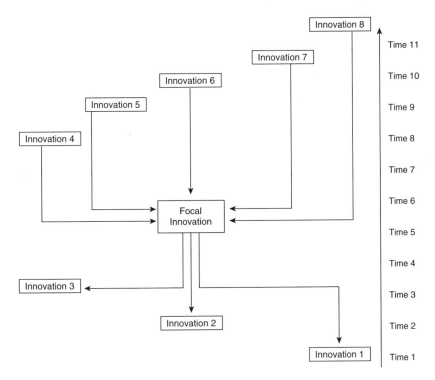

FIGURE 6.2. Hypothetical sparse niche

analogue to physical or resource space. Rather, it seems more reasonable to rely on the indirect ties in the egocentric network (i.e., the ties among the inventions to which the focal invention is connected) to reveal the level of differentiation in the technological niche.

Consider, for example, an invention that draws on diverse strands of knowledge and then becomes the technological ancestor of a highly differentiated array of inventions. That invention's egocentric network could be represented as in figure 6.2. The underlying differentiation is evidenced by the absence of technological connections among the inventions to which the focal invention is tied. The laser is perhaps an example of such an invention, because it has spawned multifarious inventions in unrelated domains, such as consumer electronics, medicine, and telecommunications. The fact that the nonfocal inventions do not share technological ties implies considerable differentiation of technological knowledge in the niche. Conversely, consider the network around an invention that draws on interconnected inventions and that spawns inventions that are themselves only slightly differentiated. An example of such an invention, drawn from our own data on the semiconductor industry, is represented in figure 6.3.

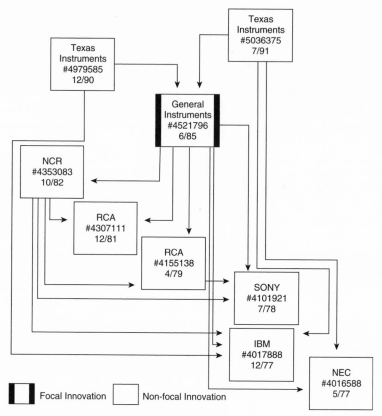

FIGURE 6.3. Niche of patent number 4521796

The number of direct ties provides no information about the level of differentiation in the technological content of the inventions within a niche. The central nodes in figures 6.2 and 6.3 are both directly connected to an equal number of inventions, and, while the direct ties are relevant to signaling processes, it is the indirect ties that provide information about differentiation and hence competitive intensity. The more indirect ties that surround a focal invention, the more the network can be seen as folding in on itself, blanketing the focal invention.

The use of indirect ties to measure differentiation can be easily derived from network theory. According to both Granovetter (1974) and Burt (1992), the information that an actor receives from two alternative contacts is redundant to the degree to which those two actors are connected. More generally, the more connections there are among the nodes within the egocentric network, the less differentiated is the informational content at each node. Thus, the greater the number of indirect ties among the inventions in a technological niche, the more the inventions can be considered to be technologically similar and the lower the likelihood that an inventor will enter that niche.

While indirect ties are the crucial structural determinant of the level of competition within the niche, direct ties are still a meaningful attribute of niche structure. Organizational and evolutionary theories of the firm (March 1988; Nelson and Winter 1982) highlight the role of local search behavior in technological evolution. The basic claim of these theories is that resource constraints and embedded organizational routines restrict the areas for invention that an organization may successfully pursue. This claim can be framed structurally by considering the number of nonfocal inventions, or alternatively the number of direct ties, within the niche. The more that the focal invention is directly connected to other inventions, the more that the focal invention is within the local search domain of other members of the technological community. Stated in terms of the structural properties of the niche, the greater the number of direct ties within the niche, the greater the likelihood of a new entrant into the niche.

Niche Attribute 3: Status

As in other domains, an actor's status in the technological domain is reflected in the deference relations among actors. The only attribute that distinguishes an actor's status in the technological domain is the content of those deference relations. When firm i chooses to build on an invention of firm j rather than on the inventions of other firms, firm i is implicitly engaging in an act of deference. Importantly, deference does not need to be any part of a firm's motive for choosing to build on a particular invention, just as deference does not need to be any part of a firm's motive for accepting a particular position on a tombstone advertisement or part of a winery's motive for using grapes from another region. However, even though deference is not the motive, deference can be the observed social consequence. If the technological community is uncertain about which nodes of the evolving network deserve attention and resources, then a direct deference tie from firm j to firm i signals that j considers the work of i as worthy of such attention. It shows that j regards the activity already undertaken by i as a better foundation for continued invention than some set of alternatives. When considered across all actors, the accumulated acts of deference are manifest as status differences.

Thus, just as status provides a signal of product quality, so it seems reasonable to suppose that status can serve as a signal of an invention's quality. In the article quoted above on the significance of flash memories, the author expresses skepticism regarding the promise of this invention. What is left unexplained, however, is why the "drum beats are growing even louder" for this technology rather than for the others that the author notes (Josephson junction and bubble memory). One possible explanation is that the inventor of flash memory technology in 1986 was Toshiba and the leading promoter of this technology was Intel Corporation. Toshiba and Intel were regarded as among the most successful and innovative firms in the semiconductor industry. Arguably the combined status of Toshiba and Intel provided an indication of the likelihood that flash memory would become an important technology.

Anecdotal evidence that a prominent organization or individual actor can bolster expectations for a product by virtue of their association with that product is prevalent. For example, IBM's entry into the personal computer market in 1981 provided the impetus for software developers to devote substantial resources to programs designed for the personal computer (Anders 1981). This example illustrates how the actions of high-status organizations can become "focal points" (see Schelling 1960) for the allocation of resources by the broader array of actors within or around a particular domain.

Some technologies may lend themselves to a market phenomenon known as demand-side increasing returns (DSIR), which reinforces this expectational dynamic. DSIR occurs whenever the value that a user derives from a product increases with the number of other users of that product; for example, the value of a word-processing program to an individual user increases with the number of other users of that word-processing program because more users implies a greater ability to share document files. (For a more extensive discussion of DSIR, see Saloner et al. 2001). While DSIR is complementary to this expectational status dynamic, DSIR is not necessary for status distinctions to engender self-reinforcing perceptions around inventions.

The general observation that an actor's status affects the attention that the actor receives from the larger community is supported by research in the sociology of science. Indeed, in this context, it is worth referencing Merton's (1968) work on the Matthew Effect since the focus of the empirical analysis was on how scientists' identities provide a biased lens through which the quality of their intellectual contributions is evaluated. When considered collectively, these examples from technological domains as well as research from the sociology of science suggest the following dynamic: if actors working in a technological area expect that a technology will be superior, they will devote more resources to that technology than to alternatives that are evaluated to be inferior. Consequently, the technologies sponsored by high-status actors are more likely to be rapidly developed than are competing ones, and they will thus appear as superior ex post despite the fact that they may not have been superior ex ante. For example, if the combined status of Toshiba and Intel leads others to devote resources to the development of flash memory rather than to competing technologies, such as ferroelectronics, then this additional flow of resources will increase the likelihood that the high expectations for flash memory, as well as the superior status of Toshiba and Intel, will be confirmed.

The fact that an actor's status is expected to lead others to favorably evaluate its inventions does not imply that a high-status actor's inventions will always, or even regularly, be of greater historical significance than a low-status actor's inventions. It implies only that on average there will be an ex post positive correlation between an actor's status and the acknowledged importance of that actor's inventions. Thus, just as status begets quality in the market domain, so status can beget quality in the technological domain. To the extent that an actor's status beckons others to enter a particular invention's niche and thus increases the likelihood that others build on its inventions, status by definition increases the contribution of an invention. To draw on another of Merton's expressions, the Matthew Effect may hold in part because status engenders a "self-fulfilling prophecy" with respect to the contribution of an invention.

The basic proposition arising from this discussion of status in the technological domain is the following: *controlling for the competitive intensity in a technological niche, the status ordering of the actors that sponsor the inventions in a technological niche serves as a tangible guide for the probability that the focal invention in that niche will become important.* Given this basic proposition as well as the other aspects of the niche that must be incorporated into an analysis, let us now turn to a consideration of how to operationalize the features of the niche as well as the process of niche entry.

MEASURING THE NICHE

Given the conception of technological evolution as an unfolding interlocking niche structure, it is necessary to have a methodology capable of identifying inventions and the technological connections between them. The approach employed herein relies on information contained in patent issues, which grant inventors the legal rights to commercially exploit their inventions. Patents provide a useful means for identifying inventions since they are granted only to products, processes, or designs that are judged by the Patent Office to be industrially useful and nonobvious to those trained in the current state of the art of the relevant technological domain. Patent applications not judged to represent novel technologies are denied.

Patents identify the technological ties between inventions. As part of the application procedure, patentees must list all previously issued U.S. patents that serve as important technological building blocks for the inventions for which they seek approval. Furthermore, it is the role of the patent examiner to verify that the lists included in the patent application encompass all relevant existing inventions. Such listings are referred to as "prior art" citations, which are an integral part of the patent process in the United States. The citation process is legally important, because it limits the claims of the patent under consideration; the technological domain of the current patent extends only to the point where the prior art ends. The inventor has a legal claim only to the aspects of the patent that do not overlap with the technological contents of the cited patents (see Office of Technology Assessment and Forecast 1976: 167).

Given the image of the ideational web in which inventions are nodes, each time a new patent is issued, the patented invention both enters existing niches (by virtue of overlapping with the technologies represented by previous patents) and represents the emergence of a new egocentric niche. As time progresses, future patented inventions may cite the focal invention, in which case its niche expands. For example, in figure 6.1 inventions 3 and 4, which were patented prior to the focal invention, are included in the niche once the focal invention is patented. These two inventions represent work that the focal invention cited as prior art. Inventions 5–7 represent later niche entrants; these inventions cited the focal invention.

A citation thus designates the focal invention as a technological precursor to a novel technology. In addition, the Office of Technology Assessment (1976) has asserted that the more citations that an invention receives, the more important that invention is in the advancement of technological knowledge. The literature has corroborated this assumption. For example, Trajtenberg (1990) found that patent citations were accurate indicators of technological importance in the computed tomography industry, and Albert et al. (1991) found a positive correlation between the number of citations that a patented invention received and the technological importance that experts ascribed to that invention. Several cross-sectional studies document a correlation between citations and economic performance. For example, Narin, Noma, and Perry (1987) found high correlations (ranging from .6 to .9) between the possession of a frequently cited patent portfolio and changes in corporate financial measures such as increases in company profits and sales (additional studies are reviewed in Basberg [1987]). In addition to these studies highlighting the relationship between citations and the (perceived) importance of an invention, the fact that citation analysis is now used by corporations to analyze the technology portfolio of their competitors, to provide insight into likely future market strategies, and to compare productivity within or between firm laboratories further supports the use of patents as proxies for innovative activity (Eerden and Saelens 1991).

Although academic research has validated the use of patent citation data as a meaningful reflection of a number of features of the innovative activities of firms, caution must still be exercised when using patents to identity inventions and the technological ties between them. Only inventions passing some threshold of inventive success are patentable. Second, even among those crossing this threshold, inventors may be less willing to patent some types of inventions than others (Levin et al. 1987). Furthermore, there are sometimes industry-specific means that inventors can use to protect their intellectual property.[4] For these reasons, it is not surprising that researchers have found interindustry variance in the tendency to patent (see Scherer 1984). To the extent that inventors do not seek patents for inventions, the use of patents to operationalize analysis of the composition and structure of the technological niche will be less encompassing. Clearly, the researcher must be sensitive to the validity of patents as indicators of inventions and the relationships among inventions in the context that is studied. With this admonition in mind, let's turn to the empirical setting for our study, the semiconductor industry.

The Semiconductor Industry

The semiconductor industry began with the invention of the point contact transistor at Bell Laboratories in 1947. The industry has evolved to include a heterogeneous population of firms, including large captive producers (e.g., IBM),[5] diversified merchant producers (e.g., Motorola), and specialized firms that concentrate on a single technology or market niche (e.g., Bipolar Integrated Technology). European and Japanese organizations have also actively participated in developing semiconductor technologies since the 1950s. In addition, while private firms have conducted a large majority of the invention in semiconductor technology, national governments and universities have also developed and patented technologies. Thus, the semiconductor industry encompasses a range of actors based in many different nations, creating technological networks that span national boundaries and organizational forms.

The data analyzed herein include all U.S. semiconductor device patents granted to worldwide semiconductor inventors and manufacturers for sixteen

---

[4] For example, in microelectronics, the industry that we examine, the Semiconductor Chip Protection Act of 1984 enables inventors to apply for copyrights to protect semiconductor mask works, which are in essence the designs of semiconductor chips' circuitry. However, there are reasons to think that inventors are still likely to seek patents for their devices. First, the period of copyright protection is only 10 years since the time at which the mask work is registered with the Copyright Office or it is first commercially exploited, which is shorter than the 17-year period of patent protection. Further, the Semiconductor Chip Protection Act does not prevent the inventor from receiving both copyright and patent protection for the same invention. Generally, it is thought that the statutory requirements for patents, novelty and nonobviousness, make patents more difficult to obtain than copyrights (for a discussion of the relationship between copyrights and patents for semiconductors, see Ladd, Leibowitz, and Joseph [1986]).

[5] Captive manufacturers are firms that produce for internal use rather than for sale on the open market. IBM is a captive producer because the vast majority of its semiconductors are consumed internally.

years, from 1976 to 1991.[6] Previous research suggests that the U.S. patent system is the most complete for analyzing international technology. The United States is widely recognized as the world's largest technological marketplace (with 50% of patents granted to foreign applicants; Albert et al. 1991). Patent information provided by the U.S. Patent Office is available back to 1976 from the Lexis/Nexis online database.

As support for the use of patents to examine technology and technological change in the semiconductor industry, it can be noted that all the landmark inventions in semiconductor technology have been patented (Wilson, Ashton, and Egan 1980). Moreover, during the majority of the time period represented in the data, certain semiconductor producers, most notably Intel and Texas Instruments (TI), aggressively litigated to protect their intellectual property. Indeed, the popular press estimated that TI earned some $1 billion in royalties from infringement lawsuits (Orenstein 1992). TI's patent royalties reached the point that the company reported them as a separate line item on its income statement. In addition, as Japanese producers gained familiarity with the U.S. legal system, they too became more assertive in filing infringement cases (for example, Fujitsu recently opted to file a countersuit against TI rather than to pay royalty fees; Helm 1992). The apparent importance that semiconductor firms placed on patents and patent rights suggests the validity of using patent information to operationalize the central concepts of this analysis.

ANALYSIS

A patent enters another patent's niche through the act of citing. Accordingly, to explore the determinants of niche entry, one models the citation rate for existing patents. Each spell begins when a patent is issued or cited and ends when it is next cited.[7] The proportional hazards model introduced by Cox

---

[6] Under the U.S. system, patents are filed according to major class and subclass. Semiconductor device patents include all subclasses of primary class 357. Patents are typically filed in one primary class/subclass combination but are also cross-classified in additional locations. The data for this analysis comprise all patents filed in primary class 357.

[7] In previous research, Toby Stuart (my frequent collaborator in this work on the semiconductor industry) and I experimented with alternative event definitions. For example, we performed analyses in which we did not end a spell when a self-citation occurred (i.e., when a focal patent was cited by its owner). This event definition can be defended on the grounds that a self-citation is substantively less meaningful than a citation from another actor, because it does not imply that an additional actor has decided to enter the niche. Based on a similar logic, we considered a second alternative in which a spell ends only if the focal patent is cited by a new actor rather than one that has previously cited the focal patent. Again, it might be that a citation from an additional actor is a more significant event than a repeat citation, because it indicates that an additional actor has chosen to enter the niche. However, only 5.3% of the spells end in self-citations, and only 4.6% of the spells end in repeat citations by nonfocal actors. Consequently, while there may be theoretical reasons for considering alternative event definitions, in practice the results are unaffected by the different definitions of the dependent variable.

(Kalbfleisch and Prentice 1980) is appropriate for such an analysis. The basic model can be specified as follows:

$$r(t) = h(t) \exp[\mathbf{XB} + \mathbf{Y}(t)\mathbf{S}], \qquad [6.1]$$

where $r(t)$ is the transition rate or hazard of niche entry, $h(t)$ *is* an unspecified baseline rate for the transition, $\mathbf{X}$ is a matrix of time-constant covariates, $\mathbf{Y}(t)$ is a matrix of time-varying covariates, and $\mathbf{B}$ and $\mathbf{S}$ are vectors of unknown regression parameters. Because $h(t)$ is an unspecified step function, the Cox model offers an extremely flexible means for modeling time dependence. While the Cox model accounts for interarrival time dependence (i.e., the time from when the patent is granted to the time at first entry and then the time between subsequent entries) with an unspecified baseline rate for the transition, the time since last arrival is not the only form of time dependence that is likely to affect the rate of citation. In addition to modeling interarrival times, it seems appropriate to include two additional clocks that can accelerate the baseline rate. The first is a variable (updated monthly) to denote the *calendar time*. The second is a variable reflecting the *age of the niche* (updated monthly). Assuming that firms are more likely to enter a niche after they become aware of it, the composite baseline should increase as a function of the time since the patent at the center of the niche was introduced. However, because the relevance of a patent should decrease with the time since it was introduced, it is also important to include an *age-squared* variable as well to allow for nonmonotonicity.

Earlier in this chapter, the theoretical discussion of the properties of a technological niche emphasized three attributes: the quality of the focal invention in a niche, the structure of relations among the inventions in the niche, and the status of the actors associated with the niche. I shall now describe the operationalization of these attributes.

The quality of the focal invention.   As has been the case in the analyses of the investment banking and wine industries, a critical analytical question is how to control for underlying quality. And, akin to the situation in the investment banking industry, the difficulty that industry observers have in inferring the comparative quality of inventions almost necessarily implies the absence of a completely adequate means to control for the quality of an invention. There are three possible ways to respond to this difficulty. One is to forgo any attempt to control for quality, under the assumption that what is not observable cannot have an effect on the likelihood of niche entry. A second approach is to treat quality differences across patents as unobserved heterogeneity and then to devise some method for controlling for this unobserved heterogeneity. A third possibility is to rely on one of the measures of quality that has been put forth in economic analyses of patents as indicators of innovative activity. In our analysis, we have chosen the second and third approaches, which both suggest the same control variable for quality.

In their discussion of unobserved heterogeneity, Heckman and Borjas (1980) noted that unobserved differences across units are likely to result in occurrence dependence. A frequently cited example of this type of unobserved heterogeneity arises in the context of research on job mobility. If there is unobserved heterogeneity across individuals in their likelihood of shifting jobs, then an occurrence-dependent term (i.e., the number of times that someone has changed jobs in the past) will have a positive effect on the rate of job mobility. Heckman and Borjas argued that one way to account for such unobserved differences is to include as a control variable the number of previous realizations of the dependent variable. Applying Heckman and Borjas's logic to the analysis of patents, one should include as a covariate *the number of times that a patent has been cited*, controlling for the time that the patent has been at risk of being cited.

While econometric work on unobserved heterogeneity suggests the inclusion of a variable denoting the number of times that the patent has been cited, so too does economic research on patents as indicators of innovative activity. In particular, Trajtenberg (1990) employed the number of citations received by a patent over a given time interval as a measure of that patent's quality. Thus, in including the number of citations received as a covariate (while also controlling for time dependence in the form of calendar time, the age of the patent, and the age of the patent squared), one is including as a covariate the measure of quality that has been put forth in the economics literature. I would not want to equate an occurrence-dependent term solely with quality differences for several reasons. First, unobserved heterogeneity could be due to other factors. Second, insofar as individual citations are acts of deference and insofar as status at the firm level is a function of accumulated acts of deference, one cannot rule out that citations to any individual patent are really a manifestation of deference to the firm. But the fact that the analysis incorporates a measure that others have used to capture quality should counter concerns that many of the results can be explained by unobserved quality differences between patents.[8]

Attributes of niche structure.   Our consideration of niche structure led to the expectation that indirect ties among the inventions in a niche should have a negative effect on the likelihood of a new entrant. The argument is that the competitive intensity in a niche is a positive function of the number of indirect ties in that niche, controlling for the number of direct ties. Therefore, a covariate in the

---

[8] Even if the citations to the patent reflect accumulated acts of deference, this variable reflects only those acts of deference directly related to the focal patent. Accordingly, if we include citations to the focal patent as one variable and citations to the firm's other patents as another variable, the latter variable will reflect status net of the deference associated with the focal invention. Accordingly, by including the citations to the focal patent as a control for the quality of that patent and/or the status effect associated with that patent, it is possible to interpret the citations to the other patents of the firm as a purer status effect. I will discuss the operationalization of this other variable shortly.

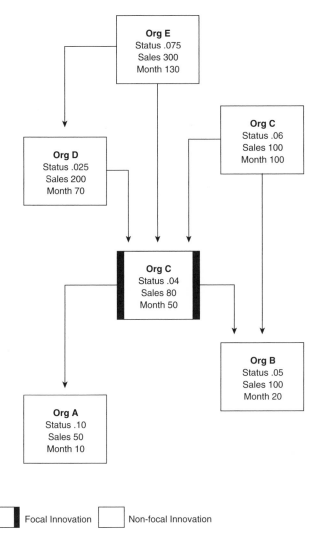

Org E
Status .075
Sales 300
Month 130

Org C
Status .06
Sales 100
Month 100

Org D
Status .025
Sales 200
Month 70

Org C
Status .04
Sales 80
Month 50

Org B
Status .05
Sales 100
Month 20

Org A
Status .10
Sales 50
Month 10

■ Focal Innovation   ☐ Non-focal Innovation

FIGURE 6.4. Hypothetical niche and spell data from which the information in table 6.1 is constructed

analysis is a count of *the number of indirect ties among the inventions in a niche* (see fig. 6.4).

The theoretical consideration of niche structure also led to the expectation that the number of direct ties in the niche would have a positive effect on the likelihood of a new entrant into the niche. Significantly, direct ties can be decomposed into two components: (1) the number of patents that the focal invention cites and (2) the number of patents that cite the focal invention. The previous discussion of quality differences across patents suggests that there is an identification problem encountered in interpreting the number of citations received by the focal invention. While the number of citations going to the focal invention could represent the degree to which the focal invention is in the local search domain of other actors, it could also be a proxy for unobserved heterogeneity or patent quality differences. Thus, this parameter cannot be given a unique interpretation.

Yet while the interpretation of the number of citations *going to* the focal patent is confounded by alternative processes for which this quantity may be a proxy, the number of citations *made by* the focal invention can be clearly interpreted. The more patents that the focal invention cites, the more that the focal invention is within the local search domain of those within the technological community.

Given the inclusion of citations made by the focal invention, it is important to reiterate that the sample includes all semiconductor device patents between 1976 and 1991. While these data provide the opportunity for a longitudinal analysis, the arbitrary lower bound of 1976 leads to left censoring. When a niche emerges, it includes not only the focal patent but also all the patents that the focal patent cites. If any of these patents were issued prior to 1976, they would be excluded from the data and thus not captured in the demarcation of the focal patent's niche. To minimize the potential biases from left censoring, semiconductor device patents issued between 1976 and 1981 were not included in the analysis as focal patents but only as potential citations of patents issued from 1982 to 1991. Given that the product life cycle in the semiconductor industry is typically estimated to be three to five years from introduction to maturity (McClean 1981–91), setting aside the first six years as "history" seems fairly conservative.[9] In total, the sample contains 4,048 patents, of which 2,983 represent focal patents (i.e., were issued after 1982).

Status (and other attributes) of niche occupants.   Recall that an actor's status at a point in time is defined in terms of the deference relations in the technological domain that signify the actor's contribution to the advancement of technological knowledge up to that time. Consistent with this definition, an actor's status is measured as a proportion related to the number of citations that the actor has received on all its semiconductor device patents during the 12-month interval prior to the month in which it introduces a patent. A greater score on this variable implies a greater contribution to the advancement of technological knowledge over that time period.

Why, one might reasonably wonder, is status not measured as a simple count of citations? Because as an actor's portfolio of patents enlarges over time, the number of patents "at risk" of a citation increases over time. If one measured status simply in terms of a count, status would increase merely as a function of time. For example, in month 16 an actor can receive citations on patents only during a 15-month time period, but in month 36 it can receive citations on patents that it

---

[9] Previous analyses included experimentation with the length of this window, and the reported results are robust across shorter and longer intervals.

issued over a 35-month time period. To correct for the expanding risk set, the number of citations to an actor over a given 12-month interval is divided by the citations to all actors during that window. As a consequence of this standardization, an actor's status can range from "0," if it received no citations during a given window, to a maximum of "1," if it received all the citations made over the previous year. In the context of our data, the highest-status organizations have scores of approximately .1, indicating that they received 10% of the citations made over a one-year period.

One might also wonder why Bonacich's $c(\alpha, \beta)$ measure is not employed to measure status. That is, just as Bonacich's measure was used to codify the deference relations in the investment banking industry, why isn't Bonacich's measure employed here? In principle, the measure could be employed. One could construct a matrix of deference relations, **R**, in which each cell, r_{ij}, represents citations from the firm on the on the row to the firm on the column. However, in order to apply Bonacich's measure to any given network, that population must be fully connected; there cannot be any fragmentation of the deference relations into disconnected groups. Because there are a large number of firms with only a few ties, the technological network fragments, and as a result, the measure is not appropriate for this particular analysis. A later analysis in this chapter will focus on deference relations involving only the largest 113 firms involved in the technological network, and this network is fully connected. In that analysis, Bonacich's measure and the proportionate measure will both be used.

As a practical measure, the major difference between the two measures is that the Bonacich measure weights the value of any citation by the status of the citer. Using Bonacich's measure, status is not only a function of the number of citations but also a function of the status of the citers, whose status is a function of the number and status of those who have cited them, and so on. The value of β determines the degree to which the effect of a citation on an actor's status is weighted by the citer's status. When $\beta = 0$, the count-based measure and the Bonacich measure are essentially identical.

To assess whether there is a positive relationship between the status of the focal organization (i.e., the owner of the focal patent) and the rate at which other organizations choose to enter its niche, the *status of the focal organization at the time of its most recent entry into the focal patent's niche* is included as a covariate. In general, the value of this covariate will be the focal organization's status at the time that the focal patent was approved. However, if the focal inventor reenters the niche by introducing a patent that cites the focal patent, we update the variable to reflect the focal actor's status at the time of its most recent entry into the niche.[10]

---

[10] Clearly, this is not the only coding rule that one might apply. One might, for example, update the focal actor's status whenever it changed. However, such a coding rule was impractical, because many actors change status monthly as new citations arrive and old citations are dropped (these are typically small changes).

Illustration of variable construction.   Figure 6.4 and table 6.1 provide an illustrative example that hopefully clarifies the definitions of the variables in the event-history analysis. Figure 6.4 presents a hypothetical niche that expands over time. Table 6.1 presents the spell data that would correspond to such a niche. The first spell begins when the focal patent is granted to organization C. At this time, organization C has a status of .04, and thus the covariate denoting the status of the focal inventor at the time of its most recent entry into the niche takes the value .04. This value implies that in the 12 months prior to month 50, the month in which the focal patent is introduced, organization C received 4 percent of all the citations made. The first spell ends when the focal patent is cited by organization D in month 70. The covariate for the status of

TABLE 6.1
Spells Constructed from the Hypothetical Niche in Figure 6.4

Variables	Spells			
	1	2	3	4
Time clocks*				
Age of patent (months)	0	20	50	80
Age of patent squared	0	400	2,500	6,400
Calendar time (months)	50	70	100	130
Unobserved quality of the focal patent				
N of patents that cite the focal patent	0	1	2	3
Attributes of actors within the niche				
Status of focal organization	.04	.04	.06	.06
Average status of nonfocal organizations whose patents are cited by the focal patent	.075	.075	.075	.075
Average status of nonfocal organizations that cite the focal patent	0	.025	.025	.05
Sales of focal organization (billions of $)	80	80	100	100
Average sales of nonfocal organizations whose patents are cited by the focal patent (billions of $)	75	75	75	75
Average sales of nonfocal organizations that cite the focal patent (billions of $)	0	200	200	250
N of alliances entered into by the focal organization	0	0	0	0
N of self-citations by the focal organization	0	0	1	1
Attributes of the niche structure				
N of indirect ties	0	0	1	2
N of patents cited by the focal patent	2	2	2	2

*Values listed are at the start of the spell.

the focal inventor remains the same for the duration of the second spell, which ends in month 100 when organization C reenters the niche with a self-citation. On account of this reentry, we update the value of the covariate of the focal inventor to reflect the fact that its status has changed from .04 to .06. This variable has a value of .06 for the duration of the third and fourth spells.

To assess the effect of the status of the nonfocal actors on the likelihood of new entrants into that niche, two additional covariates are included in the analysis: the *average status of the nonfocal inventors with patents that **are cited by** the focal patent* and the *average status of the nonfocal inventors with patents that **cite** the focal patent*. The statuses of the nonfocal inventors are divided into these two components because of the asymmetry implicit in the patent citation process. The whole notion of deference implicit in the citation process suggests that a citation from a high-status actor ought to be a more meaningful event than a citation to a high-status actor. If a high-status actor cites a focal patent, that actor implicitly acknowledges the dependence of its invention on the technologies represented by the focal patent. In contrast, if a focal patent cites the invention of a high-status actor, this implies only that the focal patent is in a technological area that the high-status actor regards as important; such a citation from the focal patent to the invention of a high-status actor does not imply any acknowledgment on the part of the high-status actor of the focal patent's contribution.

Once again, figure 6.4 and table 6.1 show how these two variables are constructed. The focal patent in figure 6.4 cites two inventions. The average status of the owners of these patents is $(.10 + .05)/2 = .075$. The average status of the nonfocal inventors cited by the focal patent maintains this value for all the spells. In contrast, the average status of the nonfocal inventors that cite the focal patent changes each time an additional organization enters the niche. In the first spell, the focal invention by definition has no citers, and thus the value of this variable is 0 until the focal invention is cited by organization D. Since organization D's status is .025, this variable has a value of .025 for the second spell. The value remains the same for the third spell since the reentry of the focal inventor into the niche does not affect this variable. However, when the focal patent is cited by organization E, this variable changes in value to .05, the average of organization D's status and organization E's status.

While status is the actor attribute of greatest theoretical interest, it is obviously not the only one that may be relevant to the process of niche entry. Another important attribute is the market presence of the organizations in the niche. Just as an organization's status may be a signal of the technological significance of its inventions, so sales may be a signal of the market significance of its inventions. There may be other reasons why an organization's market presence would affect the rate at which its technologies are developed, but I am less interested in discriminating among alternative explanations than in including market presence as a control. Because it seems reasonable to believe that sales and status will be correlated, greater confidence can be placed in a status effect if it can be shown to have explanatory power in excess of an organization's market presence. Motivated by these considerations, the analysis incorporates market sales volumes (in billions of dollars) for the merchant and captive semiconductor makers for which we were able to obtain this information. Data on the annual sales of merchant semiconductor firms between 1981 and 1991 come from Dataquest, a consultancy to firms in the high-technology industries. Data on the estimated dollar value of production volume for the major captive producers over this period were obtained from the annual status reports issued by the Integrated Circuits Engineering Corporation (McLean 1981–91). Like the measures for organizational status, the measures for organizational sales are based on the time of an organization's most recent entry into the niche. However, unlike the status measures, which are updated monthly, the sales data are available only annually. Thus, the *sales volume of the inventor of the focal patent* is measured as the sales volume in the year prior to its most recent entry into the niche. Also included in the analysis are variables representing the *average sales of all of the nonfocal organizations that are cited by the focal patent* and the *average sales of all the nonfocal organizations that cite the focal patent*. Each time a new inventor enters a niche, this variable is changed to reflect the sales of the entering organization (measured at the year prior to entry).

There are two complications with the sales data. First, although the Dataquest data account for over 90 percent of worldwide semiconductor sales and offer the most complete information available, they are not exhaustive. Dataquest attempts to collect data on all firms producing more than $10 million in sales (approximately 0.02% of the market in 1991), but it does not track sales for all firms producing less than this dollar amount. Firms not included in the database are assigned a sales volume of zero. The implicit assumption in this coding rule is that sales levels of less than $10 million are not a stronger signal of market potential than zero sales, such as would by definition be true of nonproducing assignees (e.g., universities, government agencies, etc.). As justification for this decision, it can be noted that the total sales volume in the industry ranged from $15.9 billion in 1981 to $55.5 billion in 1991, and the mean sales for a firm in the database are $473 million, so zero sales seems a sufficiently close approximation for the excluded firms. The second complication is that, although data on semiconductor patents go back to 1976, data on sales volume go back only to 1981. Excluding spells affected by missing data results in the elimination of 47 percent of the sample, quite possibly biasing the results. Therefore, missing sales data were imputed according to the multiple imputation procedure advocated by Rubin (1987).[11]

---

[11] A distinctive feature of Rubin's multiple imputation procedure is that it introduces a random component into the imputation to reflect the uncertainty about the "true" parameter values underlying the coefficients that one uses for the imputation. In our analysis, we used a regression model

Finally, there are two additional control variables incorporated into the analysis to reflect other aspects of the actors in a niche. The first is the *number of times that the focal organization cites itself.* Because a citation by the inventor of the focal patent might not represent as significant an event as a citation by an independent firm, it seems appropriate to control for self-citations in the analysis. The final included actor attribute is the total number of patent license, patent cross-license, technology exchange, and second-source agreements that the focal organization entered prior to its most recent entry into the niche.[12] The *total number of strategic alliances* is included as a control variable because such relationships seem likely to affect the degree to which the technology owned by an organization diffuses.[13] An organization's participation in interorganizational relationships should increase the amount of overlap between its innovative efforts and those of the organizations with which it is partnering, and this overlapping effort may increase the degree to which other organizations build on the focal organization's patents. The data for this variable were collected by scanning every edition of the trade publication *Electronic News*, a weekly periodical that has a section devoted to the semiconductor industry, for the time period covered by the focal patents in our study. *Electronic News* is probably the most comprehensive single source for information about collaborations among semiconductor firms.[14]

Table 6.2 presents descriptive information on the number of entries (completed spells) per patent. For example, 483 patents experienced two complete spells (i.e., two subsequent patents entered their niche). Table 6.3 presents descriptive information on critical independent variables. In addition to the means and standard deviations, table 6.3 present values for the twenty-fifth and seventy-fifth percentiles because the interquartile range is less sensitive than the standard

---

to impute the missing sales data in year $t-1$ from observed (or imputed) sales in year t. This procedure was repeated until there existed a complete data set (i.e., complete sales information for all firms going back to 1975). A second data set was generated following the same procedure. Rubin (1987) explains how parameter estimates from two or more such complete data sets can be combined to provide unbiased estimates of coefficients and their variances.

[12] Second-source arrangements are a common practice in the semiconductor industry. A formal second-source agreement occurs when one firm licenses another to manufacture one of its products, resulting in a nearly identical copy of the licensor's design. This practice helps to guarantee users that the product will be reliably supplied.

[13] Some of these agreements (cross-license and technology exchange deals) are symmetric in the sense that each firm licenses its patents or exchanges its technology with the other. The other agreements, license and second-source deals, are asymmetric, because one firm is the licensor and the other is the licensee. Because this variable is included as a control for other factors that may lead to the diffusion of an organization's technology (and hence an increase in the rate at which its patents are cited), this variable is incremented for both firms in the case of symmetric deals but only for the licensor in the case of second-source and license deals.

[14] Although *Electronic News* is the most comprehensive source for interfirm collaborations, it is unlikely that the data on alliances are complete. In particular, we suspect that we have not included some partnerships between small firms and especially small firms based outside the United States.

TABLE 6.2
Frequency of Events per Patent

N of Events	Frequency
0	1,037
1	668
2	483
3	174
4	111
5	72
6	32
7	34
8	25
9	25
10+	58

An event occurs when a subsequent patent enters a focal patent's niche; each event constitutes a completed spell.

deviation to outliers and to the assumption of normality. Table 6.3 reports the distribution for the number of indirect ties at various levels of niche size (i.e., the number of citations from the focal patent plus the number of citations to the focal patent), since the number of possible indirect ties is contingent on the number of direct ties.

Results

Hazard rate models of niche entry were estimated using TDA 5.2 (Rohwer 1993), and the results are presented in table 6.4. The coefficients reported in this table indicate how a one-unit change in an independent variable serves to multiply the rate of niche entry.

Though our main interest is in the effects of status, it is worth considering the effects of the other variables in passing. Let us first consider the results for the attributes of niche structure. As expected, the parameter estimate for the number of indirect ties in a niche is negative, indicating that an increase in the number of indirect ties reduces the rate of niche entry. Controlling for the number of direct ties in the niche, each indirect tie lowers the rate of niche entry by 4.5 percent ($\exp[-0.0464] = 0.955$). The negative coefficient as well as the level of significance for this variable suggest that the number of indirect ties does reflect the competitive intensity in the niche. Thus, technological domains that are "crowded" in the sense that the inventions in them lack differentiation are ones that potential entrants either avoid or are unable to enter.

The coefficient for the number of citations made by the focal patent has a positive effect on niche entry. This finding supports the local search hypothesis, which suggests that organizations continue to work in the domains in which they

TABLE 6.3
Descriptive Statistics for Variables

Variables	Mean	S.D.	25th Percentile	75th Percentile
Quality of the focal innovation				
N of citations received by focal patent	1.743	3.092	0	2
Attributes of niche occupants				
Status of focal inventor	.030	.024	.005	.048
Average status of nonfocal inventors cited by the focal patent	.020	.020	0	.033
Average status of nonfocal inventors that cite the focal patent	.013	.019	0	.026
Sales of focal inventor (billions of $)	.913	1.246	0	1.361
Average sales of nonfocal inventors that are cited by the focal patent (billions of $)	.335	.553	0	.415
Average sales of nonfocal inventors that cite the focal patent (billions of $)	.773	1.132	0	1.233
Self-citations of focal inventor	.453	.923	0	1
Alliances formed by focal inventor	5.789	6.976	1	8
Attributes of niche structure				
N of citations made by the focal patent	2.278	2.142	1	3
N of indirect ties:				
Niche size = 2 or 3 (N = 3,244)	.164	.440	0	0
Niche size = 4 or 5 (N = 2,154)	.617	1.010	0	1
Niche size = 6 or 7 (N = 1,171)	1.432	1.741	0	2
Niche size = 7 or 8 (N = 645)	2.403	2.592	0	3
Niche size ≥ 9 (N = 753)	5.678	5.269	2	8

have had previous successes. The more that an invention is within the local search domain of other organizational actors, the more likely is that invention to become a foundation for future technological developments.

Turning to the indicator of quality, we find that the coefficient for the number of citations received by the focal patent is positive. Because this variable is an occurrence-dependent term, one must be cautious in applying a substantive interpretation to this coefficient. However, the fact that this measure has been used in the economics literature to control alternatively for unobserved heterogeneity or quality differences across patents should increase the level of confidence in the results.

The estimate for the sales volume of the focal firm and the average of the sales volumes of the nonfocal firms in a niche both have positive effects on the rate of niche entry. The number of times that a firm cites its own patents does not have a statistically significant effect in the complete model. The final control

TABLE 6.4
Parameter Estimates for the Hazard of Niche Entry

Variables	Model 1	Model 2	Model 3
Time Clocks			
Age of patent	.0549** (.0058)	.0458** (.0058)	.0453** (.0058)
Age of patent squared	−.0001** (1.6×10^{-5})	−.0001** (1.8×10^{-5})	−.0001** (1.8×10^{-5})
Calendar time	−.0125** (.0006)	−.0086** (.0007)	−.0089** (.0007)
Quality of the focal innovation			
N of cites received by focal patent	.1118** (.0064)	.1030** (.0065)	.1019** (.0066)
Attributes of niche occupants			
Status of focal inventor	1.3937* (.6555)	1.6508** (.5934)	.7780 (.6605)
Average status of nonfocal inventors cited by the focal patent		2.1555** (.8239)	2.5329** (.8326)
Average status of nonfocal inventors that cite the focal patent		10.0709** (1.4007)	10.1462** (1.4033)
Sales of focal inventor		.0292* (.0148)	.0474** (.0151)
Average sales of nonfocal inventors cited by the focal patent		.1710** (.0332)	.1644** (.0332)
Average sales of nonfocal inventors that cite the focal patent		.0760** (.0230)	.0757** (.0231)
Self-citations of focal inventor	−.0006 (.0165)	.0382* (.0163)	.0276 (.0168)
Alliances formed by focal inventor	.0051* (.0023)	.0037 (.0022)	.0022 (.0023)
Attributes of niche structure			
N of indirect ties	−.0557** (.0078)	−.0557** (.0080)	−.0464** (.0080)
N of citations made by focal patent	.0933** (.0066)	.0692** (.0071)	.0734** (.0072)

Numbers in parentheses are standard errors.
*$p < .05$; **$p < .01$.

variable, the number of strategic alliances in which a firm participates, is positive but not statistically significant in the complete model.

Let's focus now on the variables of main substantive interest. In columns 1 and 2 of table 6.4, the status of the owner of the focal patent has a positive and statistically significant effect on the likelihood of a new entrant into the niche of the focal patent. However, when the attributes of the nonfocal inventors and the sales of the owner of the focal patent are included in the full model (col. 3), this effect is no longer statistically significant. While it seems reasonable to suppose that the lack of significance may have resulted from a high correlation between the sales and status of the owner of the focal patent, the correlation between these two variables is only .55. Thus, we cannot reject the null hypothesis that the status of the focal inventor has no independent effect on niche entry.

In contrast, the average status of the nonfocal inventors that cite the focal patent and the average status of the nonfocal inventors that are cited by the focal patent both have positive and statistically significant direct effects on niche entry in the complete model. These findings indicate that the relationships between organizations in a niche can be commensal: when patents owned by high-status actors enter a niche, they attract other inventors, thus enhancing the status of the focal actor. Moreover, the status of those who cite the focal patent has a greater effect on the hazard of niche entry than does the status of those who are cited by the focal patent. As an illustration of the difference, consider how an interquartile shift in both variables multiplies the rate of entry. An interquartile-size increase in the average status of the citers of the focal patent augments the rate of niche entry by 30 percent ($\exp[10.14 \times .026] = 1.302$). In contrast, an interquartile-size increase in the average status of those cited by the focal patent increases the rate of niche entry by only 8.7 percent ($\exp[2.53 \times .033] = 1.087$). In other words, the effect of the average status of those who cite the focal invention is more than three times the magnitude of the effect of the average status of those cited by the focal patent. The difference in the magnitudes of these coefficients is consistent with the view that a citation going to the focal invention is an explicit recognition of the importance of that invention and that a citation from the focal invention indicates only that the focal invention is proximate to the inventions of other actors.

This asymmetric effect also seems to undercut an alternative explanation for the results: the status effect may simply be a quality effect, and high-quality firms tend to cite other high-quality firms. If the higher rate of citation simply reflected the fact that higher-quality firms are more productive and more likely to cite each other, it would be difficult to understand why this effect should be asymmetric. However, such asymmetry is completely consistent with the interpretation of citations as acts of deference.

Particularly interesting is the finding that the status of the nonfocal actors has a greater direct effect on the likelihood of niche entry than does the status of the focal inventor. Even in the model for which the sales of the focal organization are excluded from the analysis (col. 2 of table 6.4), the effect of the status of the nonfocal actors is greater than the effect of the status of the focal actor. While this result was not anticipated, it is compelling to find that inventors have greater difficulty legitimizing their own inventions than drawing attention to the inventions of others. An actor's self-interest in the success of its own inventions almost undoubtedly compromises its ability to draw on its status for the purpose of attracting to its inventions the attention of other actors.

Although the status of the focal inventor has no statistically significant direct effect on the likelihood of entry, a comparison of the results in columns 1 and 3 of table 6.4 reveals an important indirect effect of the focal organization's status. In column 1, when only the attributes of the nonfocal inventors are excluded, the effect of the focal owner's status on the likelihood of niche entry is positive and statistically significant. Indeed, the magnitude of the coefficient is approximately two times greater than in the full model. This finding implies that the status of the focal inventor significantly affects the probability that higher-status (and larger) nonfocal actors will enter the niche, which in turn has a positive effect on the rate of niche entry. However, when the status and size of these nonfocal actors are included as controls, the focal owner's status has little direct effect. Together, the indirect effect of the status of the focal actor and the direct effects of the nonfocal actors underscore the importance of the sociotechnical context that is highlighted by the niche framework. The less that an actor is able to exploit its status to draw attention to its own efforts, the more that actor depends on the context in which its inventions are situated. More generally, the results point to the effect of status as a signal of invention quality in the technological domain, just as we have observed that status acts as a signal of product quality in the market domain.

LEAKAGE FROM TECHNOLOGICAL WEB TO MARKET PUMP

Having observed the impact of status in directing attention in the technological domain, we can now investigate the interesting and important question of whether there are any spillover effects from the technological web to the market pump. Does an actor's status in the technological domain increase the extent to which consumers have a higher estimation of the quality of the focal inventor's products and, if so, does it increase the flow of payments from consumers?

The most stringent test of such a spillover effect would require a mapping between the inventions in the technological domain and the products in the market domain. However, such a mapping—especially on the scale of an entire industry—would require a level of industry knowledge beyond that not only of an investigating sociologist but of practically any industry participant,

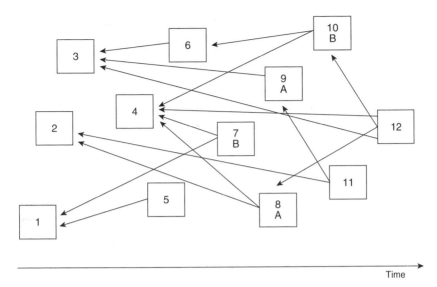

FIGURE 6.5. Hypothetical technological network focusing on the inventions of two organizations

since no individual would have a sufficiently omniscient vantage point to accurately draw all connections.

A somewhat less stringent but still informative test would involve shifting the level of analysis from that of patent niches to firm niches. That is, one can conceptualize each firm as having a niche in the technological web defined by the pattern of ties linking its inventions to the inventions of others in the technological domain. Figure 6.5 illustrates the basic idea. It represents the inventions of two organizations, A and B. Organization A has two inventions. Its position is defined by the ties of these to inventions 2, 3, and 4 and by the ties from inventions 11 and 12. Organization B's position is defined by its two inventions' ties to inventions 1, 4, and 6 and its tie from 12.

Given such a conception of a firm-level niche, one can then investigate the extent to which the payments flowing to a focal firm from the consumer side of the market are affected by its status in the technological domain. At first, it may seem that the implications of status in the technological domain for consumer payments could either be zero (if consumers do not pay attention to status dynamics in the technological domain) or positive (if consumers do pay attention). However, an actor's status arises out of imitative deference relations, and in the technological domain such deference relations have a twofold significance. On the one hand, as noted above, if the technological community is uncertain about which nodes of the evolving network deserve attention and resources, then a direct deference tie from firm *j* to firm *i* signals that *j* considers the work of i as worthy of such attention. It shows that j regards the activity already undertaken by i as a better foundation for continued invention than some set of alternatives. By building observably on another organization's invention, an organization confers a certain legitimacy or status on the innovative activity of the pioneer. If these conferrals of legitimacy and status get noticed by the relevant actors, then a direct tie from j to i improves i's fortunes. Receiving deference eases the problem of mobilizing resources to build, to sustain, and to expand organizations. Flows of deference signal controllers of resources that an organization deserves support. Earlier in this chapter we considered IBM's entry into the personal computer market as an act having this deferential significance. The entry was a signal not just to potential consumers but to software and hardware developers that this invention was one that deserved attention and resource allocation (Anderson 1995). However, at the same time that an imitative act of deference confers status, the imitative act also has the possibility of increasing competition because imitation implies greater similarity between the imitator and imitated. Insofar as an act of deference implies an increase in competition, status—the accumulated acts of deference—could potentially imply a negative flow of payments from consumers to producer. The signaling benefits of status could be counterbalanced by the implicit competition engendered by the acts of deference that give rise to status.

To be clear, not all forms of deference have both competitive and status-enhancing implications. The act of deference implied by subordination in the investment banking tombstone does not have competitive implications because of an implicit increase in similarity. However, acts of deference that imply imitation generally do have competitive implications, and accordingly, *when considered in isolation*, a direct deference tie from one actor to another has an indeterminate effect on the flow of payments to the deferred-to actor.

In order to analytically extract ourselves from this indeterminacy, it is necessary that we not consider the significance of an act of deference in isolation. Rather, we need to consider its significance in the context of a key feature of a firm's niche—the crowding of that niche. Just as crowding can be manifest at the level of the patent niche, so crowding can be manifest at the level of the firm niche. Specifically, if an organization occupies a position having few potential competitors with similar technological antecedents, then it has a more novel technology than an organization in a niche crowded with organizations with similar technical antecedents. In effect, as I have argued in earlier chapters, when there is high uncertainty about underlying quality, status is of the greatest benefit, and one would expect the greatest uncertainty when a firm finds itself in a relatively uncrowded region of the technological web, building on inventions that no other firm is building on. Conversely, the more common and redundant the organization's technology, the less a direct tie from another organization can positively affect the perceptions of that technology.

Acts of deference would therefore seem to have their most potent competitive implications in the most crowded portions of the technical space. To the extent that the firm is building on inventions on which others are also building, there is necessarily less uncertainty about the quality of its inventions and less of a signaling impact. Moreover, because the firm is building on the same inventions that others are building on, the competitive implication of the accumulated acts of deference will be most severe.

So if consumers are attending to acts of deference in the technological domain, the effect of status should depend fundamentally on the degree to which a focal firm finds itself building on well-established technological antecedents on which others are building. Formally, it is possible to capture this concept of common technological antecedents with the idea of niche overlap, a readily available analytical construct in the ecological literature (Hannan and Freeman 1989).

Niche overlap between two organizations in a technological network can be regarded as a function of the degree of common dependence on prior inventions as foundations for their research activity. Figure 6.6 presents an example in the form of a Venn diagram. Organization i's activity draws on 50 inventions in the technological network; organization j's activity builds on 100 inventions in this network; 25 inventions serve as antecedents for the innovative activity of both organizations. *Niche overlap*, denoted by α_{ij}, is the proportion of i's niche simultaneously occupied by j. In this example, $\alpha_{ij} = .5$ and $\alpha_{ji} = .25$. Note that overlaps are bounded by zero and one, and they are not necessarily symmetric.

This understanding of niche overlap as similarity in patterns of ties has strong parallels in the ecological and network literatures. Hannan and Freeman (1989) define niche overlap as similarity in profiles of dependence on resources. Burt (1992) uses the network idea of structural equivalence in exchange relations to define the competitive intensity between actors. In a work that bridges network and ecological traditions, McPherson (1983) defines niche overlap in terms of a common distribution of members across several sociodemographic characteristics. He argues that the competition between two voluntary organizations for members is directly proportional to the similarity of their memberships on sociodemographic characteristics.

The central contention from niche theory is that the greater the asymmetric niche overlap (α_{ij}), the stronger the competitive effect of organization j on organization i at time t. A like pattern of technological antecedents implies a similarity—or even redundancy—in technological competencies. The greater the overlap in technological competencies, the more that j's pursuit of its market possibilities affects the ability of organization i to pursue its opportunities.

When a focal firm's niche overlap with its competitors is considered in the aggregate, this conception of niche overlap implies that an organization's market

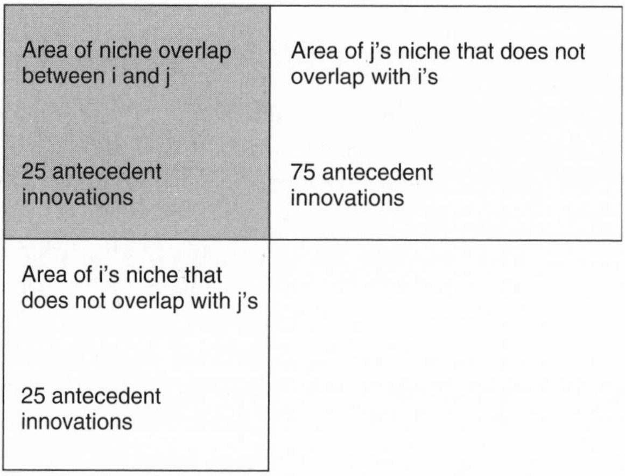

Area of niche overlap between i and j 25 antecedent innovations	Area of j's niche that does not overlap with i's 75 antecedent innovations
Area of i's niche that does not overlap with j's 25 antecedent innovations	

FIGURE 6.6. Niche overlap of two organizations

opportunities are inversely proportional to the extent of its overlaps with all other organizations in the population. In effect, at the firm level, *crowding* around an organization i's niche at time t can be understood as the sum of its niche overlaps:

$$\sum_{j=1}^{n} \alpha_{ijt, i \neq j},$$ [6.2]

where there are n organizations in the population at time t. Thus, crowding in the technological domain implies a reduction in the flow of payments from consumers to producers.

Even more important for our purposes, crowding should mediate the implications of technological status on the flow of payments from consumers. If consumers indeed attend to the imitative acts of deference, status in the technological domain should positively affect the flow of payments if a firm is in an uncrowded niche (since the signaling benefit of status is greatest in the uncrowded niche) and should negatively affect the flow of payments if the firm is in a crowded niche (since the competitive effect of imitation is layered on top of the high level of competition in the form of common citations). In effect, in a crowded field, quality is clearer, both because of the competition and because of the legitimacy indicated by the fact that the field is crowded. In less crowded fields, there is less understanding of quality, thus making the producer's status relatively more important.

To test for these effects, one can use a growth model, the type of model employed in chapter 4 for the purpose of studying the growth and decline of status

in the investment banking industry. Specifically, we can model growth in organizational sales as a function of niche overlap and status in the technological domain. Formally, the model can be specified as follows:

$$ln\left(\frac{S_{i,t+1}}{S_{it}}\right) = B_1(status) + B_2(crowding)$$

$$+ B_3(status \times crowding) + \sum_{k=4}^{K} B_k X_k,$$

[6.3]

where there are $K - 3$ control variables, and B_1, B_2, and B_3 denote the coefficients of central analytical interest. The above theoretical discussion implies
that $B_1 > 0$, $B_2 < 0$, and $B_3 < 0$.

The analysis employs the same data as the previous one. Data on firm sales
between 1981 and 1991 come from Dataquest. There were 113 firms for which
Dataquest provided sales data. Data on the firms' niches in technological space
once again come from patents.

In trying to measure the niche overlap among firms that is relevant to market
sales, an important issue is deciding on an appropriate time window for a firm's
patent portfolio. Over time, the value of most patents will tend to obsolesce as
new inventions replace old ones. Accordingly, the niche overlap that two firms
would derive from ten-year-old patents would have fewer implications for market sales than the niche overlap that the two firms would derive from patents
one or two years old. One can try to figure out some linear or curvilinear decay
function to reflect the different consequences of overlap from new and old
patents. Alternatively, one can draw a sharp cutoff at a particular number of
years—say three or five—and exclude all patents issued prior to that window
from the calculation of niche overlap scores. Such a sharp cutoff is also a decay
function; however, it is a step function rather than a smooth linear or curvilinear
decay. Absent any guidance for such a smooth curve, it seems appropriate to use
the information on product life cycle to set a sharp cutoff. As discussed above,
product life cycles in the industry are on the order of three to five years; so five
years seemed an appropriate window length. Operationally this is tantamount to
saying that an organization's current technology in year t includes all its patents
issued within a five-year window ending in the year t. Given this five-year window to define current technology, niche overlaps are based on the technological
antecedents of the patents within this window. In other words, α_{ij} represents the
overlap in citations from organization i's patents issued for the five-year window
ending in year t and organization j's patents issued over the same years.

There are two ways in which status is measured for this particular analysis. One measure, which will be labeled the unweighted measure of status, is
essentially the same as in the previous analysis. That is, it is the proportion of

all citations that are in fact citations to the focal firm.[15] In addition, because we are focusing on the largest 113 firms, it is possible to apply Bonacich's $c(\alpha,\beta)$ measure to the matrix of deference relations between firms. As noted above, Bonacich's measure can be applied only to a fully connected population of firms, and the deference relations among the top 113 firms are sufficiently dense that they do constitute a fully connected population. This second status measure will be labeled the weighted measure of status since Bonacich's measure effectively weights each act of deference by the status of the deferrer. As was the case in the investment banking study, the measure is standardized so that a value of 1 is average.

In addition to the measures for niche overlap and status, several covariates are also included. The first is simply the *total number of patents in an organization's portfolio over the five-year time window*. Patents indicate underlying technical competencies; they also have value as resources that can affect a firm's pursuit of market opportunities. So that this measure parallels the proportional measure of direct citations, it is standardized by dividing the focal organization's number of patents over the period by the total number of patents issued to all the organizations in the sample over the same period.

A second covariate of analytical interest concerns a weighted measure of the sales of a firm's technological competitors. The sales of competitors is operationalized as follows:

$$\sum_{j=1}^{n} \alpha_{ijt} S_{jt,i \neq j},$$

[6.4]

where α_{ijt} is the measure of niche overlap discussed above and S_{jt} denotes firm j's sales in year t. The measure thus represents a weighted average of the sales of a firm's set of technological competitors, with the sales of each competitor weighted proportionally to its niche overlap with the focal firm. The more that j falls in i's niche, the more that j's sales are assumed to be targeted toward the same customers. For example, if 50 percent of the patents that j cites are also cited by i, then we assume that 50 percent of j's sales are directed toward the same markets as i's sales. This weighting is obviously premised on the assumption that all of a firm's patents contribute equally to its sales. Although this assumption is not likely to be accurate in many cases, it nonetheless seems the most plausible assumption that can be made in the absence of complete data on the link between patents and sales. By comparing the effect of total sales of technological competitors with that of crowding, one can evaluate the

---

[15] The only difference between this measure and the previous one is that the window is expanded to five years to ensure consistency with the window for niche overlap. It seems hard to justify using different-length windows for different independent variables, and because a five-year window seems appropriate for niche overlap, it is being used for the measure of status.

extent to which growth rates depend more on the technological encroachment or the sales of competitors.

In addition to these control variables, indicator (i.e., "dummy") variables are included for each year and each firm. The indicator variables for each year capture any annual fluctuations in demand for semiconductors. More generally, they control for temporal autocorrelation.

The indicator variables for firms remove all between-organization variance from the analysis and thereby control for any time-invariant unobserved heterogeneity among organizations. Thus, the fixed-effect specification constrains the coefficients to be *within-organization* effects. For example, a negative effect for competitive intensity would indicate that an increase in the intensity of competition for a focal organization is associated with reductions in its growth rates. When between-organization variance is not eliminated, one needs to be much more cautious about making within-organization inferences. The apparent effects of changes might reflect enduring differences among organizations rather than changes experienced by the organizations over the analyzed period. For example, in the growth model in chapter 3, one needs to worry that there is some unobserved heterogeneity across investment banks that is driving the effect of partner status on a bank's growth in status. However, because there were only two time points at which status was measured, there were not sufficient degrees of freedom to include a dummy variable for each firm. Because the analysis in this chapter relies on annual data over a ten-year period, it is possible to do so here.

Table 6.5 presents descriptive information on the variables in the analysis. Since the analysis focuses only on within-firm variance, the table reports the bivariate within-firm correlations. Table 6.6 presents the results for the growth model using OLS. Because of some concerns about collinearity that I shall discuss subsequently as well as the two alternative measures of status, the reported results represent a set of parallel analyses. The first column includes the main effects of crowding and weighted status and an interaction effect of the two. The second column is identical to the first except that the interaction term is expressed as a product of mean-deviated values of crowding and status. The third column replaces the weighted measure of status with the unweighted measure. The fourth column replaces crowding around the technological niche with the measure of sales of technological competitors.

The first column in table 6.6 reports estimates of the main effects of crowding and (weighted) status and the interaction between them. The main effect of crowding is negative and statistically significant. The main effect of status is positive and statistically significant. The interaction effect of crowding and status is negative and significant. Thus, according to column 1, the effect of status in the technological domain is most positive when a firm's niche is least crowded, and the effect declines as the niche becomes more crowded.

TABLE 6.5
Correlations and Standard Deviations Based on Within-Firm Variation

Variables	S.D.	1	2	3	4	5	6
1. Ln(sales)	.34	1.00	.22	.22	.30	.24	−.07
2. Patents	.002		1.00	.04	.26	.50	−.03
3. Crowding	.48			1.00	.13	.10	.04
4. Weighted status	.14				1.00	.84	−.01
5. Unweighted status	.002					1.00	−.03
6. Sales of technology competitors	4.26						1.00

One methodological concern that arises is that the correlation between status and the interaction effect in column 1 is extremely high (.97). There are several ways in which this multicollinearity can be addressed. First, following Belsley, Kuh, and Welsch (1980), it is possible to calculate a set of collinearity diagnostics to examine the degree to which the estimates might be influenced by collinear relations among the independent variables. Though there are no rigid guidelines for rejecting a null hypothesis of no multicollinearity, the diagnostics revealed that the collinearity was well within conventionally accepted levels.[16] Second, one can apply various root transformations to the proportion of direct citations to reduce the correlation between status and the interaction term. The results are not reported here, but it can be noted that the results were robust across multiple alternative specifications. Third, one conventional practice for reducing the correlation between a main effect and an interaction term is to mean-deviate the variables included in the interaction. That is, one subtracts the mean value of each variable from the variable itself. So, in this case, the interaction term becomes (*crowding* − mean(*crowding*)) × (*status* − mean(*status*)). This mean deviation reduces the correlation between weighted status and the interaction to .30. The results using the interaction term comprising mean-deviated values of weighted status and crowding are reported in the second column. The effects again agree with the hypotheses. Notably, it might appear that the effect of status drops precipitously in this specification: the main effect of weighted status drops from 0.69 to 0.17 while the estimate of the interaction effect

[16] Belsley, Kuh, and Welsch's approach first scales $\mathbf{X'X}$ through singular value decomposition and then computes the eigenvalues and eigenvectors associated with this matrix. A "condition index" for the kth eigenvalue is computed, which equals the square root of the ratio of the largest eigenvalue to the kth one. If the condition index is very large, this indicates that there is a principal component of the scaled $\mathbf{X'X}$ matrix that adds little or no new information to the matrix. While there is no value that is definitively regarded as very large, Belsley, Kuh, and Welsch (1980: 105) state that "moderate to strong relations are associated with condition indices of 30 to 100." In the analysis reported in column 1, the largest condition index is 11.69, considerably below this range.

TABLE 6.6
OLS Estimates of Fixed-Effect Growth Models for Semiconductor Firms, 1985–1991

Variables	Models			
	1	*2*	*3*	*4*
Log(lagged sales)	−.35*	−.35*	−.35*	−.34*
	(.03)	(.03)	(.03)	(.03)
Crowding	−.032†	−.132*	−.036*	
	(.018)	(.043)	(.019)	
Weighted status	.69*	.17†		.02
	(.29)	(.09)		(.07)
Crowding × weighted status	−21*			
	(.09)			
[Crowding − mean(crowding)] ×		−.21*		
[W. status − mean(w. status)]		(.09)		
Unweighted status			24.65†	
			(12.69)	
Crowding × unweighted status			−6.59†	
			(3.58)	
Sales of competitors				−.008
				(.006)
Unweighted status ×				−.0001
sales of competitors				(.0010)
Firm's total patents	−.65	−.65	−1.61	3.17
	(3.79)	(3.80)	(4.35)	(3.46)
1987	.01	.01	.01	.02
	(.03)	(.03)	(.03)	(.03)
1988	.10*	.10*	.10*	.11*
	(.03)	(.03)	(.03)	(.03)
1989	−.01	−.01	−.01	−.02
	(.03)	(.03)	(.03)	(.04)
1990	.05	.05	.06	.08
	(.04)	(.04)	(.04)	(.05)
1991	.08†	.08†	.08†	−.02
	(.04)	(.04)	(.04)	(.05)
R^2 (within-firm variations)	.68	.68	.67	.67

$N = 431$. Numbers in parentheses are standard errors.
†$p < .10$; *$p < .05$

remains unchanged. However, one needs to account for the effect of the mean in interpreting the magnitude of the status coefficient. In column 1, the effect of status is $0.69 - .21 \times crowding$; in column 2 it is $0.17 - 0.21 \times (crowding - mean(crowding))$. The mean of *crowding* in the complete data set is 2.53. Thus the effect of status in this alternative formulation is on average equal to

$0.17 - 0.21 \times (crowding - 2.53) = 0.70 - 0.21 \times crowding$, nearly identical to the result in column 1. Fourth and finally, it is possible to use unweighted status as the measure of status. Although this is a less interesting measure of status and less consistent with the measure of status employed in the examination of the investment banking and wine industries, it has the advantage that the correlation of the interaction effect with status is lower than is the case for the weighted measure (.89 vs. .97). The results for the unweighted measure of status appear in the third column. As should be clear upon inspection, results in this column agree with the results in the first two columns.

Column 4 replaces competitive crowding defined in terms of technological overlaps with the sales of technological competitors. The effect of technological competitors' sales is not statistically significant. The fact that crowding exerts a stronger effect indicates that growth/decline is affected more by the technological encroachment of competitors than by the ability of those same competitors to increase their sales in the market. Given that the market for semiconductors grows throughout the period of the sample, this result should not be surprising. Under rapid market expansion, it is less likely that an organization's ability to grow is sharply delimited by the growth of its competitors. Rather, an organization's growth is determined by its ability to stake technological claims that will give it a share of the expanding market. It seems reasonable to expect that as the market for semiconductors becomes saturated, then the sales of technological competitors might have a stronger effect on growth rates.[17]

Taken together, the results in table 6.6 indicate that an organization's status in the technological domain does affect the flow of payments from consumers and this effect declines with increased crowding in the firm's technological niche. How strong are these effects? Given the presence of an interaction effect, it is most straightforward to address this question by comparing the implications of the results for various combinations of status and crowding. It seems informative to examine the effects at the first and third quartiles of the distributions of status and crowding since the first-quartile levels indicate representative "low" values and the third-quartile levels reflect representative "high" values. By comparing cases that are low on both crowding and status, those that are high on both, and those that are high on one and low on the other, we can get a better appreciation of how the status effect varies with the level of crowding. According to the growth model, the growth rate is a linear combination of the combined effects of status and crowding and the effects of the other covariates (lagged size, period effects, and other covariates). It is possible to conceptualize the latter

---

[17] In an analysis not reported here, the effects of technological crowding and sales crowding are included in the same model. When both effects are included, the effect of technological crowding is just beyond conventional levels of significance, and the effect of sales crowding is not significant.

TABLE 6.7
Combined Effect of Crowding and Weighted Status on Growth Rates

Row	Status	Crowding	Joint Effect	Net Effect of Status
1	low = .015	low = 2.10	−.096	
2	high = .453	low = 2.10	.180	row 2 − row 1 = .243
3	low = .015	high = 3.02	−.096	
4	high = .453	high = 3.02	−.071	row 4 − row 3 = .025

The "low" and "high" values of status and crowding were chosen to equal the first and third quartiles of the firm-year distributions. The calculations use the parameter estimates from col. 1 of table 6.6.

effects as comprising the baseline rate. The joint effect of crowding and status inflates or deflates the baseline rate.

Table 6.7 reports the joint effect of status and crowding implied by the estimates in the first column of table 6.6. Overall we see that the increment to the growth rate is positive only for the combination of high status and low crowding. The implied growth rate is smallest for the reverse case: low status and high crowding. From the perspective of our argument, the most interesting comparisons are those that compare the effect of status across levels of crowding (the last column of table 6.7). Consider the multipliers for firms in niches with low crowding (the first two rows of table 6.7). In this condition, high-status firms have a joint effect that exceeds that of low-status firms by 0.243. Next consider the case of niches with high crowding (the third and fourth rows of table 6.7). Here the returns to status are lower: 0.025. That is, the returns to status are only a tenth as large as in the less crowded niches.

The distributions of organizations in terms of the status and crowding of their niches suggests an interesting classification of roles in the technological development of the industry. Figure 6.7 depicts the organizations in our sample on the status and crowding dimensions. Weighted status is plotted on a logarithmic scale so that the distances between the lower-status organizations can be detected.[18] Locations in the figure correspond with particular types of roles. Organizations located toward the upper left corner can be considered brokers of new technologies. They build on technological antecedents that have been unexploited by their competitors, and they provide a distinctive foundation for the innovative activities of other organizations. Analog Devices occupied such a position in 1986. In direct contrast, organizations situated near the bottom right corner of the space are engaging in innovative activity in

[18] Because it is not possible to plot a zero point on a log axis, we replace all zero values for status with a value of 0.00001 for the purpose of plotting. In the analysis, however, the values remain zero. This figure excludes three outlying points in the lower right-hand corner that lie between 6 and 7 in competitive intensity and fall at zero on the status dimension.

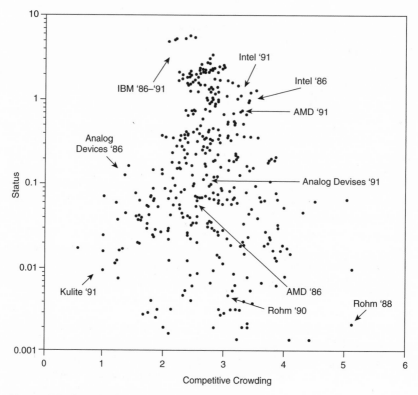

FIGURE 6.7. Organizational positions in role typology

congested regions of the technological space and are not contributing to the innovative activities of others. Rohm occupied such a role in 1990. Organizations positioned toward the upper right quadrant are leaders in well-established technologies. Intel occupied this role for nearly the entire period of the study. Finally, organizations in the lower left quadrant are, in effect, isolates, developers of technologies that are not endorsed by other organizations. Kulite Semiconductor Products in 1991 is one example of an organization in this region of the role typology.

While some firms, such as Intel and IBM, occupied a relatively consistent role throughout the entire period of our study, others shifted. The role of Advanced Micro Devices (AMD) changed rather dramatically over the period. In 1986 AMD occupied an intermediate role; it had moderate status and was exposed to moderate crowding. But, by 1991, it had moved close to Intel as a leader in a well-established technology.

This figure thus provides at least one way of characterizing a firm's location in the technological web. In so doing, it returns us to the observation with which this chapter began. Alongside the status ordering of firms pumping out services to consumers, there exists a web of inventive active that over time has an evolutionary impact on the constituent elements of that quality for which market status is in fact a signal. This technological domain has its own internal status ordering grounded in deference relations that arise as a natural by-product of a collection of firms and organizations building on one another's inventive activity. We have observed that status shapes perceptions of invention quality and, in so doing, shapes the way in which the technological web unfolds. We have also observed that this signaling effect of status in the technological domain spills over to affect payments from consumers in the market.

As the dispersion of consumer payments across firms in the market will induce differences in the ability of firms to affect the evolving technological web, the status orderings in the technological and market domains are interdependent, with each ordering influencing the other. Importantly, there are multiple mechanisms by which the resources generated by market status can enhance a firm's ability to occupy central nodes within the unfolding technological web. This study of the semiconductor industry has emphasized the extent to which status generates superior rents for research and development and, even more important, engenders an expectational dynamic in which the bets of higher-status firms attract more energy and resources from the industry as a whole and thereby yield a self-fulfilling prophecy. However, different industries may lend themselves to other mechanisms. In a study of Formula 1 racing, Fabrizio Castellucci and I (Castellucci and Podolny 2003) show that higher-status teams are able to derive greater benefit from their relationships with engine suppliers who are constantly trying to devise technological improvements to the engines; because the engine suppliers derive greater benefit from being associated with high-status teams, these suppliers will devote additional resources to their exchange relationships with the high-status teams, thereby ensuring that the high-status teams are the first to benefit from any new inventions. Future research may reveal additional mechanisms by which market status spills over into the technological domain.

Of course, as noted at the outset of this chapter, the relevance of the technological domain will vary across market contexts. In market contexts such as fashion design or investment banking, dynamics in the technological domain are likely to have less significant spillover effects between the technological and market spheres. Even while one firm may become a pioneer in the use of a particular technology, as when a particular investment bank pioneers the use of the Internet in providing services to its clients, technological inventions available to one are likely to be available to many others, and other important constituent elements of quality will exist that do not have a strong technological component.

Nevertheless, even if the technological domain will not be of equal importance in all market domains, there are clearly some contexts, such as semiconductors or biotechnology, in which a firm's position in the web of inventive activity will be one of the central determinants—if not the central determinant—of its status and success in the market. In the next chapter, we consider another instance of status distinctions in one domain spilling over and affecting on the market. Specifically, we look at how status distinctions in the social sphere can spill over to impact on the competitive dynamics in the market.

Chapter Seven

EMBEDDEDNESS AND ENTRY

THE PREVIOUS CHAPTER provided evidence as to how status in one domain—the technological arena—can spill over and affect market outcomes; this chapter focuses on how status distinctions in the social domain can have a similar spillover effect. Insofar as this chapter highlights the relevance of status distinctions in the social arena to market outcomes, it necessarily connects to the sociological literature on embeddedness. This term, which Mark Granovetter bequeathed to the field of economic sociology in a 1985 *American Journal of Sociology* article, is probably the most frequently utilized term to emerge out of economic sociology in the past twenty or thirty years. At the time of this writing, the article had amassed roughly 1,500 citations in the *Social Science Citation Index*. Granovetter introduced the term as a way to carve out a sociological perspective on economic institutions for the production, exchange, and distribution of goods and services. Granovtter sought a middle ground between oversocialized conceptions of economic institutions, which posited that their central features were programmed by the dominant cultural values in society, and undersocialized conceptions, which posited that economic institutions could be understood as the product of atomized individuals acting on their own preferences. Granovetter's middle ground is a conception of economic actors whose opportunities, constraints, and therefore actions are influenced by the network of relations that those actors do (and implicitly do not) have. Over time, the term embeddedness has been adopted by others to refer to a diffuse array of contextual effects on action, leading some scholars to try to clarify different types of embeddedness (DiMaggio and Zukin 1990).

However, at least when Granovetter first elaborated the term, he seemed to imply something very specific: there exist social systems operating alongside and interdependently with markets, and these social systems imply networks of relations and identities that induce economic action that is distinct from that in which hypothetical oversocialized or undersocialized actors would engage.

Sometimes these social systems imply dyadic obligations that lead actors to market action that simply cannot be understood apart from a consideration of the social context. So, in a 1997 study of the New York garment industry, Brian Uzzi recounts the case of a manufacturer that was relocating its production facilities to Asia and would therefore no longer need its New York contractors. The manufacturer had a strong reason to keep this information secret; once its contractors in New York found out about the impending move, they could start to lower the quality of their work since there would no longer be any promise of future business as an incentive to keep the work above a certain quality threshold. However, a number of the supplier relationships were embedded in long-term social relations, and the manufacturer felt an obligation to inform those suppliers so that they could start developing exchange relations with new manufacturers. Because these suppliers felt a similar obligation to the manufacturer, they did not lower their quality. Notably, the manufacturer did not inform its other suppliers, those with which it had no long-term social relation underlying the economic exchange.

Sometimes the social systems alongside the market imply more than dyadic obligations; rather, they imply systemic motivations and logics of behavior that can spill over and shape actions in the market. The classic illustration of such a spillover is Weber's *Protestant Ethic and the Spirit of Capitalism.* Weber argued that the Calvinist doctrine of predestination resulted in an intense desire of an individual to know if he or she was one of the "elect" who would go to heaven. Although a follower of the Calvinist doctrine did not believe that his actions could influence a choice that an omniscient God had made some time ago, an individual's achievements in this lifetime were taken to be a sign of God's favor and accordingly of the likelihood that the individual was indeed one of the elect. As a result, the desire to know about their fate provided them with the motivation to engage in a restless, ascetic accumulation of wealth, continually reinvesting rather than consuming their profits.

In a study of what they label as industry peer networks (IPNs), Zuckerman and Sgourev (2003) offer another example of how motivations grounded in a social system outside the boundaries of the market can spill over and affect market behavior. IPNs are associations in which members are all from the same industry but do not actively compete with one another, because they all operate in different geographic markets. Accordingly, while these network associations are centered on work-related information, the pattern of ties implied by these associations is by definition beyond the boundaries of any particular market in which a member might compete. IPNs are characterized by strong friendship bonds and considerable knowledge transfer between members. To facilitate this knowledge transfer, the IPNs provide considerable information for internal benchmarking activity.

Interestingly, members of these IPNs comment that this benchmarking has motivational significance; in interviews, members of IPNs report that their concern about their position in the pecking order within the IPN causes them to work harder than they otherwise would. There are good reasons to be skeptical about self-reports regarding the source of motivation, but Zuckerman and Sourev collect systematic survey data from those who do and those who do not belong to IPNs, and these additional data are consistent with the motivational significance that IPN members ascribe to the benchmarking. Thus, in ways that are reminiscent of Weber's account of the Calvinists, market competition by itself does not generate sufficient motivation to engage in long-run profit-maximizing behavior. The IPN members implicitly acknowledge that they would be satisfied with lower levels of economic performance in the market if they did not participate in the IPN. So, again, we observe an instance in which motivations in a social system outside the bounds of the market spill over and alter behavior within the market.

Finally, in a study of emerging patterns of exchange in Renaissance Italy, Padgett and McLean (forthcoming) argue that logics of social exchange in the social and political spheres can become the basis for logics of market exchange. They find that the pattern of economic partnerships borrowed a cross-neighborhood, within-class logic from the pattern of marriage relations, whereas commercial credit relations adopted the same-neighborhood, cross-class logic of clientage relations.

Thus, just as the previous chapter posited the existence of an evolving technological network alongside and affecting exchanges within the markets, so the embeddedness perspective implies the existence of an evolving social network alongside and affecting the market. Moreover, just as the previous chapter emphasized an interdependence and at least loose correspondence between identities in the market and identities in a well-defined technological domain, so the embeddedness perspective emphasizes an interdependence and loose correspondence between market identities and well-defined identities in the social domain.

Following in this broad line of work, this chapter provides a unique illustration of this interdependence between social and market identities by showing how the social status of a firm's leading figure can serve as a signal on which that firm's competitors rely. The chapter provides evidence that, at least in certain markets, industry incumbents will look to the social status of those leading a newly entered firm as a signal of whether that firm will behave in a responsible or cooperative manner (here, "cooperative manner" refers to the potential entrant's willingness to participate in explicit or tacit agreements regarding pricing or production volumes).

This particular line of inquiry has its motivation and point of departure in the long-standing observation, going back to Adam Smith in *Wealth of Nations*, that competitors can benefit from explicit or tacit collusion. While the topic of collusion among competitors is a central one in Industrial Organizations (IO) economics, it has also received attention from organizational scholars and sociologists (Pfeffer and Salancik 1978; Baker and Faulkner 1993). Sometimes this cooperation among the producers in a market is explicit, involving active communication among an organized group of competitors typically referred to as a cartel. OPEC is probably the best-known example of a cartel today. Sometimes such cooperation is tacit, whereby competitors are allowed to make public announcements of their intended pricing decisions but are prohibited by law from actively engaging one another in a coordinated attempt to regulate prices or production volumes. Notably, although explicit communication makes cooperation easier, cooperation is by no means assured. Over the years, there have been many times when OPEC members have been unable to agree on prices and production volumes, leading the price of oil to fall.

Accordingly, if incumbents in an industry are generally able to behave cooperatively, a new entrant is a source of concern. If the new entrant decides it would rather expand market share than participate in the collusive agreement, it could upset the cooperative equilibrium. Even if the new entrant has no intention of expanding market share, the cooperative equilibrium could be destabilized if any of the incumbents believe that the new entrant might try to do so. Fearing that the new entrant will be uncooperative, an incumbent may seek to "beat the entrant to the punch," lowering prices to preserve market share that the incumbent fears the new entrant will take, and once one incumbent lowers prices, the rest of those in the industry will feel pressure to do the same.

The central proposition of this chapter is that *the social status of the leading figure of a new firm in a market can serve as a tangible basis for incumbents' calculations of the likelihood that they will be able to arrive at an agreement with the entrant regarding what restraints on competitive behavior are normatively appropriate and/or in their common interest.* The lower the entrant's social status, the more that the incumbents will doubt the possibility of reaching such a common understanding and the more that they will try to drive the entrant from the market through what is known as predatory pricing. By way of providing support for this proposition, I will first review economic work on predatory pricing and sociological work on business groups. Following the review of this literature, I will then provide an empirical test of this proposition in an analysis of the predatory pricing of three British shipping cartels, which collectively span the years 1879 to 1929.

THE ECONOMIC LITERATURE ON PREDATORY PRICING

Predatory pricing is the practice of charging extremely low prices in the short term in the hopes of being able to raise prices in the long term once a particular firm or set of firms are excluded from the market. Perhaps in part due to limited empirical evidence, predatory pricing has been a topic of lively debate among legal experts and economists. On the one hand, a number of scholars (e.g., Bork 1978; McGee 1980) are extremely skeptical that profitable predation could exist. A predation strategy is profitable only when high prices can be maintained after the exit of the victim. These scholars believe strongly that competition will limit postexit excess profits. If so, it would never be rational for an incumbent or set of incumbents to lose money to drive out the entrant.

A number of economists have developed formal models that specify conditions under which it would be rational for incumbent firms to prey on an entrant. Ordover and Saloner (1989) identify three broad classes of motivations for predation: reputation, long purse, and signaling. Reputation models (e.g., Milgrom and Roberts 1982) are explicitly dynamic and allow an incumbent to create a reputation for aggressive behavior that effectively deters further entry. The long purse explanation for predation is quite old but has been given new credibility by models such as those of Fudenberg and Tirole (1985) and Bolton and Scharfstein (1990) that draw on asymmetric information and agency to create a situation whereby firms can be driven out of the market for lack of capital. Finally, the incumbent may need to credibly signal market or firm-specific information such as low demand or low costs to the entrant, perhaps in order to merge with the entrant at a favorable price and thus control industry capacity (Saloner 1987).

Empirical research identifying instances of predatory pricing largely focuses on historical data; more modern evidence is rare owing to the prevalence of antitrust laws. Burns (1986) examines how prominent firms in the American tobacco industry engaged in predatory pricing at the opening of the twentieth century to reduce the cost of acquiring rivals. Genesove and Mullin (1997) calculate the marginal cost of the Sugar Trust in the same period very precisely and show that the dominant incumbent, a near monopolist, set prices below cost in an effort to either drive out or purchase aggressive entrants. Levin and Weiman (1994) produce similar evidence, showing that Southern Bell priced below cost in areas where it competed with rivals. Scott Morton (1997) shows that entrants with more resources face a lower likelihood that the cartel will respond to their entry with predation, suggesting that the most important strength of an entrant is financial resources. In a more modern example, Lerner (1995) documents that disk drive firms choose lower prices for products that neighbor the products of financially constrained firms and argues that this represents a type of long purse predation.

Economists have not paid much attention to how the social status or, more generally, the identity of a new entrant affects predatory pricing. While the term reputation is employed in economic models of predatory pricing, the concept of reputation in these models is further removed from the concept of status than is the concept of reputation employed in economic models of product quality and discussed in chapter 5. In economic models of predation, the term reputation refers to the perception of an actor—typically a firm—whose behavior proves that the actor is willing and able to engage in a price war.

SOCIAL STATUS AND PREDATION

While sociologists have not focused on predatory pricing per se, sociologists frequently examine more general processes of competition and conflict and, in doing so, have drawn attention to the significance of social identity as a determinant of causes of, consequences of, and bounds on that conflict.[1] In his work on business groups, Granovetter (1995) offers an initial theoretical foundation for the relevance of social status to the inclusion or exclusion of a firm from a market-based association of producers, such as a cartel. Granovetter emphasizes the importance of a "moral community" to the successful operation of a cartel. A business group such as a cartel constitutes a "moral community" to the extent that "trustworthy behavior can be expected, normative standards understood, and opportunism forgone." Drawing on several historical examples, Granovetter argues that the presence of a "renegade" individual who heads a business operation in the market but who is personally outside the moral community threatens the ability of a cartel to set terms of trade and establish pooling arrangements unilaterally.

There are several ways in which a renegade owner might constitute a threat to the viability of the cartel. First, the "renegade" might simply have different incentives for certain types of behavior, different information about the world and expectations about actions of commercial partners, or a different discount rate than other cartel members. Second, because the renegade is not part of the moral community, miscommunications may be more likely to arise, and these miscommunications could easily result in a lack of trust. Third, a renegade owner might constitute more of a threat because the renegade's position outside the moral community implies less ability to implement social sanctions against the renegade. If an entrant is part of the same social community as the incumbents, the incumbents have the option to sanction or reward the newcomer socially. This additional disciplinary instrument may help sustain collusion.

Granovetter's emphasis on moral community does not directly imply that social status will be the sole signal on which incumbents will rely to make inferences about an entrant's potential for contributing to the moral community. Rather, it implies that any basis of social homophily between the entrant and incumbents will increase the likelihood that incumbents will expect that the entrant can make a positive contribution to the moral community. For example, it also implies that common geography could be a signal on which incumbents would focus, and in the actual empirical analysis that follows, common geography is one of the variables incorporated into the analysis of the likelihood that the incumbents in a British shipping cartel will engage the entrant in a price war.

---

[1] Gould (1995); Olzak, Shanahan, and McEneany (1996). See also the references in chapter 2 to Elias and Scotson's ethnographic work on status dynamics within a community.

However, while Granovetter's emphasis on moral community does not imply that social status will be the sole signal to which incumbents will look, it does suggest the importance of social status when the major members of the business group are of high status. Indeed, across the diverse array of business groups from Asia, Europe, and the Americas that Granovetter (1995) references, it seems clear that the members of these groups are invariably of extremely high status. Similarly, the major incumbents in the British shipping cartels studied below are invariably of high status. Therefore, while Granovetter's discussion of business groups implies that status will be a signal only when the major incumbents are high-status, this qualification does not seem to be a particularly restrictive boundary condition, since the leaders of well-established corporations in an industry are likely to be high-status.

In a historical study of the British shipping industry using the analytical tools of network theory and information economics, Gordon Boyce (1995) presents evidence that the personal network of a shipowner and others' opinion of him were important to that person's business success:

> Early steam operators reduced the cost of devising contracts by operating within networks, or bands of individuals bound by interpersonal knowledge (knowledge gained through kinship, religious ties, or local presence). . . . Repeat contracting based on reciprocity generated trust and co-operation. Members co-operated in the hope of generating a stream of future contracts. Co-operation depended on each party taking a long-term view of their economic relationship. Over time, network participants acquired reputations for being dependable co-operators. Reputation was a form of implicit communication, it conveyed judgments about a person to other people who lacked first-hand knowledge of the subject. (p. 3)

Note that Boyce's use of the term reputation is much closer to the notion of status developed in this book than to the notion of reputation in predation models. If renegade producers outside the moral community undercut the possibility for mutually beneficial collusion, it follows that incumbents should seek to drive from the market—or not accept—those individuals whom they believe will fail to participate in the moral community. The people in the community described by Boyce cultivated productive contacts and, implicitly, while doing so excluded those who did not fit their criteria.

As will be discussed further below, shipping cartels were not easy to run. Cartel members had to meet as a group to make decisions; when the members disagreed, lengthy—and therefore costly—negotiations produced a compromise or a conflict. Unresolved conflicts took the form of expensive price wars. Since the future was highly uncertain and owners could not draw up a formal contract on every possible contingency, common information and incentives among incumbents as well as social ties and good communication were valuable in reducing the cost of future negotiations and promoting the successful functioning of the cartel.

While generally concerned with collectivities that span a number of markets and industrial sectors, the sociological literature on the social structure of the business elite provides additional support for this claim that social status and commonality of background facilitate cooperation among the heads of economic enterprises (Useem 1984; Domhoff 1967). In his work on the diffusion of hostile takeovers in the market for corporate control, Hirsch (1986) observes that the initial proponents of this acquisition strategy were low-status individuals from outside the corporate elite. Hirsch concludes that much of the initial opposition to the hostile acquisition strategy was due to the fact that this acquisition strategy allowed outsiders to acquire assets controlled by more established insiders without the consent of those insiders. More to the point, in an example that relates to the social bases for collusion within a market more than across markets, Glasberg (1981) describes how the larger banking community collectively acted to prevent the hostile takeover of a major bank by a low-status outsider.

The clear implication of this line of research is that conflict between a set of established firms and a potential challenger is a function of the social identity of the challenger. The lower the challenger's social status and the more the challenger's background differs from that of the incumbents, the more the established firms will seek to exclude the challenger from their domain. Predatory pricing is one means by which established firms may collectively pursue this path of exclusion. To the extent that social status signals a willingness and ability to uphold the "moral community" of the cartel, high social status of an entrant should lower the likelihood of a price war.

However, even though social status might affect entry via the signaling mechanism that has been emphasized throughout this book, there are other reasons that status might affect entry, and these other reasons might have little if anything to do with signaling. For example, members of a cartel might simply place value on associating with those who are high-status irrespective of the signaling value of status. Or, social status might imply some form of political capital, such as ties to Parliament, to which the cartel members would like to have access. Status might also give an owner influence with a merchant association, again providing a tie from which the conference might benefit.

Status might also imply kinship relations or bank relations that are indeed indicators of extended "deep pockets." As noted above, economic models have shown how the depth of an entrant's pockets affects the likelihood of a price war. Indeed, a common method of starting or growing a shipping line during this period was for the main owner/manager to sell shares in his ship(s) to his extended family and neighbors. Thus, equity holders of a line might be a couple of brothers, a brother-in-law, an uncle, a supplier, and a neighbor. The total financial strength of the line depended on all its owners as well as their relationships with the local bank. Boyce (1995) reports that "bank officials not only used financial data, they also relied on direct communication, personal references, and traditional indicators of substance, such as land, titles, and occupational links" (p. 229).

Yet, while there is undoubtedly a correlation between social status and wealth, the correlation is not perfect. As sociologists have long emphasized (Weber 1948), not all forms of wealth accumulation result in equally high social status, and even when wealth results in status, there is typically a long lag between the initial wealth accumulation and the attainment of high social status. Shipowners with high status were those who had had wealth long enough to develop connections, engage in philanthropy, become elected to Parliament, and so on. A successful individual might become rich over a few years, but that did not earn him high social status according to the standard of the times or our metric. However, his children would grow up in a different social circle, enjoy expensive schooling, marry into wealth, and would certainly have high social status. Later generations in a wealthy family would have a more lucrative personal network (siblings, in-laws, and neighbors) than a nouveau riche entrepreneur.

However, even if status is imperfectly correlated with the depth of an individual's pockets, it is obviously important to tease apart the signaling effect from either the status consumption effect or the deep pocket effect, just as it has been important to tease apart the signaling effect of status from effects of quality in previous analyses throughout this book. The empirical analysis below will include model specifications that will enable us to assess whether some considerable component of the status effect is due to the signaling mechanism.

BRITISH SHIPPING CARTELS

We now turn to the systematic empirical analysis, focusing on the behavior of British shipping cartels between 1879 and 1929. Beginning in the 1870s and continuing to the present day, rate schedules and shipping capacity for overseas freight on a number of trade routes were set by shipping conferences—associations (or cartels) of deep-sea merchant or passenger shipping lines. Each main trade route between regions (which might have branch routes and/or multiple ports at each end) had its own shipping conference organization, composed of anywhere from two to fifteen or more shipping lines that served the route.

The analysis covers three conference agreements over fifty years. Two of the three conferences governed trade routes from the United Kingdom to British colonies (South Africa and India). The third conference agreement covered trade from the United Kingdom to the Far East (Hong Kong, Japan, and the North China coast). These three conferences were chosen because they existed on important trade routes and were stable in the period before World War II.

Other conferences had less significant volumes of trade or fell apart completely at one or more points because of trade fluctuations or internal disputes. The wealth flowing to and from British colonies in this time period ensured that the firms, owners, and conditions on these routes were important. They were therefore written about in both scholarly works and the popular press, which makes systematic data gathering possible.

Most of the participants in these conference agreements were British. This high proportion of British members reflects not only the fact that the United Kingdom was an end point on each of the three routes; it is also reflective of the extent to which British shipping companies dominated shipping worldwide. British shipping companies carried over 50 percent of world trade and owned a similar percentage of world tonnage at the start of the sample period (Aldcroft 1968).

The shipping lines in our data could own one or multiple ships and operate on one or multiple routes. A line could therefore be a member of more than one conference. These conferences were completely legal entities that were not restricted in their actions during the time of the sample.[2] The members of the shipping conference would collectively determine cargo rates and sailing schedules to which each member line would adhere. Often the cartels would also allocate market shares of specific types of goods and determine the exact ports that would be served by each member line. To protect their monopoly over specific trade routes, the conferences would typically create switching costs that penalized merchants if they used an entrant line. This "deferred rebate" created a fairly effective barrier to entry, which was necessary because entry is attractive in a market where a cartel is successfully sustaining higher-than-competitive prices.[3]

Cheating by members of the cartel was not a significant problem for conferences. It was nearly impossible to expand capacity—that is, add ships to the predetermined sailing schedule—without being detected. Perhaps the most plausible way to cheat on a conference agreement would have been to offer a potential customer a lower rate than the agreement allowed in order to get the customer to switch from using one of the other conference lines. However, since such switching behavior on the part of the customer was easily observable, it was quite difficult to violate the pricing agreements without being detected. Additionally, the conference members often divided by type of good, port, or particular customer (functionally the same thing in many cases) so that competing for business was not an option. Moreover, most conferences

---

[2] They still exist and are legal, but now face some restrictions on behavior in some nations.

[3] The terms of the "deferred rebate" would usually be as follows: a customer would receive back a fixed percentage (usually 10%) of its total freight bill over a six-month period *if* the customer used only the services of conference members over the six-month period and over a further six- or nine-month waiting period. The purpose of the deferred rebate was to create a strong incentive for existing customers *not* to patronize a new entrant, even if it was offering low rates.

shared revenues in some way. Such pooling practices reduced the incentive to cheat in order to gain market share since the cheater could keep only a fraction of the profits from the additional cargo. Shipowners controlled competition with the contracts described above and others. Data on the complete web of contacts between lines are not available, but since the conference agreement was arguably the most important and overarching agreement, deviations from this agreement clearly indicate internal or external conflict.

These three shipping conferences were able to set prices well above cost and control shipments such that members were probably earning what would be considered abnormally high profits (for detailed evidence see Scott Morton 1997). A consequence of the high prices and rapid growth of the industry was that cartels would often find themselves confronted by new entrants who wished to benefit from the collective arrangement. Sometimes these entrants were encouraged or actively supported by local merchant organizations that wanted more competition and lower prices. Unless the cartel accommodated the new entrant by providing the entrant with a share of the trade route that the entrant considered appropriate, the entrant could seek to win market share by undercutting the prices charged by the cartel. When facing a new entrant, the cartel had two options. It could accommodate the new entrant, or it could pursue a price war by either preemptively or reactively cutting prices so low that the new entrant would decide that its continued presence in the market would be unprofitable.

While external shipping lines were a significant threat to cartel stability, internal disagreements among incumbents were equally important. Especially since status is supposed to be a signal of whether a newly admitted owner would provoke a disagreement, it is important to consider the nature of these internal disagreements in some detail. In a rapidly changing environment, the potential for conflict over rates and schedules was considerable. There was no simple, obvious way to set rates or to determine how the schedule could be "fairly" allocated across all member lines. Each type of good had a different rate that was often nonlinear in quantity, and each pair of ports had its own rate. Moreover, shipping lines were of different sizes and carried different sorts of goods from different regions of the country. At any given time, the demand for or supply of a particular product would be growing or declining. A source of supply might sprout in a colonial country or in another British port because of a new railroad connection. Alternatively, a newly discovered, cheaper source of supply might wipe out a profitable trading opportunity in a matter of a few years. Previous allocations made by product or port would seem unfair in light of market changes. Some lines would gain from a change while others would lose, and so negotiations would take place.

It is hard to overstate how difficult it was for these shipping lines to agree on the division of the market. Correspondence from the period, such as the letter in exhibit 7.1, illustrates how long and vigorously the member firms negotiated over each change. As a result, while these cartels would rarely fall apart

EXHIBIT 7.1
Letter illustrating contract negotiation within cartel

26 November 1936   Union-Castle Lines
With Mr. D. Storrar's Compliments

We understand that the proposal of the West Coast Lines for the participation of the Blue Star Line in a comprehensive rotation of sailings from Liverpool was that they should transfer six of their schedule dates to the Blue Star Line, the Clan Line giving up four and the Ellerman and Harrison Lines one each. The Clan Line describe this as 'a most inequitable sacrifice' on their part and suggest that 'the burden must be shared proportionately.' To achieve this object they propose that four sailings of the Union-Castle Line from the East Coast be transferred to the Houston Line from the East Coast. This proposal has been rejected by the Union-Castle Line and the Clan Line state that unless it is accepted the West Coast Lines cannot admit the Blue Star Line to a rotation of sailings from Liverpool.

As an alternative 'for discussion,' the Harrison Line suggest that the loss by the Clan Ellerman Harrison Lines of the six sailings from the West Coast should be borne in proportion to the number of sailings dispatched by the four 'groups' of interests as follows:

Union-Castle Group	2.504 sailings
Clan Group	1.654 sailings
Ellerman Group	1.008 sailings
Harrison Line	0.834 sailings

They then propose not that the Union-Castle Line should merely give up 2.5 sailings per annum but that they should hand these 2.5 sailings over to the Clan Group. By reducing their present scheduled sailings as proposed and taking six Blue Star vessels into the rotation, the West Coast Lines would be abandoning six sailings but not transferring them to any other Line. In abandoning these six sailings they would be reducing the number of Blue Star sailings by four and thus lessening the actual and potential competition of the Blue Star Line on the West Coast.

It would be something quite new to regulate Conference arrangements according to groups. Hitherto the Conference has always worked on the basis of the individual interests specified in the 1904 Agreement. It is suggested that because the Union-Castle 'Group' has no sailings from the West Coast it sacrifices nothing. In reality it suffers more than the other Lines because of the small cargo capacity of its passenger vessels, the additional 5/- per ton which shippers have to pay on cargo by the Mail vessels and the increasing trend of shipments to the West Coast ports, and it has also had to make sacrifices on the Continent (without compensation) to prevent trouble with the German and Dutch Lines. If there is to be a re-arrangement of sailings as between 'Groups' or as between the West Coast Lines and the East Coast Lines, then the new arrangement, if it is to be 'fair to all,' should provide for the Union-Castle having an interest on the West Coast.

With regard to the admission of the Blue Star Line into a rota, the West Coast Lines seem to regard their present schedule as unalterable, but it should be remembered that this schedule only became operative this year. From 1921 to 1933 the West Coast Lines dispatched 54/53 ships per annum. In 1934 they had 60 sailings, in 1935, 84 sailings and in 1936 they will have 88 sailings. The East Coast sailings have not been similarly increased and assuming the 'Group' theory is to be accepted the Union-Castle is the only interest which has not participated in these additional sailings . . . the Clan Line state that years ago they foresaw the desire of the Blue Star Line to enter the South African trade and they increased their sailings in anticipation. In any case if the West Coast Lines give up dates for the whole 10 sailings of the Blue Star Line they would still be despatching 19 ships more than they did in 1934 and 24 more than in the years 1921 to 1933. The East Coast Lines are despatching approximately the same number of vessels as in 1934.

The Union-Castle have had no voice in deciding the number and order of sailings from the West Coast and it is not reasonable to expect them to suffer through any reduction or re-arrangement of those sailings. As matters stand they consider the sailings from the East and West Coast must be treated separately as they have been in the past. They think an arrangement with the Blue Star is possible of achievement on the East Coast by equally spacing all sailings up to the limit of two per week, any balance to be superimposed, but the Blue Star have indicated that they attach much more importance to an arrangement on the West Coast.

due to cheating, price wars did disrupt cartels. A determined incumbent firm that wished to alter the existing division of profits would threaten to start a price war. If the other cartel members did not give in, the disputant might begin a price war. Although we have no *direct* examples of disputes that arose from differences in social background, the negotiations that ensued each time the environment changed required delicate give-and-take, and favors owed between lines could last across generations of owner-managers.

ANALYSIS

Data and Measures

The data employed in this analysis are collected from histories of shipping companies, general histories of shipping, or histories of specific ports. The data were first collected as part of an analysis by Scott Morton (1997), in which she focused on the economic rationales for price wars. More detailed information on the specific sources for the data can be found in that article, but the sources include correspondence among cartel members, which is housed at the Shipping Records Archive of Glasgow University; quantitative information on shipping tonnage, reported in Lloyd's Register of Shipping; as well as more than forty histories focusing on individuals, firms, or routes relevant to the operation of the shipping cartels.

Over the time period of the analysis, the three conferences confronted 61 potential challenges to their agreements. Of these 61 challenges, 4 are dropped from the analysis because of insufficient data on the challenger and a further 8 not used because the price wars were caused by disputes within the cartel rather than by the appearance of a new entrant. The resulting data set contains 49 cases of a new entrant attempting to capture a place in an existing shipping cartel.

For each potential challenger, a conference decided whether to engage the entrant in a price war or to accommodate the challenger's desire to conduct traffic on the trade route under conditions that were not consistent with the conference agreement as perceived by the incumbent firms. The outcome of this decision is the dependent variable in our analysis. The relationship between the potential entrant and the conference is characterized as a price war when the historical sources describe a sharp commercial conflict between the parties that includes price cuts.

Sometimes the texts use the term "price war" in describing vigorous price decreases in the history of the firm or market, but not always. Other common descriptions are "sharp price decreases" or "rates dropped by 40%." This analysis follows Scott Morton (1997) and classifies price drops in excess of 30 percent as price wars. Of the 49 events on which there are sufficiently complete data to conduct at least some analyses, 15 are categorized as price wars.

The economic strength of the entrant is captured by several variables. *Total tonnage* is the total number of gross tons of shipping that the challenger owns measured in millions of tons; all the tonnage need not be on the route governed by the conference. Total tonnage is positively correlated with financial and other resources. For example, the largest shipping lines had considerable cash reserves used for ship purchasing and self-insurance of their existing fleets.[4] Larger size increased the ability of a firm to spread risk, gain easier access to financing, and purchase new ships at favorable prices. Size was also positively associated with the likelihood that the challenger would or could compete with cartel members on routes other than those governed by the conference agreement. For all these reasons, larger size made a firm a stronger combatant. Since a stronger combatant can, almost by definition, wage a longer and hence more costly price war, larger size should lower the likelihood of a price war.

A firm is coded as "new" if the firm had existed for fewer than five years at the time of the challenge. A young challenger was unlikely to have the cash and insurance reserves common to the established shipping firms at the time. The conference would likely think that its own reserves were greater than those of the new challenger. A young firm would also lack a loyal customer base and a reputation, and would likely not be competing with the incumbents in multiple markets. For these reasons, lack of experience in the industry is likely to have a positive effect on the likelihood of a price war. One might question the dichotomization of this variable; however, the rationale is straightforward. For this analysis, it is important to capture the distinction between young and old firms. More continuous measures of "newness" such as age of the firm or logged age of the firm should not (and do not) have a significant effect on the likelihood of a price war. The specific rationale for the five-year break is that a firm could not build up insurance reserves and a customer base in that time; it is relatively short compared with the business cycle, and yet a significant number of entrants were younger than five years.

Obviously, the variable of greatest interest analytical interest is *social status*. Specifically, we are interested in whether the owner/manager of the entrant would have been considered to have high social status by his peers. The writers of the historical sources used by Scott Morton for her initial analysis were very attuned to the status of owners even though they did not always include all the facts one would like to know. Many of the sources were written around the Second World War, and many of the authors were British; they thus grew up in a context in which they were especially sensitive to status distinctions and in which such distinctions were worth noting as part of any historical

---

[4] Boyce (1995: 225) notes that firms accumulated both public reserves of cash to help in downturns as well as secret reserves that the public and rivals did not know about. Again, this sort of resource would give an established firm deeper pockets than a young firm.

record. Consequently owners are described in ways that reveal their status. One might be characterized as being from "a prominent family in Yorkshire that founded the University of X"; another might be noted as being a knight; a third might be identified as a member of Parliament. Such descriptions are taken as evidence that an owner possessed high social status. Since the industry was so important to the nation during the sample period, owners were celebrities, and any notable feature of their lives, such as those mentioned in the examples above, was of general interest and commented on. Therefore, the lack of a description of family background or accomplishments probably indicates there were none. Accordingly, while systematic data on status are lacking, it is possible to code individuals as "high-status" if the historical record provides some information of a high-status position in society and to code individuals as "low-status" if there are no such earmarks in any of the historical sources.

Given the numerous, fine gradations of status in British society, it is important to point out that "high status" is a relative term. For the purposes of this analysis, high-status entrants are not members of the aristocracy.[5] British aristocracy of the time owned land and did not engage in business. Rather, shipping owners were almost all members of the British merchant class and had "high status" or not compared with others in that class. However, the industrial revolution and the wealth it created caused social change. When British shipping produced more millionaires and half millionaires than any other industry in Britain, its owners began to be awarded inheritable titles. Whether a person's status changed because that person received an official title or simply attained local prominence, we acknowledge that social status was not constant across a lifetime. Many of our owners worked their way up from humble beginnings. Cases of entry early in the careers of these owners are coded "low-status." However, after many years of success and wealth, that same owner late in life, or his sons, would be coded "high-status" if they attempted to enter a new route.

Unfortunately, the historical sources provide much too sparse information to construct any kind of network of challenger and participant contact, or to document the strength of social ties between the challenger and the participants in the conference agreement. However, it is possible to circumvent the problem of measuring similarity of social status because of key characteristics of our sample of cartels. As mentioned above, these cartels were successful and operated on economically and politically important trade routes. The owners of established conference lines therefore generally were already

---

[5] The period that we study is one in which social mobility increased dramatically. Boyce (1995: 295) reports that "the rapidity of wealth accumulation by shipowners is striking." "First generation owners also achieved conspicuous mobility in terms of honours." However, "only 14 honours were bestowed upon shipowners before 1900, and just one man attained a peerage. Shipowners participated in the post-1900 proliferation of titles." Of the 65 titles given to owners in Boyce's sample, 41 went to first-generation owners. Thus, the entrants in our sample may have earned titles after the entry incident we study.

"high-status" by virtue of belonging to the cartel. Membership immediately gave an owner a large impact on the economy and a role in public discourse." Thus an entrant is a better match for the three cartels studied here if its owner had high status.

Of the 49 challengers, 11 were high-status. With the exception of one German line, all these high-status entrants were British. (Non-British firms tended to be government-run or heavily associated with the government, and therefore the leading figures were often bureaucrats.) Of the 10 high-status British challengers, 4 were knights.

Although status is obviously the aspect of social identity that is of the greatest interest, it was noted above that other bases of social homophily could also influence a cartel's decision to admit an entrant or engage the entrant in a price war. A common home location seems to be especially important. All owners lived in the home port of their shipping line in order to better manage its affairs and participate in the civic life of the town. Boyce writes of owner/manager Charles Cayzer, "Cayzer's son suggested that the Clan Line transfer its headquarters to the capital to gain prestige, facilitate conference dealings, and develop wider social ties. However, citing other firms like Harrisons and Anchor, Cayzer senior decided to retain his Glasgow base to preserve ties with sources of cargo, secure lower operating costs, and maintain the firm's 'identity with its place of origin' " (Boyce 1995: 289). Boyce's evidence is consistent with the hypothesis that a similar background or origin would lower the likelihood of a price war because a common origin implies greater potential for continued cooperation. However, unlike social status, there are reasons to think that a commonality on this aspect of identity could be problematic for cooperation. Conference participants stood to lose more market share to a challenger whose operations served a similar set of customers. A line's home port was the origin for most of its voyages, and most of its cargo would originate from manufacturing firms in the local area (or the area accessible by railroad). Thus if an entrant started up a service from an incumbent's home port, it is highly likely it would be stealing business from the incumbent, as the quotation above implies.

This type of reasoning also applies to non-British cartel entrants. For example, a German line would be much less likely to become a major exporter of British goods than a British line. Therefore, from an economic perspective, one would predict that a predominantly British cartel would give up less in market share and might even find the total "pie" increased if it admitted a German entrant rather than a British entrant. Under those circumstances, it might be more likely to start a price war against the British firm.

Given that a common home port and common nationality could have either reduced or increased the likelihood that cartel members would engage an entrant in a price war, one cannot arrive at a clear ex ante prediction about the net result of these variables. Indeed, if we consider both home port and nationality as variables, it is clearly possible that the effect of one variable could be positive and the other negative, since there is no reason to believe that the community-enhancing and competitive effects of common background should decline with social/geographical distance at the same rate. However, while it is not possible to predict a negative coefficient for nationality or local port, it is possible to assert that an observed negative effect will be an indication that the community-enhancing effects of common background are relevant to the likelihood of a price war. Moreover, regardless of the ultimate effect of common port and common nationality on the likelihood of a price war, it is important to at least include these variables as controls.

British nationality is coded 1 if the entering firm was British and 0 otherwise. Since the majority of all conference participants were British, a British identity implies a greater commonality of background between the challenger and the adherents to the agreement. *Same home port* is coded 1 if the challenger's home port was the same as that of the majority of conference participants. London was the home port for the majority of conference participants in the South African cartel. Liverpool was the home port for the majority of conference participants in the Indian cartel. There was no clearly predominant home port for the Far East conference. The home port for British participants in this cartel was rather evenly divided between London, Liverpool, and Glasgow. Accordingly, this variable is coded 0 for all challengers to the Far East conference agreement.

Route tonnage is included as another measure of the costs and benefits of a price war. *Route tonnage* is the number of gross tons that the entrant placed on the route measured in million of tons. The amount of tonnage the entrant placed on the route determined the maximum volume of trade that the cartel could lose. A greater potential loss of profits would have lowered the opportunity cost of any type of price war. As a consequence, a higher route tonnage should increase a price war's likelihood. It is important to highlight the fact that route tonnage is not a measure of an entrant firm's strength, especially given the inclusion of *total tonnage* in the analysis; rather, it is a measure of the potential losses that the cartel could suffer by allowing the continued operation of the entrant on the route that its conference governed. For example, if a firm already operating several routes entered a new route by putting some of its ships there, its *total tonnage* will show up in the analysis as being greater than its *route tonnage*.

Dummy variables are included for whether or not the particular entry event occurred on the trade route governed by the United Kingdom–India conference or the United Kingdom–Japan conference. (The United Kingdom–South Africa conference is the residual category.) These variables control for differences in the propensities of the various cartels to engage in a price war. The calendar year of the entry event is also an explanatory variable; it controls for learning over time or other linear changes in the equilibrium.

Results

Tables 7.1a and 7.1b report the summary statistics for the full sample and the sample without price wars caused by internal disputes. Table 7.2 reports simple tabulations of the main variables of interest in conjunction with the war event. In this contingency table framework, one can see that entrants that were new and lacked status were involved in a disproportionate percentage of price wars. Table 7.3 reports the correlations between the various explanatory variables and their significance. High *status* is significantly correlated with *time*, *age*, *local*, and *British*. The highest significant correlation with *status* is age, at .49; this correlation arises because the oldest firms had existed for multiple generations, by which time the descendants of the founders had achieved high status.

As the dependent variable is dichotomous, it can be appropriately estimated with either a logit or a probit model. The analyses in this chapter employ the latter of these two models, and table 7.4 presents the regression results. The effect of social status is negative (and significant at the .1 level), as predicted. To assess the marginal effect of status on the probability of a price war, it is necessary to multiply the status coefficient by the normal probability density function (pdf) value at the average index in the data set. The pdf value for column 1 is 0.294. Accordingly, the marginal effect on the probability of a price war for an owner moving from regular to high status is over 40 percent. Social status clearly had a large impact on the probability of a price war.

As discussed above, this status coefficient potentially denotes multiple effects. Although status may have constituted a signal that a potential entrant would uphold the moral community underlying the cartel, there are other possible

TABLE 7.1a
Summary Statistics for Sample with No Internal Disputes

Variables: Characteristics of Potential Target	Obs.	Mean	S.D.	Min.	Max.
War	49	.306	.466	0	1
Age	49	29.6	32.3	0	135
New firm	49	.286	.456	0	1
Route tonnage	49	29,105	24,703	1,449	126,000
Total tonnage	49	86,851	116,158	1,449	598,203
High social status	49	.224	.422	0	1
Same local port	49	.286	.456	0	1
British	49	.612	.492	0	1
Time	49	18.0	12.7	1	56
UK–India cartel	49	.245	.434	0	1
UK–Far East cartel	49	.245	.434	0	1

TABLE 7.1b
Summary Statistics for the Full Sample

Variables: Characteristics of Potential Target	Obs.	Mean	S.D.	Min.	Max.
War	58	.397	.493	0	1
Age	59	31.5	34.6	0	157
New firm	59	.237	.429	0	1
Route tonnage	57	32,840	27,845	1,449	12,600
Total tonnage	58	90,917	110,334	1,449	59,820
High social status	59	.203	.406	0	1
Same home port	59	.288	.457	0	1
British	59	.593	.495	0	1
Time	59	18	12.05	1	56
UK–India cartel	59	.288	.457	0	1
UK–Far East cartel	59	.288	.457	0	1

interpretations of the status coefficient. One alternative interpretation is that high status denotes that the stronger financial resources of individuals associated with the entrant protected the entrant from predation. Note, however, that for the long purse/financial resources interpretation to be correct, social status needs to be positively correlated with financial resources that (1) are not reflected in either the total tonnage of the challenger's firm, the tonnage capacity that the challenger had on the particular route, or the age of the firm but (2) are still relevant to the strength of the challenger's shipping operation. Of course, even if the presence of these controls helps to rule out a financial interpretation of the status coefficient, other interpretations are still possible. For example, cartel members may simply have valued association with high-status others as a consumption good, or status may have been an indicator of political capital.

In order to distinguish the signaling explanation from these others, we should examine the extent to which the effect of status on a price war is contingent on the age of the entering firm. If status was a signal of an individual's willingness to join the moral community, then the magnitude of this effect should decline with the age of the entering firm. The older an entering firm, the more cartel members would have had other bases for inferring the likelihood that the owner of the firm would be a willing member of the moral community underlying the cartel. On the other hand, if status was valued only as an end in itself, and/or represented an entrée to some political capital, and/or was a proxy for economic resources of an entrant, then the effect of status should not be contingent on the age of the firm.

The inclusion of the interaction between age and status in column 2 helps to tease apart these alternative interpretations. The main effect for status again has a negative coefficient and is significant at the .05 level. One can interpret this

TABLE 7.2
Tabulations of *Status*, *New*, and *War*

	Status	*No Status*
No war	9	25
War	2	13
	British	*Not British*
No war	23	11
War	7	8
	Home Port	*Not Home Port*
No war	25	9
War	10	5
	Not New	*New*
No war	28	6
War	7	8
	Status	*No Status*
Not new	9	26
New	2	12

TABLE 7.3
Correlations between Independent Variables

Variables	Firm New	Tons	Status	Age	Local	Route British	Tons
Total tonnage	−.322[†]						
Status	−.084	.053					
Age	−.494[†]	.236[†]	.494[†]				
Local	.085	.049	.329[†]	.006			
British	−.025	−.088	.247[†]	.224	.527[†]		
Route tonnage	−.272[†]	.346[†]	−.007	.186	−.133	.031	
Time	.000	.491[†]	.307[†]	.073	−.110	−.127	.317

[†] $p < .10$

main effect as the status effect for a firm of age 0. Age is also negative and significant at the .1 level. Interestingly, the interaction between age and status is positive and significant at the .1 level; old firms appear to obtain less of an advantage from status than do young firms. If status were solely a proxy for economic or political resources, this result would imply that an owner's financial

TABLE 7.4
Determinants of Price War

Variables	Model 1	Model 2
Economic resources of potential new firm	.805†	—
	(.541)	
Total tonnage of potential target	$-6.22 \times 10^{-6\dagger}$	4.42×10^{-6}
	(4.72×10^{-6})	(4.76×10^{-6})
Identity of potential target	-1.54*	-3.06*
Status of potential target	(.81)	(1.41)
Status of potential target $\times$ age	—	.056*
		(.030)
Age	—	$-.045$*
		(.027)
Same home port	2.16†	2.24*
	(.93)	(.981)
Potential British target	$-.98$*	$-.922^\dagger$
	(.60)	(.639)
Control variables	$1.81 \times 10^{-5\dagger}$	1.43×10^{-5}
Route tonnage of potential target	(1.28×10^{-5})	(1.32×10^{-5})
Far East–UK cartel	1.33†	1.44*
	(.88)	(.894)
India–UK cartel	1.11†	.399
	(.78)	(.619)
Time (years)	.039	.045*
	(.025)	(.026)
Intercept	-1.90*	-1.03
	(.85)	(.824)
Log-likelihood	-22.20	-21.06
ϕ(XB) for marginal effect	.294	.270
N	49	49

Numbers in parentheses are standard errors. The default cartel is South Africa–UK. The standard normal density is evaluated using the estimated coefficients and the mean values of the variables.

$^\dagger p < .10$, one-tailed test; *$p < .05$, one-tailed test

or political strength mattered more when his firm was young than when it was old. Such an interpretation seems difficult to sustain. Similarly, if cartel members simply valued status as an end in itself, the value that they placed on status should be age-invariant. However, the positive interaction is quite consistent with an interpretation of status as a signal of future cooperation. The older the entering firm, the more likely that incumbents had an alternative basis—the past behavior of that firm in other markets and cartels—for inferring whether the entrant would be a cooperative member of their organization.

Of course, such evidence that status was a signal of future behavior does not rule out the possibility that status may also have been a proxy for the financial resources of kin or that status may have been valued as an end in itself. Indeed, the magnitude of the main effect for status relative to the magnitude of the interaction term would suggest that these alternative interpretations of the status effect are valid. The magnitude of the overall status effect in column 2 is $(-3.06 + 0.056 \times age)$. The status effect does not cross 0 until the firm is over fifty years old. Thus, even after twenty or thirty years—which would seem to be a sufficiently long time to infer cooperative behavior on some basis other than status—there remains a positive status effect.[6] The reason for including the interaction term is not to rule out all possible alternative interpretations of a main status effect; rather, it is simply to examine whether there is some evidence for a signaling story in the data. Since there are so few observations relative to explanatory variables, we estimated simpler specifications as well as those reported and found evidence for the signal interpretation there as well. A regression of war on only age, age $\times$ status, and status yields coefficients on those variables very similar to those in the more complete specification. However, status is not an overwhelmingly strong predictor of war; regressing war on status results only in a negative but insignificant coefficient on status. Therefore, the strongest effect of status is on young entrants. Table 7.2 also addresses this point.

Returning to the results in column 1, we observe that being based in the same home port increases the probability of a price war; being British, however, lowers the likelihood of a price war. It therefore seems that the competitive effects of similar origin outweighed the community-enhancing effects of similar origin at the level of the home port, but the community-enhancing effects of similar origin may have outweighed the competitive effects at the level of nationality. Again, while this combination of effects could have been predicted ex ante, the existence of a positive effect for same nationality remains noteworthy insofar as it does suggest benefits of a common background at some level.

To summarize the results related to status, an entrant-owner with high social status was approximately 40 percent less likely to trigger a price war than an entrant of ordinary status. This result is consistent with social status being a proxy for family wealth (or deep pockets), being a consumption good for other cartel members, and being a good indication of the future cooperation of the entrant in upholding the "moral community" of the cartel. Potentially all these

---

[6] The mean entrant age is 30, the median is 20, the maximum is 135, and the 75th percentile is 51 years. Most entrants in the data were in the age range where high social status was helpful.

explanations were operating for the entrants in our data set. To try to separate out evidence for the third explanation, the moral community, a term for the interaction between social status and age as an explanatory variable was included in the analysis. The effect of social status in reducing the probability of predation declines with age. There is no simple explanation for why this should be the case if social status is merely a proxy for wealth or if it is a consumption good. Thus, the interaction effect provides evidence that the cartel members used an entrant's history to decide if that entrant would be a cooperative cartel member, but if the entrant was very young, they had to rely on social cues, such as social status.

In pointing to how the social status of a shipping line's owner influenced how the shipping line was treated by rivals, this chapter provides an illustration of the embeddedness of economic action. At the same time, one may reasonably wonder how idiosyncratic this particular result is. It clearly does not seem reasonable to expect that a CEO's status will always be a salient determinant of the intensity of competition that the CEO's firm faces. Nor does it seem reasonable to expect that a CEO's status will always be a salient determinant of whether a firm is able to participate in a "moral community" of producers in a market. In fact, although there has been no systematic attempt to explore the prevalence of moral communities across markets, it seems likely that most markets probably do not even have a moral community at their center. A "moral community" undoubtedly requires a certain amount of interaction among competitors, and not all markets will be equally conducive to such interaction.

However, even though the setting analyzed in this chapter may have some unique features, two observations can be made. First, even if the status of individuals is not relevant to market entry in a particular context, this does not mean that the concept of status is irrelevant; rather, it means that one might wish to look for the effects of status at the level of the firm. In an examination of the entry of commercial banks into investment banking markets, Jensen (2003a, 2003b) shows that the status of those entrants affects the opportunities that they realize in the investment banking markets.

Second, although there is reason to expect that social status will not always be as relevant to market dynamics as it seems to have been in British shipping cartels in the last third of the nineteenth century and the first third of the twentieth century, there are more recent examples of similar dynamics. For example, in motivating the relevance of social status to market dynamics earlier in this chapter, I referenced the work of Hirsch (1986) and Glasberg (1981). Hirsch concludes that much of the initial opposition to hostile takeovers in the United States in the 1960s and 1970s was due to the fact that the initial proponents of this acquisition strategy were low-status individuals from outside the corporate elite. The high-status insiders used economic and political tactics to prevent the low-status individuals from acquiring corporate assets that would have constituted an entrée into the elite ranks. However, a decade later, in the 1980s, the hostile takeover reemerged as a corporate tactic; the only difference was that the proponents of hostile takeovers were now members of the corporate elite.

Glasberg (1981) as well as Brooks (1973) examine one particular case of a hostile takeover attempt and find evidence quite consistent with Hirsch's broader account. Specifically, they explore how elites of the banking world in New York engaged in a coordinated effort to prevent Saul Steinberg, the CEO of the computer-leasing company Leasco, from taking over Chemical Bank, a New York company. Congressional investigations and interviews suggest that the CEO of Chemical Bank worked with others in the banking establishment to prevent Steinberg from being able to join their ranks. While it is not possible to completely list Chemical Bank's alleged tactics—some legal and some illegal—without delving into the operational details of hostile takeovers, one example is that the CEO of Chemical Bank called the chairman of one of Leasco's major creditors, who in turn informed Steinberg that "a Leasco attempt to take over Chemical would not be a good thing for banking." Ultimately, Steinberg and Leasco were defeated in their attempt to take over Chemical Bank; in reflecting on the way in which the banking community conspired against him, Steinberg commented, "I always knew there was an Establishment—I just used to think I was part of it" (Brooks 1973: 259).

In the terms of this chapter, Steinberg reflected a potential threat to the moral community of the New York banks. Thus, as recently as the 1960s and 1980s, there is evidence that the effects of social status spilled over into the market for corporate control. So while these social status effects will clearly not be relevant in every market context, we know that they have been relevant in some, and it would a mistake to simply assume that dynamics like those in the British shipping cartels are idiosyncratic.

In addition to providing support for the concept of the social embeddedness of market behavior, this chapter—along with the previous one—shows the relevance of status dynamics across multiple domains for market evolution. In the previous chapter, we observed how status distinctions in the technological domain can spill over and affect the evolving perception of what constitutes high and low quality. In this chapter, we observed how status distinctions in the social domain can affect which producers are able to enter a particular market. The next chapter continues the concern with evolutionary dynamics by looking at the phenomenon of firm exit. In examining this phenomenon, we will return to looking at status in the market rather than status in a related domain. We will also return to looking at the industry that we examined in chapters 3 and 4—the investment banking industry. However, we will look at the investment banking industry over a much longer time frame to better capture the evolutionary dynamics around exit.

Chapter Eight

AN EVOLUTIONARY PERSPECTIVE
ON STATUS SEGREGATION

IN CHAPTER FOUR, we focused on the extent of status segregation as one of the defining characteristics of a status ordering. We observed that the greater the uncertainty that market actors confront regarding the quality of their potential exchange partners, the greater the extent of status-based homophily in exchange relations. While this tendency toward status homophily is one way in which status segregation can be realized, it is not the only one. Another is in terms of divides in the status ordering, in which those below a threshold have little or no contact with those above the threshold. In other words, one can adopt a more micro-level or macro-level vantage point from which to examine status segregation. In the micro level, one focuses on the extent to which there is a divide or at least a thinning out in key parts of the status ordering and considers the extent to which these divides or thin patches relate to other characteristics of competing firms, such as size, age, and so on. In a study of competition among law schools, Saunder (2004) looks at how the "shape" of the status distribution changed when a key third party—*US News and World Report* (USNWR)—increased the number of law schools that it ranked. When USNWR ranked only a small number of elite schools, the status distribution was divided into a small number of elite schools (fewer than twenty-five) and a large number of nonelites that could all claim to be just beyond elite status; however, when USNWR increased the number of schools that it ranked and created a second, third, and fourth tier between the top twenty-five and the others, then the vast majority of nonelite schools found that they could no longer claim status that was just below the top twenty-five and, accordingly, faced increasing scrutiny from key constituencies.

With his analysis, Saunder draws our attention to how a particular institutional factor—third-party evaluators—can influence the shape and key divides in a status ordering. In this chapter, I will focus on evolutionary processes that give rise to status segregation of a very similar sort. The vast majority of what sociologists have to say about the evolution of markets and industries comes from one paradigmatic approach within the sociology of organizations—organizational ecology. The approach, initially pioneered by Michael Hannan and John Freeman (1977, 1989), is the most well-developed paradigm within the sociology of organizations; in fact, it may be the most well-developed paradigm within the entire discipline.

There are a number of evolutionary processes toward which organizational ecology draws our attention. For example, the density-dependent model of organization competition has highlighted the relationship between the density (i.e., number) of organizations in an industry and the vital rates in that industry, such as the rate of organizational foundings or failures (Hannan and Carroll 1992). Organizational ecology has also done much to illuminate how organizational properties, such as age or size, interact with features of the environment to affect the organization's likelihood of failure (Carroll and Hannan 2000). For our purposes, one particularly noteworthy model within this perspective is Glenn Carroll's (1985) resource-partitioning model, which highlights dynamics of competition and market segmentation when two conditions hold: (1) firms occupy a series of interdependent niches on a given dimension that is important to their competitive strength, and (2) firms have limits on the extent to which they can expand from their location on this dimension. Though the single dimension on which Carroll focuses is what is called niche width—a term denoting the degree to which a firm is a specialist or a generalist—these two conditions imply the relevance of Carroll's model to the status-based model of market competition, in which firms are locked into a series of interdependent niches along the status dimension.

I will begin this chapter by reviewing the essential elements of Carroll's resource-partitioning model. I show how a concern with status can be integrated into the basic model by allowing the dynamics of competition and segmentation that Carroll posits for the single dimension of niche width to play out on the dimensions of niche width and status simultaneously. As we shall see, when these dynamics are allowed to occur on these two dimensions, an interesting empirical question is whether status or niche width becomes a more salient basis of segregation. Is a firm more highly constrained in its movement along the status dimension or more highly constrained in its movement on the dimension of niche width? The answer to this question has important implications for understanding the way in which patterns of competition evolve over the history of an industry. To explore these ideas empirically, we will return to the investment banking industry. However, because the resource partitioning model draws attention to evolutionary dynamics that occur over an industry's emergence and maturation, we need to focus on an earlier time period than that studied in chapters 3 and 4. Specifically, we focus on the competition among investment banks in the investment-grade market between the years 1920 and 1949.

THE RESOURCE-PARTITIONING MODEL

Although Carroll first elaborated the resource-partitioning model in 1985, the model has undergone considerable development since its initial statement, and probably no version can be said to be the definitive formulation. Therefore, in reviewing the model, I will try to elaborate a specification that is broadly representative.

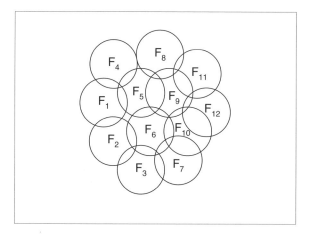

FIGURE 8.1a. Resource space—unconcentrated mass market

In focusing on market dynamics related to niche width, the model begins with a conception of market demand that can be divided into a "center" and a "peripheral" region. The center is a region of relatively homogeneous demand in which economies of scale and scope become a fundamental determinant of the competitive strength of a firm. As a result, generalists tend to dominate in this region of the market. The peripheral region, on the other hand, is characterized by a plethora of niches, each of which is characterized by its own unique set of tastes and preferences. In these smaller niches, economies of scale and scope are not the central determinant of the competitive strength of a given firm. Rather, the extent to which the firm appeals to the idiosyncratic preferences associated with that particular niche determines its competitive strength. Accordingly, specialists tend to dominate these peripheral regions.

Given this conception of the market, the resource-partitioning model focuses on how market concentration relates to the mortality rates of specialist and generalist organizations. It is well acknowledged that markets generally become more concentrated over time (Carroll 1985, 1997; Klepper and Graddy 1990). By definition, increasing concentration implies that a smaller number of firms are acquiring a larger share of the market.

Intuitively, one might expect that increasing concentration would be positively related to the mortality rates of specialists and inversely related to the mortality rates of generalists. Carroll argues that this intuition is misleading. To explain why, Carroll adopts an evolutionary perspective. In the early history of a market, there are perhaps a dozen or so generalists seeking to achieve the economies of scale and scope necessary to dominate the market's center, as depicted in figure 8.1a. Since the center is crowded, these generalists expand by developing niches that are located somewhat in the center and somewhat in

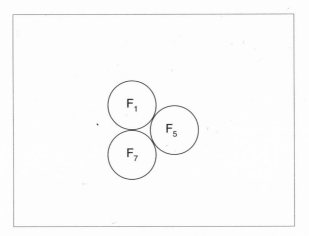

FIGURE 8.1b. Resource space—concentrated mass market

the periphery. Over time, a war of attrition unfolds, with the one or few generalists that possess the greatest scale and scope eventually dominating the market. Diseconomies of scale and scope beyond a certain size and breadth, combined with highly idiosyncratic preferences in the periphery, prohibit the few surviving generalists from serving the mass of demand in the center of the market and also serving the peripheral regions formerly occupied by the large number of generalists.

As the winners of this war of attrition expand and move to the center of the market, some of the peripheral market demand formerly served by smaller generalists becomes open to specialists, as in figure 8.1b. Since market concentration is almost exclusively a function of the war of attrition among generalists, the consequence of an increase in market concentration is the opposite of that suggested by intuition. For generalists, increasing concentration implies an increase in mortality rates. Almost by definition, increasing concentration means that one or a few generalists eliminate the rest of the generalists from the market. For specialists, however, increasing market concentration implies a reduction in mortality rates. On average, a decline in the number of large generalists reduces the competition that specialists face in the more peripheral regions. Instead of competing with generalists and specialists in these more peripheral regions, specialists are now competing only with other specialists. Studies in a number of industries have provided support for the central prediction of the resource-partitioning model (Carroll 1985; Barnett and Carroll 1987; Lomi 1995; Mitchell 1995). Perhaps most notably, in his original 1985 article, Carroll predicted the emergence of the microbrewery movement based on his observation of the consolidation of the beer industry at the time. While there are many sociological models that can explain events after the fact, the number that can provide the basis for successful prediction of industry events is much more limited.

INTEGRATING NICHE WIDTH AND STATUS

Informal observation of multiple markets suggests that niche width and status are rarely orthogonal. While the correlation between status and niche width may be either positive or negative, there is often a correlation. For example, in professional services such as consulting, accounting, or the law, the highest-status organizations tend to be large generalists offering a broad product range and serving diverse clients (Han 1994; Phillips 2001; chapters 3 and 4 of this book). In other industries such as fashion, publishing, beer, or automobiles, the highest-status firms frequently have products tailored toward an elite or specific clientele. The observation that niche width and status are often correlated is consistent with White's insight that the relationship between volume and quality is a central though varying feature of the role structure of a market (White 1981). Finally, Carroll and Swaminathan (2000) and Zuckerman and Kim (2003) also observe relationships between status and niche width.

More systematic evidence of a relationship between niche width and status comes from the data that will be used for the analysis in this chapter—the primary securities market in the U.S. investment banking industry between 1920 and 1949. While a fuller description of the data is available below, I will note now that status is once again measured as it was in chapters 3 and 4—using the information codified in tombstone advertisements. Niche width is measured with a Herfindahl-like measure of the industry diversity of the corporate issuers for which a bank is an underwriter. I will discuss the specifics of this measure of niche width in greater detail in the context of a more systematic analysis below, but generally speaking, if a bank underwrites the securities of corporations across a large number of industries, that bank is a generalist. If the bank tends to underwrite the securities of corporations across only a few industries, it is a specialist.

Given these operationalizations of status and niche width, figure 8.2 depicts the distribution of generalists and specialists by status. Each observation represents one "bank-year." Generalists are defined as those banks that are above the mean on the Herfindahl-like measure of industry diversity, and specialists are categorized as those banks that are below the mean on this diversity measure. The figure clearly reveals a positive relationship between niche width and status. In fact, the correlation across all the observations is .50. While the number of banks in the highest status range is obviously lower than the number of banks in the lowest status range, the proportion of generalists at a given level increases with status.

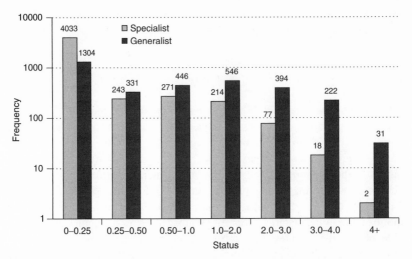

FIGURE 8.2. Location of specialists and generalists along the status distribution

   Given the general observation of a systematic interdependence between status and niche width that can be either positive or negative, it is tempting to ask about causes of the relationship. Why is the relationship between niche width and status positive in some markets and negative in others? It seems difficult to develop a conclusive answer to this question; however, because status must be positively correlated with quality, clearly the answer turns in part on the relationship between a firm's niche width and quality. If being a large generalist tends to imply a quality level that is the lowest common denominator across a range of specialist products, then the relationship between niche width and quality is likely to be negative. On the other hand, if being a large generalist implies the ability to produce at a level of quality that smaller specialist organizations cannot match, then the relationship between status and niche width is likely to be positive.[1] In the case of the U.S. investment banking industry and the primary securities markets, the positive relationship can be explained largely by the capabilities that a bank must possess in order to manage an

---

[1] One can posit a signaling dynamic around niche width that would reinforce an underlying relationship between niche width and quality. So, even if a firm has capabilities that allow it to counterbalance any negative effects of niche width on quality, the firm may find itself unable to earn returns that compensate for the higher costs of making a high-quality product. Firms like Gallo Winery or Anheuser-Busch help to illustrate the point. Industry observers generally acknowledge that both firms are capable of making exceptionally high-quality products; however, both firms confront the fact that the quality of wine or beer is assumed to be dependent on craftlike methods that are extremely difficult to practice on a large scale. As a result, even though such firms might represent exceptions to the prevailing relationship between niche width and quality, these firms will find it difficult to overcome expectations of quality premised on niche width.

underwriting of one of the higher-status issuers. When we considered the institutional details of the investment banking industry in chapter 3, we observed that a bank's market presence had a positive impact on the quality of its underwriting activities. The same was true more than a half century before. Hayes and colleagues (Hayes 1971, 1979; Hayes, Spence, and Van Praag Marks 1983) noted that in the early part of the twentieth century, the larger and implicitly higher-status corporate issuers required unprecedented sums of financial capital in order to finance their growth on a national scale. As a result, a bank could distinguish itself in this market segment simply on the basis of an ability to place these considerable sums of securities. The capability depended not on knowledge of a particular industry but on the presence of extensive ties to investors, especially large institutional investors. However, as Hayes and coworkers also noted, this focus on building a capability in large-volume placements left smaller geographic and industry-specific market segments, where firms could distinguish themselves by focusing on particular niches (Hayes, Spence, and Van Praag Marks 1983). In effect, there were greater scope economies in the higher-status niches than in the lower-status niches, giving rise to the correlation observed in figure 8.2.

To conceptualize the way in which competition plays out simultaneously on the dimensions of niche width and status, it is helpful to begin within an image of a "resource-status" space that combines the essential features of the status hierarchy in the status-based model of market competition and the resource space in Carroll's resource-partitioning model. While one could depict such a space in multiple ways, figures 8.3a and 8.3b provide one possible representation. The resource-status space is wrapped around a sphere or globe. The north pole represents the highest status point, the south pole represents the lowest status point, and the intervening latitudes can be considered status bands. Longitudinal divisions denote heterogeneity in tastes. Two organizations at the same latitude are to be considered identical in status; two organizations at the same longitude are to be understood as competing for the same tastes or preferences. There is generally greater crowding in the lower-status ranges than in the higher-status ranges because each status gradation represents an entry barrier to status levels above. This greater crowding at the lower levels is quite consistent with the status distributions observed in the investment banking and wine industries as well as that observed in Han's (1994) study of the audit services market.

Niches are rectangular because tastes and status are each arrayed along one dimension, though the actual shape of the niches does affect the basic argument.[2] Consistent with Carroll's notion of a center, occupied by large generalists, and

[2] Péli and Nooteboom (1999) have argued that niches in resource space should be understood to be spheres or hyperspheres, rather than n-dimensional rectangles as in McPherson's representation (McPherson 1983). Because figure 8.3 represents only one resource dimension, both the sphere and the rectangle converge to a line in that one dimension.

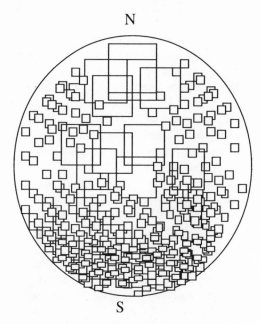

FIGURE 8.3a. Resource-status space where generalists are on average higher in status than specialists

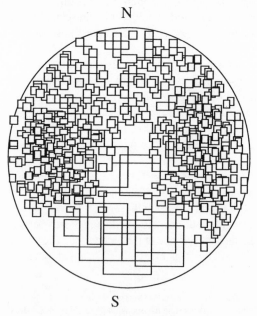

FIGURE 8.3b. Resource-status space where specialists are on average higher in status than generalists

a periphery, occupied by small specialists, the generalists are horizontally segregated, or located within a restricted set of longitudinal coordinates on the sphere. A correlation between niche width and status implies that organizations of different niche width are segregated not only horizontally but vertically as well. Organizations of different niche width are systematically distributed across the different latitudes. In professional service markets like the investment banking industry (fig. 8.3a), the large generalists are located primarily in the northern hemisphere. On the other hand, in markets like the fashion or beer industry (fig. 8.3b), the large generalists are concentrated in the southern latitudes. Following the resource-partitioning model, we assume that economies of scale and scope are dominant sources of advantage in the regions occupied by generalists. In contrast, in the region occupied by specialists, the dominant source of advantage is the appeal to a particular need or taste.

Underlying this image of a resource-status space are two assumptions; one is critical to the propositions that will be tested, and the other is less critical. The critical assumption is the following: *competition is localized along both the vertical and the horizontal dimensions.* Organizations compete with other firms only to the extent that their positions on the sphere overlap. As an example, one can think about automobile manufacturers being arrayed in resource space in terms of vehicle types: sports car, family car, luxury car, and so on. One can view those manufacturers as being arrayed in terms of status. For example, in the sports car segment, Mazda with its Miata might be at a lower-status ranking, whereas Ferrari and Lamborghini might be at a higher-status ranking. In this particular example, our framework implicitly posits that Ferrari competes more intensely with makers of other sports cars than with automobile manufacturers that may specialize in family or luxury cars. Likewise, Ferrari competes more intensely with Lamborghini than it does with Mazda. While this assumption is critical, the assumption follows directly from both the status-based and resource-partitioning models. Both models posit the localization of competition: the status model posits localization along the vertical dimension, while the resource-partitioning model posits localization of competition along the horizontal dimension.

The less critical assumption is that heterogeneity in resource space begins to converge at the highest and lowest status levels. This assumption is implicit in specifying the resource-status space as a sphere in which longitudes converge at the poles. The implication of the spherical shape is, first, that the exceptionally high-status firms offer products or services that possess qualities desired by all constituencies regardless of their particular tastes and preferences and, second, that the lowest-status firms offer products or services that possess qualities regarded as undesirable by all constituencies regardless of their particular tastes. If one were uncomfortable with this assumption, then one could represent the resource-status space as a cylinder rather than a sphere. However, unlike the first assumption, this second assumption will not affect any of the hypotheses being elaborated in this chapter.

Having laid out this general image, it is now possible to consider the theoretical implications of integrating a concern with status and niche width. Because the investment banking industry is one in which there is a positive correlation between niche width and status, we shall focus on the resource-status space represented in figure 8.3a, where there is also a positive correlation between status and niche width.

Consider the mortality rates of a generalist and specialist located near the southern end of the sphere. Since this is the part of the resource space where there are returns for specialization, it naturally follows that the mortality rates of generalists should exceed the mortality rates of specialists. Now consider how an increase in status (i.e., a shift northward in the resource-status space) affects the mortality rates of both the specialist and the generalist. The economic advantages of status uncovered in earlier chapters leads to the expection that the mortality rates of both specialists and generalists should generally decline with an increase in status. As noted above, the higher-status regions tend to be less crowded, as each status gradation can be regarded as an entry barrier to the status gradations above it. However, there are good reasons to believe that specialists and generalists will not benefit equally from the increment in status. As an organization shifts northward, it increasingly finds itself in a location within the resource-status space in which economies of scope and scale can be realized more easily. Therefore, while both the generalist and specialist may benefit from an increase in status, the generalist will benefit more since it is moving to a region of the resource-status space that favors a broad niche width. In the northernmost locations, the mortality rates of the generalist will eventually fall below those of the specialist. This line of argument thus implies the following contingent hypothesis: *When economies of scale and scope are greater in the higher-status segments than in the lower-status segments, the benefit of a given status increment should increase with niche width (i.e., there should be a negative interaction between status and niche width on the mortality rate).*

Figure 8.4 provides an illustration of the hypothesized relationship between status and mortality rate for hypothetical specialist and generalist organizations. Importantly, the hypothesized relationship hinges on the existence of greater economies of scale and scope in the high-status regions of the resource-status space than in the low-status regions.

Since this hypothesis is premised on the assumption that there are greater economies of scale or scope in the high-status regions of the market, one might reasonably ask: what if the opposite holds? What if there are greater economies of scale or scope in the low-status region of the market? In this case, an increase in status will yield greater benefits for the specialist than the generalist since the increment implies a shift out of the range of the market where the generalist derives the greatest benefit.

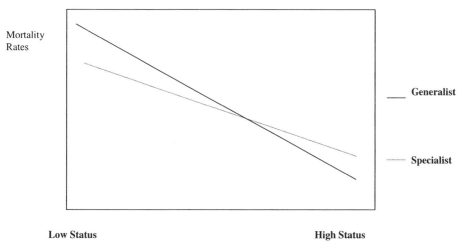

Mortality
Rates

___ **Generalist**

······· **Specialist**

Low Status   **High Status**

FIGURE 8.4. Relationship between niche width and mortality rates where there are greater scope or scale economies in the higher-status niches

In the beer-brewing industry, for instance, one would expect movement by a generalist into higher-status areas of the resource-status space to harm the expanding generalist. As the generalist moves to a higher-status region of the segment, it finds itself in a region of the space that is not as conducive to scale or scope economies (due to the fact that the ability to signal craftlike production quality is inversely proportional to volume in this elite segment). The shifting generalist suffers since it is moving to a region of the resource-status space that favors a narrow niche width rather than a broad niche width. Carroll and Swaminathan (2000) make a very similar argument in their examination of the microbrewery movement. *Accordingly, when economies of scale and scope are greater in the lower-status regions than in the higher-status regions, the benefit of a given increment in status should decline with niche width (i.e., there is a positive interaction between status and niche width on the mortality rate).*

While these two contingent hypotheses have been framed at an abstract level to reflect their generalizability, it is possible to present a more concrete realization of these two contingent hypotheses in any particular instance. For example, in the investment banking industry, the "southern" end of the resource-status space is the location in which banks are competing for opportunities to underwrite small, low-status issuers. In this part of the resource space, there are returns for specialization. Small, low-status issuers are relatively unknown by investors and, accordingly, a bank with a focus on this particular industry is able to provide a more compelling argument to investors that it can evaluate the financial soundness of the low-status firms in this industry. In this segment of the market specialists will tend to dominate generalists. As a bank's status increases, it begins to play a significant role in the underwriting of moderate- and high-status issuers, and there is less benefit associated with specialization. Investors are less worried about the financial soundness of the moderate- and high-status issuers than about the financial soundness of their low-status counterparts. Instead, because the issuers are now larger, the primary concern is the ability of the investment bank to place a large volume of securities regardless of the industry from which the issuing firm comes. In this segment of the market there is a "virtuous circle" underlying the placement of a large volume of securities. The more that a bank becomes a primary underwriter for a diverse set of issuers from a broad cross section of industries, the easier it will be for the bank to form ties to large institutional investors seeking to build a large, broad investment portfolio. The easier it is for investment banks to form these ties to institutional investors, the easier it is for these banks to place the large volume of securities being issued by the moderate- and high-status firms. Thus, as a bank's status increases, the returns for niche width should increase. Or, as stated in the first contingent hypothesis above, there should be a positive interaction between status and niche width on a bank's performance in the underwriting markets.

This hypothesized interaction of status and niche width on mortality rates is one implication of integrating the status-based model with the resource-partitioning model. We now consider a second implication, one pertaining to the resource-partitioning model's hypothesized effect of market concentration. Recall that in the resource-partitioning model an increase in market concentration implies that a few large generalists expand their niches. Figure 8.5 represents a hypothetical resource-status space in which the relationship between niche width and status is positive. Let us assume that the two generalists denoted by an E in the figure are the ones that start to expand their niche. Being among the larger and higher-status generalists, these two firms are at an advantage in the war of attrition.

As these generalists expand, what space will they occupy? The resource-partitioning model specifies that they will move into the space occupied by other generalists. In the imagery of figures 8.3 and 8.5, the expanding generalists will remain in the area of the resource-status space dominated by generalists (i.e., they will encroach upward and downward into the region of the resource-status space occupied by the generalists). However, because they do not fully take over the space occupied by the other generalists, the vertical expansion opens up resource space for the specialists.

The status-based model, however, posits that high-status firms will be reluctant to expand vertically downward since doing so undercuts their own status. In the imagery of figures 8.3 and 8.5, to the extent that an organization expands its niche, it will expand horizontally for the most part, moving into the niches of the high-status generalists and specialists. However, because these

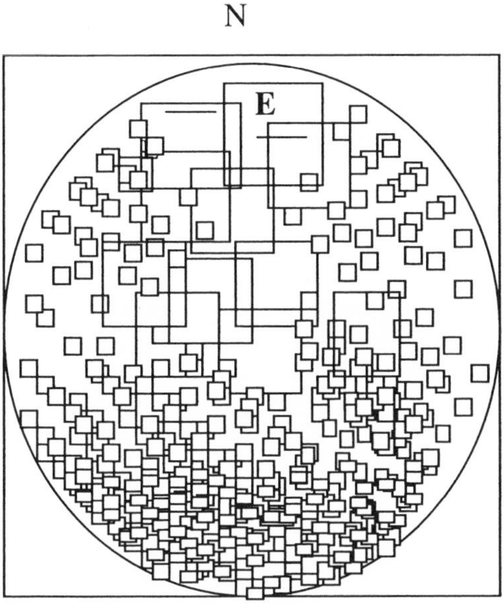

FIGURE 8.5. Resource-status space with expanding generalists

high-status generalists cannot expand too far downward without undercutting their own status, they do not completely take over the space occupied by the slightly lower-status competitors that they eliminate from the market. The expansion of the higher-status firms thus lowers crowding in the lower-status ranges and reduces the mortality rates of lower-status firms.

Even in markets where the relationship between niche width and status is negative, the status-based model also predicts expansion within a status gradation, rather than expansion into different status ranges. Large, expanding generalists might wish to expand into the higher-status ranges, but their lack of status inhibits their ability to move into the higher-status band. To the extent that generalists expand, they must do so primarily within their particular status band. Therefore, regardless of whether the expanding generalists are high-status or low-status, the status-based model implies status-localized competition and the following hypothesis. *In a market where economies of scale and scope are greater (lower) in the higher-status region of the market, an increase in market concentration decreases the mortality rates of low-status (high-status) firms and increases the mortality rates of high-status (low-status) firms.*

This hypothesis is premised on the assumption that status is valued as a signal. The less important that status is as a signal, the more the largest generalists will cut across status gradations and enter the niches of the other generalists. Conversely, the more important status is as a signal, the less the expanding generalists will traverse status gradations in the resource-status space and the more the results will be consistent with this hypothesis.

With that observation, we turn to the empirical study of the primary securities markets in the United States between 1920 and 1949. If status was an important signal during this time, then one would expect that an increase in market concentration would imply the expansion of the largest firms into the niches of other high-status banks, regardless of whether those other high-status banks were generalists or specialists. As these high-status banks were eliminated from the market, some space in the resource-status space opened up for the moderate- and low-status banks. On the other hand, if status was not an important signal during this time, then one would expect that the high-status generalists expanded into the niches occupied by other generalists since these would have been the niches in which economies of scale and scope were of greatest value.

EMPIRICAL ANALYSIS: INVESTMENT BANKING, 1920–1949

The sample for this analysis is the population of investment banks involved in underwriting between 1920 and 1949; the outcome on which we will focus is the exit of firms from this industry. When one's sample starts at a time point that is subsequent to the start of the population or subsequent to the birth of some subset of firms within the sample, then the data are said to be "left-censored" (Tuma and Hannan 1984). Organizational ecologists have been extremely concerned about the problems of making statistical inferences when one's sample includes left-censored data. Accordingly, in seeking to integrate the status-based model into the context of an ecological analysis, it seems important to collect the data at what could reasonably be said to be considered the beginning of the industry.

Of course, there is rarely an official birth date for an industry; individuals or firms may be involved episodically in some form of activity for some time before that activity can be said to constitute the basis of a functioning market or industry. Though there were a number of U.S. investment banks at the beginning of the twentieth century, underwriting activity was relatively sporadic. Historical accounts lead to the conclusion that underwriting syndicates did not become a common mechanism for raising capital until about 1920 (Carosso 1970). Accordingly, 1920 seems an appropriate year to designate as the birth of the underwriting industry as it came to be constituted. An additional, though related, reason for starting the analysis in 1920 is that this was the earliest year for which we could obtain reliable exit information on the population of firms. Until the formation of syndicates, there was not systematic record keeping on the existence of firms and, accordingly, no systematic basis for coding exit.

Although collecting data from this period allows us to focus on evolutionary dynamics to which the resource-partitioning model draws attention, one perhaps obvious fact should be noted: there is not as much detailed information on banks and security offerings during this period as during the 1980s. Thus, whereas the analyses in chapters 3 and 4 included considerable detailed information on underwriting spread and bond ratings of issuers, it is not possible to get comparable data from this earlier period.

Information on the population of investment banks involved in underwriting between 1920 and 1949 came from a variety of sources. The population was derived by consulting tombstone advertisements that appeared in the *Wall Street Journal* between 1919 and 1948.[3] This selection procedure resulted in a final set of 6,606 tombstone advertisements between 1919 and 1949. Investment banks with headquarters outside the United States and Canada were deleted from the sample since systematic organizational-level data for banks outside North America were not available. The tombstones over this period yielded a list of 1,973 North American banks; collectively these 1,973 banks represented 10,950 bank-years of data, yielding an average of $10,950/1,973 = 5.54$ years that a bank was in the population. The sample was concluded in 1949 because this time period seemed sufficient to examine the market dynamics of interest.[4]

Another source for information on investment banks was Standard & Poor's *Security Dealers of North America*, published at semiannual intervals beginning in 1920 (Standard & Poor's, 1920–1950). Though this source is probably the most complete listing of investment banks over the time period of the study, it does not distinguish between those banks that were involved in underwriting activity and those that were not. The number of investment banks not involved in underwriting activity far exceeded the number involved. Therefore, this source provides information on a number of organization-level variables, but it is not appropriate for determining the boundaries on the population.

---

[3] Only those tombstones detailing the public offerings of securities providing *new* funding were used for the purpose of determining the population. Announcements of refunding issues, private placements, and advisory activities concerning mergers and acquisitions were all excluded.

[4] One might wonder why it was possible to collect so many more tombstone advertisements for this period than for the 1980s. That is, in chapters 3 and 4, data collection was limited to only a few hundred tombstones because of the practical constraints of time, but in this chapter over 6,000 tombstone advertisements were collected. The reason is that the number of banks on a typical tombstone advertisement during this period was considerably smaller than the number in the 1980s. During this period, one does not observe massive syndicates with over 100 banks; tombstone advertisements with fewer than a dozen banks are quite common during this period, and the coding time is more a function of the number of bank appearances than the number of tombstone advertisements. If one were to compare the number of bank appearances across the data sets, then the data sets would be more comparable in terms of size.

In addition to delimiting the set of banks constituting the population of under-writers, the tombstone advertisements between 1919 and 1948 provided the information to determine status and niche width. Finally, the tombstone advertisements were used to acquire information on the number of offerings in which a bank was involved and on the dollar volume of security offerings for which a bank was lead underwriter.

The publication *Security Dealers of North America* contains information enabling the coding of organizational-level data on year of founding and legal form. Though the directory is the most complete record of investment banks in the United States, the founding year is not listed for every bank in the sample. For some banks whose founding year is not listed, it was possible to obtain this information from bank anniversaries announced in the *Wall Street Journal*. However, it was still not possible to determine the founding year for 324 banks (16%). With respect to legal form, the listing for each bank indicates whether it was organized as a partnership or as a corporation.

In this analysis, a bank is considered at risk for exit beginning with its initial appearance in a tombstone. Since a bank can exist for many years before it first appears in a tombstone, including a bank in the risk set before its first tombstone appearance would introduce bias into the estimates. A bank's "underwriting life history" therefore begins with its entrance into the set of tombstone banks.

Dependent Variable: Exit from Underwriting in the Primary Securities Markets

Because we are focusing on the primary securities markets and because banks could engage in activities other than underwriting, our outcome of interest is the exit of the bank from the primary securities market rather than failure of the entire organization. For the 10,950 bank-years in our data, there are a total of 2,714 exit events. Obviously, failure of the bank is one of the reasons that a bank would have exited the primary securities market. However, it is not the only reason. In addition, a bank may have exited because it simply chose to exclude underwriting from the set of activities in which it engaged.

Since banks did not announce the date of their exit from underwriting, the only reliable indicator of exit is a bank's *lack of* participation in an underwriting syndicate over some time period. A bank is considered at risk of exit in year t only if it appeared in a tombstone advertisement in the previous year. A bank is coded as exiting the underwriting market in year t when it did not participate in underwriting in year t. Of the 2,714 exit events, 152 were due to failure. Obviously, there is some arbitrariness in coding an exit as a one-year departure. The one-year time period is convenient and sensible because the time-varying covariates in the analysis are generally updated on an annual basis.

Especially given that the analysis in chapters 3 and 4 focused on important differences between the investment-grade and non-investment-grade markets, one might reasonably ask why this analysis focuses on exit from underwriting rather than on the exit from different primary securities markets. Even though the non-investment-grade debt market would not exist for many more decades, equity and debt were still recognized as separate forms of security issues. The reason is relatively straightforward. As noted above, underwriting syndicates started to appear with some regularity only around 1920; there was relatively little differentiation between the two markets. Historical accounts would write about the emergence of underwriting activity without writing separately about underwriting of equity and debt; accordingly, during this time period, it seems more reasonable to think of originating equity and originating debt as constituting one primary securities market.

Independent Variables

For the purpose of analyzing exit, any independent variables are lagged a year. Obviously, the variables of central analytical interest are status, niche width, and market concentration, but a number of other variables are included as control variables.

Status.   Status is measured the same way that it was measured in chapters 3 and 4—by applying Bonacich's $c(\alpha,\beta)$ measure to the tombstone advertisements.

Niche width (NW).   Specialism and generalism are relevant to competition in the investment banking industry. For the purpose of this analysis, niche width will be chacterized in terms of the diversity of industries among the issuers for which the bank served as underwriter. While probably not the only dimension of resource utilization for characterizing niche width, industry diversity is an important one. On the one hand, some investment banks had established reputations as specialists in particular industries. In the early twentieth century, Kuhn Loeb rose to prominence on its underwriting of railroad issues. Similarly, Halsey Stuart gained prominence by focusing on issues for public utilities, motion picture companies, and publication corporations (Carosso 1970). Many banks concentrated their relationship building and maintenance activities to target particular industries.

On the other hand, some investment banks underwrote firms in many industries. Until the end of the 1920s, J. P. Morgan, arguably the highest-status bank of the early history of investment banking, underwrote for issuers in many industries. This background suggests that information on the diversity of industries for which a bank underwrote offers one reasonable conceptualization of the niche width of an investment bank. While one might point to regional specialization as another possible basis for identifying niche width, the empirical analysis does not incorporate a measure of regional specialization for two reasons. First, while there are clearly banks that were regional specialists, regional specialization has more relevance to the location of a bank's investor clients than the issuers whose syndicates the bank would join. For example, Kidder Peabody, based in Boston during the period of the study, had primarily New England investment clients, but it did not participate only in syndicates that underwrote New England firms (Carosso 1970). While Kidder Peabody was perhaps more likely to take a lead management or comanagement position if the firm making the offering was a New England firm, it participated as a syndicate member on offerings for firms from across the United States. The second reason for not defining niche width according to regional specialization follows from the first. Because "regional specialists" did not restrict their syndicate participation to firms located in their particular region, it is practically quite difficult to measure regional specialization.

The level of heterogeneity of a bank's syndicate participation across industries can be measured from information on tombstones. Since the name of the issuer of the securities always appeared on the tombstone, it is possible to determine the primary industry in which the issuer's activities occurred. During the period of the study, tombstones often indicated the primary industry of the issuer. Even when this was not the case, it is relatively easy to assign issuers to an industry. Drawing on the Standard Industrial Classification system, we constructed a twenty-three-industry category code. Given these categories, the niche width for bank i can be defined as follows:

$$NW_{it} = 1 - \sum_{j=1}^{23} \left(\frac{\tau_{jt}}{n_t} \right)^2,$$

where NW_{it} is the niche width of firm i in year t, τ_{jt} equals the number of syndicate participations for firm i in industry category j in year t, and n_t equals the total number of syndicate participations for bank i in year t. If a bank's syndication activities are concentrated entirely in one industry, its niche width equals 0. A bank with a niche width of 0 is a "pure" specialist; that is, the bank's syndication activities are concentrated in one category. The more that a bank's syndication activities are equally dispersed across all the categories, the more closely its niche width approaches 1.

Market concentration (HI).   This variable measures the Herfindahl index of the volume that banks underwrote as lead managers. Formally, the measure is defined as follows:

$$HI_t = \sum_{i=1}^{n} S_{it}^2,$$

where S_{it} equals the proportion of underwriting volume in year t for which bank i was lead manager. This variable is updated annually and is lagged one year.

Environmental variables.   Market and institutional conditions over the history of the investment banking industry may systematically affect the likelihood of exit from the primary securities markets. Historical accounts of U.S. investment banking (Waterman 1958; Longstreet and Hess 1967; Miller 1967; Carosso 1970) identify several periods across which one would expect the hazard of exit to vary: the Depression (1929–1934), post-Depression regulatory reform (1935–1941), U.S. involvement in World War II (1942–1945) and, finally, post–World War II (1946–1949). These historical periods are associated with substantial shifts in the institutional and/or competitive environments of the U.S. investment banking industry. Accordingly, indicator variables for all these time periods except one are included in the analysis; the residual category in this analysis is the period from 1920 to 1928.[5]

Another environmental variable incorporated into the analysis is the volume of capital issues in the United States. Total underwriting activity is measured using annual estimates of total foreign and domestic stock and bond issues (in hundreds of millions of dollars) published in the *Statistical Abstract of the United States* (U.S. Department of Commerce, various years).

As noted at the outset of this chapter, ecological analysis has highlighted the importance of density (i.e., the number of firms in an industry) as a critical driver of the vital rates for a population. Accordingly, density is included as an environmental variable in the analysis. Density is defined as the total number of firms that appeared in tombstones in the previous year. The variable is lagged by one year to ensure exogeneity.

Organizational variables.   Control variables are included for several organizational characteristics that may systematically affect mortality rates—specifically, age, legal form, and market volume.

Because of missing data on age for some banks as well as some substantive distinctions in the way that a firm can exit a market, modeling the effects of age is complicated. Age effects are accordingly measured in four ways. The first measure of age is the bank's actual *age*, measured from the time of founding. Second, since some banks did not immediately participate in underwriting activities when they were founded, a second age variable is included in the analysis which reflects a bank's "incubation" period between its founding and its first observable appearance in a syndicate. This variable is labeled *age at*

---

[5] As with most analyses involving indicator variables for historical periods, there exists some degree of judgment in determining the dividing points for the historical periods. Additional analyses were conducted in which the dividing points were shifted by a year. The results are generally robust across these alternative codings, suggesting that the dividing points are sensible.

first tombstone. The value of this variable remains fixed over the duration of the bank's inclusion in the risk set. The third measure of age is a *risk-set clock.* This measure captures the number of years a bank has been at risk of exit, either by failure or by departure. The clock is reset to 0 after each departure event. The fourth measure of age is *total number of years in the risk set.* This measure is the sum of the bank's risk-set clocks across multiple appearances in the risk set. A bank can appear in the risk set more than once, for instance, if it exits from underwriting for a two-year period and then returns.

Conflicting empirical results on age dependence suggest that one may want to refrain from using parametric models that do not allow for complex relationships between age and departure from the market.[6] This intuition seems most relevant to the waiting-time measure of age. Thus, the effect of the risk-set clock is allowed to vary across time segments, but the effect remains constant within each segment. The risk-set clock is divided into seven segments: 0–2, 2–4, 4–7, 7–10, 10–15, 15–20, and more than 20 years.

As discussed above, there is not complete information on the founding years of the investment banks. In 16 percent of the observations, information on year of founding is simply missing. For a subset of these observations (9 percent of the population), there is evidence from the *Wall Street Journal* that the banks existed in the decade prior to 1919, the first year of data. For this 9 percent, the founding information is left-censored. Indicator variables are used to denote missing observations of each type.[7]

During the observation period, investment banks assumed two legal forms, the *partnership* and the corporation. To examine whether legal form had any effect on the likelihood of organizational exit, banks organized as partnerships were coded 1, while banks organized as corporations were coded 0. This variable is updated annually and is lagged one year.

Underwriting volume was measured as in the analyses in the earlier chapters— the natural log of the volume of securities underwritten by a bank as lead manager during a given year. More specifically, since a number of banks in the data led no issues and since the log of 0 is undefined, the variable is actually the log of underwriting volume + 1.

---

[6] However, see Carroll and Hannan (2000) for a theoretical attempt to reconcile these conflicting empirical findings.

[7] For all observations with missing information on year of founding, the age variable denoting the *risk-set clock* was calculated in the same way that it was calculated for observations on which we had full information: time since first observable appearance in a syndicate beginning with 1919. Likewise, the age variable denoting *age at first tombstone* was set to 0 for these same observations. This coding scheme allows us to interpret the effect of the incubation variable as the effect of incubation years for those observations on which we have full information. The indicator variables will indicate whether or not there is any systematic difference between the exit rates of those firms on which there is missing age information and those on which there is complete age information. Finally, for the observations with no determinable founding date, *age* was counted beginning with the bank's first appearance in a tombstone. Thus, *age* and *age at first tombstone* are equal in such cases.

The *number of times a bank served as lead manager* on securities issues during a given year was included as a final organizational covariate. Both underwriting volume and lead manager count were derived from the information contained in the tombstone advertisements.

Results

The hazard of exit is estimated using a piecewise constant exponential model implementation in TDA 5.2 (Rohwer 1993). A piecewise model is appropriate when organizations begin before the sample period, as left-censoring can introduce bias into many other parametric hazard rate models (Guo 1993). One additional feature of the piecewise model is that the effect of time can be allowed to vary over preselected ranges. Baseline probabilities are estimated for each time period.

Table 8.1 presents descriptive statistics for the data. Each observation represents one organization-year. Table 8.2 presents correlations among the variables. The correlation between status and niche width is worth noting. Consistent with what we observed in figure 8.2, generalists tend to be higher-status than specialists, though investment banks of narrow and broad niche width are common at all points in the status distribution. Table 8.3 presents the results

TABLE 8.1
Descriptive Statistics for Investment Banking, 1920–1949

	Mean	*S.D.*	*Min.*	*Max.*
1. Risk-set clock	2.64	3.98	0	30
2. Total number of years in risk set	6.09	6.47	0	30
3. Age	19.33	22.46	0	163
4. Age at first tombstone	10.96	18.67	0	162
5. Founding year missing	.16	.37	0	1
6. Left-censored	.18	.38	0	1
7. Capital issues in U.S. ($100 millions)	65.68	28.29	10.54	115.92
8. Density/100	3.15	1.12	.99	5.32
9. Partnership	.50	.50	0	1
10. Log(volume as lead manager)	3.01	6.19	0	20.86
11. Number of issues as lead manager	.60	2.79	0	120
12. Status	.35	.78	0	5.26
13. Niche width	.24	.31	0	.92
14. Market concentration	.09	.04	0	.22
15. Niche width × market concentration	.02	.03	0	.14
16. Status × market concentration	.03	.08	0	.75
17. Status × niche width	.26	.59	0	4.17

10,950 yearly spells

TABLE 8.2
Pearson Correlation Coefficients

	1	2	3	4	5	6	7	8	9	10	11	12	13	14	15	16
1. Risk-set clock																
2. Total number of years in risk set	.67															
3. Age	.33	.48														
4. Age at first tombstone	.14	.18	.93													
5. Founding year missing	-.00*	.07	-.16	-.24												
6. Left-censored	.30	.40	.43	.25	.24											
7. Capital issues in U.S.	.06	.02	.00*	.00*	-.01*	-.06										
8. Density/100	.14	.18	.06	-.02*	-.20	-.18	.58									
9. Partnership	.05	.07	.22	.22	-.09	.10	.02	.01*								
10. Log(volume as lead manager)	.38	.26	.17	.10	.02	.24	-.03	.03	.03							
11. Number of issues as lead manager	.38	.22	.10	.02	-.01*	.13	.02	.03	-.03	.50						
12. Status	.59	.46	.30	.17	.02*	.30	.00*	.04	.01*	.55	.49					
13. Niche width	.49	.42	.24	.11	.00*	.28	.11	.10	.05	.41	.28	.50				
14. Market concentration	-.00*	.06	.02	-.00*	-.05	-.02	-.25	-.14	.01*	-.05	-.01*	-.01*	-.05			
15. Niche width × market concentration	.47	.43	.23	.09	.00*	-.24	-.07	.10	.05	.37	.27	.46	.91	.19		
16. Status × market concentration	.56	.45	.27	.15	.00*	.26	-.03	.02	.01*	.50	.46	.92	.44	.14	.52	
17. Status × niche width	.55	.43	.26	.14	-.00*	.30	.05	.06	.01*	.51	.50	.88	.63	.02*	.58	.78

10,950 yearly spells
*Not significant at .05 level

TABLE 8.3
Piecewise Constant Exponential Models of Investment Bank Exit, 1920–1949

Variables	Model 1	Model 2	Model 3	Model 4	Model 5	Model 6
Risk-set clock (in years)						
0–2	−2.725** (.153)	−1.638** (.196)	−1.626** (.196)	−1.659** (.197)	−1.563** (.198)	−1.579** (.198)
2–4	−2.442** (.160)	−1.627** (.201)	−1.629** (.202)	−1.653** (.202)	−1.549** (.203)	−1.567** (.203)
4–7	−1.696** (.163)	−.783** (.203)	−.772** (.203)	−.807** (.204)	−.697** (.205)	−.715** (.205)
7–10	−.789** (.172)	.256 (.213)	.291 (.213)	.230 (.213)	.348 (.214)	.329 (.215)
10–15	−.539** (.181)	1.773** (.221)	1.868** (.222)	1.748** (.222)	1.875** (.223)	1.855** (.224)
15–20	2.056** (.209)	3.588** (.248)	3.688** (.249)	3.567** (.249)	3.715** (.250)	3.694** (.251)
>20	4.148** (.224)	5.944** (.265)	6.091** (.268)	5.096** (.266)	6.099** (.268)	6.068** (.269)
Total number of years in risk set	−.220*** (.006)	−.271** (.007)	−.266** (.007)	−.271** (.007)	−.270** (.007)	−.271** (.007)
Age	−.285** (.006)	−.313** (.007)	−.323** (.007)	−.313** (.007)	−.317** (.007)	−.316** (.007)
Age at first tombstone	.286** (.007)	.315** (.007)	.324** (.008)	.315** (.007)	.319** (.007)	.318** (.007)
Founding year missing	.299** (.059)	.308** (.059)	.261** (.059)	.312** (.059)	.307** (.059)	.309** (.059)
Left-censored	−.249** (.082)	−.406** (.083)	−.318** (.081)	−.404* (.083)	−.398** (.083)	−.397** (.083)
Periods						
Depression (1929–34)	−.281** (.093)	−.167 (.095)	−.157 (.094)	−.154 (.095)	−.174 (.095)	−.168 (.095)
Regulation (1935–41)	−.565** (.101)	−.412** (.106)	−.419** (.105)	−.409** (.106)	−.396** (.106)	−.396** (.106)
World War II (1942–45)	−.603** (.127)	−.550** (.129)	−.567** (.129)	−.546** (.129)	−.538** (.129)	−.537** (.129)
Post–World War II (1946–50)	−.982** (.136)	−.907** (.151)	−.895** (.151)	−.918** (.151)	−.892** (.151)	−.898** (.151)
Capital issues in U.S.	−.006** (.001)	−.007** (.001)	−.007** (.001)	−.007** (.001)	−.007** (.001)	−.007** (.001)
Density/100	.306** (.028)	.275** (.029)	.277** (.029)	.277** (.029)	.275** (.029)	.276** (.029)

TABLE 8.3 (*continued*)
Piecewise Constant Exponential Models of Investment Bank Exit, 1920–1949

Variables	Model 1	Model 2	Model 3	Model 4	Model 5	Model 6
Partnership	.019 (.040)	-.003 (.040)	.006 (.040)	-.005 (.040)	-.006 (.040)	-.007 (.040)
Log(volume as lead manager)	.332** (.032)	.197** (.035)	.133** (.036)	.194** (.035)	.193** (.036)	.192** (.036)
Log(volume as lead manager)²	-.018** (.002)	-.011** (.003)	.007** (.003)	-.011** (.003)	-.011** (.003)	-.011** (.003)
Number of issues as lead manager	-.201** (.054)	-.332** (.061)	-.339** (.063)	-.339** (.061)	-.351** (.061)	-.353** (.061)
Market concentration (*HI*)		-.651 (.648)	-.897** (.652)	-.631 (.651)	-1.615* (.672)	-1.527** (.676)
Niche width (*NW*)		1.759** (.045)	1.960** (.049)	1.496** (.103)	1.758** (.045)	1.632** (.108)
Status (*STATUS*)		-.609** (.059)	.306** (.057)	-.635** (.063)	-1.108** (.119)	-1.066** (.124)
STATUS × *NW*			-3.603** (.246)			
NW × *HI*				3.054** (1.094)		1.469 (1.145)
STATUS × *HI*					5.938** (1.074)	5.467** (1.146)
Log-likelihood	-8485.12	-7573.25	-7401.14	-7569.28	-7560.23	-7559.40
χ^2 (against baseline)		1823.74**	2167.96**	1831.68**	1849.78**	1851.44**
χ^2 (against previous)		1823.74**	344.22**	7.94**	26.04**	27.70**

Numbers in parentheses are standard errors.

*$p < .05$; ** $p < .01$

for piecewise exponential models of organizational exit. The first column in table 8.3 shows the baseline model that includes the period effects and control variables. Looking first at the operational measures of age, we see that the risk of exit increases with waiting time. With the exception of one period (7–10 years), the effects are statistically significant. At the same time, the risk of exit declines with the total number of years that a bank has spent in the risk set. Age at first tombstone, left-censoring, and missing information about the founding year increase the likelihood of exit. Yet because of the data limitations on organizational age, one needs to be extremely cautious in interpreting the results and implications of the various age measures.

As one would expect, a higher volume of capital issues reduces the likelihood of exit. For instance, a $200 million increase in yearly underwriting activity slightly decreases the likelihood of exit: $\exp(-0.006 \times 2) = 0.988$. Increasing density in the underwriting market elevates the likelihood of exit.

There are two measures of organizational size: underwriting volume and the number of issues as lead manager. Because these variables are included as control variables, it seemed important to find the specification of these variables that provided the best fit to the data. A better fit would provide a more meaningful baseline against which to test the main effects for the variables of substantive interest. Repeated analyses looking at linear and quadratic effects for both measures of size were conducted. The combination of variables reported in column 1 provided the best fit to the data.

The number of issues as lead manager is statistically significant. Banks that acted as lead manager have a lower rate of exit. Underwriting volume has a curvilinear effect on exit. Initially, the exit rate begins to rise, then levels off and declines. Only banks with an underwriting volume as lead manager above $10,240,000 in one year have a lower exit rate than banks with $0 in underwriting volume as a lead manager. Just by itself, this latter result implies the difficulty of being a middle-of-the-road firm, between the smaller specialists and larger generalists.

The model in column 2 adds the main effects of market concentration, status, and niche width. Market concentration does not have a significant effect on the exit rate. Consistent with previous research demonstrating the benefits of status, status lowers an organization's hazard of exit. One way to understand the benefit of status is to compare various values of status. A one-standard-deviation increase in status from a value of 0 lowers the likelihood of exit by almost 40 percent: $\exp(-0.609 \times 0.78) = 0.622$. The effects of the control variables are largely the same as in the previous model, with one notable exception. The baseline exit rate during the Depression is no longer even marginally significant. The model is a statistically significant improvement in fit over the baseline model ($\chi^2 = 1823.74$, d.f. $= 3$, $p < .01$).

The model in column 3 examines the interaction of status and niche width. According to the resource-status space hypothesis, firms with a broader niche width will benefit more from status than will firms with a narrower niche width. The interaction lowers the likelihood of exit and is significant. Therefore, consistent with the resource-status space hypothesis, a given increment in status reduces the likelihood of exit the broader a firm's niche width. The model is a statistically significant improvement in fit over model 2 ($\chi^2 = 344.22$, d.f. $= 1, p < .01$).

It is noteworthy that when this interaction is included, the main effect for status becomes positive and statistically significant. Thus, for a firm whose niche width is 0 (i.e., all offerings are for firms in the same industry), increments in status have a positive effect on mortality, suggesting the strong risk to which such narrow specialists exposed themselves when they moved into segments where economies of scale and scope had greater benefits.

The model in column 4 adds the interaction of niche width and market concentration. The main effects of both status and niche width on organizational exit remain significant ($p < .01$). Because there is an interaction between niche width and market concentration, the coefficient for market concentration denotes the effect of concentration for firms with a niche width of 0 (i.e., a pure specialist). Following from the resource-partitioning hypothesis, we expect that increasing market concentration would lower the exit rate of pure specialists. Though the coefficient is in the expected direction, it is not statistically significant. The interaction between niche width and market concentration is positive and statistically significant; accordingly, the resource-partitioning hypothesis receives support.

The model in column 5 examines whether there is status-based partitioning in the market. To do so, the model adds an interaction between status and market concentration to the specification in model 2. The model is a statistically significant improvement in fit over model 2 ($\chi^2 = 26.04$, d.f. $= 1, p < .01$). The coefficient for market concentration is -1.615. Since there is an interaction between market concentration and status in this model, this coefficient denotes the effect of market concentration when status equals 0.

The significant negative coefficient signifies that increasing market concentration has a negative effect on the exit of organizations with a status of 0. The positive interaction between market concentration and status indicates that the higher an organization's status, the stronger the positive effect of market concentration on the hazard of exit.

As status increases, the effect of increasing concentration on exit switches from negative to positive. Using a p level of .05, it is straightforward to show that the effect of market concentration on exit is significantly greater than 0 when status takes on a value above 0.62.[8] That is, for all firms whose status is

---

[8] To test for the value at which the effect of status is greater than 0, one first specifies the effect of market concentration on life chances when interacted with status, which (in model 5) is $-1.615 + 5.938 \times STATUS$. The standard error associated with this joint effect is the square root of the sum of the variances associated with each of the coefficients minus twice the covariance of the coefficient estimates. This standard error equals 1.04. Accordingly, it is straightforward to show that this effect is significantly greater than 0 for all status values greater than 0.62.

greater than 0.62, the expansion of the highest-status firms has a positive effect on exit. While this value of 0.62 is significantly higher than the mean of 0.17, it is still somewhat surprising that the expansion of the highest-status firms, whose status is in the range from 3 to 4, would have a negative effect on firms whose status is as low as 0.62. In the full model in column 6, the value at which the null can be rejected is somewhat higher, but not significantly so. It is perhaps important to remember that the estimates for the main effect of concentration and the interaction between concentration and status have some uncertainty associated with them. If the "true" main effect were one standard deviation below the −1.615 value and the "true" interaction effect were also one standard deviation below the value of 5.938, then the null could be rejected only for those banks with a status approximately greater than 0.9. Such a cutoff would represent only the top forty or so banks in any given year. Thus, while one needs to interpret the point estimates cautiously, the results point to a partitioning based on status.

Finally, column 6 in table 8.3 reports the interaction effect of market concentration and status along with the interaction effect of market concentration and niche width. In this model, the interaction of status and market concentration remains significant while the interaction of niche width and market concentration becomes insignificant. This notable result indicates that the previously significant interaction of market concentration and niche width is spurious. That interaction, which indicates partitioning on the basis of niche width, appeared significant because the possibility of partitioning on the basis of status was not considered.

Even though partitioning on the basis of status dominates partitioning on the basis of niche width in this particular analysis, there are good reasons to believe that this will not always be the case. In chapter 4, we observed that stratification on the basis of status was inversely related to market uncertainty. In contrast, the level of uncertainty is not likely to affect the extent to which niche width is a salient basis of stratification, since scale and scope economies will be technologically determined. Accordingly, over time one would expect some of the partitioning on the basis of status to give way to partitioning on the basis of niche width.

Obviously, such a conclusion is necessarily speculative; however, regardless of whether status or niche width is a more important basis for stratification in a particular context, this analysis suggests that the basic dynamic of Carroll's resource-partitioning model is more general than was stated in its original formulation. Carroll posited that as industries evolve, increasing concentration implies the elimination of "middle-of-the-road" firms, which in turn benefits the peripheral firms that compete with the "middle-of-the-road" firms but are in a completely different niche than the market leaders. Whereas Carroll formulated his model with reference to niche width, I asserted that the basic dynamic that he posits can apply to another organizational dimension or property whenever two conditions hold: (1) firms occupy a series of interdependent niches along that dimension, and (2) firms have limits on the extent to which they can expand from their location on this dimension. The analysis of the investment banking industries discussed in this chapter provides empirical evidence that this dynamic can be applied to status. Additional research could perhaps point to even further dimensions.

Probably the most general implication of this chapter is that it provides a further illustration of how a consideration of status dynamics is also compatible with a focus on market evolution. To foreshadow a point to which I shall return in the conclusion, the Matthew Effect implies that status dynamics are inherently stabilizing and self-reinforcing. While it is certainly true that a signaling mechanism does imply an equilibrating dynamic, this chapter as well as the previous two should hopefully illustrate that an analytical focus on status dynamics is compatible with a focus on market evolution. Chapter 5 showed how status could illuminate the technological underpinnings of the way in which market quality changes over time. Chapter 6 documented how status could illuminate dynamics around market entry, and this chapter shows how the status lens is relevant to understanding the implications of increasing concentration in the market as well as market exit. Although we are still a far way from an encompassing statement of how the inherently self-reinforcing properties of the status-based model link to various facets of market evolution, these three chapters provide some valuable analytical leads.

Chapter Nine

UNCERTAINTY RECONSIDERED

As we have investigated the significance of status as a signal, the concept of uncertainty has been central. In the first two chapters, I essentially argued that market uncertainty is the raison d'être of status as a signal; in the empirical chapters that followed, we observed that the market consequences of status are contingent on the underlying level of uncertainty.

In drawing out these implications of market uncertainty, I have—at least until this chapter—adopted a conception of uncertainty that can be largely reduced to the asymmetry between information known by an actor taking on the role of an evaluator and information known by an actor who is the target of the evaluation. While the evaluator is uncertain about the true quality of the target actor's actions, products, services, or efforts, the target actor is not uncertain. So, for example, the examination of the investment banking industry rested on the assumption an investment bank's potential exchange partners were uncertain about the quality of a bank's services, but there was no assumption that the bank itself was uncertain of the quality of services that it would or could provide to potential exchange partners. Similarly, the study of the wine industry rested on the assumption that consumers were uncertain as to the quality of a winery's bottle, but there was no assumption that the winery faced uncertainty about the quality of wine that it could or did produce.

In this chapter, I would like to focus on situations in which the target of evaluation confronts uncertainty about how to organize its resources to provide quality at a desired level. In so doing, I will introduce a distinction between two types of uncertainty: *altercentric uncertainty*, the uncertainty that an evaluator has about qualities of a target being evaluated, and *egocentric uncertainty*, the uncertainty that the target of the evaluation has about which combinations of inputs and resource allocation decisions will yield products or services above a desired level of quality. Given this distinction, it should be clear that altercentric uncertainty is the type of uncertainty posited in the empirical analyses that have appeared in the preceding chapters in this book. As an example of egocentric uncertainty, consider the uncertainty confronted by an automobile producer whose resource allocation decisions will result in a vehicle that is perceived by some set of buyers to provide considerable value.

The presence of egocentric uncertainty does not preclude altercentric uncertainty. At the same time that the automobile manufacturer is trying to decide which combination of inputs and resource allocation decisions will result in

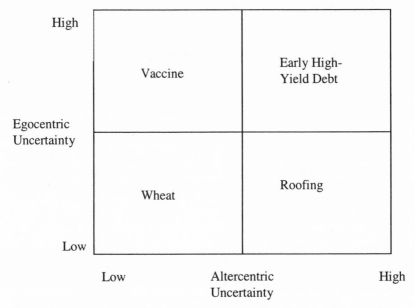

FIGURE 9.1. Illustrative markets arrayed by altercentric and egocentric uncertainty

a vehicle at a desired level of quality, consumers or possibly other constituencies, such as potential alliance partners, are trying to make inferences about the quality of goods or services that the producer presents to them in the market.

However, just as one type of uncertainty does not necessarily preclude the other, so one type of uncertainty does not necessitate the other. It is possible to consider contexts that are high on one type of uncertainty but low on others. For example, consider the four markets represented in figure 9.1, beginning with the market for a particular vaccine, such as polio or smallpox, in the upper left-hand quadrant. The most salient source of uncertainty in this market is in that which underlies the development of the vaccine. Once the vaccine is developed and is given regulatory approval, there is little uncertainty on the part of consumers as to whether they will benefit from the invention. Accordingly, a market for a vaccine is one that rates high on egocentric uncertainty but low on altercentric uncertainty. Alternatively, consider the market in the lower right-hand corner, a regional market for roofers. "Roofing technology" is relatively well understood, and while roofers may face some uncertainty as to who needs a roof in any particular year, they can be confident that every homeowner will need repair work or a replacement every twenty years or so. By sending out fliers or advertising in the yellow pages, they can be assured of reaching a constituency with a demand for their service. However, because an individual consumer only infrequently enters the market, the consumer is generally unaware of the quality-based distinctions among roofers. The consumer may be able to alleviate some of this uncertainty through consultation with others who have recently had roof repairs; however, the need for such consultation is an illustration of the basic point. Only through such search and consultation can the consumer's relatively high level of uncertainty be reduced. Accordingly, this is a market that is relatively low in egocentric uncertainty but relatively high in altercentric uncertainty. Many of the standard "asymmetric information" models in economics, such as the reputation or signaling models considered in earlier chapters, assume market conditions that are implicitly high on altercentric uncertainty and low on egocentric uncertainty. However, such asymmetric information is not the only condition that would imply this combination of altercentric and egocentric uncertainty. Another instance of this combination occurs in "conspicuous consumption" markets, in which buyers purchase goods not so much for their inherent quality but in order to demonstrate that they are part of an elite that consumes a particular brand. In this case, the uncertainty of the buyers is less about the inherent quality of the good and more about the trends in tastes and fashion that will lead one brand or style to become identified with elite status.

Finally, there are some markets that may be high or low in both egocentric and altercentric uncertainty. Particularly during the time of its emergence, the market for non-investment-grade debt was arguably high in both types even though egocentric uncertainty probably declined rapidly after Drexel and then the major investment banks better understood with whom and at what volume the securities could be placed.

Although altercentric uncertainty has been the type of uncertainty that has been implicit in the previous chapters in this book, it is important to consider the distinction between altercentric uncertainty and egocentric uncertainty in some detail if only because the conception of egocentric uncertainty is actually more prevalent in the sociological and organizational literatures. Even though the actual terminology of egocentric uncertainty is not employed, it is fair to say that the "Carnegie School" and its behavioral theory of the firm is fundamentally concerned with how best to organize a firm given the presence of egocentric uncertainty. Notions such as "satisficing search behavior" and the "garbage can theory" of decision-making all arise from an image of firms that do not know how best to organize inputs and allocate resources internally to produce a desired output. Similarly, much of the literature on information flow in networks assumes the perspective of a focal actor trying to assess what combinations of resources are most critical to the realization of the actor's goals rather than trying to make inferences about the quality of other actors.

Given the analytical distinction between altercentric and egocentric uncertainty, my basic claim is the following: whereas *altercentric uncertainty* in a market enhances the value of a high-status position, *egocentric uncertainty* in a market actually undercuts the value of occupying a high-status position. There are two reasons why this is the case. The first reason follows directly from a consideration of one of the primary mechanisms by which status generates advantage. The second reason follows from a consideration of the type of network position whose value is actually enhanced by egocentric uncertainty. We shall consider each of these reasons in turn.

As we have observed, the advantage of status rests at least in part on the fact that potential exchange partners would prefer to enter into an exchange relation with a high-status rather than a low-status producer. To oversimplify somewhat, ceteris paribus, the highest-status producer should essentially have its choice of exchange partner. To be sure, the highest-status producer may have reason to avoid entering into exchange relations with some potential exchange partners. The highest-status producer may wish to avoid exchange relations with a low-status actor either because the producer believes the low-status actor to be of low quality or because the producer is simply concerned that the affiliation with a low-status actor will lower the producer's own status. Yet, what is important is that the highest-status producer has greater discretion than other producers in choosing an exchange partner. While the highest-status producer may generally wish to avoid entering an exchange relation with low-status others, the highest-status producer may also decide on occasion that the potential benefits of such a relation outweigh the potential costs.

The value of such enhanced access is contingent on the extent to which the high-status producer is able to ascertain what combination of exchange relations will actually result in a superior-quality product or service. A higher-status producer may have greater access to upstream suppliers, providers of financial capital, human capital, and alliance partners, but unless the producer knows what combination of those relations will result in a higher-quality product, the enhanced access is of little value.

Since a market segment that is high in egocentric uncertainty is by definition one in which the producer is not certain what combination of inputs is likely to result in the most desirable output, status is of little value in such a context. When egocentric uncertainty is high, a producer does not know how it should best use the enhanced access that status provides.

This observation is perhaps best captured by framing the matching process of markets in terms of a queuing imagery. Imagine that producers queue up for whatever exchange opportunities they would like to pursue, and their position in the queue is a function of their desirability as an exchange partner. To the extent that others prefer to enter into an exchange relation with a higher-status rather than a lower-status producer, then ceteris paribus the highest-status producer should be at the front of the queue, the second highest-status producer should be next in line, and so on. However, when egocentric uncertainty is high, the highest-status producer does not know for which exchange opportunities it should queue up. As a result, in the high egocentric uncertainty context, its status is of little value; in contrast, in the low egocentric uncertainty context, there is tremendous benefit in being able to be at the front of the queue. Thus, one reason that status is of little benefit in a context of high egocentric uncertainty is that high-status actors do not know on which exchange relations they should spend their status, and as a result high-status firms should seek to avoid markets or market segments in which egocentric uncertainty is high.

While the above reason is perhaps a sufficient explanation for why high-status firms would seek to avoid contexts in which egocentric uncertainty is high, there is a second reason that comes from Burt's (1992) theory of structural holes. Burt uses the term "structural holes" to refer to a network position in which an actor's exchange partners are disconnected from one another. In effect, the actor is the hub at the center of an otherwise disconnected exchange network. Burt argues that the network position yielding the most information benefits is a network rich in structural holes. By being connected to actors who are themselves otherwise disconnected, a focal actor is exposed to a broader variety of information more quickly than if the actor were part of a clique of densely connected actors, and when the actor is uncertain as to how to allocate resources, more rapid access to a broader array of information is a tremendous advantage.

Though Burt does not use the concept of egocentric uncertainty in discussing the information benefits of structural holes, it seems clear that this conception of uncertainty is strongly aligned to his understanding of information benefits. The structural holes in a focal actor's network are not a basis for others to make inferences about the actor; rather they determine the extent to which the focal actor overcomes uncertainty about how to best act to realize his or her interest.[1]

Thus, the automobile manufacturer that has alliances with manufacturers who are otherwise disconnected is more likely to have access to information that will enhance the quality of its vehicles than the automobile manufacturer

---

[1] In the earliest formulation of his structural hole argument, Burt (1992) also suggested that structural holes in ego's network might be valuable in establishing a broad, positive reputation. If ego is connected only to a small, tightly bound clique of individuals, then there are at most only these few individuals who will be exposed to ego's reputation. Conversely, if ego is connected to a large number of individuals who are themselves disconnected, then ego can more easily establish a broad, positive reputation. If this relationship between structural holes and reputation exists, then the value of structural holes would also be enhanced by altercentric uncertainty. When altercentric uncertainty is high, those with many structural holes in their network would have a reputational advantage over those with few structural holes in their network. However, research by Burt and Knez (1995) finds that a broad, expansive network is not more conducive to a positive reputation. A broad, expansive network reduces the variance in an actor's reputation across a set of alters, but it does not improve the mean reputation across those alters. That is, actors with many structural holes in their network are less likely to have a very negative reputation, but they are also less likely to have a very positive reputation. As the number of structural holes in an actor's network increases, so does the probability that the actor will have a middle-of-the-road reputation. Since structural holes do not have a positive effect on an actor's reputation, the value of structural holes is enhanced only by egocentric uncertainty and not by altercentric uncertainty.

that is tightly tied to one or two other manufacturers based in the same city or country. The value of structural holes in reducing egocentric uncertainty is made even clearer when one assumes a context in which there is no egocentric uncertainty. If the automobile manufacturer had perfect information on the tastes of consumers and the production methods of competitors that were most conducive to manufacturing high-quality cars, then there would be no information to be gained from structural holes. Indeed, for this reason, Burt has argued that the informational benefits of structural holes are necessarily fleeting; as information diffuses through a market, those with initial access to that information will gradually cease to possess any competitive advantage. However, there is a tension between maximizing the structural holes in one's network and maximizing one's status since status maximization implies status-based homophily and a maximization of structural holes implies building ties across (otherwise disconnected) status boundaries. Thus, not only does egocentric uncertainty reduce the value of status; egocentric uncertainty creates competitive pressure to develop a network that will lead high-status actors to develop ties that dilute their own status. As a consequence, to the extent that an actor is high-status and wishes to preserve its status, the actor will need to sort out of markets or market segments that are high in egocentric uncertainty.

While this discussion of the different types of uncertainty and different types of network position is undeniably abstract, a simple example should help to reinforce the basic claims. Consider a college or university department making decisions about the hiring of faculty. The department enters into exchange relations in the academic labor market with the hope of offering some combination of research and teaching excellence that is valued by the various constituencies that provide the larger college or university of which it is a part with funds (i.e., incoming students, alumni, grant-making institutions, etc.).

With some oversimplification, one can think about the department's hiring decisions as taking place in one of two market segments: a junior segment, consisting of newly minted PhDs, and a senior segment, consisting of those who have held an academic position for a number of years and most likely have tenure at their current institution. Since more information is known about the individuals in the senior segment than in the junior segment, the junior segment is obviously one that is relatively high in egocentric uncertainty for the department, and the senior segment is obviously one that is relatively low.

We can now think about the personal ties of a department into its field as constituting the network of that department. The information provided by these ties can be used in evaluating the candidates in their respective market segments, and the network position of the department within the broader discipline can be characterized in terms of the volume of structural holes and status. A department with a network that is rich in structural holes is one in which the members of that department are connected to a large number of disconnected others within the field. A department with a high-status network is one in which the ties of its faculty members are primarily to (other) high-status departments.

The claim that structural holes alleviate egocentric uncertainty implies that the more structural holes in the department's joint personal network, the better that department will be in making hiring decisions in the junior segment. The personal information yielded by such a network will be helpful in this context in which there is typically little tangible information on which to make a hiring decision. In contrast, a network laden with structural holes will be of comparatively little value in the senior segment, since there exists a detailed research and teaching history on which to base evaluations that is independent of the personal information yielded through the network. Since such a department would clearly benefit from participating to a greater degree in the junior market than in the senior market, one would expect that over time such a department would devote more and more of its hiring efforts to the junior market and less and less of its time to the senior market.

The claim that status alleviates altercentric uncertainty implies that the greater the status of the department, the more the department will be at an advantage in bidding for talent in the senior segment. While status may also be of some advantage in the junior segment, the high-status department faces much greater uncertainty as to whom it should use its status to attract. As a result, departments with networks possessing numerous structural holes will tend to shift more of their hiring to the junior market, and high-status departments will tend to shift more of their hiring to the senior segment.

A reader familiar with the network conceptions of status and structural holes might reasonably ask whether status and structural holes could have these apparently opposite effects on selection of market segments. It seems reasonable to anticipate a high correlation between an actor's status and the presence of structural holes in the actor's network. An actor with many structural holes in his or her network of exchange relations is, by definition, an actor that is quite prominent in the larger network of relationships—serving as a bridge and boundary spanner across numerous diverse cliques within the larger structure.

However, even if one expects that high-status actors will have a disproportionate number of holes in their network or that Burt's entrepreneurs will generally be high-status actors, the conceptual difference between a high-status network position and a position with many structural holes is sufficient for there to often exist a real trade-off between the formation of ties that will add structural holes to the network and ties that will augment the actor's status. Consider again the example of the high-status academic department. To the extent that the focal department has ties primarily to other high-status departments, the members of the focal department can maintain or perhaps even increase the department's status by building ties to another high-status department that is tied to other departments to whom the focal department is tied. Alternatively, the focal department can attempt to build ties to a middle-status or perhaps lower-status department to which no member of the focal department is currently tied. The first would be the more status-enhancing or status-maintaining option; the second option would be more consistent with maximizing the number of structural holes.

It is important to note that, in asserting that actors possessing networks with considerable structural holes will sort into market segments that are high in egocentric uncertainty and that high-status actors will shift into segments that are low in this type of uncertainty, I do not need to assume that market actors are cognizant of how the features of their network allow them to confront the problems of egocentric uncertainty. The linkage between network pattern and market segment requires only that firms respond to reinforcement of poor or strong performance across various segments. For example, a high-status firm need only be aware that its activities in a high egocentric uncertainty segment are yielding a comparatively low return and that it therefore should direct resources toward the low egocentric uncertainty segment. The firm does not need to be aware that its status is of less use in a high egocentric uncertainty segment.

Notably, if such reinforcement is the primary driver behind the shift in segment, there is value in empirically distinguishing "focused" firms, whose fate is determined primarily by their performance in closely related markets or market segments, from diversified firms, whose fate is determined by performance across a broad array of relatively distinct markets.

The business units of diversified firms will be relatively insulated from the costs of a mismatch between network and market segment since the continued viability of the unit depends not simply on its own actions but on the actions of other business units within the firm (Milgrom and Roberts 1992). This observation leads naturally to the empirical analysis.

To test these basic claims regarding the contingent effects of status and structural holes, I focus on the venture capital market, a market in which there is considerable altercentric uncertainty across all market segments and considerable variance in egocentric uncertainty between markets segments. This variation in egocentric uncertainty allows for a test of the basic hypotheses. While the vast majority of "producers" in this market are venture capitalists, there are a significant number of other entities—companies, investment banks, diversified financial firms—that try to decide which entrepreneurial firms they should fund and which they should not. As a consequence, in conducting the analysis, it will be important to attend to whether the claims apply primarily to the venture capital firms or to these more diversified institutions.

THE EMPIRICAL CONTEXT: VENTURE CAPITAL

In venture capital markets, venture capitalists occupy an intermediary or broker role between investors and entrepreneurial companies in need of financial capital.[2] A venture capital firm enacts this brokerage role by first raising money from the investors and placing the raised money into a fund. The fund is organized as a partnership, with the senior members of the venture capital firm serving as general partners and the investors as limited partners. The venture capital firm invests the fund's money in entrepreneurial companies in exchange for an ownership stake. At the end of a fixed period of time, usually seven to ten years, the fund is dissolved. The venture capital firm takes a fraction of the proceeds, usually about 20 percent, and distributes the remainder to the limited partners in proportion to their original investment in the fund.

Venture capital firms are evaluated on their ability to generate high returns for their limited partners by successfully investing the fund's resources. A venture capital firm may be managing more than one fund at a time, but the returns to the limited partner are based solely on the performance of the fund in which she or he invested. The more successful a fund, that is, the higher the return on investment paid to the limited partners at liquidation, the easier it is for a venture capitalist to raise money for subsequent funds. Moreover, venture capital firms with a history of delivering extraordinary returns on investment to their limited partners not only find it easier to raise funds but also can increase the fraction of the proceeds that they keep for themselves.

For the purpose of this analysis, I regard investors as "consumers" and venture capital firms as "producers." From the perspective of the venture capitalist, the venture capital markets are characterized by both high egocentric uncertainty and high altercentric uncertainty, where investors constitute the critical "alters." Neither the investors nor the venture capitalists are highly certain of the benefit that they will derive from any particular investment. Even though some of the uncertainty associated with investments in this market can be "priced away" and thus transformed into risk, there remains considerable uncertainty in these markets that is difficult if not impossible to price. Venture capital emerged as an institution largely because traditional financing institutions were unwilling to invest in entrepreneurial firms lacking collateral. The origins of venture capital are thus indicative of the generally high level of egocentric and altercentric uncertainty in this particular market. In background interviews for this chapter, venture capitalists were quite open about the fact that there exist no reliable quantitative formulas for evaluating the risk associated with their investments.

A venture capital firm's quality is determined by its ability to make superior investment decisions in the context of this uncertainty. The venture capital firm must learn to identify characteristics of an entrepreneurial firm that increase the likelihood that the start-up will emerge as a success. In evaluating an entrepreneurial firm's chances for success, the venture capitalist will

---

[2] This section draws heavily on the description of the venture capital industry in Podolny and Feldman (1997).

typically consider numerous factors. For example, the venture capital firm must assess the entrepreneurial firm's technology, the managerial ability of the firm's founders, the dynamics of the market(s) in which the entrepreneurial firm hopes to compete, and the potential responsiveness of the financial markets to a public offering of the entrepreneurial firm's equity.

While it should now be clear that the venture capital markets are characterized by a high level of altercentric and egocentric uncertainty, it is equally important to note that there is variance in the level of egocentric uncertainty across investments. To understand the basis for this variance, it is necessary to review in somewhat more detail how start-ups raise capital from venture capitalists. Entrepreneurial firms generally raise money in "rounds." That is, entrepreneurial companies do not receive a continuous flow of payments from venture capitalists. Rather, they seek financing over some discrete time period. At the end of the time period, the process is then repeated. In some rounds, a firm may require more money than any one venture capital firm is willing to invest. In these cases, multiple firms may invest in a given round.

Rounds can be categorized into stages. For the purpose of this analysis, I divide rounds into three stages. Start-ups that do not have a viable product are regarded as being in the first stage. At this stage, the entrepreneurial firm may have little more than an idea or concept for a product. At least some of the financing in this stage is referred to as "seed" or "start-up" financing. Once an entrepreneurial firm establishes the viability of its product, that firm may pursue financing for the commercial manufacturing and sales of its product. I denote such financing as second-stage financing. Second-stage financing takes place after a company has initiated production but typically before the company has become profitable. Finally, the company enters third-stage financing when it is profitable and is pursuing capital for further expansion. As a company progresses through the various stages, its value increases. From the perspective of the venture capital firm, that is, from the perspective of an investor purchasing equity in a company, the highest returns are to be found when a company that was financed in the earliest stage proves to be successful. Because there is less uncertainty in the later stages, the returns from a successful late-stage investment are smaller.

An entrepreneurial company does not necessarily begin to receive financing in a seed or a start-up round, and a company need not go through all stages of financing before being acquired or going public. For example, because they have high capital needs in the product development stage, biotechnology firms typically go public long before they have a marketable product.

On the other side of the market, a venture capital firm need not invest in a firm in the earliest stage in order to make an investment in a later stage. However, once a firm makes its initial investment, it obviously has privileged access to information about the firm, and accordingly the uncertainty around a reinvestment decision is very different from the uncertainty around an initial investment decision. This fact has important implications for the empirical analysis. In examining the investment patterns of venture capital firms, I will focus only on initial investments made in a start-up, since the initial investment generally implies a high likelihood that the firm will invest if and when others make subsequent investments in the firm.

More generally, for the purposes of this article, what is important about these stages is that they provide a basis for categorizing investments in terms of the egocentric uncertainty faced by the venture capitalist at the time of the resource allocation decision. The later the stage of the investment at which a venture capitalist first becomes involved with a startup, the less uncertainty the venture capital firm confronts regarding the outcome of an investment decision.

MODEL

To explore the extent to which variation in egocentric uncertainty leads high-status firms and firms rich in structural holes to sort into different market segments, I propose the following model:

$$\overline{R_{i,t+1}} = \alpha H_{i,t} + \beta S_{i,t} + \sum_{k=1}^{n} \gamma_k + \sigma_i + \tau_t + \varepsilon_{i,t+1},$$

where $\overline{R_{i,t+1}}$ denotes the average stage of firm i's initial investments in year $t+1$, $H_{i,t}$ denotes a measure of the structural holes in firm i's network in year t, $S_{i,t}$ signifies the status of venture capitalist i in year t, γ_k represents a set of control variables, σ_i indicates a firm-specific effect for venture capital firm i, and τ_t reflects a time-specific effect for year t. Given this specification, the discussion of status implies that $\beta > 0$, and the discussion of Burt's theory of structural holes implies that $\alpha < 0$. That is, the higher a firm's status, the later the stage in which the firm invests. Conversely, the more structural holes in a firm's network, the earlier the stage in which the firm first invests in a start-up.

The model can be estimated using conventional ordinary least squares (OLS) techniques for the analysis of panel data. The firm-specific effect σ_i absorbs all the between-firm variance in the model estimation. As a consequence, the estimates of the other terms are not confounded by any unobserved variables that are time-invariant. Moreover, the absorption of between-firm variance with these firm effects gives us greater confidence that the changes in the values of the independent variables at time t are temporally followed by a change in the outcome measure at time $t+1$. Absent these firm-specific effects, one might worry that there is some unobserved attribute that varies across firms and leads firms with a disproportionate number of structural holes (at time t) to also have a disproportionate number of early-stage investments (at time $t+1$). However, because only within-firm variance is used in the estimation of the network effects, we can rule out the confounding effects of any unobserved variables that systematically differ across firms.

ANALYSIS

The data for this examination were obtained from the Securities Data Corporation's (SDC) Venture Economics database. The SDC collects information on numerous financial markets and then sells this information to the various financial communities. The SDC assimilates the information in the Venture Economics database from both public and private sources. Venture capitalists use these data to obtain benchmarks for their performance, and entrepreneurs use these data to better understand venture capitalists' investment preferences.

Though the SDC has information on entrepreneurial start-ups dating back to the early 1970s, data from the 1970s are extremely scant, raising the possibility that much of the data from this time period are missing. Because of concerns about the scantness of the data during the early period, I limit the analysis to the time period between 1981 and 1996, inclusive, though I also use data from 1980 for the purpose of constructing independent variables that rely on a one-year historical "window."

In addition to deciding on an appropriate time period for the analysis, one also needs to decide which actors to include in the population of "producers" making resource allocation decisions. The SDC Venture Economics database includes information on the investments of venture capital firms as well as information on the investments of diversified financial institutions, nonprofit organizations such as governments and universities, and wealthy individuals. Some of these entities only make episodic investments and accordingly appear in the data only a few times. Since the network and identity of an actor making only infrequent investments is not meaningfully bound to the venture capital community, it seems important to exclude those actors who make only infrequent investments in this market. As a selection rule, I require that an actor make at least five investments in year t (i.e., the lagged year) to be included in the population for that particular year. Such a selection threshold seems conservative; that is, I am including actors for whom venture capital is most likely not a principal form of economic activity. However, it seems preferable to err on the side of inclusion rather than exclusion.

Even with this selection rule, one ends up with a number of actors in the analysis that are not venture capital firms. Using a variety of archival sources, I categorized entities investing in start-ups into seven categories: venture capital firms, consumer banks (e.g., First Boston), investment banks (e.g., Goldman Sachs), nonbank financial institutions such as insurance companies or investment funds (e.g., Fidelity, Allstate Insurance), nonfinancial firms (e.g., Apple

Computer, Raytheon Corporation), nonprofit institutions such as governmental organizations or universities, and, finally, individual investors. For the sake of exposition, I refer to all the actors as venture capitalists insofar as they are all making decisions about which start-ups to fund. However, being a venture capitalist obviously does not imply that an actor is a venture capital firm.

Table 9.1 reports the distribution of actors across the various categories. Despite consulting a number of sources, I could not classify approximately 12 percent of the investing entities. The first column lists the number of actors in each category. The second column lists the number of actor-years in each category, and the third column lists the number of investments with each category. (The actor-years need not be consecutive, but for the vast majority of actors they are consecutive.) As noted above, one would expect the theory discussed above to apply most strongly to those entities whose primary form of economic activity is venture capital. The more that a decision-making entity is subject to competitive stimuli from outside the venture capital markets, the less that the competitive dynamics within this market should lead to the sorting processes specified in the hypotheses. Accordingly, I conduct the analyses with the population of investing entities defined in three ways: (1) only U.S.-based venture capital firms ($N = 248$), (2) U.S.-based venture capital firms and other U.S.-based financial institutions ($N = 238 + 13 + 18 + 7 = 276$), and (3) all entities making more than five investments in year t ($N = 387$). If reinforcement-based learning is the driving mechanism behind the sorting process, one would expect to find the strongest effects of network on sorting in the subsample of dedicated venture capital firms, somewhat weaker effects in the sample that includes all financial firms, and the weakest effects in the full population.[3]

TABLE 9.1
Categories of Financial Supporters of Start-ups

Financial Supporters	N	N × T	N of Investments
Venture capitalist	248	1,788	9,853
Investment bank	13	126	1,129
Diversified financial	18	101	670
Consumer bank	7	41	204
Governmental organization	2	5	26
Nonfinancial firm	28	163	1,607
Individuals	10	57	262
Uncertain	50	204	770
Total N	387	2,485	13,547

[3] One might reasonably ask why I do not simply construct interaction effects by type of firm. The reason is that the inclusion of firm-specific effects precludes the estimation of such interaction effects.

Dependent Variable

Average investment stage.   Measuring the average stage of a venture capitalist's investments is straightforward. The SDC Venture Economics database categorizes investments into the three investment stages discussed
above. To reiterate, an entrepreneurial firm is considered a first-stage investment when it does not yet have a viable product. It is identified as a second-
stage investment when it has a viable product but is not yet able to profitably
manufacture and distribute the product. Finally, the entrepreneurial firm is
categorized as a third-stage investment when it is generating a profit. Table 9.2
reports the distribution of investments across the stages. As should be clear,
there is a strong decline in the number of stage 3 investments. This implies that
the vast majority of firms either go public or fail before becoming profitable.

I assign first-stage investments a value of 1, second-stage investments a value
of 2, and third-stage investments a value of 3. I then add up the values associated with a firm's investments in a given year and divide by the total number
of investments. The range of this variable is accordingly 1–3.

There are two concerns that one can have about this dependent variable.
First, because the stages are simply ordinal, there is an obvious arbitrariness
in assuming that the interval distance between the values for stage 1 and 2 is
identical to the interval distance between the values for stage 2 and stage 3.
That is, one could just as easily assign stage 1 investments a value of 0.5 rather
than a value of 1, and such a change would obviously affect the value of the
dependent variable and accordingly the point estimates in the analysis. Second, because the dependent variable is bounded at 1 and 3, heteroscedasticity
is a concern. On account of these two issues, I conduct the analyses with a second dependent variable—the proportion of investments that are *not* in stage 1.[4]
Because this variable is a proportion, heteroscedasticity is less of a concern,

TABLE 9.2
Distribution of Funding by Stage

	N of Investments
Stage 1	7,525
Stage 2	4,706
Stage 3	1,300
Total	13,531

[4] I used the proportion *not* in stage 1, rather than proportion in stage 1, as the dependent variable so that the hypothesized coefficients vary in the same direction as when the dependent variable is average investment stage. With both dependent variables, a higher value means that the
firm has a portfolio of investments that is more shifted to the later rounds.

and because the proportion implicitly dichotomizes the coding of investments into those that are in stage 1 and those that are not in this stage, interval distance is not a concern. Of course, this outcome measure is not as sensitive to stratification in the later rounds. However, to the extent that the results are robust across both outcome measures, we can be relatively confident in the analyses.

Independent Variables

Status. To measure the status of the venture capital firms in year t, I construct a matrix based on the joint involvement of venture capitalists in financing entrepreneurial start-ups. That is, I construct a matrix $\mathbf{R_t}$ in which cell R_{ijt} denotes the number of times that venture capitalists i and j jointly financed a start-up in year t. Given $\mathbf{R_t}$, I then calculate status scores based on Bonacich's $c(\alpha,\beta)$ measure, just as in the studies of the investment banking, wine, and semiconductor industries.

Given this specification, a venture capitalist's status is a function of the number and status of the firms with which it jointly finances start-ups; the status of these financing partners is in turn a function of the number and status of their syndicate partners, and so on. Particularly given that I include the number of deals in which a venture capitalist has participated as a control variable in the analysis (see below), this status measure reflects the extent to which a firm has financing partners who are "players."

One concern with this measure is that joint-financing arrangements do not convey a strong of a sense of deference, as for example in the investment banking tombstones. Moreover, at each stage, one of the investing venture capital firms is typically designated as the venture capital firm, and such a lead role would seem to imply deference of others to the lead firm. Unfortunately, the SDC data do not contain information on which firm occupies the lead position. Although a few data sources do provide information on which firm occupies a lead position, these data sources are not nearly as complete as the SDC data. However, while I remain somewhat concerned about the symmetry of the ties employed in this particular measure, conversations with those in the industry provide at least anecdotal support for the use of this particular measure. Lower-status venture capitalists express a strong desire to be included in deals financed primarily by higher-status firms, and higher-status venture capitalists occasionally refuse to finance a venture if that venture is receiving financing from a lower-status venture capitalist. In effect, to be high-status is to be an insider; to be a low-status actor is to be an outsider, and joint financing constitutes a symmetrical form of deference in which each venture capitalist acknowledges the standing of the others that are included in the deal. (Descriptive information reported in table 9.3 provides more information on the distribution of the status score.)

TABLE 9.3
Descriptive Statistics for Venture Capital Market, 1981–1996

Variables	Average Investment	25th Percentile	Median	75th Percentile
Stage	1.56 (.46)	1.20	1.50	1.90
Structural holes	.83 (.17)	.81	.88	.93
Status	.11 (.16)	.01	.04	.13
N of deals	34.8 (39.8)	11.0	22.0	43.0
N of funds	2.24 (1.74)	1.00	2.00	3.00

$N \times T = 2{,}470$. Total $N \times T$ (investor-years) for this table is 15 less than the corresponding total in table 9.1 because of missing data on average investment stage for 15 investor-years. Numbers in parentheses are standard deviations.

Structural holes. To measure the structural holes in a venture capitalist's network, I follow Burt (1992) and define the structural holes in the actor's network as follows:

$$H_i = 1 - \sum_j \left(p_{ij} + \sum_q p_{iq} p_{qj} \right)^2, \quad i \neq j \neq q,$$

where p_{ij} denotes the proportion of i's network that is invested in the relation with j, and p_{qi} indicates the proportion of q's network that is invested in its relation with i.[5] As i is connected to an infinite number of others who are themselves disconnected (i.e., there are a plethora of holes in i's network), H_i approaches 1. If i is connected to only one other actor (i.e., there are no holes in i's network), $H_i = 0$.[6] For the purposes of this analysis, I identify a venture capitalist's network from the venture capitalist's joint involvement in financing entrepreneurial start-ups. That is, when venture capitalist i invests in the same start-up as venture capitalist j, I code that joint participation as a tie between i and j. Therefore, H_i is a positive function of the number of different venture capitalists with which i is involved and the extent to which those other venture capitalists themselves invest in numerous, different start-ups.

---

[5] While I use H_i to denote the structural holes, it is worth noting that Burt's analyses employ a variable that he labels as C_i, the constraint in actor i. C_i simply equals $1 - H_i$. I prefer H_i because it is directionally consistent with his theoretical construct of structural holes, but because network software, such as UCINET, calculates C_i rather than H_i, this difference is worth noting.

[6] Though the vast majority of egocentric network configurations give rise to scores between 0 and 1, it is worth noting that one can construct examples of egocentric networks that can have a score as low as −1. For example, assume ego i has two contacts to which he devotes an equal amount of his total relational strength. In this case, $p_{ij} = p_{iq} = 0.5$ for both contacts. Assume further that both contacts focus their entire network on each other; so $p_{qj} = 1$ for both contacts. In this case, the value in the parentheses would equal 1 for each contact, and H_i would therefore equal −1.

Conversely, if i makes a small number of investments and the other venture capitalists in these investments constitute a clique with identical investment patterns, then H_i will be relatively low.

Because I am examining changes in the stage in which venture capital firms invest over time, I allow the venture capitalist's network to vary over time and identify the structural holes in actor i's network at time t as H_{it}. I use a moving "one-year window" to identify ties among venture capitalists. That is, venture capitalist i and venture capitalist j have a tie if they jointly financed a start-up in the same year. Burt's autonomy measure allows for a continuous measure of tie strength. For the purpose of the analysis, I weight a tie between two venture capitalists by the number of deals that they jointly finance.

Control variables. I include two control variables in the analysis. First, I include the number of investments (N of deals) made by the venture capitalist in year t. There are several reasons to include this variable as a control variable. First, to the extent that there is evidence consistent with the elaborated hypotheses, I would like to disentangle the effects of status and structural holes from the volume of activity in which a venture capitalist is engaged. It is possible that at least some observed network effects could be the spurious consequence of the volume of activity in which a venture capitalist participates. Second, the number of deals in which an actor is engaged is a measure of an actor's experience, and to the extent that the actor learns from experience, an actor's total amount of investments should reduce the uncertainty that it confronts in making subsequent investment decisions. Since there is more egocentric uncertainty and thus more to learn about investing in the early stages than in the late stages, I would expect that such learning from experience would have a greater effect on a firm's ability to make judicious early-stage investments than judicious late-stage investments. In effect, whereas status should push firms to make more late-stage investments, experience—like structural holes—should push actors to engage in a high proportion of early-stage investments.

A second control variable is the number of funds (N of funds) from which a venture capital firm makes investments in year t. As noted above, a venture capital firm can have more than one fund from which it makes investments at any particular time. There are three reasons for including this control variable. The first two reasons are similar to the reasons for including the lagged number of deals as a control variable. As with number of deals, lagged number of funds is likely to be an indicator of both size and experience. To the extent that the number of funds is an indicator of size, I want to distinguish any potential structural hole and status effects from a possible size effect. To the extent that the number of funds is an indicator of experience, the number of funds should have a negative effect on the average stage of a venture capital firm's investment. The third reason for including this control variable is to rule out an alternative explanation for the hypothesized effect of status. I have argued that high-status firms should be more likely to make late-stage investments because status is most valuable in those market segments in which a firm knows how to best leverage its status in forming exchange relations. However, if higher-status firms generally have access to more financial resources than lower-status firms, high-status firms may be forced to make more late-stage investments because—with the notable exception of biotechnology start-ups—early-stage investments generally have small capital requirements. For example, the capital requirements for a first-stage software company, which is engaged in the development of a product, are typically much less than the capital requirements of a second- or third-stage software company, which must either put together or at least outsource manufacturing and distribution functions. Put simply, the high-status firms may simply have too much money to invest in early-stage firms. In short, there are at least two reasons to expect that the effect of the number of funds will be positive and at least one reason to expect that the effect will be negative. Since I include this variable only as a control, I do not hypothesize as to whether the negative or positive effect should be stronger.

Finally, in addition to these two control variables, I include firm-specific effects, σ_τ, and period-specific effects, τ_t. These effects simply control for unobserved heterogeneity that would be common either to all the observations drawn from a particular firm or to all the observations drawn from a particular year.

Results

Table 9.3 presents the descriptive statistics for both the dependent and explanatory variables. Table 9.4 reports the bivariate correlations between the main explanatory variables in the analysis. It is noteworthy that the correlation between structural holes and status is 0.23. While the correlation is statistically significant, it should be clear that the two measures are empirically distinguishable.

TABLE 9.4
Correlations of Explanatory Variables

Variables	Status	N of Deals	N of Funds
Structural holes	.23	.26	.19
Status		.71	.55
N of deals			.75
N of funds			

All correlations are statistically significant at the $p < .05$ level.

Table 9.5 depicts the regression results when the population includes only identified venture capital firms. Models 1 and 2 respectively exclude either status or structural holes; models 3 and 4 represent the complete model. The difference between models 3 and 4 is in the dependent variable. In model 3, the dependent variable is average investment stage. In model 4, the dependent variable is proportion of investments not in stage 1. Looking first at the control variables, we find that the number of deals done over the last year does not have a significant effect on average round of investment. Number of funds does have a significant negative effect in the first column, when status is excluded from the analysis. However, the variable becomes marginally insignificant when status is included. Turning to the main effects, we see that the results are consistent with the basic hypotheses. The fact that these results are based on within-firm variance is especially noteworthy. Because all cross-sectional variation is removed owing to the inclusion of the fixed effects for each firm, the results show how a firm's investment decisions change as the firm's network changes. As a venture capital firm acquires a "deal-flow" network that is characterized by numerous structural holes, the firm makes a greater proportion of its investments in the earlier stages. As the firm acquires a network that is indicative of greater status, it makes a greater proportion of its investments in the later round. Notably, the results are robust with respect to the different operationalizations of the dependent variable.

TABLE 9.5
Effect of Explanatory Variables on Investment Stage Distribution with Only Venture Capital Firms Included in Population

	Model			
Variables	1	2	3	4
Structural holes	−.14*	—	−.14*	−.12*
	(.07)		(.07)	(.05)
Status	—	.22*	.22*	.13*
		(.10)	(.11)	(.08)
N of deals	2.9×10^{-4}	4.5×10^{-4}	3.2×10^{-4}	4.9×10^{-4}
	(5.8×10^{-4})	(6.5×10^{-4})	(6.5×10^{-4})	(4.9×10^{-4})
N of funds	−.02**	−.02	−.02	−.014
	(.01)	(−.012)	(−.012)	(.009)

$N = 1,783$. Dependent variable for cols. 1–3 is average investment stage. Dependent variable for col. 4 is proportion of investments not in stage 1. Indicator variables for years are not reported but are included in all models. Numbers in parentheses are standard errors.

$*p < .05$, one-tailed test; $**p < .05$, two-tailed test

However, because both operationalizations of the dependent variable are ratio variables, there is some ambiguity in how to interpret shifts in the variable. A positive shift could imply an increase in the numerator, a decrease in the denominator, or both. For example, simply by looking at the dependent variable, we cannot tell if high-status firms are undertaking fewer early-stage investments, more late-stage investments, or both. However, the control variable for number of deals helps to resolve this ambiguity. Because number of deals is not significantly related to average investment stage, those firms that add late-stage investments must be reducing their early-stage investments. Similarly, those firms that are increasing their number of early-stage investments are reducing the number of late-stage investments. Thus, the structural hole effect implies a true shift from late stage to early stage, and the status effect implies a true shift from early stage to late stage.[7]

Table 9.6 reports the results for the full model with average investment stage as the dependent variable. However, the population is defined in three different ways. For the results in column 1, the population is defined only as venture capital firms. Accordingly, the results in this column are identical to the results in column 3 in table 9.5. Column 2 reports results when the population

TABLE 9.6
Effect of Explanatory Variables on Investment Stage Distribution with Different Population Definitions

Variables	Venture Capital Firms	All Financial Firms	All Firms
Structural holes	−.14*	−.14*	−.06
	(.07)	(.06)	(.06)
Status	.22*	.15*	.11
	(.11)	(.09)	(.08)
N of deals	3.23×10^{-4}	1.9×10^{-4}	1.5×10^{-4}
	6.5×10^{-4}	4.4×10^{-4}	4.7×10^{-4}
N of funds	−.02	−.016	−.015
	(−.012)	(.01)	(.010)
$N \times T$	1,783	2,046	2,470

Numbers in parentheses are standard errors.
*$p < .05$, one-tailed test

[7] To the extent that there is reason to worry about reverse causality, it is possible to provide a check by repeating the analysis but rearranging the temporal sequencing of the variables. Specifically, one can perform the analysis with average investment stage at time t and the network variables measured at $t + 1$. The coefficients associated with the network variables are insignificant, with both t-ratios less than 1. This check provides some added confidence that the causality flows in the hypothesized direction.

is defined as all financial institutions making investments in start-ups, and column 3 reports the results when the population is defined to include all actors making investments in start-ups. The effects are weaker—indeed, they are not statistically significant—when the population is defined to include all actors. The results are significant when the population is defined as all financial institutions, but the positive effect of status nonetheless declines. As noted earlier, such a pattern of results is consistent with a reinforcement-based mechanism. Relatively diversified actors, whose financial success is not strongly linked to their financial investments, are not nearly as responsive to the pressures to sort into a market niche in which their network fits the level of egocentric uncertainty.[8]

These results are notable in that they are suggestive of a distinction between two types of uncertainty that can underlie market decision and action. Whereas the previous eight chapters have focused on a type of uncertainty that is central to signaling models and that we can now label as altercentric uncertainty, this chapter has introduced the concept of egocentric uncertainty. It seems

[8] While the results in table 9.6 are consistent with the predicted status effect, one might still question why high-status venture capitalists move to the later stages. One's argument might go something like the following: while there is less egocentric uncertainty in the later stages than in the earlier stages, there is presumably also less altercentric uncertainty. Accordingly, while the ability of high-status venture capitalists to discriminate good from bad investments goes up in the later stages, the ability of investors to discriminate between good and bad investments presumably also increases. Investors therefore do not need to rely on the signal of status as much when they invest in late-stage investments as when they invest in early-stage investments. Thus, even a high-status venture capitalist cannot as easily capture the rents from that status. An increment in status accordingly would seem to have an indeterminate effect on average investment stage. However, such a concern is based on a false premise. As noted above, whereas venture capitalists make investments in individual start-ups, the investors who provide financial capital to the venture capitalists generally do not. Rather, they put their money into a venture fund, and the venture capitalist managing that fund distributes the financial capital across a range of companies. Because investors typically put their money into this fund before they know which companies at which stages will be financed and because the fund is aggregated across multiple investments, the investor is not nearly as sensitive to shifts in uncertainty across investments as the venture capitalist. So, while egocentric uncertainty—the uncertainty of the venture capitalist—varies considerably from the early stage to the last stage, altercentric uncertainty can generally be regarded as constant. There is then no countervailing uncertainty-induced cause for high-status firms to shift to the early stages.

Given that the high-status firms clearly sort into the market segment in which it is easiest for them to leverage their status, it would obviously be comforting to find some evidence that venture capitalists (VCs) derive positive monetary returns from status. At least some suggestive evidence comes from David Hsu (forthcoming), who looks at a unique sample of entrepreneurs who receive multiple bids for financing from venture capitalists. Hsu finds high-"reputation" VCs are more likely to have their bids accepted, and he finds that accepted offers are often 10% to 14% lower than the bids of low-"reputation" VCs. The only difficulty in directly tying Hsu's findings to my own is that Hsu's operationalization of reputation is an amalgam of status and reputation indicators, and therefore it is not possible to conclude what fraction of the effect can truly be called a status effect. Still, the results are highly suggestive.

reasonable to speculate that the distinction between altercentric and egocentric uncertainty is not limited to market contexts. For example, consider a political arena—say, a legislature. Each politician within the legislature has bills that she wishes to pass, but in order to win approval, she must win the support of a majority of her colleagues. Just as one can apply the concepts of egocentric and altercentric uncertainty to the market, so one could apply egocentric and altercentric uncertainty to this domain. For example, in putting forward a bill on some complex topic like health care, a legislator may face considerable egocentric uncertainty in trying to design a bill that will yield the outcome that she desires. There is also altercentric uncertainty; the colleagues of the legislator proposing the bill may have doubts as to the "quality" of the bill (i.e., whether the bill's espoused potential will be realized). As in the market, these types of uncertainty are analytically distinguishable. For example, the legislator may have no uncertainty about the actual impact of the bill either because the bill is not very complex or because the legislator has considerable knowledge of the issue. However, if the legislative arena is characterized by considerable mistrust, there may nonetheless be considerable altercentric uncertainty. As in the market case, one would expect that a network rich in structural holes would be especially helpful in resolving egocentric uncertainty, whereas a high-status network would be especially helpful in overcoming the doubts of colleagues that would arise in a situation of high altercentric uncertainty.

With respect to the market, the introduction of the distinction obviously poses a number of questions for future research. For example, are there any trends that can be observed in the way that egocentric and altercentric uncertainty evolve over time? One would expect that producers would probably resolve their uncertainty about how to combine resources to yield quality products and services before consumers could hope to resolve their uncertainty regarding stable differences across producers in terms of that quality. However, as noted at the outset of this chapter, market contexts can vary in the extent to which they are high or low in the two types of uncertainty, and there are some market contexts that can be high in egocentric uncertainty and low in altercentric uncertainty. Accordingly, the relationship between the two types of uncertainty cannot simply be reduced to a statement such as the level of egocentric uncertainty determines the lower bound on the level of altercentric uncertainty. Drawing on the parameters of his $W(y)$ model, White (2002a) shows how it is possible to analytically model the joint implications of these two types of uncertainty. With respect to the way in which these two types of uncertainty relate to status, the concluding chapter provides both some conclusions and some leads for future research.

Chapter Ten

CONCLUSION

EVERY DISCIPLINE has fundamental images on which its practitioners rely to make sense of the world. These fundamental images shape the questions that are asked and accordingly the paths of inquiry that are followed. Given the neoclassical imagery of a market as defined by intersecting supply and demand curves in a price-quantity trade-off plane, the fundamental questions center on how modifications to those supply and demand curves affect the location of the intersecting point relative to where that point would be under idealized conditions of perfect competition. So, for example, the impact of monopoly or a minimum wage is explored and understood in terms of that basic shift. Given the game-theoretic imagery of decision trees, in which sequential choice points among interacting actors lead to payoffs at the end of the tree, the central line of inquiry is relating market or organization decisions to incentives, and incentives to action. The ultimate objective is to understand how changes in design alter actions through their effects on incentives.

Sociology begins with different images, and different questions follow. This book has drawn on one of sociology's central images, that of a status ordering, and this particular imagery invites specific questions. When turned to the market, the imagery leads to the following series of interrelated questions:

- What are the primary market mechanisms by which a status ordering in the market is sustained?
- How do status distinctions in other related domains spill over into the market and affect market competition?
- What inequalities in economic rewards are engendered by the status ordering?
- What environmental conditions determine whether the engendered economic inequalities are greater or less?

The research in this book offers answers to these four questions; let's consider each question in turn.

What are the primary market mechanisms by which a status ordering in the market is sustained?

Beginning with the conception of status as a signal of quality that leaks through deference and exchange relations, we have observed three market mechanisms for sustaining the status ordering in the market: (1) cost disparities that prevent a low-status actor from offering a given quality of service at a price comparable to that offered by a high-status actor, (2) pricing disparities between a high-status and low-status actor that implicitly allow the higher-status actor to outbid the lower-status actor for the same quality of inputs, and (3) status homophily in the pattern of exchange relations.

We observed evidence of all three mechanisms in the analysis of the investment banking industry, and we observed evidence of the second mechanism in the study of the wine industry. The inverse relation between spread and status for small debt offerings strongly suggested that high-status banks have lower costs for offering a given quality of service (mechanism 1). The positive returns to status for larger, more complicated debt offerings constituted evidence that the higher-status banks can command a superior price when there is sufficient altercentic uncertainty, and this superior price ensures that they should be able to outbid lower-status competitors for the same factor inputs (mechanism 2). The wine industry provided additional evidence of this second mechanism. Wineries with a history of affiliations to high-status regions obtained greater returns for a given quality of inputs than wineries with a history of affiliations to low-status regions. The status-based homophily in the debt markets as well as the growth models of status revealed that banks are reluctant to engage in exchanges with lower-status others and, to the degree that they do so, their status is reduced accordingly (mechanism 3). This third mechanism seems especially important in differentiating the signal of market status from other signals or from reputation since this third mechanism is indicative of the fact that status leaks through exchange relations.

How do status distinctions in other related domains spill over into the market and affect market competition?

Status acts as a signal of underlying qualities not simply within the product market itself—with consumers on one side and producers on the other—but also within related, interdependent spheres. So in chapter 6 we observed that high-status firms exert a disproportionate influence on the way in which technology and therefore the underlying determinants of market quality evolve by showing deference to some inventions and not others. Moreover, when a firm occupies a niche in which there was uncertainty about the quality of inventions in that niche, a firm's status in the technological domain is a signal of quality that positively affects its sales growth. In effect, status distinctions in the technological domain spill over into the market domain, affecting the flow of consumer payments, and insofar as those actors with greater technological status find it easier to attract economic resources in the market, they will be able to bring greater economic rewards back to the technological domain— rewards that will only reinforce the extent to which the higher-status actors in the technological domain can drive the way in which the technological web unfolds. Similarly, in chapter 7, we saw that under some circumstances a correspondence will arise between the social status of individuals and the market status of firms. Higher social status becomes a basis for entrée into a market, and insofar as entrée into the market enhances the flow of financial resources to the individual, these additional resources should only augment the degree to which an individual can preserve or perhaps enhance his or her social status.

One can imagine other domains—besides the social or technological—in which the same status distinctions among firms play themselves out. For example, in chapter 2, we noted that one of the reasons that market status lowers the transaction costs of producing a good of a given quality is that, ceteris paribus, individuals would prefer to work for a higher-status firm rather than a lower-status firm. Thus, status distinctions in the product/service market create distinctions in the labor market, which in turn help to reinforce those status distinctions in the product/service market.

One can even think of adjacent product markets as constituting another related, interdependent sphere. So, when the non-investment-grade market arose, a bank's status in the investment-grade market was probably the most important determinant of its status position in the non-investment-grade market. We also observed discrepancies; Drexel Burnham Lambert clearly occupied a higher status position in the non-investment-grade market owing to the fact that it pioneered this market. However, the fact remains that status seems to spill over between markets. Higher status in the non-investment-grade market yields economic benefits translating into higher status in the investment-grade market, which reciprocally augments the bank's position in the non-investment-grade market.

We thus are left with an image of the status ordering of firms as participants in a number of interdependent, self-reinforcing spheres. Figure 10.1 is a Venn diagram depiction of this interdependence. While the position that a firm occupies in one sphere is not necessarily identical to the position that a firm occupies in another, the ever-present positive spillover effects of status between spheres implies a correspondence or lock-in of the status ordering across the different spheres. Such an image thus reveals the broader context in which the three status-order-sustaining mechanisms in the market operate.

What inequalities in economic rewards are engendered by the status ordering?

The answer to this question follows directly from the three identified market mechanisms associated with the first question and the cross-domain lock-in identified in the second question. The mechanisms of lower costs and higher prices are in and of themselves sources of economic inequality. The mechanism of status-based homophily in exchange relations implies market segmentation, with lower-status firms being relegated to the less desirable segments. The relatively greater control that high-status firms enjoy over the evolution of technology and quality implies that higher-status firms will earn greater returns on their investments in research and development.

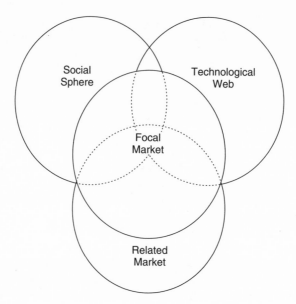

FIGURE 10.1. Interdependent spheres for market producers

Research by others reveals additional sources of economic inequality be-yond those posited in this book. Perhaps the most notable is work that has sought to document the relevance of the "middle-status conformity" hypothesis to markets (Han 1994; Phillips and Zuckerman 2001). This research under-scores ways in which the highest-status actors in a market are able to break from industry norms without risking the loss of their status. Especially insofar as experimentation and departure from industry norms is important to long-term adaptability, this research points to additional reasons the status ordering will be self-sustaining. While the lowest-status actors have no status to lose and are therefore also able to break from industry norms, they typically lack the resources to benefit from this freedom.

Obviously, not all economic inequalities will be equally germane in all contexts. Indeed, some of the sources of inequality, such as price and market segmentation—are fungible. To the degree to which higher-status firms seek to extract a higher price, they may end up ceding a larger share of the market to lower-status firms, making the low-status segment more desirable than it would otherwise be. (Of course, a higher-status firm would presumably choose to ex-tract a higher price from a smaller market segment only if it felt that the gains in margin offset the loss in market share.)

Presumably one direction for future research will be to try to identify what circumstances lead a particular manifestation of economic inequality to be more salient in a given market context. The various empirical analyses have provided a few leads. However, in order to provide a conclusive delineation of those leads, it is necessary to consider the answer to the fourth question.

What environmental conditions determine whether the engendered economic inequalities are greater or less?

Uncertainty—or, more specifically (using the terminology introduced in chapter 9), altercentric uncertainty—has obviously been the central environmental variable affecting the extent of economic inequality engendered by status. In the analysis of the investment banking industry, we saw that the spread that a bank earned for underwriting a security increased with the uncertainty of investors. In the analysis of the semiconductor industry, we saw that a firm's status had a stronger impact on its revenue growth when the firm was in a technological niche in which there was presumably a comparatively high level of uncertainty about the quality of that technology. In the analysis of the British shipping cartels, we observed that status had more of an impact on whether the firm was admitted to a (lucrative) cartel when the entrant was younger and therefore implicitly had less of a history from which the cartel could infer its true quality.

Notably, while the investment banking industry provided evidence that the impact of status on margins is a positive function of altercentric uncertainty, the investment banking industry also provided evidence that altercentric uncertainty reduces a high-status firm's willingness to expand its market presence into lower-status niches. On average, higher-status banks were much more reluctant to expand their market presence in the non-investment-grade market than in the investment-grade market. But, perhaps the most compelling evidence that a firm's willingness to expand its market presence is a function of altercentric uncertainty came from the longitudinal look at the non-investment-grade market. As the non-investment-grade market matured and the altercentric uncertainty declined, the higher-status banks were more likely to enter into management-comanagement relations with lower-status partners.

Because the analysis of the investment banking industry revealed that an increase in altercentric uncertainty is associated with an increase in a high-status firm's margins but a decrease in a high-status firm's market share, this particular analysis provides a lead as to how the economic inequality engendered by status will differ across different contexts. At high levels of altercentric uncertainty, the high-status firms are earning such large margins that they are reluctant to risk a loss of status through the expansion of market share. However, at more moderate levels of altercentric uncertainty, the margins from status will be lower and accordingly firms will be more willing to risk some loss of status through some expansion of share. Of course, at low levels of altercentric uncertainty, there are minimal returns from status. Thus, consideration of this first environmental condition not only provides some insight into when the economic inequality engendered by status will be the greatest; it also provides some insight into what form that inequality will take in a particular context.

Having considered the example of turquoise in the jewelry markets in the opening chapter, it is now convenient to return to that example. We observed different high-status jewelry stores undertaking different responses. The question of whether it is prudent to go down-market depends on one's belief about the state of altercentric uncertainty in the market. In the case of turquoise, are there any institutional changes in the market leading consumers to become more sophisticated? Are consumers better able to discern true quality when they see it? Or, do they still depend strongly on a jeweler's status as a signal that a particular jewel is worth the price being asked? If consumers are no more sophisticated today than in the past, then the jewelers are probably prudent to avoid the low-status association that will come from trading in turquoise. However, the frequency of intercontinental travel as well as the proliferation of information and the creation of a global market through the Internet mean that consumers are in a better position to judge the wares from their local jeweler. Given such changes, it seems that the high-status jewelers are probably better off trying to realize the benefit of economic status through market share than through higher margins from a selected segment. The approach of Eiseman Jewels, which was willing to sell turquoise acquired through an extensive search for high-quality items, seems more appropriate to the changed environment. The approach of Lane, which refused to sell any turquoise, or Tiffany, which refused to expand its collection in response to the increase in demand, seems incongruent with institutional changes that imply declining altercentric uncertainty.

It should not be surprising that altercentric uncertainty is the central environmental variable determining the returns from status. Given the conception of status as a signal and given the fact that the value of a signal hinges on asymmetric information in the form of altercentric uncertainty, it follows that this should be one of the major—if not the major—variables determining the relevance of status. Of course, other variables also play a role.

In the previous chapter, we observed indirect evidence that egocentric uncertainty affects the extent to which high-status firms can preserve their status and hence ensure greater returns over time. When egocentric uncertainty is high, high-status firms should have an especially difficult time selecting exchange partners that will enable them to reproduce their status. Accordingly, we observed that the higher-status venture capitalists sort into those segments of the market in which egocentric uncertainty is comparatively low.

Finally, in addition to these two types of uncertainty, chapter 8 revealed a third environmental variable affecting the inequality in economic rewards—the increasing concentration of the market over time. Taking a cue from Glenn Carroll's resource-partitioning model, we noted that a common feature of evolving markets is increasing concentration. At least in the investment banking industry, this increasing concentration is a consequence of the highest-status

firms expanding into the niches of the medium-status firms. The greater competitive thrust upon the medium-status firms ultimately alleviates some of the
competitive pressures on the lowest-status firms. Thus, over time, the middle
of the status distribution falls out, leaving a few high-status firms with considerable economic rewards and a large number of very low-status firms with few
economic rewards.

It is unclear whether this third environmental variable is entirely separable
from the first. One of the reasons that high-status firms might increase their
market share is that there will generally be a reduction in altercentric uncertainty over time. However, there are undeniably other drivers of concentration
besides declining altercentric uncertainty, such as scale economies or network
economies. Accordingly, it seems appropriate to separate out concentration as
a third relevant environmental variable.

Further work may obviously point to other environmental variables that determine why status is more relevant in some contexts than in others. However,
regardless of these additional factors, the following conclusion seems justified
by the foregoing analyses: *if status is relevant, it is an inherently conservative,
stabilizing force.* As revealed in the studies of investment banking and the
wine industry, producers cannot escape this self-reproducing dynamic by trying to rely on other signals, such as size (in the case of investment banking) or
reputation (in the case of wine). Status ultimately provides the lens through
which another signal—like reputation—is viewed; accordingly, a firm's reputation for quality eventually becomes aligned with the quality that its status
signals. Thus, the signaling dynamics within the market and the spillover activities across the domains with which the market is interdependent underscore the applicability of the Matthew Effect.

KEY METHODOLOGICAL CONCERNS INVOLVED IN
INVESTIGATING STATUS DYNAMICS

While elucidating some of the questions and answers that follow from the
image of status ordering has been one of the objectives of this book, another
objective has been to underscore the methodological concerns that must be addressed when analyzing status dynamics in markets. At least in my view, there
are two that are primary. The first and most obvious is that any observed effects of status may be spurious unless the researcher adequately controls for
the effect of quality. Of course, status is a signal precisely because quality is
difficult to observe; therefore, the researcher is left with the unenviable task of
trying to control for something that cannot be observed. While it is tempting to
set the concern aside by arguing that any difficulty that the researcher may have
in controlling for quality is indicative of the difficulty that market actors have
in perceiving quality, such a response by itself is clearly not adequate to this

concern. Even if much of the data available to market participants comes in the form of nonsystematic observations or anecdotes, the market participants clearly will have some basis for estimating quality independently of a firm's position in the status ordering. Thus, one does need to think seriously about ways to control for quality, reputation, or the important alternative indicators of quality besides status.

The various empirical analyses have pointed to different ways in which one can address this methodological problem. So, the analyses of status dynamics in the investment banking industry lacked a measure of quality but included a control for the most significant alternative signal to status—underwriting volume. Because the volume of underwriting activity has a positive impact on quality and because industry participants clearly devote considerable effort to tracking volume as an indicator of quality, this seemed to be the best proxy for quality perceptions arising independently of the status ordering. The wine industry obviously afforded the best measure of quality owing to the availability of data from blind taste tests. In the analysis of the semiconductor industry, unobserved quality was controlled through econometric proxies. So, in the analysis of whether a patent is cited, an occurrence-dependent term—the number of times that the patent has been previously cited—was included as a control. In the analysis of firms' revenue growth, a fixed effect term was included as a control for any time-invariant quality differences across firms. The analysis of the venture capital industry also relied on fixed effect controls. Obviously, no control is perfect; there is always likely to be some unmeasured discrepancy between systematic indicators and unsystematic perceptions of market participants. Which approach is best will obviously depend on the data available in that case; however, the more seriously one attempts to control for quality, reputation, and/or alternative indicators of quality, the more confidence one can have in one's results.

The second generic methodological concern is identifying those deference relations that best define the status ordering. Clearly, one's ability to do so depends on one's institutional knowledge of the market of interest. Even given a high degree of institutional knowledge across many contexts, there will be tremendous differences across contexts in terms of the systematic availability and codifiability of those deference relations. Such differences imply a trade-off. On the one hand, one could continue to analyze only those industries—like the investment banking industry up through the late 1980s—in which one has exceptional indicators of status-defining deference relations. However, a continued reliance on a small number of industries would invite questions about the generalizability of the findings. Moreover, restricting one's focus to a few industries would undercut one's ability to explore a diverse array of economic outcomes since some industries may contain exceptional data on certain economic outcomes (e.g., predatory pricing) but less than optimal data on status. At the same time, one cannot just pick whatever measure seems to be best in a particular industry and assert that it is necessarily above some minimum threshold of adequacy. If one's measure of status is likely to raise questions or concerns, then ideally one might find some perceptual correlates to corroborate one's measure, as was done in the wine study. However, since the sociological view of status is fundamentally grounded in deference *relations*, such perceptual correlates should probably never be regarded as a substitute for behavioral indicators.

EMERGING QUESTIONS FOR FUTURE RESEARCH ON STATUS

This book seeks to address the four questions elaborated above. However, these are not the only questions that follow from the image of the market as a status hierarchy. There are potentially a number of such questions, but here I will focus on three that seem especially intriguing going forward.

What are the determinants of the "shape" of the status distribution?

Through the analyses in chapter 4 and chapter 8, I attempted to distinguish a micro-level perspective on status segregation from a macro-level perspective on status segregation. The former conceptualizes status segregation in terms of a tendency toward status-based homophily; the latter implies a concern with the overall shape of the status distribution. We know that altercentric uncertainty is an especially important determinant of the general tendency, and we know that partitioning processes associated with market concentration affect the overall shape as the presence of larger firms makes middle-status positions increasingly less viable. Moreover, as perhaps indicated by the distribution of status scores in the various markets studied in this work, we know that the distribution of status generally seems to be log-normal, with a small number of very high-status firms and a larger number of low-status firms. However, above and beyond the basic log-normal shape of the status ordering and the partitioning processes that affect the relative size of the middle of the distribution, there seems considerable potential for exploring how a variety of institutional and cognitive factors can influence the formation of break points in the distribution that have significant economic consequences for the firms (Saunder 2004).

How does the status ordering of individuals within the labor market affect market competition?

As previously noted, one of the interdependent spheres in which firms participate is the labor market, and in many labor markets there are status distinctions among the participants—status distinctions grounded in the deference and exchange relations among those labor market participants. Though the examination of British shipping cartels in chapter 8 integrated social status into the study of market competition, social status is not identical to labor market or occupational status. Status distinctions arise among those in a particular industry or occupation as a signal of the individual's quality of work. In fields as diverse as engineering, acting, and law, there are some individuals who receive considerable deference and others who receive little. In his study of Hollywood composers, Faulker (2003) highlights a number of clear status groups among composers.

In my view, some of the most provocative current work on status seems attentive to how the status ordering of individuals within an occupation affects market competition. For example, Greta Hsu (2003) finds that when there is no well-defined understanding of quality in a market (and presumably therefore no tangible basis on which firms can construct a status ordering), the labor market status of producers seems to take on added importance in guiding market decisions. In a study of investment banking research analysts, Groysberg, Polzer, and Elfenbein (2003) find that having too many stars (i.e., high-status individuals) can hamper an organization's performance; however, higher-status firms seem to have a higher carrying capacity for stars. That is, the higher the status of the firm, the more that the firm can sustain a large number of high-status individuals without negative consequences. Finally, in another example of how occupational status affects market competition, Huckman (2003) looks at the propensity of hospitals to treat coronary artery disease with one of two rival treatments, either a coronary bypass procedure or angioplasty. Different medical specialists perform the different procedures; cardiac surgeons perform bypasses, and cardiologists perform angioplasties. After controlling for many factors that would explain the technological choice, Huckman finds that the likelihood that a hospital will use one of the two treatments is strongly affected by how the professional status of the hospital's cardiac surgeons compares with the professional status of the cardiologists. If the cardiac surgeons have greater professional status in their field than the cardiologists have in theirs, then the hospital is more likely to treat the patient with a coronary bypass; conversely, if the cardiologists have comparatively greater status, then the hospital is more likely to treat the patient with an angioplasty. Such work all points to cross-level status dynamics, in which the status of individuals affects the market choices of firms.

To what degree can a sensitivity to status dynamics provide insight into the boundaries between firms and markets?

At least since Williamson wrote *Markets and Hierarchies* (1975), one of the central questions for those studying economic institutions has been the "boundary of the firm" question: Why do some exchanges occur in markets and some in hierarchies? I believe that a consideration of status dynamics can help provide some insight into the question, though I will state at the outset that my thoughts here are highly speculative.

My reason for believing that status processes could be relevant to the boundary-of-the-firm question is that we now know that status processes are extremely germane to governance processes in both markets and firms. This book has revealed the self-reproducing nature of status orderings to be of fundamental importance as a governance or control mechanism in markets—constraining who can exchange with whom as well as the terms of trade associated with exchanges. Similarly, work by social exchange theorists (Blau 1955, 1989; Homans 1951) shows that informal status distinctions have played a fundamental governance role within organizations.

For the purpose of illustration, I will reference Blau's (1955) account in *Dynamics of Bureaucracy*. In that work, Blau observes a federal bureau whose purpose was to audit firms to assure compliance with two federal laws. The bureau consisted of eighteen individuals: one supervisor, sixteen auditors, and one clerk. The supervisor determined which auditors would be assigned to which cases. Each audit involved interviews with the employers and samples of employees, an examination of firm records, a determination of the degree of compliance with the laws, and (if the firm did not meet the requirements of these laws) negotiations with the employer as to what type of action ought to be taken to guarantee reparations and compliance. Most audits were relatively straightforward, requiring no more than a few days. Indeed, the average time spent on an audit was seventeen hours. However, some audits could be more complicated and involved, sometimes taking several months.

Regardless of how complicated a case might be, the supervisor would never assign more than one person to a case. An extensive set of legal rules and court decisions provided guidance for the auditor. Indeed, the constant source of reference for each agent was a thousand-page manual of regulations. Should that manual not suffice, the agent then turned to two shelves of "administrative explications" and court opinions. If this written material did not afford a satisfactory solution, the agent was not supposed to turn to other agents for advice but was supposed to consult the supervisor directly. The supervisor told Blau, "They are not permitted to consult other agents. If they have a problem, they have to take it up with me"(p. 127).

A couple of features of the situation are worth noting. First, while most cases were probably routine, a substantial minority were quite complicated. Since the complexity of a case was not revealed until the audit began, the agency could not reliably anticipate the difficulty that a case would present. The agency was thus confronted with a control problem: how to best coordinate activities and anticipate uncertainties. The supervisor's solution to the problem was one of reliance on a formal hierarchy. That is, the supervisor decided that the best way to coordinate activity and respond to unforeseen contingencies was to formally designate a hierarchy in the agency with the supervisor himself as the central node of that hierarchy.

However, from his observations of the agency, Blau concludes that on average each agent had five contacts per hour with his colleagues, and while some of these conversations were personal in nature, many were work related. These work-related interactions ranged from queries that could be answered in one simple sentence to prolonged dialogues over highly complex cases.

Even more important, Blau observes that the pattern and content of communication was far from random; rather, it reflected an underlying status ordering among those in the auditing group. Agents solved the problem of control by using the status of counterparts as signals of the quality of their advice. Conversely, just as agents relied on the status of others as a guide to action, so they relied on their own status as a guide to appropriate behavior. Middle- to low-status actors refrained from making novel suggestions, because such suggestions would be ignored or ridiculed by the group; in effect, their status determined the perceptions of the quality of their ideas, and they therefore did not seek to invest in or produce ideas whose quality would be incommensurate with their status. High-status actors, however, were willing to introduce innovative ideas to the group because their status was a cue to others that they ought to grant approval to the idea. Thus, while there was an element of hierarchy in this system, it was not the hierarchy of formal authority; it was—like the hierarchy within the market—a hierarchy that emerged endogenously from the status-based interactions of individuals.

There are some differences between the status orderings that arise within firms and the status orderings that arise within markets. First, the status orderings that arise out of the social exchange within firms tend to be based on a more diverse set of contents flowing back and forth between individuals. Some individuals may be able to improve their status by offering humor or social support along with advice; in contrast, the status orderings that arise within markets are based on a more restricted set of contents. Second, an explicit pricing mechanism is generally more central in the exchanges that take place within markets than within firms; whereas there are few exchange partners in a market who do not devote at least some time to calculating the monetary value of their transfer of resources, there are often many transactions within firms for which such calculation is completely suspended.

However, such distinctions should not be overstated. As Eccles and Crane (1988) note in their study of the investment banking industry, there are a diverse array of informal activities that banks will perform for their clients that can augment the quality of what they provide. Moreover, as Uzzi (1997) emphasizes, calculation can be suspended in long-term market relations. Eccles and White (1988) observe pricing mechanisms can be introduced into the organizations as a way to facilitate exchange even though essential features of the pricing mechanisms within firms are more likely to be contested as illegitimate. Therefore, while on average there are differences between the way in which status orderings in markets and status orderings in firms operate, it is probably better to characterize these differences in terms of tendencies rather than dichotomies.

Just as sociological work in the 1950s and 1960s pointed to the centrality of status processes to governance and control within organizations, so we now have observed considerable evidence pointing to the role of status processes in governance and control across a diverse array of market contexts.

The parallels are noteworthy not only in their own right but because of their implications for when a transaction should occur within a firm and when it should occur within a market. The most noted answer to this question comes from transaction cost economics. Scholars within this tradition argue that transactions should occur within the boundary of the firm when the transaction costs in the firm are lower, and they should occur within the market when the transaction costs of the market are lower. Of course, such a statement is vacuous unless the scholars specify circumstances in which the transaction costs in the market are lower than the transaction costs in the firm and vice versa.

Markets have comparatively low transaction costs when there are a large number of buyers and sellers and when buyers and sellers have the knowledge and the ability to easily switch to a new exchange partner if they are dissatisfied with their current exchange partner. In effect, markets tend to have comparatively low transaction costs to the degree to which they approximate the neoclassical model of perfect competition. In such circumstances, buyers and sellers are strongly motivated to behave in ways in which there are joint gains from trade, and—unlike the situation in a hierarchy—there is no costly bureaucracy overseeing these transactions.

The transaction costs in markets rise considerably when there are a small number of buyers and sellers and/or buyers cannot easily switch to a new exchange partner if they are dissatisfied with their current exchange partner. In such circumstances, buyers and sellers worry that a potential exchange partner will behave opportunistically—that is, exploit the fact that the buyer or seller has no easily available alternatives. The only way in which market actors can alleviate these worries is either by not entering into an exchange or by devising a long, complicated contract to cover all the possible contingencies that could arise with the opportunistic exchange partner. (Of course, even if a long, complicated contract is written, a market actor may still worry that the potential exchange partner will be willing to behave opportunistically up to the point at which the actor is indifferent between pursuing a legal grievance and accepting the opportunistic behavior.) Both the alternative of withdrawing from the market and the alternative of writing a long, complex contract are costly. The first alternative is costly in terms of the forgone gains from trade; the second alternative is costly in terms of the time and resources devoted to specifying detailed contingencies in a contract. In such circumstances, the costs of hierarchy are comparatively low because the authority contained within the hierarchy is able to force a transaction and prevent the opportunistic behavior in which independent parties would engage.

Granovetter (1985) offers two criticisms of transaction cost economics. First, he criticizes the approach for assuming that comparative efficiency considerations are sufficient to explain why a particular institutional arrangement arises. One can point to many inefficient institutional arrangements that persist; comparative efficiency is not a sufficient explanation for why a particular arrangement exists. Second, he criticizes transaction cost economics for adopting an undersocialized conception of the market and oversocialized conception of the firm.

While not disagreeing with the first of these criticisms, I would like to set it aside and focus on the second. In recognizing the parallel importance of status to governance in markets and firms, it is possible to give some added specificity to this second criticism. If status plays a fundamental role in the governance structure of both markets and firms, then transaction cost economics is fundamentally misspecifying the choice. In adopting the neoclassical imagery of the market, transaction cost economics overstates the degree to which buyers and sellers have the discretion to choose from many exchange partners; in identifying hierarchy with formal authority, transaction cost economics overstates the degree to which transactions within a firm can be forced.

Yet, to simply observe that the choice is misspecified does not in and of itself address the question that transaction cost economics aims to answer: what determines whether an exchange occurs within the market or within the boundaries of the firm? The common relevance of status to governance in markets and firms would seem to indicate that there is a high degree of indeterminacy. However (and *here* is where I engage in truly indulgent speculation), I believe that the beginnings of an answer can be found by returning to White's metaphor of the market pump, which I referenced in chapter 7.

To repeat, the basic idea behind the metaphor is that the efficiency of a market depends on the extent to which the differentiated order of producers acts as a rapid sorting mechanism, enabling previously dispersed activities and materials to congeal into differentiated products whose quality is sufficiently easy to infer that market actors can rapidly find their appropriate exchange partner. Disparate actors flow in, connect, then are pumped out "satisficed." To be sure, the actors may quickly reappear for added exchanges, but ultimately the efficiency of the market is judged by the velocity of exchange.

This concept of velocity is probably undertheorized in our understanding of markets even though a number of markets seem to have indicators that suggest the importance of velocity. For example, the unemployment rate or the average time that a house is on the market can both be interpreted as measures of velocity. Within production markets, producer inventory is an analogous measure. All these measures relate to the length of time that resources are in the market without leaving the market. However, while all these measures tap into velocity, they are necessarily one-sided. The unemployment rate does not reflect the time that employers spend searching; the average time that a house is on the market does not reflect the time that buyers spend searching; similarly, measures of producer inventory, such as the volume of cars in dealer lots, do not reflect the search time of buyers.

As I noted in chapter 7, the image of the market as a status ordering is completely consistent with the metaphor of the pump insofar as the status ordering provides the information to reduce search time and thereby drive rapid exchange. However, at this point, I would like to make a further claim: the concept of velocity can be regarded as an efficiency criterion by which a status ordering is judged. Such an argument echoes Baker's (1984) pathbreaking examination of market efficiencies in commodity exchanges. As noted in the first chapter, Baker studied the relationship between the number of traders of a security and the price volatility of that security. Traders responded to the search problems induced by a large number of potential exchange partners by restricting their exchanges to a relatively small number of partners. They developed search procedures that enabled them to quickly begin and end the search for an exchange partner, and these search procedures resulted in market segmentation. In effect, from the perspective of the traders (rather than from the perspective of neoclassical theory), an open market—which would increase search time and hence slow the velocity of exchanges—was less efficient than a segmented search. The obvious difference between Baker's account and the account that I am offering is that Baker does not attend to the degree to which the segmentation does or does not conform to a hierarchical pattern.

So, let's return to the boundary question: to the degree that the status ordering in a market creates focal points that lower the time that actors are seeking to consummate exchanges, the market is behaving efficiently. However, to the degree that buyers are devoting considerable time to finding producers and to the degree that producers are left with large inventories or unutilized workers, then the producers will have an incentive to try to increase the velocity of exchange by bringing some subset of exchanges within the boundaries of the firm.

To be sure, just as with the original explanation provided by transaction cost economics, one wants to avoid assuming that efficiency concerns are sufficient explanations for the movement of a transaction across the firm/market boundary. However, it is nonetheless possible to think of an ecology of status orderings—competing with one another—in terms of their capacity for the quick consummation of exchanges. Status orderings within firms will generally be characterized by a more diverse array of exchanged contents, and they will generally lack an uncontroversial pricing mechanism. Status orderings within markets will generally be characterized by a more restrictive set of exchange contents and a more legitimate pricing mechanism.

Especially when there are large numbers of buyers and sellers, one would expect that market-based status orderings would come to dominate firm-based status orderings if only for the reason suggested by transaction cost economics: they lack administrative overhead, and an uncontested pricing mechanism is clearly of tremendous assistance in facilitating exchange.

What are the conditions under which the status ordering within a firm would dominate? Again, the answer to such a question is necessarily speculative. However, with that caveat in mind, the self-reproducing nature of status orderings implies that there should be no endogenous reason why a status ordering would unravel, causing exchanges to leave the confines of the market and become enshrouded within the boundaries of a firm. Thus, we need to look either to exogenous features of the environment that would make it difficult for a status ordering to be established, to exogenous shocks that could cause the status ordering to be disconfirmed, or to the challenges of trying to conduct exchanges in a context that precedes the emergence of a stable status ordering. So, for example, we know that contexts high in egocentric uncertainty do not lend themselves to a stable status ordering. Moreover, when new markets emerge, it may take time for status orderings to evolve, and in such contexts one might expect more transactions to be pulled within the boundaries of a formal organization than left to an open market. Work on business groups is relevant here since there is considerable research showing that emerging economies tend to be dominated by vertically integrated business groups rather than markets (Granovetter 1995). In general, scholars have suggested that the absence of a well-developed legal infrastructure is the reason for such firms. However, the lack of a stable sorting into a status ordering may be another reason. Finally, exogenous shocks could always be a reason why status signals within a market could be disconfirmed. Revolutionary technological shifts are probably the best example, but exogenous shocks obviously can be generated from a variety of domains; legal changes, such as the introduction of shelf registration in the primary security markets (discussed in chapter 3), can become a reason that the status ordering starts to unravel. When such exogenous shocks unravel status orderings, more transactions may become situated within vertically integrated relations—either formally within firm boundaries or informally within long-term relations in which alternatives are at most episodically considered. To the extent that these transactions are removed from the market, their velocity becomes driven by status dynamics within the firm or long-term relations.

I feel compelled to reemphasize the speculative nature of this status-based answer to the boundary-of-the-firm question. However, speculation is obviously an essential ingredient in any future research, and while sociologists have been quite critical of the answer put forth by transaction cost economics, it is probably safe to say that sociology has not offered a particular strong alternative answer to this very important question. Though sociologists have emphasized what Durkheim (1933) called the "non-contractual elements of contracts"—especially highlighting the role of trust in facilitating market exchanges (Granovetter 1985; Uzzi 1997)—there is no theory of when trust will be sufficiently present in a market to induce the market (rather than a hierarchy) to be the preferred governance mechanism for an exchange. We know that trust seems to be associated with the density of social ties among individuals (Coleman 1988; Portes and Sensenbrenner 1993), but there is no evidence (or even theory) that we observe more market-governed transactions in contexts where the density of social ties is higher. Perhaps consideration of status dynamics will facilitate the development of a sociological alternative to the contingent theory of economics.

FINAL REMARKS

In this conclusion, I have tried to emphasize specifics—specific questions that arise from reliance on the image of a status ordering in markets, specific answers that flow from these questions, and specific methodological concerns that arise as a consequence of the investigation. I have also focused on specific questions that seem to hold special promise for future research on status processes in the market. However, I will finish with a more general observation. While this book has focused on status dynamics in particular, one broader implication of this work is the importance of the problem of predictability as a point of departure for the sociological inquiry into markets.

In his book *The Cement of Society* (1989), Jon Elster points to two fundamental problems of order that human institutions must solve—the problem of cooperation and the problem of predictability. From Durkheim's *Division of Labor* through recent work elaborating Granovetter's conception of embeddedness (Uzzi 1997; Raub and Weesie 1990), sociologists looking at the market have been primarily concerned with the first of these two problems. However, a consideration of status follows clearly from a consideration of the problem of predictability. In drawing on the problem of predictability as the analytical point of departure, the status-based model has a common link to research in organizational sociology that looks to how directorate ties alleviate the uncertainty that firms confront in making decisions (Davis 1991; Haunschild 1994). Even more directly, the foundation in the problem of predictability provides a common underpinning for the status-based model and some of the more cutting-edge research in the field of economic sociology as it is now unfolding (White 2002; Kocak 2003; Zuckerman 1999; Strang and Macy 2001). Based on a consideration of this range of work, it seems that there is considerable potential for the continued application of sociological reasoning to this second fundamental problem of order.

BIBLIOGRAPHY

Abolafia, Mitchel Y. 1996. *Making Markets: Opportunism and Restraint on Wall Street.* Cambridge, MA: Harvard University Press.

Adler, Patricia, and Peter Adler. 1984. *The Social Dynamics of Financial Markets.* Greenwich, CT: JAI Press.

Albert, M. B., D. Avery, F. Narin, and P. McAllister. 1991. "Direct Validation of Citation Counts as Indicators of Industrially Important Patents." *Research Policy* 20:251–59.

Aldcroft, D. H. 1968. *The Development of British Industry and Foreign Competition, 1875–1914.* London: Allen and Unwin.

Altman, Edward. 1989. "Measuring Corporate Bond Mortality and Performance." *Journal of Finance* 44:902–922.

Amerine, Maynard A. 1984. "Sensory Evaluation or How to Taste Wine." Pp. 448–452 in D. Muscatine, M. A. Amerine, and B. Thompson (eds.), *The Book of California Wine.* Berkeley: University of California Press.

Anders, George. 1981. "Experts Say IBM's Entry Will Buoy Already Booming Software Industry." *Wall Street Journal* (August 19).

Anderson, Philip. 1995. "The Microcomputer Industry." Pp. 37–58 in Glenn R. Carroll and Michael T. Hannan (eds.), *Organizations in Industry: Strategy, Structure, and Selection.* New York: Oxford University Press.

Anderson, Philip, and Michael Tushman. 1990. "Technological Discontinuities and Dominant Designs: A Cyclical Model of Technological Change." *Administrative Science Quarterly* 35 (1): 604–633.

Asch, Solomon E. 1940. "Studies in the Principles of Judgments and Attitudes II: Determination of Judgments by Group and by Ego Standards." *Journal of Social Psychology* 12:433–465.

Asquith, Paul, David W. Mullins, Jr., and Eric D. Wolff. 1989. "Original Issue High Yield Bond: Aging Analyses of Defaults, Exchanges, and Calls." *Journal of Finance* 44 (4): 923–952.

Bain, Joe S. 1956. *Barriers to New Competition.* Cambridge, MA: Harvard University Press.

Baker, Wayne E. 1984. "The Social Structure of a National Securities Market." *American Journal of Sociology* 89:775–811.

Baker, Wayne E., and Robert R. Faulkner. 1993. "The Social Organization of Conspiracy: Illegal Networks in the Heavy Electrical Equipment Industry." *American Sociological Review* 58:837–860.

Barnett, William P. 1994. "The Liability of Collective Action: Growth and Change among Early Telephone Companies." Pp. 337–354 in J. Baum and J. Singh (eds), *Evolutionary Dynamics Of Organizations.* New York: Oxford University Press.

Barnett, William P., and Glenn R. Carroll. 1987. "Competition and Mutualism among Early Telephone Companies." *Administrative Science Quarterly* 32:400–421.

Barron, David N., Elizabeth West, and Michael T. Hannan. 1994. "A Time to Grow and a Time to Die: Growth and Mortality of Credit Unions in New York City, 1914–1990." *American Journal of Sociology* 100 (2): 381–422.

Basberg, Bjorn L. 1987. "Patents and the Measure of Technological Change." *Research Policy* 16:131–141.

Baum, Joel A. C., and Christine Oliver. 1992. "Institutional Embeddedness and the Dynamics of Organizational Populations." *American Sociological Review* 57 (4): 540–559.

Beckert, Jens. 2002. *Beyond the Market: The Social Foundations of Economic Efficiency.* Princeton, NJ: Princeton University Press.

Belsley, David A., Edwin Kuh, and Roy E. Welsch. 1980. *Regression Diagnostics.* New York: Wiley.

Benjamin, Beth A., and Joel M. Podolny. 1999. "Status, Quality, and Social Order in the California Wine Industry, 1981–1991." *Administrative Science Quarterly* 44 (3): 563–589.

Berger, Joseph, M. Hamit Fisek, Robert Z. Norman, and Morris Zelditch, Jr. 1977. *Status Characteristics and Social Interaction: An Expectation States Approach.* New York: Elsevier.

Berk, Richard A. 1983. "An Introduction to Sample Selection Bias in Sociological Data." *American Sociological Review* 48:386–398.

Blau, Peter M. 1955. *The Dynamics of Bureaucracy: A Study of Interpersonal Relations in Two Government Agencies.* Chicago: University of Chicago Press.

Blau, Peter M. 1964. *Exchange and Power in Social Life.* New Brunswick, NJ: Transaction.

Blume, Marshall E., and Donald B. Keim. 1987. "Lower-Grade Bonds: Their Risks and Returns." *Financial Analysts Journal* 43:26–33.

Bolton, Patrick, and David Scharfstein. 1990. "A Theory of Predation Based on Agency Problems in Financial Contracting." *American Economic Review* 80:93–106.

Bonacich, Philip. 1987. "Power and Centrality: A Family of Measures." *American Journal of Sociology* 92:1170–1183.

Bork, Robert. 1978. *The Antitrust Paradox.* New York: Basic Books.

Bourdieu, Pierre. 1984. *Distinction: A Social Critique of the Judgement of Taste,* translated by Richard Nice. Cambridge, MA: Harvard University Press.

Bowles, Samuel, and Herbert Gintis. 1976. *Schooling in Capitalist America: Educational Reform and the Contradictions of Economic Life.* New York: Basic Books.

Boyce, Gordon. 1995. *Information, Mediation, and Institutional Development: The Rise of Large-Scale Enterprise in British Shipping, 1870–1919.* Manchester, England: Manchester University Press.

Brodsky, Marc H. 1990. "Progress in Galium Arsenide Semiconductors." *Scientific American* (February), pp. 68–75.

Brooks, John. 1973. *The Go-Go Years.* New York: Weybright and Talley.

Burns, Malcolm R. 1986. "Predatory Pricing and the Acquisition Cost of Competitors." *Journal of Political Economy* 94:266–296.

Burrough, Bryan, and John Helyar. 1990. Barbarians at the Gate: The Fall of RJR Nabisco. New York: Harper & Row.

Burt, Ronald S. 1992. *Structural Holes: The Social Structure of Competition.* Cambridge, MA: Harvard University Press.

Burt, Ronald S., and Mark Knez. 1995. "Kinds of Third-Party Effects on Trust." *Rationality and Society* 7:255–292.

Camerer, Colin. 1995. "Individual Decision Making." Pp. 587–703 in J. H. Kagal and A. E. Roth (eds.), *Handbook of Experimental Economics.* Princeton, NJ: Princeton University Press.

Camic, Charles. 1992. "Reputation and Predecessor Selection: Parsons and the Institutionalists." *American Sociological Review* 57:421–445.

Carosso, Vincent P. 1970. *Investment Banking in America, a History.* Cambridge, MA: Harvard University Press.

Carroll, Glenn R. 1985. "Concentration and Specialization: Dynamics of Niche Width in Populations of Organizations." *American Journal of Sociology* 90: 1262–1283.

Carroll, Glenn R. 1997. "Long-Term Evolutionary Change in Organizational Populations." *Industrial and Corporate Change* 6:119–143.

Carroll, Glenn R., and Michael T. Hannan. 2000. *The Demography of Organizational Populations.* Princeton, NJ: Princeton University Press.

Carroll, Glenn R., and Anand Swaminathan. 2000. "Why the Microbrewery Movement: Organizational Dynamics of Resource Partitioning in the U.S. Brewing Industry." *American Journal of Sociology* 106:715–762.

Carruthers, Bruce G. 1996. *City of Capital: Politics and Markets in the English Financial Revolution.* Princeton, NJ: Princeton University Press.

Castellucci, Fabrizio, and Joel M. Podolny. 2003. "The Dynamics of Position, Capability, and Market Competition." Harvard Business School Working Paper.

Chernow, Ron. 1990. *The House of Morgan: An American Banking Dynasty and the Rise of Modern Finance.* New York: Touchstone.

Chevalier, Judith A. 2000. "What Do We Know about Cross-Subsidization? Evidence from the Investment Policies of Merging Firms." University of Chicago GSB and NBER Working Paper.

Christensen, Clayton M. 1997. *The Innovator's Dilemma: When New Technologies Cause Great Firms to Fail.* Boston: Harvard Business School Press.

Cohen, Michael D., James G. March, and Johan P. Olsen. 1972. "A Garbage Can Model of Organizational Choice." *Administrative Science Quarterly* 17:1–25.

Coleman, James S. 1988. "Social Capital in the Creation of Human Capital." *American Journal of Sociology* 94:S95–S120.

Cox, David R. 1966. *Statistical Analyses of Series of Events.* New York: Wiley.

Dannefer, Dale. 1987. "Aging as Intracohort Differentiation: Accentuation, the Matthew Effect, and the Life Course." *Sociological Forum* 2:211–236.

Davis, Gerald F. 1991. "Agents without Principles? The Spread of the Poison Pill through the Intercorporate Network." *Administrative Science Quarterly* 36 (4): 583–613.

Davis, Gerald F., and Mark S. Mizruchi. 1999. "The Money Center Cannot Hold: Commercial Banks in the U.S. System of Corporate Governance." *Administrative Science Quarterly* 44 (2): 215–239.

DiMaggio, Paul, and Sharon Zukin. 1990. "Introduction." In Paul DiMaggio and Sharon Zukin (eds.), *Structures of Capital: The Social Organization of Economic Life.* Cambridge: Cambridge University Press.

Dobbin, Frank. 1994. *Forging Industrial Policy: The United States, Britian, and France in the Railway Age.* Cambridge: Cambridge University Press.

Domhoff, William G. 1967. *Who Rules America?* Englewood Cliffs, NJ: Prentice Hall.

Dumont, Louis. 1981. *Homo Hierarchicus: The Caste System and Its Implications,* translated by Basia M. Gulati. Chicago: University of Chicago Press.

Durkheim, Émile. 1933. *The Division of Labor in Society.* New York: Free Press.

Eccles, Robert G., and Dwight Crane. 1988. *Doing Deals: Investment Banks at Work.* Boston: Harvard Business School Press.

Eccles, Robert G., and Harrison C. White. 1988. "Price and Authority in Inter–Profit Center Transactions." *American Journal of Sociology* 94:S17–S51.

Eerden, C. van der, and F. H. Saelens. 1991. "The Use of Science and Technology Indicators in Strategic Planning." *Long Range Planning* 24 (3): 18–25.

Elias, Norbert, and John Scotson. 1994. *The Established and the Outsiders,* 2nd ed. London: Sage.

Elster, Jon. 1989. *The Cement of Society: A Study of Social Order.* Cambridge: Cambridge University Press.

Espeland, Wendy N., and Mitchell L. Stevens. 1998. "Commensuration as a Social Process." *Annual Review of Sociology* 24:313–343.

Fama, Eugene F. 1970. "Efficient Capital Markets: Review of Theory and Empirical Work." *Journal of Finance* 25 (2): 383–423.

Faulkner, Robert R. 2003. *Music on Demand: Composers and Careers in the Hollywood Film Industry.* New Brunswick, NJ: Transaction.

Figiel, Richard. 1991. "Is There Gout de Terroir out There? Findings of the First Annual Grand Harvest Awards: Charting the Sensory Landscape of America's Viticultural Areas." *Vineyard and Winery Management* (March–April), pp. 32–34.

Fligstein, Neil. 2001. *The Architecture of Markets: An Economic Sociology of Twenty-first Century Capitalist Societies.* Princeton, NJ: Princeton University Press.

Fombrun, Charles, and Mark Shanley. 1990. "What's in a Name? Reputation Building and Corporate Strategy." *Academy of Management Journal* 33:233–258.

Frank, Robert H. 1985. *Choosing the Right Pond: Human Behavior and the Quest for Status.* Oxford: Oxford University Press.

Fudenberg, Drew, and Jan Tirole. 1985. "Predation without Reputation." MIT Department of Economics Working Paper #377.

Genesove, David, and Wallace P. Mullin. 1997. "Predation and Its Rate of Return: The Sugar Industry, 1887–1914." MIT Department of Economics Working Paper.

Gilder, George. 1989. *Microcosm.* New York: Simon & Schuster.

Glasberg, D. S. 1981. "Corporate Power and Control: The Case of Leasco Corporation versus Chemical Bank." *Social Problems* 29:104–116.

Goode, William J. 1978. *The Celebration of Heroes: Prestige as a Social Control System.* Berkeley: University of California Press.

Gould, Roger V. 1995. *Insurgent Identities.* Chicago: University of Chicago Press.

Gould, Roger V. 2001. "The Origin of Status Hierarchies: A Formal Theory and Empirical Test." *American Journal of Sociology* 107:1143–1178.

Granovetter, Mark S. 1974. *Getting a Job.* Cambridge, MA: Harvard University Press.

Granovetter, Mark S. 1985. "Economic Action and Social Structure: The Problem of Embeddedness." *American Journal of Sociology* 91:481–510.

Granovetter, Mark S. 1995. "Coase Revisited: Business Groups in the Modern Economy." *Industrial and Corporate Change* 4:93–131.

Granovetter, Mark S., and Richard Swedberg. 1992. *The Sociology of Economic Life.* Boulder, CO: Westview Press.

Groysberg, Boris, Jeff Polzer, and Hillary A. Elfenbein. 2003. "Too Many Cooks." Harvard Business School Working Paper.

Guo, Guang. 1993. "Event History Analysis for Left-truncated Data." in P. V. Marsden (ed.), *Sociological Methodology*. Cambridge, MA: Blackwell.

Han, Shin-Kap. 1994. "Mimetic Isomorphism and Its Effect on the Audit Services Market." *Social Forces* 73:637–663.

Hannan, Michael T., and Glenn R. Carroll. 1992. *Dynamics of Organizational Populations: Density, Legitimation, and Competition*. New York: Oxford University Press.

Hannan, Michael T., and John Freeman. 1977. "The Population Ecology of Organizations." *American Journal of Sociology* 82:929–964.

Hannan, Michael T., and John Freeman. 1989. *Organizational Ecology*. Cambridge, MA: Harvard University Press.

Haunschild, Pamela R. 1994. "How Much Is That Company Worth? Interorganizational Relationships, Uncertainty, and Acquisition Premiums." *Administrative Science Quarterly* 39 (3): 391–411.

Hawley, Amos. 1950. *Human Ecology*. New York: Ronald Press.

Hayek, Friedrich A. 1949. "The Meaning of Competition." *Individualism and Economic Order*. London: Routledge & Kegan Paul.

Hayes, Samuel L. 1971. "Investment Banking: Power Structure in Flux." *Harvard Business Review* (March–June), pp. 136–152.

Hayes, Samuel L. 1979. "The Transformation of Investment Banking." *Harvard Business Review* (January–February), pp. 153–170.

Hayes, Samuel L. III, A. Michael Spence, and D. Van Praag Marks. 1983. *Competition in the Investment Banking Industry*. Cambridge, MA: Harvard University Press.

Heckman, James J., and George J. Borjas. 1980. "Does Unemployment Cause Future Unemployment: Definitions, Questions, and Answers from a Continuous Time Model of Heterogeneity and State Dependence." *Economica* 47:247–283.

Helm, Leslie. 1992. "U.S. Japan Battle of the Patents." *Los Angeles Times* (April 24).

Hewitt, John P., and Randall Stokes. 1975. "Disclaimers." *American Sociological Review* 40:1–11.

Hirsch, Fred. 1976. *The Social Limits to Growth*. Cambridge, MA: Harvard University Press.

Hirsch, Paul M. 1986. "From Ambushes to Golden Parachutes: Corporate Takeovers as an Instance of Cultural Framing and Institutional Integration." *American Journal of Sociology* 91:800–837.

Holt, Douglas B. 2004. *How Brands Become Icons: The Principles of Cultural Branding*. Boston: Harvard Business School Press.

Homans, George C. 1951. *The Human Group*. London: Routledge & Kegan Paul.

Hovland, Carl I., Irving L. Janis, and Harold Kelley. 1953. *Communication and Persuasion*. New Haven, CT: Yale University Press.

Hsu, Greta. 2003. "The Structure of Quality in Market Contexts." Ph.D. dissertation, Stanford University.

Hsu, David. Forthcoming. "Why Do Entrepreneurs Pay for Venture Capital Affiliation?" *Journal of Finance*.

Huckman, Robert S. 2003. "The Utilization of Competing Technologies within the Firm: Evidence from Cardiac Procedures." *Management Science* 49:599–617.

Hughes, Thomas P. 1987. "The Evolution of Large Technological Systems." Pp. 51–82 in Wiebe E. Bijker, Thomas P. Hughes, and Trevor J. Pinch (eds.), *The social Construction of Technical Systems.* Cambridge, MA: MIT Press.

Jensen, Michael. 2003a. "The Reproduction of Status Hierarchies: Status Descrimination in Market Entry." Michigan Business School Working Paper.

Jensen, Michael. 2003b. "The Role of Network Resources in Market Entry: Commercial Banks' Entry into Investment Banking, 1991–1997." Michigan Business School Working Paper.

Johnston, John. 1960. *Statistical Cost Analysis.* New York: McGraw-Hill.

Johnston, John. 1984. *Econometric Methods*, 3rd ed. New York: McGraw-Hill.

Kadlec, David J. 1986 . "Will the Sun Ever Shine on Merrill's Investment Bankers?" *Investment Dealer's Digest* 52 (April 21).

Kalblfleisch, John D., and Ross L. Prentice. 1980. *The Statistical Analysis of Failure Time Data.* New York: Wiley.

Kanter, Rosabeth M. 1977. *Men and Women of the Corporation.* New York: Basic Books.

Kerckhoff, Alan C., and Elizabeth Glennie. 1999. "The Matthew Effect in American Education." *Research in Sociology of Education & Socialization* 12:35–66.

Klepper, Steven, and Elizabeth Graddy. 1990. "The Evolution of New Industries and Market Structure." *RAND Journal of Economics* 21:27–44

Knight, Frank H. 1921. *Risk, Uncertainty, and Profit.* Boston, MA: Houghton Mifflin.

Kocak, Ozgecan. 2003. "Social Orders of Exchange: Problems of Valuation and the Emergence of Social Order in Markets." Ph.D. dissertation, Stanford University.

Kollock, Peter. 1994. "The Emergence of Exchange Structures: An Experimental Study of Uncertainty, Commitment, and Trust." *American Journal of Sociology* 100 (2): 313–345.

Kramer, Matt. 1992. *Making Sense of California Wine.* New York: Morrow.

Kreps, David M., and Evan L. Porteus. 1978. "Temporal Resolution of Uncertainty and Dynamic Choice Theory." *Econometrica* 46:185–200.

Ladd, David, David E. Leibowitz, and Bruce G. Joseph. 1986. *Protection for the Semiconductor Chip Masks in the United States.* Weinheim: Verlag Chemie.

Latour, Bruno. 1987. *Science in Action.* Cambridge, MA: Harvard University Press.

Lerner, Josh. 1995. "Pricing and Financial Resources: An Analysis of the Disk Drive Industry, 1980–88." *Review of Economics and Statistics* 77:585–598.

Levin, Richard, and David F. Weiman. 1994. "Preying for Monopoly? The Case of Southern Bell Telephone Company, 1894–1912." *Journal of Political Economy* 102: 103–126.

Levin, Richard C., Alvin K. Klevorick, Richard R. Nelson, and Sidney G. Winter. 1987. "Appropriating the Returns from Industrial Research and Development." *Brookings Paper on Economic Activity.* Washington, DC: Brookings Insititution.

Lewin, Kurt. 1935. *Dynamic Theory of Personality.* New York: McGraw-Hill.

Link, Bruce, and Barry Milcarek. 1980. "Selection Factors in the Dispensation of Therapy: The Matthew Effect in the Allocation of Mental Health Resources." *Journal of Health & Social Behavior* 213:279–290.

Lomi, Alessandro. 1995. "The Population and Community Ecology of Organizational Founding: Italian Cooperative Banks." *European Sociological Review* 11:75–98.

Longstreet, J. R., and A. P. Hess, Jr. 1967. "Characteristics of Corporate New Issues in the Post-SEC Period." In I. Friend, J. R. Longstreet, M. Mendelson, E. Miller, and

A. P. Hess, Jr. (eds.), *Investment Banking and the New Issues Market*. Cleveland: The World Publishing Company.

Manfreda, John, and Richard Mendelson. 1988. "U.S. Wine Law." Manuscript. Sonoma County Wine Library, Healdsburg, CA.

Mansson, Sven-Axel, and U.-C. Hedin. 1999. "Breaking the Matthew Effect on Women Leaving Prostitution." *International Journal of Social Welfare* 81:67–77.

March, James G. 1988. *Decisions in Organizations*. New York: Basil Blackwell.

McClean, William J., ed. 1981–91. *Status: A Report on the Integrated Circuit Industry*. Scottsdale, AZ: Integrated Circuit Engineering Corporation.

McGee, John S. 1980. "Predatory Pricing Revisited." *Journal of Law and Economics* 23:289–330.

McPherson, Miller J. 1983. "An Ecology of Affiliation." *American Sociological Review* 48:519–532.

Merton, Robert K. 1968. "The Matthew Effect in Science." *Science* 159:56–63.

Milgrom, Paul R., and John Roberts. 1982. "Predation, Reputation, and Entry Deterrence." *Journal of Economic Theory* 27:280–312.

Milgrom, Paul R., and John Roberts. 1992. *Economics, Organization, and Management*. Englewood Cliffs, NJ: Prentice Hall.

Miller, E. 1967. "Background and Structure of the Industry." In I. Friend, J. R. Longstreet, M. Mendelson, E. Miller, and A. P. Hess, Jr. (eds.), *Investment Banking and the New Issues Market*. Cleveland: The World Publishing Company.

Mitchell, Will. 1995. "Medical Diagnostic Imaging Manufacturers." In Glenn R. Carroll and Michael T. Hannan (eds.), *Organizations in Industry: Strategy and Structure*. New York: Oxford Unversity Press.

Mizruchi, Mark S., and Linda Brewster Stearns. 1994. "A Longitudinal Study of Borrowing by Large American Corporations." *Administrative Science Quarterly* 39:118–140.

Mizruchi, Mark S., and Linda Brewster Stearns. 2001. "Getting Deals Done: The Use of Social Networks in Bank Decision-Making." *American Sociological Review* 66:647–671.

Monroe, Ann. 1986. "Just Like Film Stars, Wall Streeters Battle to Get Top Billing." *Wall Street Journal*, January 15, p. 1.

Moulton, Kirby. 1984. "The Economics of Wine in California." Pp. 380–405 in D. Muscatine, M. A. Amerine, and B. Thompson (eds.), *The Book of California Wine*. Berkeley: University of California Press.

Narin, Francis, Elliot Noma, and Ross Perry. 1987. "Patents a Indicators of Corporate Technological Strength." *Research Policy* 16:143–155.

Nelson, Richard R., and Sidney G. Winter. 1982. *An Evolutionary Theory of Economic Change*. Cambridge, MA: Belknap Press.

Office of Technology Assessment and Forecast, U.S. Department of Commerce, Patent and Trademark Office. 1976. *Technology Assessment and Forecast*, 6th ed. Washington, DC: Government Printing Office.

Okowa, Willie J. 1989. "The Matthew Effect, Ake's Defense Radicalism and Urban Bias in Nigerian Development Planning." *Scandinavian Journal of Development Alternatives* 84:31–38.

Olzak, Susan, S. Shanahan, and E. H. McEneany. 1996. "Poverty, Segregation, and Race Riots, 1960–1993." *American Sociological Review* 61:590–613.

Ordover, Janusz A., and Garth Saloner. 1989. "Predation, Monopolization, and Antitrust." In R. Schmalensee and R. Willig (eds.), *Handbook of Industrial Organization.* New York: North-Holland.

Orenstein, Susan. 1992. "Japanese Companies Shift Gears, Fight in Court." *Legal Times* (June 22).

Padgett, John F., and Paul McLean. Forthcoming. "Economic and Social Exchange in Renaissance Florence." *American Journal of Sociology.*

Park, Douglas Y., and Joel M. Podolny. 2000. "The Competitive Dynamics of Status and Niche Width: US Investment Banking, 1920–1949." *Industrial and Corporate Change* 9:377–414.

Parsons, Talcott. 1963. "On the Concept of Influence." *Public Opinions Quarterly* 27:37–92.

Péli, Gabor, and Bart Nooteboom. 1999. "Market Partitioning and the Geometry of the Resource Space." *American Journal of Sociology* 104:1132–1153.

Pfeffer, Jeffrey, and Gerald R. Salancik. 1978. *The External Control of Organizations.* New York: Harper & Row.

Phillips, Damon J. 2001. "The Promotion Paradox: Mortality and Employee Promotion Chances in Silicon Valley Law Firms, 1946–1996." *American Journal of Sociology* 106:1058–1098.

Phillips, Damon J., and Ezra W. Zuckerman. 2001. "Middle Status Conformity: Theoretical Restatement and Empirical Demonstration in Two Markets." *American Journal of Sociology* 107:379–429.

Pinch, Trevor J., and Wiebe E. Bijker. 1987. "The Social Construction of Facts and Artifacts." Pp. 17–50 in Wiebe E. Bijker, Thomas P. Hughes, and Trevor J. Pinch (eds.), *The Social Construction of Technical Systems*, Cambridge, MA: MIT Press.

Podolny, Joel M. 1993. "A Status-Based Model of Market Competition." *American Journal of Sociology* 98:829–872.

Podolny, Joel M. 1994. "Market Uncertainty and the Social Character of Economic Exchange." *Administrative Science Quarterly* 39:458–483.

Podolny, Joel M. 2001. "Networks as the Pipes and Prisms of the Market." *American Journal of Sociology* 107:33–60.

Podolny, Joel M., and Andrew Feldman. 1997. "Choosing Ties from the Inside of a Prism: Egocentric Uncertainty and Status in the Venture Capital Markets." Stanford University, Graduate School of Business Working Paper.

Podolny, Joel M., and Greta Hsu. 2003. "Quality, Exchange, and Knightian Uncertainty." Pp. 77–106 in Vincent Buskens, Werner Raub, and Chris Snijders (eds.), *The Governance of Relations in Markets and Organizations.* Amsterdam: JAI Press.

Podolny, Joel M., and Fiona M. Scott Morton. 1999. "Social Status, Entry and Predation: The Case of British Shipping Cartels, 1879–1929." *Journal of Industrial Economics* 47:41–67.

Podolny, Joel M., and Damon J. Phillips. 1996. "The Dynamics of Organizational Status." *Industrial and Corporate Change* 5:453–472.

Podolny, Joel M., and Toby E. Stuart. 1995. "A Role-Based Ecology of Technological Change." *American Journal of Sociology* 100:1224–1260.

Podolny, Joel M., Toby E. Stuart, and Michael T. Hannan. 1996. "Networks, Knowledge, and Niches: Competition in the Worldwide Semiconductor Industry, 1984–1991." *American Journal of Sociology* 102:659–689.

Polanyi, Karl. 1944. *The Great Transformation*. New York: Rinehart & Co.

Portes, Alejandro, and Julia Sensenbrenner. 1993. "Embeddedness and Immigration: Notes on the Social Determinants of Economic Action." *The American Journal of Sociology* 98:1320–1350.

Powell, Walter W. 1985. *Getting into Print: The Decision-Making Process in Scholarly Publishing*. Chicago: University of Chicago Press.

Rao, Hayagreeva, Gerald F. Davis, and Andrew Ward. 2000. "Embeddedness, Social Identity, and Mobility: Why Firms Leave the NASDAQ and Join the New York Stock Exchange." *Administrative Science Quarterly* 45:268–292.

Raub, Werner, and Jeroen Weesie. 1990. "Reputation and Efficiency in Social Interactions: An Example of Network Effects." *American Journal of Sociology* 96:626–654.

Ristelhueber, Robert. 1993. "Time for a Reality Check." *Electronic Business*, p. 99.

Robinson, David T., and Toby E. Stuart. 2003. "Network Effects in the Governance of Biotech Strategic Alliances." Columbia Business School Working Paper.

Rohwer, Götz. 1993. *Transition Data Analysis*, ver 5.2. Institut für Empirische und Angewandte Soziologie, Universität Bremen.

Ross, Lee, and Richard E. Nisbett. 1991. *The Person and Situation: Perspectives of Social Psychology*. New York: McGraw-Hill.

Rubin, Donald B. 1987. *Multiple Imputation for Nonresponse in Surveys*. New York: Wiley.

Saloner, Garth. 1987. "Predation, Merger, and Incomplete Information." *The RAND Journal of Economics* 18:165–186.

Saloner, Garth, Andrea Shepard, and Joel Podolny. 2001. *Strategic Management*. New York: Wiley, pp. 305–317.

Saunder, Michael. 2004. "Third Parties and Status Position." Northwestern University Working Paper.

Schelling, Thomas. 1960. *The Strategy of Conflict*. Cambridge, MA: Harvard University Press.

Scherer, Frederic M. 1984. *Innovation and Growth: Schumpeterian Perspectives*. Cambridge, MA: MIT Press.

Scott Morton, Fiona M. 1997. "Entry and Predation: British Shipping Cartels, 1879–1929." *Journal of Economics and Management Strategy* 6:679–724.

Shapiro, Carl. 1983. "Premiums for High Quality Products as Returns to Reputation." *Quarterly Journal of Economics* 98:659–679.

Spence, A. Michael. 1974. *Market Signaling: Informational Transfer in Hiring and Related Processes*. Cambridge, MA: Harvard University Press.

Standard & Poor's. 1920–1950. *Security Dealers of North America*. New York: Standard & Poor's Corporation.

Stevens, Mark. 1991. *The Big Six: The Selling Out of America's Top Accounting Firms*. New York: Simon & Schuster.

Strang, David, and Michael W. Macy. 2001. " 'In Search of Excellence': Fads, Success Stories, and Adaptive Emulation." *American Journal of Sociology* 107:147–182.

Stuller, Jay, and Glen Martin. 1989. *Through the Grapevine: The Great Story behind America's Eight Billion Dollar Wine Industry*. New York: Wynwood Press.

Swedberg, Richard. 2003. *Principles of Economic Sociology*. Princeton, NJ: Princeton University Press.

Thaler, Richard. H. 1994. *The Winner's Curse: Paradoxes and Anomolies of Economic Life*. Princeton, NJ: Princeton University Press.

Thompson, Bob. 1984. "The Critics Look at California Wines." Pp. 486–536 in D. Muscatine, M. A. Amerine, and B. Thompson (eds.), *The Book of California Wine*. Berkeley: University of California Press.

Trajtenberg, Manuel. 1990. "A Penny for Your Quotes: Patent Citations and the Value of Information." *Rand Journal of Economics* 21 (1): 172–187.

Tripas, Mary, and Giovanni Gavetti. 2000. "Capabilities, Cognition and Inertia: Evidence from Digital Imaging." Harvard Business School Working Paper Series, No. 00-067, 2000.

Tuma, Nancy B., and Michael T. Hannan. 1984. *Social Dynamics: Models and Methods*. Orlando, FL: Academic Press.

Useem, Michael. 1984. *The Inner Circle: Large Corporations and the Rise of Business Political Activity in the U.S. and U.K.* New York: Oxford University Press.

Uzzi, Brian. 1997. "Networks and the Paradox of Embeddedness." *Administrative Science Quarterly* 42:35–67.

Uzzi, Brian, and Ryon Lancaster. 2004. "Embeddedness and the Price of Legal Services in the Large Law Firm Market." *American Sociological Review* (forthcoming).

Veblen, Thorstein. 1953. *The Theory of the Leisure Class*. New York: New American Library.

Walberg, Herbert, and Shiow-Ling Tsai. 1983. "Matthew Effects in Education." *American Research Journal* 20:359–373.

Waterman, Merwin H. 1958. *Investment Banking Functions: Their Evolution and Adaptation to Business Finance*. Ann Arbor, MI: University of Michigan Press.

Weber, Max. 1948. "Class, Status, and Party." Pp. 180–195 in H. H. Gerth and C. Wright Mills, (eds.), *From Max Weber*. Oxford: Oxford University Press.

Weber, Max. 1978. *Economy and Society,* edited by Guenther Roth and Claus Wittich. Berkeley: University of California Press.

White, Harrison C. 1981. "Where Do Markets Come From?" *American Journal of Sociology* 87:517–547.

White, Harrison C. 2002a. "Manipulation Versus Niches within Market Networks?" Cambridge Colloquium on Complexity and Social Networks Working Paper.

White, Harrison C. 2002b. *Markets from Networks: Socioeconomic Models of Production*. Princeton, NJ: Princeton University Press.

Whyte, William. 1981. *Street Corner Society: The Social Order of an Italian Slum*, 3rd ed. Chicago: University of Chicago Press.

Williamson, Oliver E. 1975. *Markets and Hierarchies*. New York: Free Press.

Williamson, Oliver E. 1985. *The Economic Institutions of Capitalism*. New York: Free Press.

Wilson, Robert W., Peter K. Ashton, and Thomas P. Egan. 1980. *Innovation, Competition, and Government Policy in the Seminconductor Industry*. Toronto: Lexington Books.

Zelizer, Viviana. 1994. *The Social Meaning of Money*. New York: Basic Books.

Zuckerman, Ezra W. 1999. "The Categorical Imperative: Securities Analysts and the Legitimacy Discount." *American Journal of Sociology* 104 (5): 1398–1438.

Zuckerman, Ezra W. 2000. "Focusing the Corporate Product: Securities Analysts and De-diversification." *Administrative Science Quarterly* 45:591–619.

Zuckerman, Ezra W., and Tai-Young Kim. 2003. "The Critical Trade-off: Identity Assign-
ment and Box Office Success in the Feature Film Industry." *Industrial and Corporate
Change* 12:27–67.
Zuckerman, Ezra W., and Stoyan Sgourev. 2003. "Peer Capitalism: The Role of Parallel
Relationships in the Market Economy." MIT Sloan School Working Paper.

CREDITS

CHAPTERS 3 through 9 draw in part from the following articles. I would like to thank the various copyright holders for their permission to use the previously published material.

Podolny, Joel M. 1993. "A Status-Based Model of Market Competition." *American Journal of Sociology* 98 (4): 829–872.
Original article published by University of Chicago Press and is © 1993 by the University of Chicago. All rights reserved.

Podolny, Joel M. 1994. "Market Uncertainty and the Social Character of Economic Exchange." *Administrative Science Quarterly* 39 (3): 458–483.
Original article © Johnson Graduate School of Management, Cornell University, and is used by permission.

Podolny, Joel M., and Toby E. Stuart. 1995. "A Role-Based Ecology of Technological Change." *American Journal of Sociology* 100 (5): 1224–1260.
Original article published by University of Chicago Press and is © 1995 by the University of Chicago. All rights reserved.

Podolny, Joel M., Toby E. Stuart, and Michael T. Hannan. 1996. "Networks, Knowledge, and Niches: Competition in the Worldwide Semiconductor Industry, 1984–1991." *American Journal of Sociology* 102 (3): 659–689.
Original article published by University of Chicago Press and is © 1996 by the University of Chicago. All rights reserved.

Podolny, Joel M., and Damon J. Phillips. 1996. "The Dynamics of Organizational Status." *Industrial and Corporate Change* 5 (2): 453–472.
Original article was published by Oxford University Press, and is used by permission.

Benjamin, Beth A., and Joel M. Podolny. 1999. "Status, Quality, and Social Order in the California Wine Industry, 1981–1991." *Administrative Science Quarterly* 44 (3): 563–589.
Original article © Johnson Graduate School of Management, Cornell University, and is used by permission.

Podolny, Joel M., and Fiona Scott Morton. 1999. "Social Status, Entry and Predation: The Case of British Shipping Cartels, 1879–1929." *Journal of Industrial Economics* 47 (1): 41–67.
Original article was published by Blackwell Publishing, Ltd.

Park, Douglas Y., and Joel M. Podolny. 2000. "The Competitive Dynamics of Status and Niche Width: US Investment Banking, 1920–1949." *Industrial and Corporate Change* 9 (3): 377–414.
Original article was published by Oxford University Press, and is used by permission.

Podolny, Joel M. 2001. "Networks as the Pipes and Prisms of the Market." American Journal of Sociology 107 (1): 33–60.
Original article published by University of Chicago Press and is © 2001 by the University of Chicago. All rights reserved.

INDEX

ABD Securities, 49
Advanced Micro Devices (AMD), 172
advertising: costs of, 28, 53–54; tombstone, 47–52, 56–58, 69–73, 80, 89, 213–14, 216
Albert, M. B., 144
Alcohol, Tobacco and Firearms, Bureau of (ATF), 111–12, 114–15
altercentric uncertainty. *See* uncertainty, altercentric
American Securities Corporation, 49
Anderson, P., 134n
Anheuser-Busch, 204n
appellation system, 111–12
AT&T, 51–52
ATF. *See* Alcohol, Tobacco and Firearms, Bureau of

Bache Halsey Stuart, 51–52
Bain, J. S., 32n
Baker, Wayne E., 4–5, 263
banking, investment. *See* investment banking industry
basis point, 56
Baum, Joel A. C., 5
Becker, Gary, 31n
Beckert, Jens, 3
Bell Laboratories, 145
Belsley, David A., 122n, 168
Berk, Richard A., 58
Blau, Peter M., 8, 11, 37, 259–60
Bolton, P., 179
Bonacich's measure, 57–58, 89, 114, 151, 166, 215
bond ratings, 60
Borjas, George J., 91, 148
boundary of the firm question, 258–65
Bourdieu, Pierre, 11
Bowles, Samuel, 106
Boyce, Gordon, 181–83, 188–89n, 190
brand, 8, 15–16
British shipping cartels. *See* shipping cartels
Brooks, John, 198
bulge bracket, 47n5, 49
Burns, M. R., 179
Burt, Ronald S.: and differentiation of informational content at nodes, 140; and

egocentric niche, terminology for, 135n; and structural equivalence in exchange relations, 163; and structural holes, theory of, 4, 8, 231–33, 237, 242–43

California wine industry. *See* wine industry
Camic, Charles, 105
Carroll, Glenn, 200–203, 205, 209, 225, 254
Carruthers, Bruce G., 3
cartels, 177–78, 180. *See also* shipping cartels
Castellucci, Fabrizio, 173
Cayzer, Charles, 190
Chemical Bank, 198
Christensen, Clayton M., 134n
Chrysler Corporation, 47–49
commensuration, 3
competitive intensity, 138–40, 163
concentration in evolving markets. *See* market concentration
Connoisseur's Guide to California Wine, 109–11, 118, 126
conspicuous consumption, 16, 25, 129–30, 229
convertible securities, 61
Cox, David R., 91, 146–47
Crane, Dwight, 2, 56, 260
crowding: firm niche, at the level of, 162–64, 167–72; patent niche, at the level of, 156; sales, 170n. *See also* market concentration

Dataquest, 154, 165
Davis, Gerald F., 5
Dean Witter Reynolds, 49
debt: investment-grade distinguished from non-investment-grade (junk), 42, 68–69; junk bonds (*see* junk bond market). *See also* investment banking industry
deference relations: competitive and status-enhancing implications of, 161–62; defined, 14; status and, 14–15; technological domain, conferring status in, 162–63, 166. *See also* inequality
demand-side increasing returns (DSIR), 142
DeMarco, Steve, 12
diamonds, criteria for assessing, 19n
diseconomies of scale, 31–32